GunDigest® Book of

SHOTGUNS

ASSEMBLY/DISASSEMBLY

3rd EDITION

Kevin Muramatsu

Published by

Gun Digest® Books, an imprint of F+W Media, Inc.
Krause Publications • 700 East State Street • Iola, WI 54990-0001
715-445-2214 • 888-457-2873
www.krausebooks.com

To order books or other products call toll-free 1-800-258-0929
or visit us online at www.gundigeststore.com

CAUTION: Technical data presented here, particularly technical data on the handloading and on firearms adjustment and alteration, inevitably reflects individual experience with particular equipment and components under specific circumstances the reader cannot duplicate exactly. Such data presentations therefore should be used for guidance only and caution. F+W Media, Inc., accepts no responsibility for results obtained using this data.

ISBN-13: 978-1-4402-3071-4
ISBN-10: 1-4402-3071-4

Cover Design by Al West
Designed by Tom Nelsen
Edited by Corrina Peterson

Printed in the United States of America

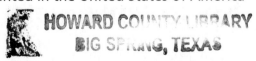

Introduction

Shotguns cover many arenas and utilities. And unlike the previous edition of this book series, the many differing types of shotguns, whether it be semiautomatic, pump, or break action, they are all covered in this book. In the last five years, there have been a few interesting things going on in the shotgun world. The AK-47 based Saiga shotguns have become very popular in several categories and remain in high demand. This is a perfect example of taking a functional rifle and doing something else with the action. Just as a Remington 870 and a 7600 are very, very similar, differing mostly in what goes down the bore and how it feeds, the Saiga is literally the fat twin of the AK.

Truly, the majority of current designs are more mature versions of previous models. However, even then, there are often enough a great enough dissimilarity of parts and functions that newer updated instructions may be necessary. Furthermore, the ownership of many companies has changed back and forth, with name brands being owned by other name brands that were formerly unrelated. A perfect example would be the Benelli/Franchi/Stoeger relationship. Franchi and Stoeger are wholly owned subsidiaries of Benelli, and both use Benelli's Inertia Driven operating system in their semiauto shotguns, but the remaining configurations of the firearms can be completely different, and thus justify separate takedown instructions. This can even be witnessed within the same brand. Benelli's line of shotguns, such as the Super Black Eagle function very similarly or identically with their new Vinci and Super Vinci Line. However the Vinci has an eloquent quick disassembly/field strip that makes the Vinci significantly easier to maintain, and thus an entirely different set of instructions will be found here as well. Then you have things like the Kel-Tec KSG, which is something completely off-the-deep-end original.

This book and its siblings in the Disassembly/Reassembly series are written so that the mystery in firearm disassembly can be at least partially diffused. Obviously not every single shotgun ever made will fit into these pages, for three major reasons. First, it is desirable that the most common models be present. Secondly, beyond the common models (of which many are interrelated) there are those interesting types that catch attention or are just simply the ones that happen to be available to the particular gunsmith author.

The take down steps herein can be invaluable to the professional and the lay person, and to manufacturers. Many gun owners like to work on their own firearms, and this is usually a good thing, since a man who understands how his gun works will likely take better care of it, resulting in a better maintained and therefore, safer gun. This gun owner will be more likely to identify malfunctions or breakdowns, and then institute simple repairs. Following the steps in this book will greatly assist the shotgun owner in disassembly, because unfortunately, there are many examples where what seems the logical choice is really not the correct choice, and going in that direction will result in damage to the firearm or to the owner. It is this author's desire to prevent such occurrences. Use this manual to assist you in your shotgun maintenance.

The steps in this book are designed to be as linear as possible. When disassembling the shotgun, simply follow the steps in the order given. The reader will note that the reassembly tips are far fewer than the given steps for disassembly. The reassembly can generally be accomplished by reinstalling the parts in the reverse order of the disassembly. If there are deviations, these deviations are noted. The use of a digital camera is priceless. It should be standard practice when disassembling a gun for the first time that images be taken of each step. It's astounding how the "oh nuts" moment becomes an "oh yeah, I see how it was" moment. A cheap 2-4 megapixel camera is sufficient.

There is a fair selection of basic tools needed for the disassembly of the firearms in this book. Punches of various sorts, such as roll pin punches, starter punches, and standard drift punches are necessities. Small hammers for tapping (not pounding) and a diverse selection of screwdrivers and hex wrenches (standard and metric) will also be needed. Of particular importance is the use of screwdrivers with hollow ground tips, not the standard taper type tips. These types of things are noted in the tools section.

We will not go over, every single time, that one should triple check to ensure the gun is unloaded: but we will just this once, right now. Do not ever work on a loaded firearm. Remove the magazine, empty the chamber. On tube fed models, visually check the loading port, and finger the follower to make sure it is indeed the follower. Check every chamber on a break open/hinge gun.

When removing screws, use the proper sized tool. Many nicer guns, particularly double barrels, have engraving that often incorporates the features of the screw head. Be sure the screw properly lines up during reassembly. Forceps or tweezers come in handy, as they help remind you to not pry anything out of a slot. There's a better way to do it. You don't want to leave a mark in the finish, or an extra line in an engraving pattern. Generally, greater force results in greater damage, with little to no result. Use safety glasses, since you don't want springs stuck in your eyes, and wait till you get home to your well lit workbench before you take it apart. Read the manuals supplied with the firearm; you might even find a schematic to help you out in the last few pages.

In the last pages of this book is a cross referencing index. Many of these guns have branched into similar models for different uses, but all of which are pretty much the same when being taken apart and put back together. Fortunately, there are a lot of common trends, such as in fire control designs, takedown methods, and ignition methods, and many guns are so closely related to others that if you do not find your specific model of shotgun, then flipping through this manual may still assist you by providing a basis of knowledge by which other somewhat similar guns operate. Still the index is quite expansive, referencing many hundreds more guns than can be covered in the preceding pages.

It is recommended that the user of this manual also acquire an even larger tome published by FW Media/Krause Publications, called the Gun Digest Book of Exploded Gun Drawings. Sometimes a simple drawing can be incredibly informative, many showing the exact placement and direction of insertion with simple lines on paper.

Kevin Muramatsu
Somewhere in the Twin Cities
Somewhere in Minnesota
March, 2012

Contents

Every writer has someone that supports, encourages, and assists in many other ways. Often it is a spouse; such as it is in this case. My wife Rachel puts up with my procrastination, my terse impatient directions when taking pictures, yet still brings me the hot chocolate without me even making a request. It is to Rachel that this book is dedicated.

Acknowledgements

I would like to express my appreciation to a few folks whose help was quite valuable in completing this book. They were instrumental in the acquisition of these shotguns and the answering of questions.

The Wolf's Den Gun Shop in Hugo, MN, was pivotal in the loan of several guns used in this book. Also of great note were Jody and the gang from North Country Marketing here in MN, who kindly provided several of the newer Browning models. Furthermore, Derek Kellgren from Kel-Tec, Caleb Siedlecki from RSR Group, Bruce Pierson, Bonnie Tetzlaff for paying me, and Corrina Peterson from F&W for editing this book, and Mike Keller for assuming some of my unrelated work load.

A Note on Reassembly

Most of the shotguns covered in this book can be reassembled by simply reversing the order of disassembly, carefully replacing the parts in the same manner they were removed. In a few instances, special instructions are required, and these are listed with each gun under "Reassembly Tips." In certain cases, reassembly photos are also provided.

If there are no special instructions or photos with a particular gun, you may assume that it can just be reassembled in reverse order. During disassembly, note the relationship of all parts and springs, take digital photos of the installed arrangements, and lay them out on the workbench in the order they were removed. By following this procedure, and referring to your own digital images, you should have no difficulty.

Tools

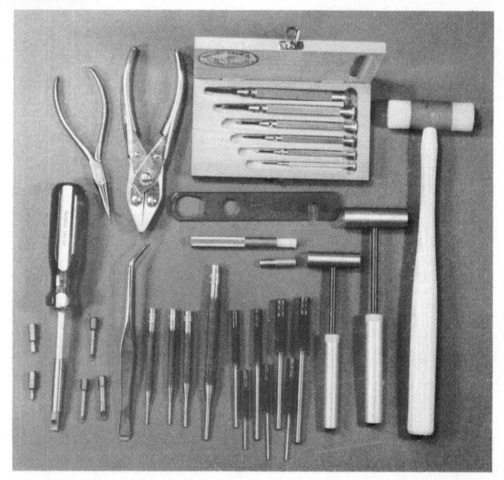

Countless firearms, old and new, bear the marks, burrs and gouges that are the result of using the wrong tools for taking them apart. In the interest of preventing this sort of thing, I am including here a group of tools that are the best types for the disassembly of shotguns. Except for the few shop-made tools for special purposes, all of those shown here are available from one of these sources.

Brownells Inc.
Route 2, Box 1,
200 S. Front St.
Montezuma, Iowa 50171

B-Square Company
P.O. Box 11281
Fort Worth, Texas 761092

General Instructions:

Screwdrivers: Always be sure the blade of the screwdriver exactly fits the slot in the screw head, both in thickness and in width. If you don't have one that fits, grind or file the tip until it does. You may ruin a few screwdrivers, but better them than the screws on a fine shotgun.

Slave pins: There are several references in this book to slave pins, and some non-gunsmith readers may not be familiar with the term. A slave pin is simply a short length of rod stock (in some cases, a section of a nail will

do) which is used to keep two parts, or a part and a spring, together during reassembly. The slave pin must be slightly smaller in diameter than the hole in the part, so it will push out easily as the original pin is driven in to retain the part. When making a slave pin, its length should be slightly less than the width of the part in which it is being used, and the ends of the pin should be rounded or beveled.

Sights: Nearly all dovetail-mounted sights are drifted out toward the right, using a nylon, aluminum, or brass drift punch.

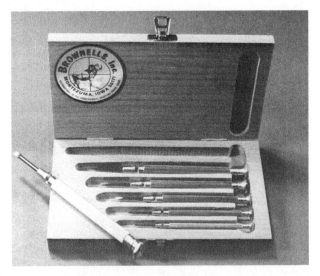

1. The tiniest of these fine German instrument screwdrivers from Brownells is too small for most gun work, but you'll see the rest of them used frequently throughout the book. There are many tight places where these will come in handy.

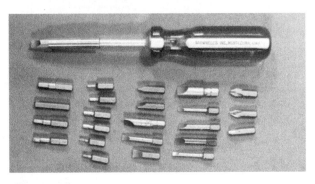

2. When a larger screwdriver is needed, this set from Brownells covers a wide range of blade sizes and also has Phillips- and Allen-type inserts. The tips are held in place by a strong magnet, yet are easily changed. These tips are very hard. With enough force you might manage to break one, but they'll never bend.

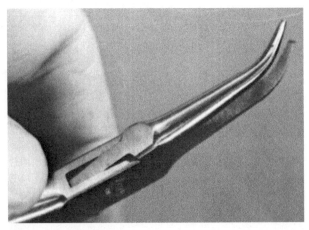

3. You should have at least one good pair of bent sharpnosed pliers. These, from Brownells, have a box joint and smooth inner faces to help prevent marring.

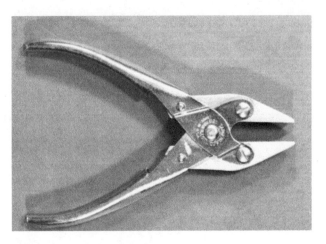

4. For heavier gripping, these Bernard parallel-jaw pliers from Brownells have smooth-faced jaw-pieces of unhardened steel to prevent marring of parts.

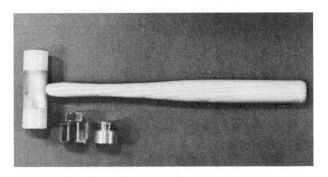

5. For situations where a non-marring rap is needed, this hammer from Brownells is ideal. It is shown with nylon faces on the head, but other faces of plastic and brass are also available. All are easily replaceable.

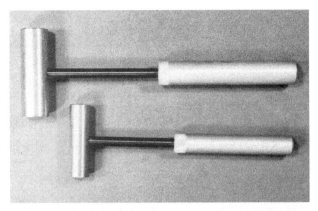

6. For drifting out pins, these small all-metal hammers from B-Square are the best I've seen. Two sizes (weights) are available and they're well worth the modest cost.

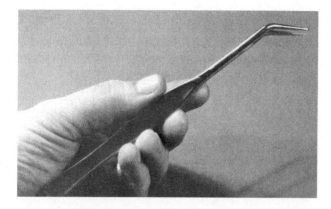

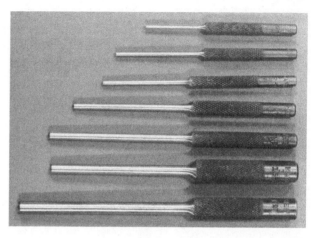

7. For situations where reach and accessibility are beyond the capabilities of sharp-nosed pliers, a pair of large sharp-nosed forceps (tweezers) will be invaluable.

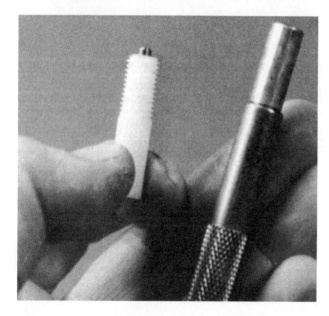

8. One of the most-used tools in my shop is this nylon tipped drift punch, shown with an optional brass tip in place on the handle. It has a steel pin inside the nylon tip for strength. From Brownells, and absolutely essential.

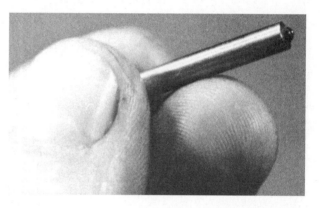

10. These punches by Mayhew are designed specifically for roll pins and have a projection at the center of the tip to fit the hollow center of a roll pin, driving it out without deformation of the ends. From Brownells.

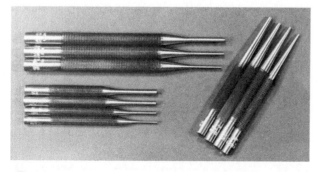

9. A good set of drift punches will prevent a lot of marred pins. These, from Brownells, are made by Mayhew. The tapered punches at the right are for starting pins, the others for pushing them through. Two sizes are available-4 inches or 6 inches.

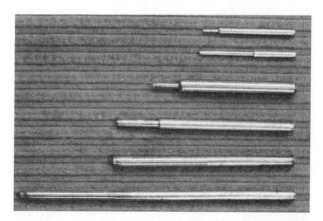

11. Some of the necessary tools are easily made in the shop. These non-marring drift punches were made from three sizes of welder's brazing rod.

12. This firing pin bushing spanner wrench from B-Square adjusts to fit all bushing holes, from 3/16" to 7/16" spacing. The pins are replaceable.

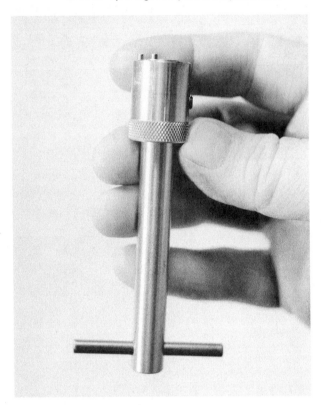

14. A digital camera, even a cheap low resolution model can be invaluable. The ability to take a quick, free photo of anything that you are doing for reference is a modern convenience that one would be foolish to neglect.

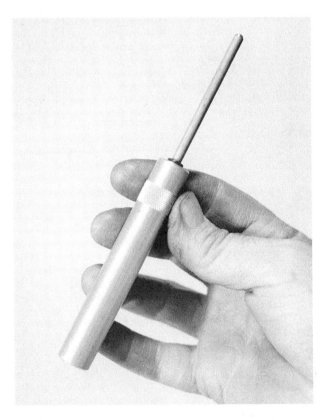

13. Designed to fit the Winchester Model 12, this forend cap nut wrench from Brownells is also usable on several other slide-action shotguns.

15. Conceived by former Gun Digest associate editor, Bob Anderson for B-Square, this handy tool is designed for pushing out the trigger group retaining cross pins in the Remington shotguns, and will work on several others. A rubber ring at the base of the shaft protects the side of the receiver.

16. Another of the B-Square stock wrenches, this short version is designed especially for the Remington Model 870, but will work on several other guns.

18. For restaking the shell stops on several of the Remington shotguns, this heavy tool from B-Square makes an awkward job a simple operation.

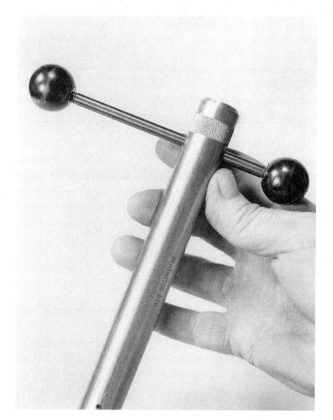

17. This wrench from B-Square is for easy removal of the deeply recessed forend cap nut on the Remington Model 870.

Akdal MKA 1919

Data: Akdal MKA 1919
Origin: Turkey
Manufacturer: Eksen Arms, Inc., Istanbul, Turkey
Gauges: 12
Magazine Capacity: 5 rounds
Overall Length: 40.5 inches
Height: 7.5 inches
Barrel Length: 19.7 inches
Weight: 6.5 pounds

Unveiled early in 2012, the MKA 1919 is a product designed to fit right into the modern sporting rifle lineup, except that it is a shotgun. Anyone familiar with an AR-15 can skillfully operate this example as the controls and handling are the same, though the takedown procedure is quite different. Still, it is a magazine fed, semi-automatic 12 gauge shotgun shooting 2 ¾" and 3" shells, with a price tag well under 1K, and as such became quite in demand as soon as it was released. A highly refined modification was produced by Firebird Precision for competition use, and while most of the parts and thus some of the disassembly were altered, these steps should be sufficient for those customized versions.

Disassembly:

1. With the magazine removed and the bolt closed, unscrew the front handguard cap and remove it from the shotgun.

2. Remove the handguard plate so that it is freely hanging on the barrel.

3. Remove the handguard halves.

4. Remove the knurled lock nut, then the gas regulator and gas regulator spring which sits behind the nut, then the stainless steel bushing/seal which sits behind the regulator spring and rests in the front of the barrel ring.

5. Pull the bolt slightly to the rear to unlock the bolt, then pull the barrel from the receiver.

6. Pull the piston from the rear of the barrel ring.

7. The front sight assembly can be removed by loosening this set screw and the two clamp screws beneath the barrel, however it is not necessary to do so unless repair is warranted.

8. Remove the carry handle/rear sight.

9. Take the buttpad off the stock. It is retained by two screws.

10. The upper and lower receivers can be separated by inserting a long hex driver into the buttstock to unscrew the bolt.

11. Leaving the bolt screwed in a few turns, tap the extension with a rubber mallet (Picture A) until the receivers start to separate (Picture B).

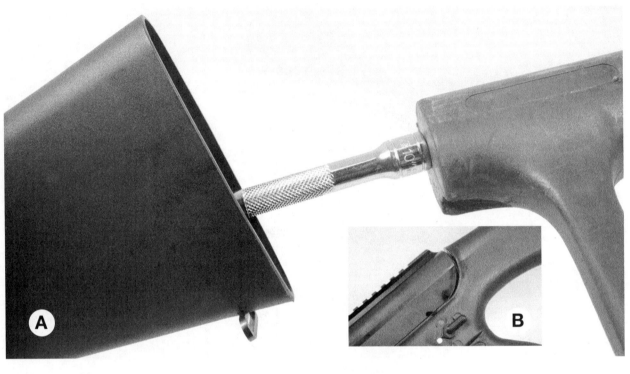

12. While holding the bolt slightly back to clear the feed ramp, pull the upper receiver up and forward to separate it from the lower.

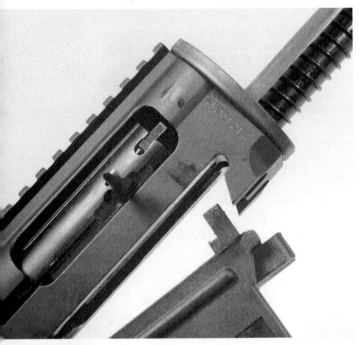

13. While holding the bolt assembly slightly to the rear, align the round section of the charging handle hole in the bolt with the charging handle and pull the handle from the bolt.

14. While firmly holding the bolt rails, slowly pull the bolt assembly out of the upper receiver to the front. The recoil spring can also be removed at this time.

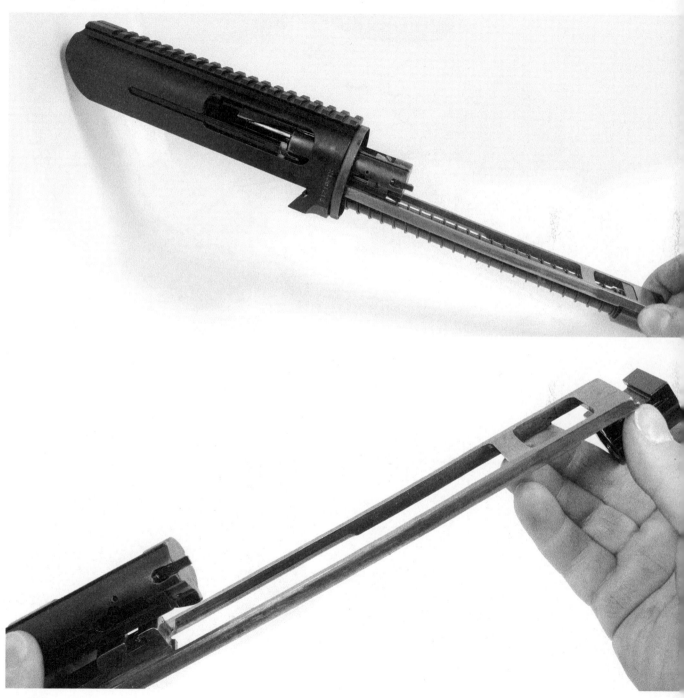

15. The bolt can be separated from the bolt carrier, and the carrier seat can be removed from the front of the bolt carrier's rails.

16. The extractor pin can be driven out from bottom to top to release the extractor, extractor detent, and spring.

17. Drive out this pin from top to bottom to release the firing pin and firing pin return spring. This will also release the bolt locking lug.

18. To remove the hammer, drive out this splined pin from left to right.

19. Remove this screw from the left receiver wall. The screw contains an integral detent. Once this screw is removed, the safety lever can be taken out of the receiver to the left.

20. Drive out this splined pin from left to right to remove the trigger and trigger spring. The trigger, disconnector, and their two associated springs can then be withdrawn up and out of the lower receiver.

22. The bolt catch, spring, and buffer can be removed by driving out this spring pin. The bolt catch housing is pressed into the lower and need not be removed.

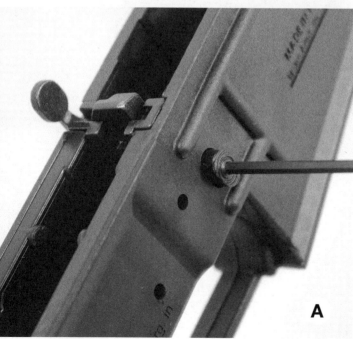

A

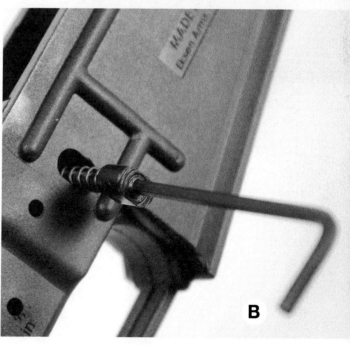

B

21. Use a hex key to remove the hex screw in the magazine catch button (Picture A). When the screw releases, the screw and the magazine catch spring will come out to the right (Picture B), and the magazine catch will fall out to the left.

Reassembly tips:

1. When reattaching the upper receiver to the lower receiver, the bolt must be withdrawn slightly to allow clearance for the feed ramp to enter the upper receiver.

Benelli Model 121 M1

Similar/Identical Pattern Guns

The same basic assembly/disassembly steps for the Benelli Model 121 M1 also apply to the following guns:

Benelli Standard Autoloader

Benelli Model 121 Slug

Data:	Benelli Model 121 Ml
Origin:	Italy
Manufacturer:	Benelli Armi, S.p.A.,Urbino
Gauge:	12
Magazine capacity:	7 rounds
Overall length:	39-3/4 inches
Barrel length:	19-5/8 inches
Weight:	7 lbs. 3 oz.

The Benelli semi-auto shotgun has an unusual action, using neither gas nor long recoil. Instead, it has a prop-type locking bar that is released by a rebounding bolt head-a unique system. Importation and sales in the U.S. were formerly handled by Heckler & Koch, Inc. The present importer is Benelli U.S.A..

Disassembly:

1. Loosen the cross screw in the magazine tube hanger loop at the muzzle, and slide the hanger off toward the front. Cycle the action to cock the internal hammer, and set the safety in the on-safe position. Unscrew the knurled retaining nut at the front of the forend, and remove the nut and the sling loop toward the front. The nut unscrews counter-clockwise (front view).

2. Remove the barrel, upper receiver, and forend toward the front. If the gun is new and tight, it may be necessary to pull the bolt half-way back and release it several times, to start the assembly forward.

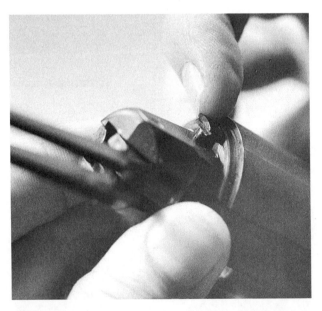

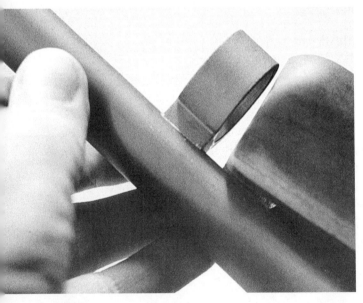

3. Tip the rear of the forend wood away from the barrel, and remove the forend downward and toward the rear. Remove the spacer ring and spring ring from the recess at the front of the forend. The rings will be released as the wood is taken off, so take care that they aren't lost.

4. Move the bolt all the way to the rear of the receiver, and pull out the firing pin retainer toward the right. A fingernail notch is provided in the head of the T-shaped retainer, and no tools are needed. Remove the firing pin and its return spring toward the rear.

5. Remove the cocking handle toward the right, and remove the bolt assembly toward the rear. The ejector, which is also the bolt guide, is welded in place inside the receiver, and is not removable.

6. Remove the locking bar from the underside of the bolt carrier, outward and toward the rear.

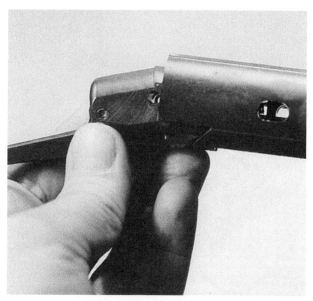

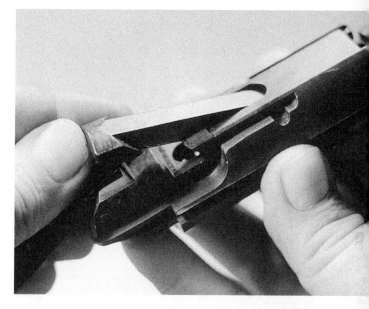

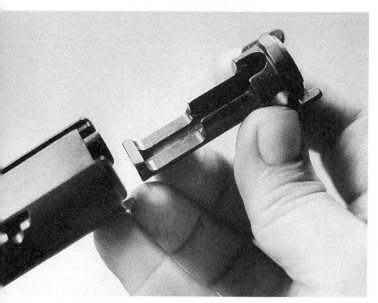

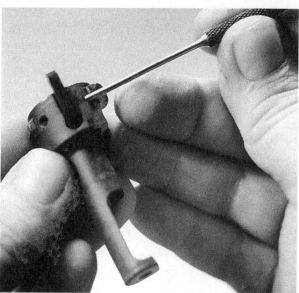

7. Remove the bolt head from the front of the bolt carrier. Remove the heavy bolt head spring toward the front.

8. The extractor and its coil spring are retained on the right side of the bolt head by a vertical roll pin. Restrain the extractor, and drift out the pin in either direction. Remove the extractor and spring toward the right.

9. The recoil spring connector strut is retained at the lower rear of the bolt carrier by a cross pin that is riveted on both sides. Unless removal is necessary for repair, this pin should be left in place.

10. Drift out the roll pin at the lower rear of the lower receiver, directly above the safety. Push the carrier latch, and tip the carrier up to its raised position. Use a nylon-tipped drift punch to nudge the trigger group downward at the rear. Be sure the carrier stays elevated, or it will be damaged.

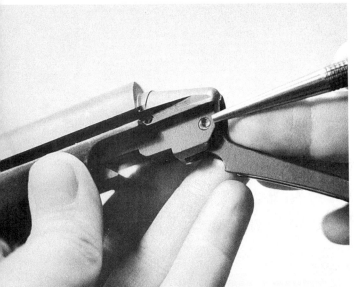

11. When the trigger group is free, remove it downward and toward the rear.

12. Grip the front of the carrier spring guide firmly, and move it toward the rear to detach it from its cross pin in the carrier dog. Slowly release the spring tension, and remove the guide, spring, and spring base from the trigger group.

13. The carrier pivot is retained on both sides of the group by C-clips, but only one has to be taken off. Remove the C-clip from either side, restraining it as it is pried from its groove to prevent loss. Remove the carrier pivot from the trigger group.

14. Remove the carrier upward.

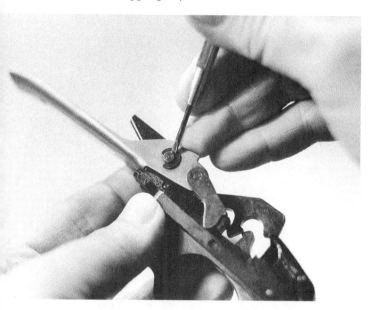

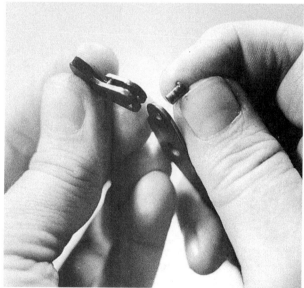

15. The carrier dog pivot is easily removed, and the dog is then detached from the carrier. The pivot is held in place by the side of the group unit when the carrier is in place, and is freed as the carrier is taken off, so take care that it isn't lost.

16. Move the safety to the off-safe position, pull the trigger, and ease the hammer over forward, beyond its normal fired position. The hammer spring and follower can now be removed upward.

17. Pull out the hammer pivot toward the right, and remove the hammer upward.

18. Restrain the trigger, and drift out the trigger pin toward the right.

19. Remove the trigger assembly upward. The trigger spring is easily detached from the front of the trigger. The secondary sear, or disconnector, and its plunger and spring can be removed from the trigger by pushing out its cross pin. Caution: Control the plunger and spring as the pin is taken out

20. Hold a fingertip over the hole on top of the group at the rear to arrest the safety spring, and drift the small cross pin at upper rear toward the right until the hole is cleared. Remove the safety spring and plunger upward, and push out the safety button toward either side. If the plunger fails to come out with the spring, tap the trigger group on the workbench to free it. The other small cross pin at the rear of the group is a limit pin for the trigger. It retains no part, and need not be removed in normal takedown.

21. The carrier latch and its spring are retained inside the right wall of the lower receiver by a vertical pin which is pushed out upward. Only half of the lower tip of the pin is accessible, and a very small screwdriver or an opened paper clip should be used to push the pin. Restrain the carrier latch.

22. After the pin is pushed out, remove the carrier latch from the lower receiver. The spring is easily detached from the carrier latch, if necessary.

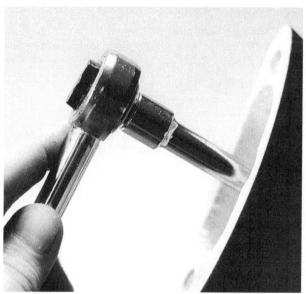

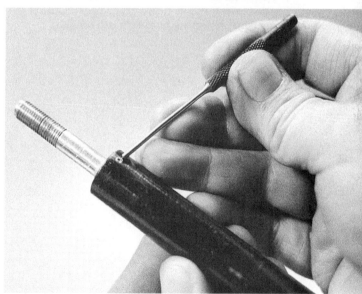

23. An ordinary socket wrench can be used to remove the nut under the buttplate that retains the stock. The exact size of the nut is 13mm, but if no metric socket is available, a standard 1/2-inch socket will work. Take off the nut, lock washer, and spacer washer, and remove the buttstock toward the rear.

24. Drifting out the vertical roll pin at the rear of the recoil spring housing will release the stock mounting bolt for removal toward the rear. Caution: The stock bolt is also the retainer for the recoil spring, so restrain it during removal Take out the spring and follower toward the rear. No attempt should be made to remove the spring housing or the magazine assembly from the lower receiver.

Reassembly Tips:

1. Remove the trigger assembly upward. The trigger spring is easily detached from the front of the trigger. The secondary sear, or disconnector, and its plunger and spring can be removed from the trigger by pushing out its cross pin. Caution: Control the plunger and spring as the pin is taken out

2. When replacing the carrier spring base in its recess on the left side of the trigger group, note that the hole in the base is off-center. The end nearest to the hole must go toward the outside-that is, to the left. Also, the flat face of the base goes to the front.

The bolt head must be pushed to its rear position in the carrier before the cocking handle can be re-inserted.

When replacing the two rings in the front of the forend, the plain ring goes in first, and the spring ring at the front.

When moving the barrel and receiver assembly toward the rear, be sure the rear tip of the recoil spring strut on the bolt carrier engages the cup of the spring follower.

Benelli Nova

Similar/Identical Pattern Guns:

The same basic assembly/disassembly steps for the Benelli Nova also apply to the following guns:

Nova Slug Gun   **Rifled Slug Gun**

Data:	Benelli Nova
Origin:	Italy
Manufacturer:	Benelli Armi, Urbino, Italy
Gauges:	12 only
Magazine capacity:	4 rounds (2 3/4-inch shells) 3 rounds (3 1/2-inch shells)
Overall length:	49-1/2 inches
Barrel length:	28 inches (others offered)
Weight:	8 pounds

An excellent exercise in modern design and polymer construction, the Benelli Nova was introduced in 1999. One of its notable features is a magazine cutoff button that is located at center underside on the forend, allowing a load change with the other rounds kept in reserve. Overall, the Nova is a beautifully-engineered design.

Disassembly:

1. Cycle the action to cock the internal hammer, and set the manual safety in on-safe position. Unscrew the magazine end cap. Operate the slide latch, and move the bolt slightly toward the rear. Remove the barrel toward the front.

2. Use a drift punch, or the provided nose on the magazine end cap, to start the trigger group cross pins out toward the left.

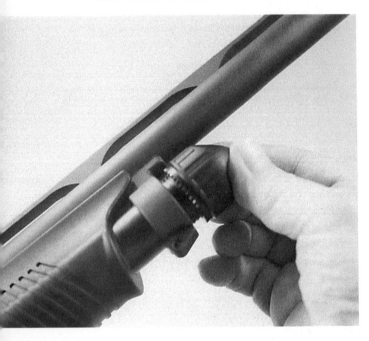

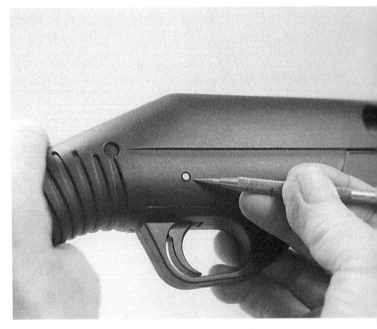

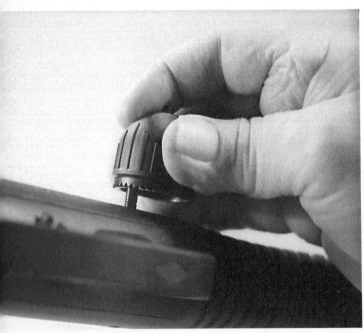

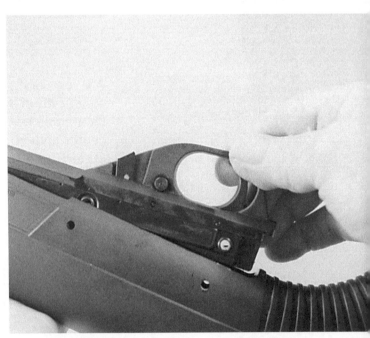

3. You can drift the pins all the way out, or use the flange on the inside of the magazine end cap to pull them out. Note, for reassembly, that the cross pins are not of equal length.

4. Tilt the trigger group downward at the rear, and take it out rearward and downward.

5. Push on the top of the action bars to tilt them away from their engagement with the bolt, and take out the action slide assembly toward the front.

6. The action bars are retained in the forearm by two short pins that are not routinely removable.

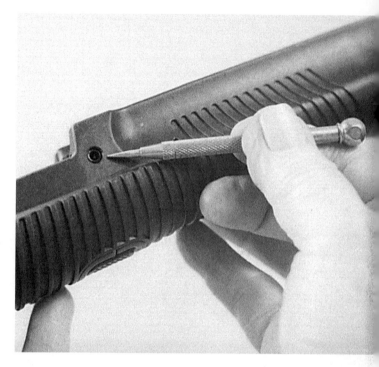

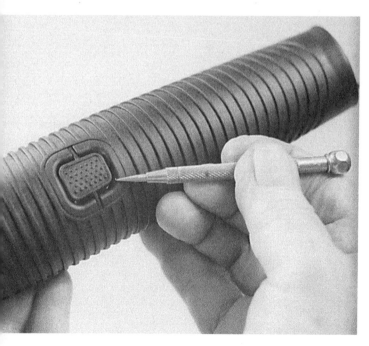

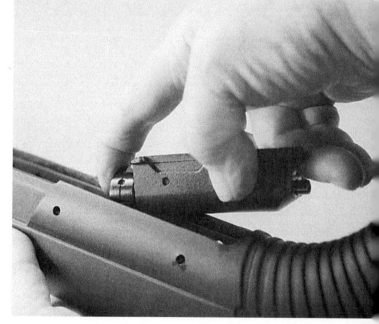

7. The magazine cutoff button can be taken out, inward, by inserting a tool inside to depress its detent plunger. Caution: control the plunger and its coil spring.

8. With the bolt at the rear of the receiver, compress the bolt head into the bolt body, and lift the assembly out.

9. By repeatedly drawing back the ejector and releasing it to strike its roll-pin retainer, it is possible to push out the pin, and remove the ejector and its long coil spring. If this is done, keep a finger near the retainer pin, to arrest it and prevent loss.

10. The magazine spring and follower can be removed in the usual way, by prying out the retainer at the outer end of the tube. **Caution:** *Control the retainer and spring.*

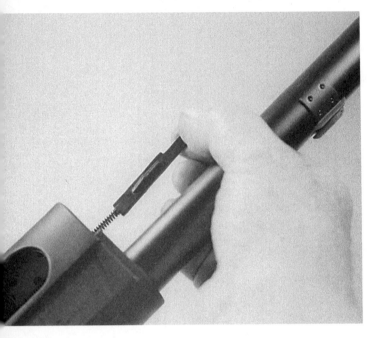

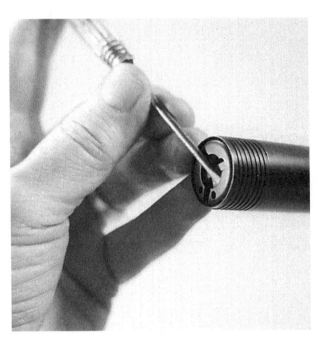

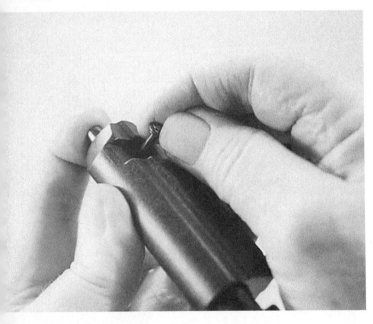

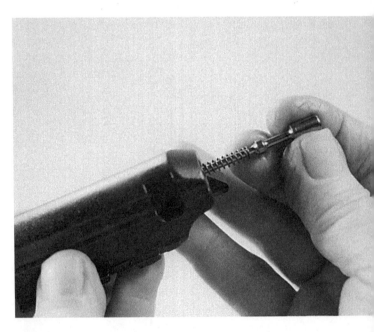

11. Restrain the firing pin, and pull out the firing pin retainer. Note that the retainer has a rubber 0-ring at its head, and be sure this isn't dislodged.

12. Remove the firing pin and its spring.

13. It is possible, if necessary for repair, to drift out the large cross pin that retains the bolt head in the bolt. The pin, however, is heavily factory-staked in place. In normal takedown, it should be left in place. If it must be taken out, it is drifted toward the left, in the direction of its staked head.

14. The extractor is pivoted and retained by a roll-pin, which is drifted out downward. Restrain the extractor during removal, and take out the extractor and its coil springs

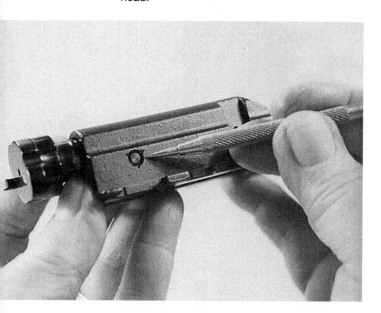

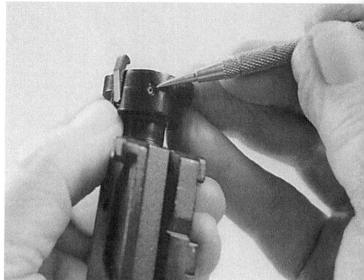

15. Restrain the hammer, pull the trigger, and ease the hammer down to fired position. Insert a sharp tool beneath the rounded part of the spring clips on the left end of the trigger group cross-pin sleeves, and tip off both spring clips. Restrain them, and take care that these small parts are not lost.

16. Moving it evenly at front and rear, remove the left sideplate. The front portion of the sideplate is the secondary shell stop.

17. Using a rod or drift of appropriate size, push the front cross-pin sleeve just far enough toward the right to free the hammer.

18. Remove the hammer upward.

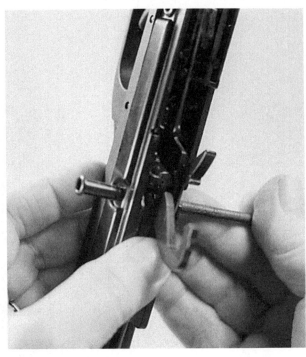

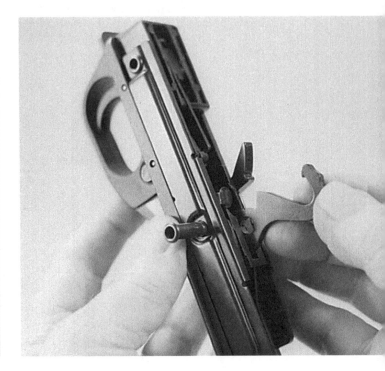

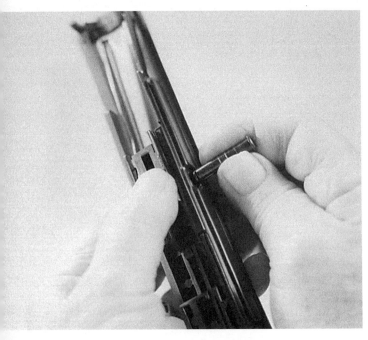

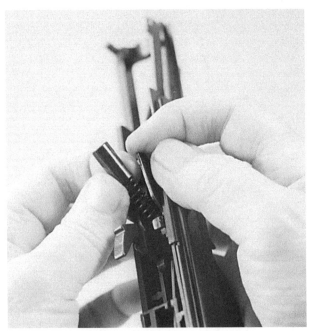

19. Restrain the bolt latch and hammer spring, and remove the front cross-pin sleeve toward the right.

20. Move the bolt latch slightly rearward, and slowly release the hammer spring tension. Remove the hammer spring and plunger upward.

21. Remove the rear cross-pin sleeve and take off the right sideplate. Note that the front of the sideplate is the primary shell stop, and that it has a tab that engages a recess inside the front extension of the trigger group housing.

22. Move the carrier assembly forward, and tip it downward for removal. Note that the carrier dog retaining pivot is held in place only when in its slot in the group housing, so take care that it doesn't fall out.

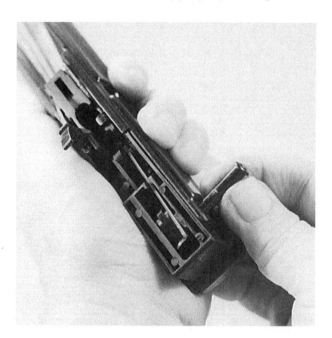

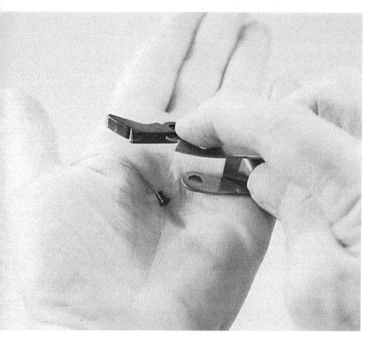

23. Turn the carrier over your hand, and the dog pivot will fall into your palm. The dog can now be taken off.

24. Remove the carrier plunger and spring.

25. Push out the trigger cross pin.

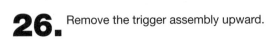

26. Remove the trigger assembly upward.

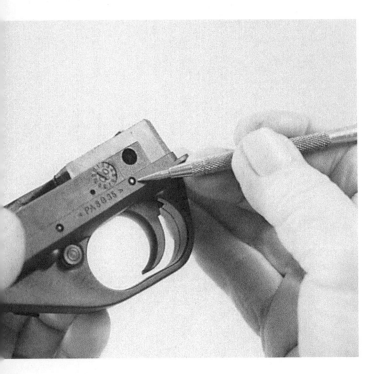

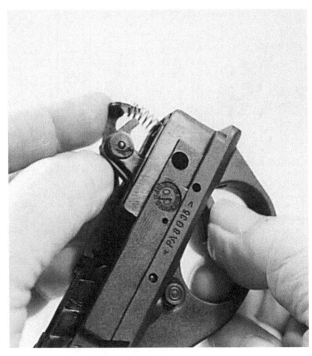

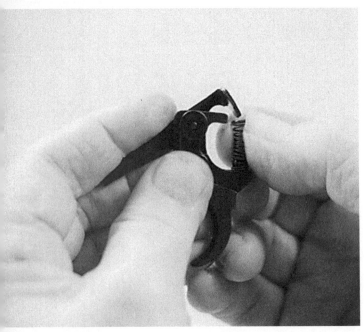

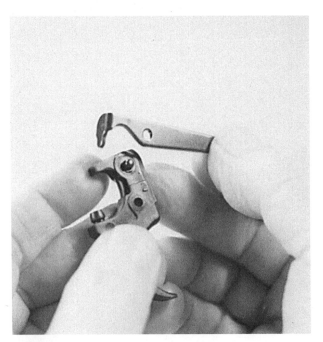

27. Detach the trigger spring from its stud on the disconnector. Turn it clockwise (top view) to remove it from the trigger stud.

28. The disconnector is easily lifted off its pivot pin on the trigger. The pin should be left in place.

29. Use a small tool to push the bolt latch spring retaining pin outward for removal. Restrain the spring, as it may or may not fit tightly in its recess.

30. Remove the bolt latch spring, moving it forward and upward.

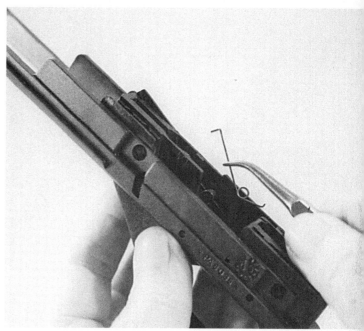

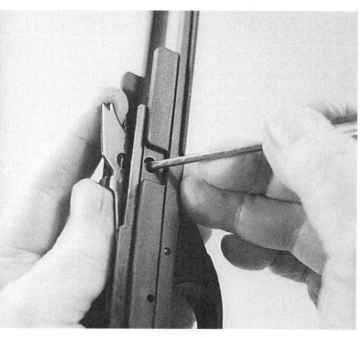

31. The bolt latch can now be removed upward. Because its lower tip is angled slightly outward, it will have to be gently pried.

32. Restrain the sear, and push out the sear cross pin.

33. Remove the sear and its coil spring upward.

1. When re-installing the rear cross-pin sleeve, the trigger must be pulled slightly to clear.

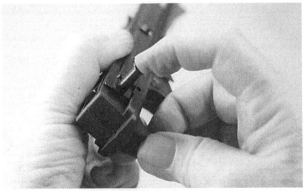

2. Insert the front cross-pin sleeve in small increments, getting it through the carrier arm, the bolt latch, the hammer, and so on. Remember to install the hammer spring and plunger before putting in the bolt latch.

34. If removal of the manual safety is necessary for repair, put the button in on-safe position, and insert a small tool with an L-shaped tip, such as the dental tool shown, to depress its plunger and spring. The safety button is then easily pushed out. **Caution:** *Keep the plunger and spring under control.*

3. Remember that the bolt head must be compressed into the bolt body for reinsertion into the receiver, Be sure the lugs on the action slide bars mate properly with their recesses on the bolt.

Benelli Super Black Eagle II

Similar/Identical Pattern Guns:

The same basic assembly/disassembly steps for the Benelli Super Black Eagle II also apply to the following guns:

Benelli Super Black Eagle	**Benelli Sport II**
Benelli M1	**Benelli Cordoba**
Benelli M2	**Benelli Montefeltro**
Benelli SuperSport	

Data: Benelli Super Black Eagle II
Origin: Italy
Manufacturer: Benelli Armi, Urbino, Italy
Gauges: 12
Overall Length: 47.6 inches
Height: 7.5 inches
Barrel Length: 26 inches
Weight: 7 lbs. 3 oz.

Benelli's flagship line in the U.S.A. is the Super Black Eagle II series. Available in black, multiple camouflage patterns, or with wooden stocks, it is a very popular, low recoil, low profile, semiautomatic shotgun. The SBE II, like most modern Benelli models, uses a lightweight "inertia driven" means of operation, not relying on gas operation, or blowback or recoil means either. The SBE II, Cordoba, SuperSport, and Sport II all feature upper receivers that disassemble along with the barrel. The rest of the Benelli line utilizes one-piece receivers. There is also some variation in the magazine cap designs among the various models, but, regardless, there should be no trouble disassembling them. The rest of the steps are very close to the same in all models and these steps will apply.

Disassembly:

1. Remove the magazine cap from the magazine tube.

2. With the bolt closed, pull the barrel and forend forward off the receiver and magazine tube. The bolt assembly will accompany the barrel and upper receiver.

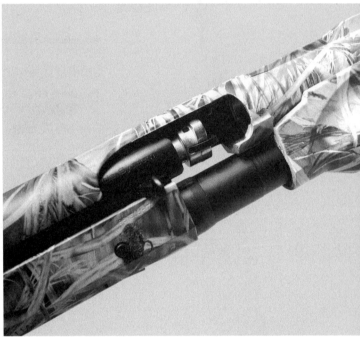

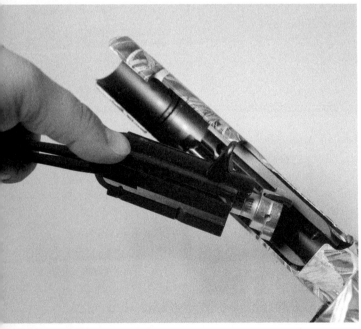

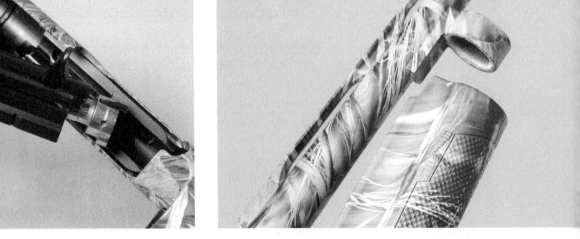

3. Pull the bolt assembly from the upper receiver/barrel.

4. Remove the forend from the barrel by pulling it rearward off the barrel ring.

5. The ejector can be removed by first displacing this spring off its post and removing it. The ejector can then be pulled out to the rear by lifting its rearmost portion to clear the receiver. As this is a tight fit and will likely result in cosmetic damage to the inside of the receiver, it is not advised unless the ejector is broken and needs replacement.

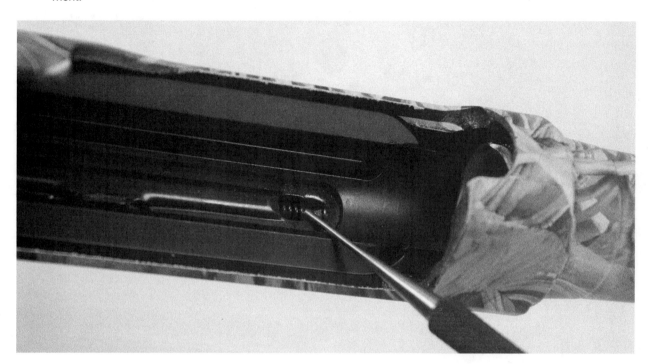

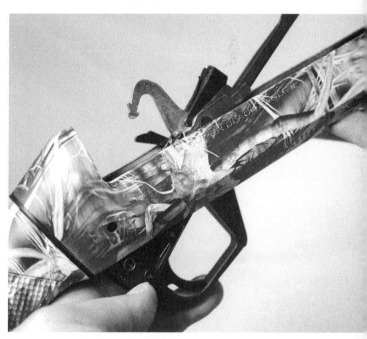

6. Press out the trigger guard pin.

7. To remove the trigger guard assembly, depress the carrier latch button and pull the trigger guard down. It will rotate around and pull out the bottom rear of the receiver.

8. The buttpad can be removed by hand. Do this to expose the stock bolt. The bolt and lock washer beneath it bear against a locking plate that establishes cast and drop for the stock. Remove the bolt, washer, and plate, recording the orientation of the plate.

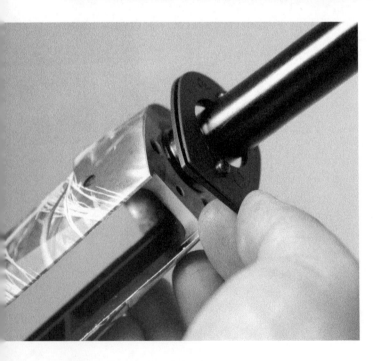

9. Remove the buttstock. In front of the stock, between the stock and the receiver are drop and cast shims.

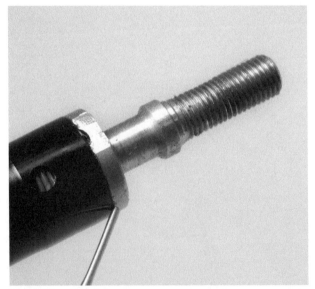

10. The recoil spring and follower assembly can be removed from the recoil spring tube by removing this cap. However, this cap is very tightly screwed in with threadlocker, and removal is unadvised without the need to repair. The tube itself can be unscrewed from the receiver, but this is also not recommended outside of the factory.

11. Use snap ring pliers to remove the magazine spring seal ring. The magazine plug, spring, and follower will follow. Control the spring.

12. The carrier latch assembly and its spring can be removed by driving out this pin.

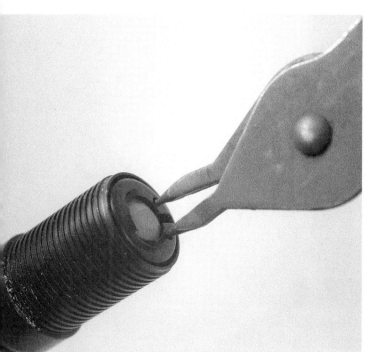

13. Depress the bolt head slightly until the bolt handle can be pulled from the bolt body.

14. Pull the firing pin retaining pin from the bolt assembly and withdraw the firing pin and spring out of the rear of the assembly.

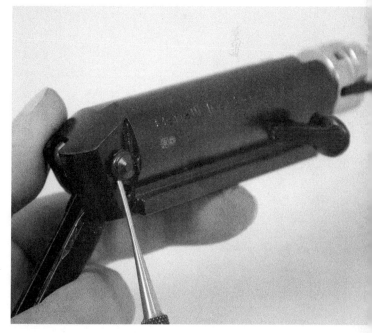

15. Pull out the cam pin.

16. Remove the bolt and inertia spring behind it.

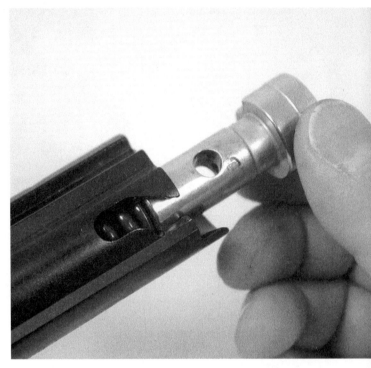

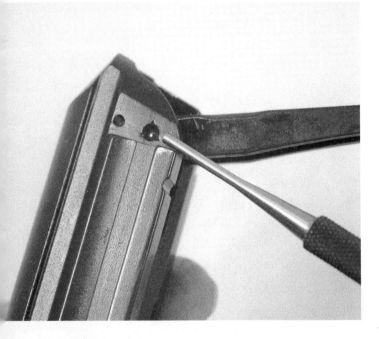

17. The link pin is staked in place but can be driven out if repair of the link is necessary.

18. Displace the carrier drop lever spring to the left, off of the lever.

19. Remove the bolt latch pin and spring. The rear anchor point is a washer that is retained only by the spring pressure.

21. Push out the trigger pin slightly to release the carrier drop lever spring, then fully to release the trigger. Remove the trigger from the trigger guard.

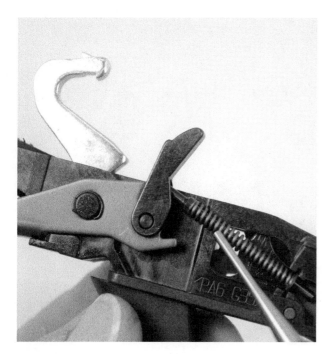

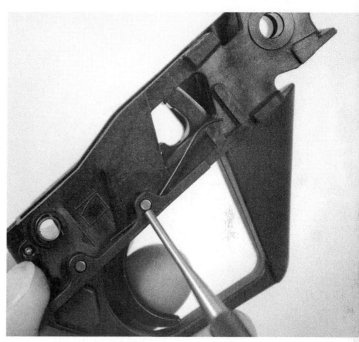

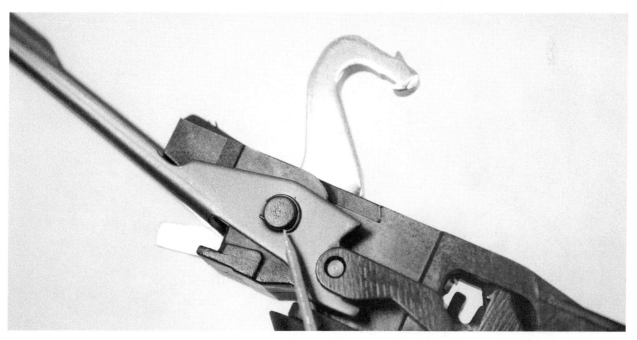

20. Remove this spring clip from the hammer pin. Push the hammer pin out to the right. This will free the carrier, hammer, and carrier drop lever, in that order. These parts can be removed from the trigger guard. The hammer spring is still compressed, so control the hammer and carrier drop lever. Also remove the hammer spring and plunger.

22. The trigger stop pin and the trigger guard pin bushing above it need not be removed unless replacement is warranted.

23. This roll pin can be removed to take out the safety detent and spring. The safety button can then be pushed out to either direction.

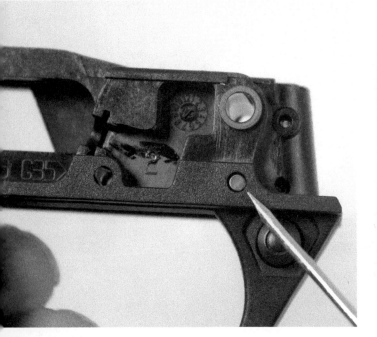

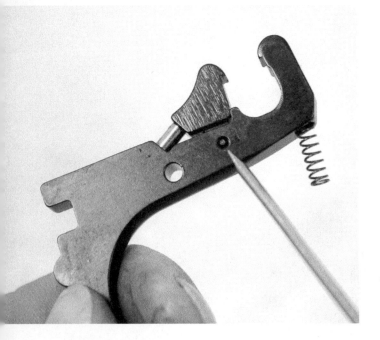

24. The disconnector can be removed by pushing out this pin.

Reassembly Tips:

1. The scribed line in the cam pin of the bolt should face the rear when reinstalled.

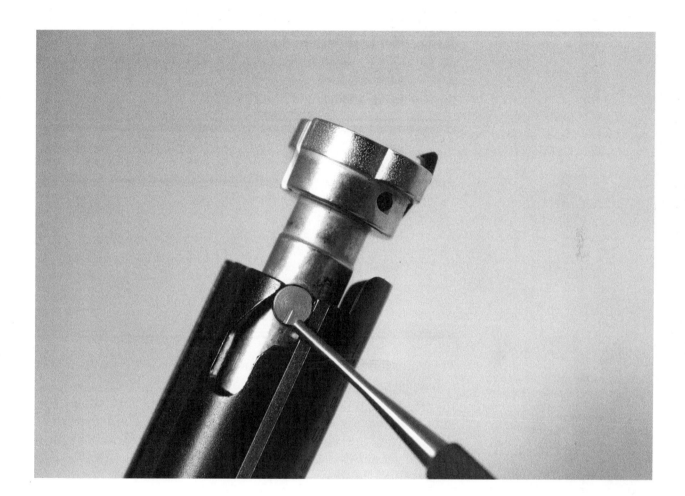

Benelli Vinci

Similar/Identical Pattern Guns:

The following basic assembly/disassembly steps for the Benelli Vinci can also be used for the following guns:

Benelli Super Vinci

Data:	Benelli Vinci
Origin:	Italy
Manufacturer:	Benelli Armi, Urbino, Italy
Gauges:	12
Overall Length:	47.5 inches
Height:	7.5 inches
Barrel Length:	26 inches
Weight:	7 lbs. 15 oz.

The Vinci and the Super Vinci are innovative examples of modular construction. With just a couple of motions the entire assembly breaks apart into three major subassemblies. This allows the gun to be quickly configured for various tasks. The Super Vinci differs from the Vinci by having a 3.5" chamber and slightly altered cosmetics. Both are available in black and camouflage.

Disassembly:

1. Depress the forend button and rotate the magazine tube cap counterclockwise until the gun carriage (forend) separates. Remove the carriage from the action.

2. Rotate the buttstock 90 degrees to separate it from the action.

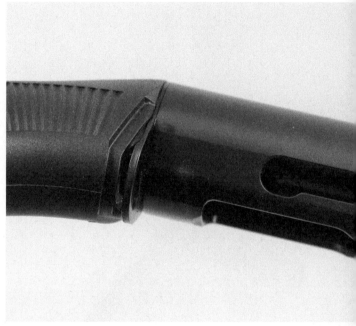

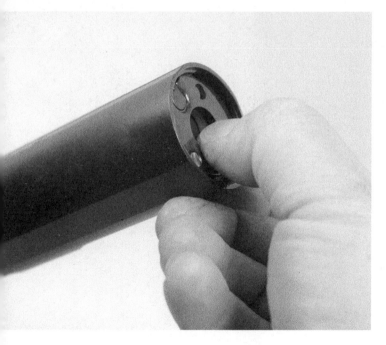

3. Push down on the bolt stop to unlock the bolt assembly.

4. Pull the bolt assembly to its rearward extent, then pull out the bolt handle.

5. Remove the bolt assembly completely from the action.

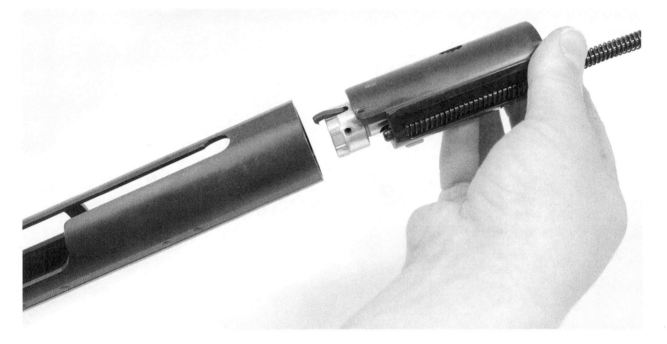

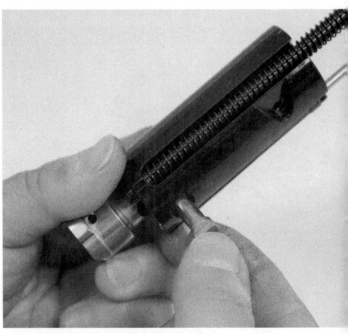

6. Pull the firing pin retaining pin out to the left. This will free the firing pin and firing pin spring to be removed from the back of the bolt carrier.

7. This is the locking (bolt) head pin. Pull it out to release the locking head.

8. Pull the locking head from the front of the bolt carrier. The inertia spring will follow.

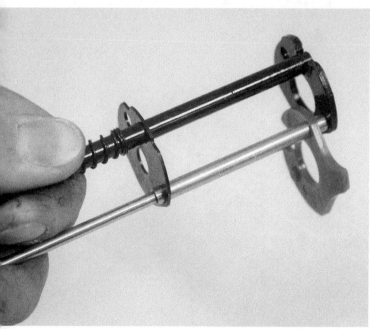

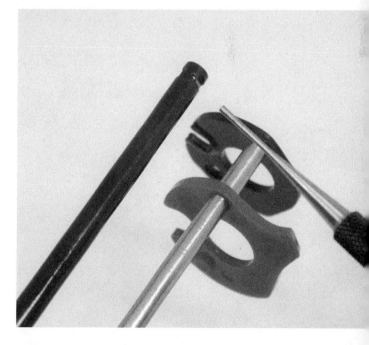

9. Pull the bolt return spring forward, releasing tension on the bolt shoulder-plate. Then pull the plate forward to allow the rubber insert to rotate out from between the plate and the ejector guide pin and plate.

10. Rotate the ejector pin plate off the bolt spring plunger pin (recoil spring guide rod).

11. Pull the ejector pin from the bolt body. Then remove the bolt return spring and the bolt shoulder plate. This spring is still highly compressed so control these parts as they are removed.

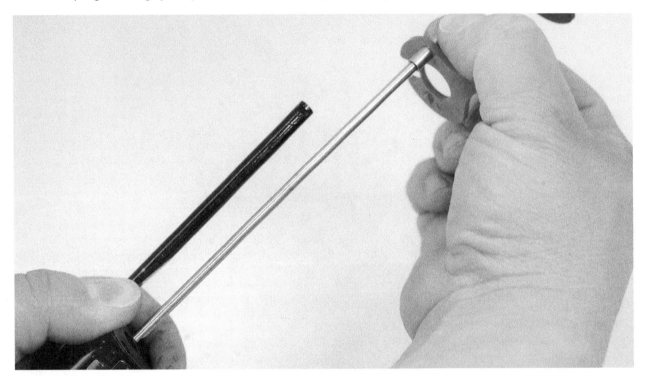

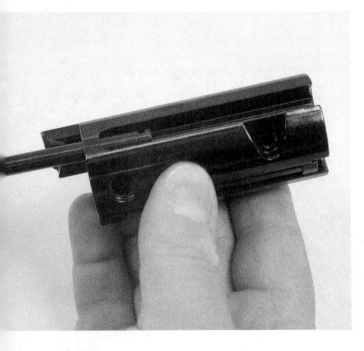

12. The guide rod can then be pulled from the front of the bolt.

13. Driving out this pin will allow the long tubular ejector to be removed from the bolt channel it slides in.

14. Drive out this pin to remove the extractor and spring.

15. Drive out the trigger guard pin to release the trigger group assembly.

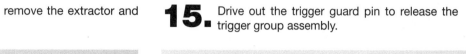

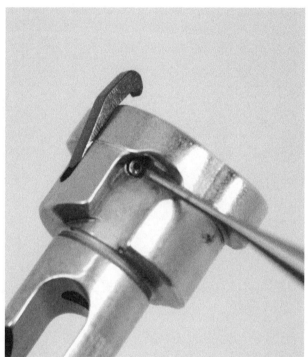

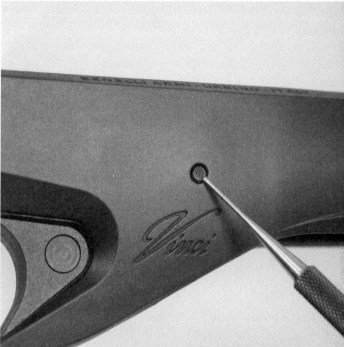

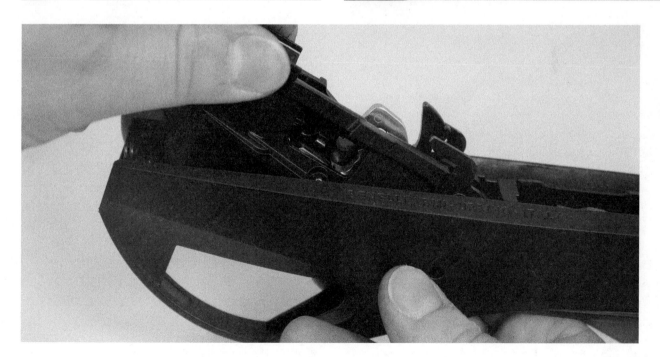

16. Lift the trigger group assembly from the carriage.

17. Remove this spring clip that holds the pin bushing in place (Picture A). Then lift the left carriage fixing plate from the trigger assembly (Picture B).

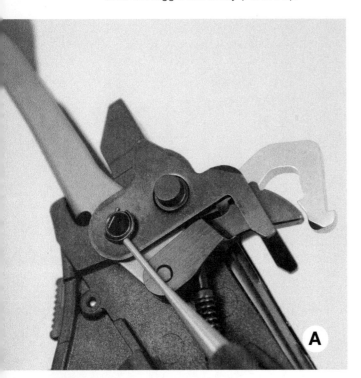

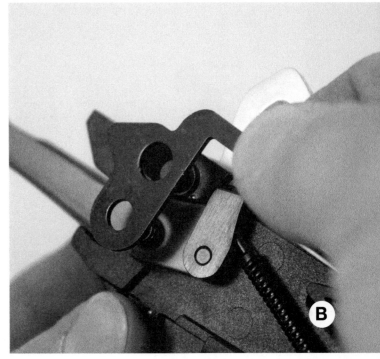

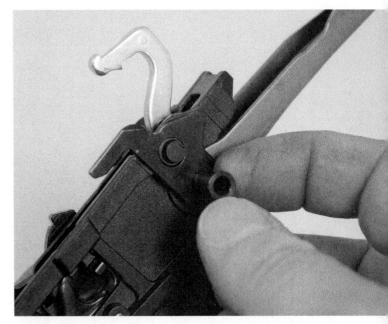

18. Remove the carrier spring and bolt latch pin from the left side of the assembly. The rear of the pin is retained by a washer. Pull back on the head of the pin and move it to the left to remove spring compression.

19. Pull the pin bushing out to the right of the assembly. As this is done, both the carrier with bolt stop and the hammer will be released from the trigger assembly. As the bushing is fully removed, the right carriage fixing plate will also be freed.

20. The hammer assembly consists of the hammer, link pin, right and left side links, the link plate (which holds the links together at the back), and the hammer spring. These parts are easily separated, if necessary.

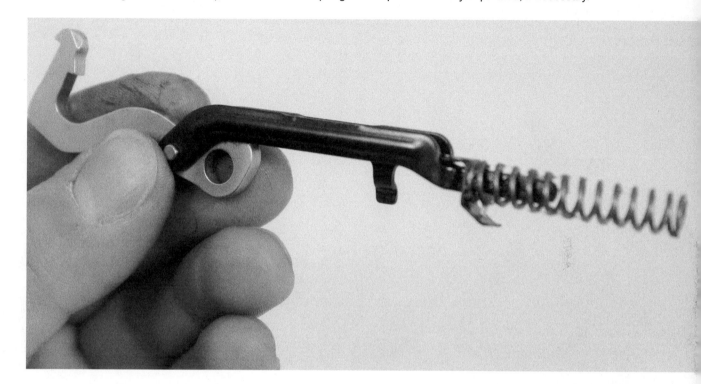

21. Remove this set screw and the identical screw on the left side to release the hammer spring cap, to be removed from the back of the trigger guard.

22. Drive out this pin to release the sear/disconnector assembly. Lift the assembly forward and up to clear the trigger guard.

23. The sear and sear spring can be separated from the disconnector by pushing out this bushing.

24. Drive out this pin to free the trigger. Remove the trigger by pulling it down and out of the trigger guard.

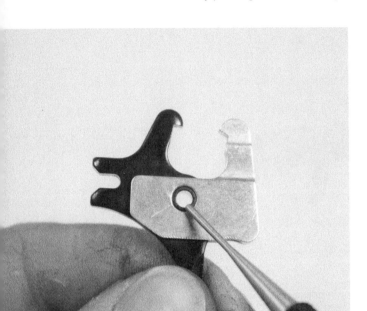

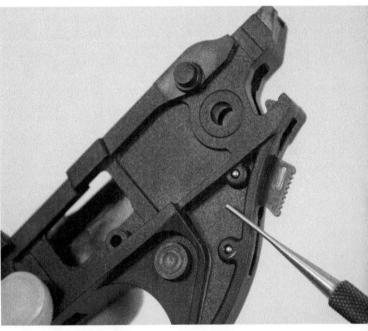

25. The trigger spring and plunger can be removed from the front of the trigger, as can the disconnector trigger roller pin.

26. Push out both of these pins to free the cartridge drop lever and spring.

27. This is difficult to show in a picture. The safety button can be removed by using a long probe to depress the safety spring plunger to clear the button, which can then be removed to either side. The plunger and spring can be removed by inverting the trigger guard.

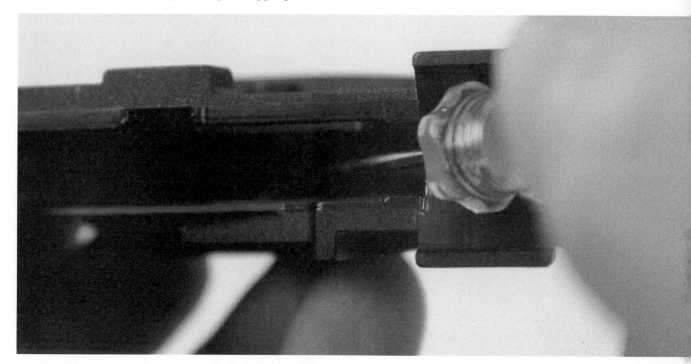

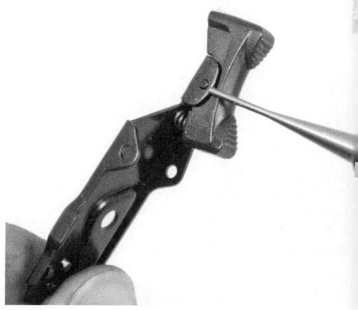

28. Lift this pin out to release the carrier latch assembly and spring.

29. The carrier latch button, spring, and latch can be separated by pushing out this pin.

30. By fully depressing the forend button, the entire magazine tube assembly can be pulled from the front of the carriage.

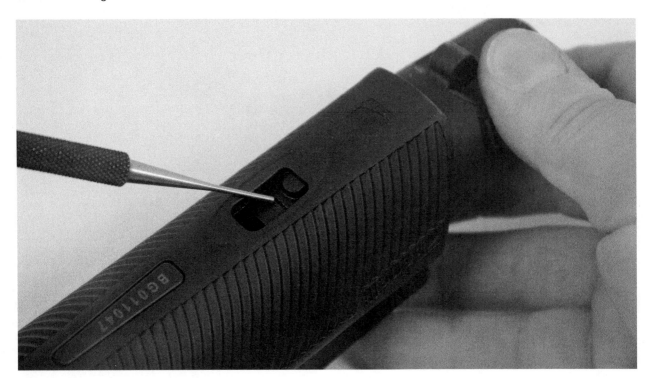

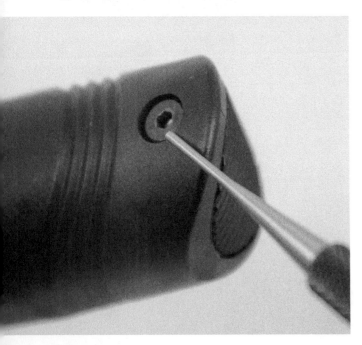

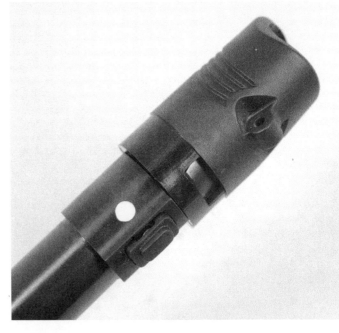

31. Remove this screw on the top of the magazine tube module to release the cap. Below the cap is the magazine plug, magazine spring, and follower.

32. If necessary, the rest of the magazine tube module should be replaced as an assembly, and should not be disassembled.

33. Beneath this nut and its associated washers lies one of several possible drop change plates and the stock lock ring. The plate can be exchanged for other plates with differing dimensions, but other than for that task, or to swap butt pads or cheek risers, the buttstock should not be disassembled.

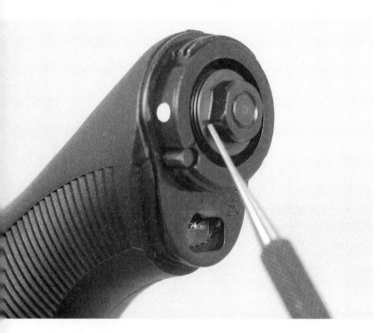

Reassembly Tips:

1. When reinstalling the cartridge drop lever, first insert the spring into its channel, then insert the lever into its slot. It is easier to reinstall the forward upper pin first, then rotate the lever down and in for the second pin.

Beretta Model A303

Similar/Identical Pattern Guns:

The same basic assembly/disassembly steps for the Beretta Model A303 also apply to the following guns:

Beretta Model AL-2   **Beretta Model AL-3**

Beretta Model A301   **Beretta Model A302**

Data:	Beretta Model A303
Origin:	Italy
Manufacturer:	Armi Beretta S.p.A. Gardone, V.T. (Brescia)
Gauges:	12
Magazine capacity:	2 rounds
Overall length:	44 inches (with 24-inch barrel)
Barrel length:	24, 26, 28, 30 & 32 inches
Weight:	6½ pounds to 7-½ pounds

The original Model A303 was introduced in 1983, and in 1989 a Sporting Clays version was offered, with a wide barrel rib and different stock dimensions. Also, in 1989, the A303 Upland Model was introduced. In 12-gauge only, it has a shorter barrel and an English-style buttstock. The earlier guns, the AL-2, AL-3, A301 and A302, are essentially the same, mechanically.

Disassembly:

1. Lock the action open, and set the safety in on-safe position. Unscrew and remove the forend cap.

2. Slide the forend off toward the front.

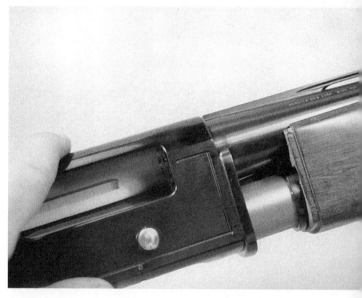

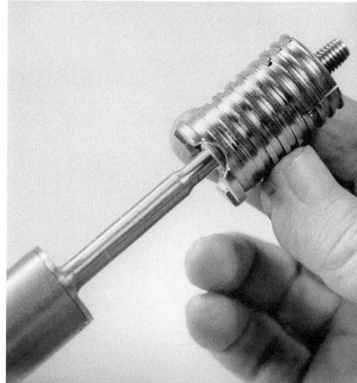

3. Remove the barrel toward the front.

4. Remove the gas piston.

5. The bushing inside the piston is retained by a ring-clip. This is not removed in normal takedown, only for repair.

6. Restrain the bolt, press the release button, and ease the bolt to forward position. Grip the cocking handle firmly, and remove it toward the right.

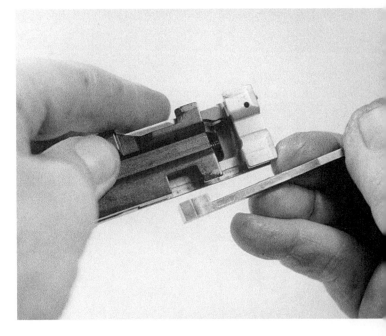

7. Move the action slide assembly forward, while pushing gently on the rear of the bolt, and remove the bolt and action slide.

8. Detach the bolt from the action slide.

9. Detach the slide plate and spring strut from the bolt.

10. Push out the cross pin, and detach the strut from the slide plate.

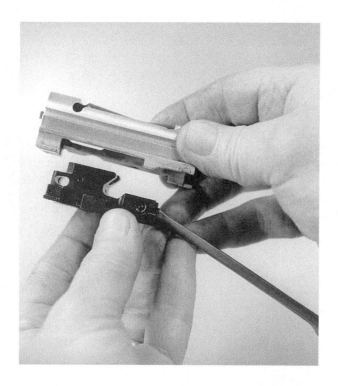

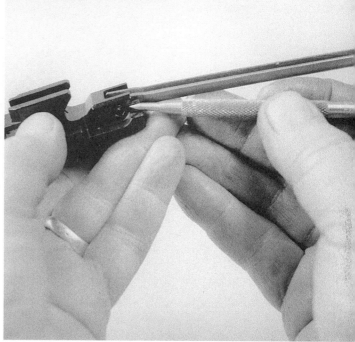

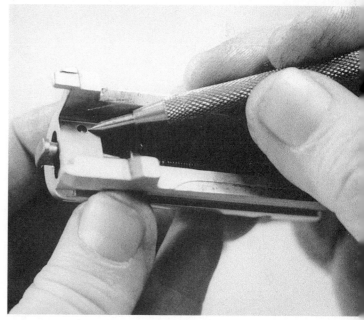

11. A roll cross pin retains the bolt handle retaining plunger and spring. If this assembly is removed, restrain the spring.

12. The firing pin and its return spring are retained by a vertical pin on the right side of the bolt at the rear. The pin must be drifted out upward. After removal of the firing pin, the locking block can be turned upward, and is taken out toward the left.

13. The extractor and its coil spring are retained by a vertical pin on the right side of the bolt at the front. The pin is drifted out upward. It is lightly staked at the top, and should be re-staked on reassembly.

14. Depress the carrier stop button toward the rear, allowing the carrier to drop lower.

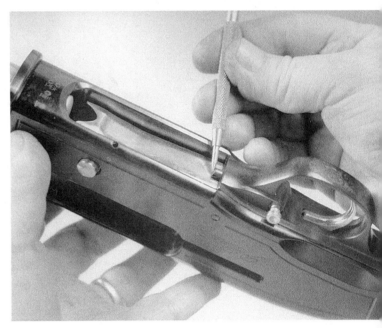

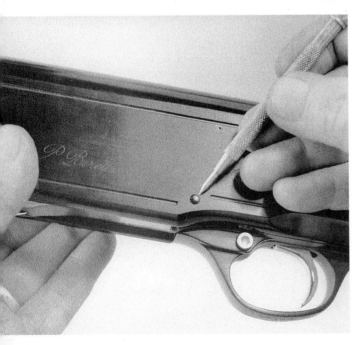

15. With a non-marring tool, push out the trigger group retaining pin.

16. Depress the carrier latch button, and move the trigger group forward and downward for removal.

17. With the carrier in the fully lowered position, grip the carrier spring firmly, and compress it slightly rearward while moving the semi-circular attachment at the front upward, to disengage it from the recess in the carrier. Remove the spring, guide, and attachment piece.

18. Remove the spring base.

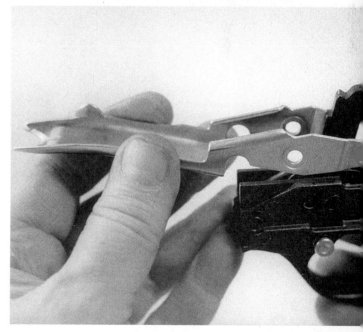

19. Push out the carrier pivot pin.

20. Remove the carrier upward.

21. The carrier dog pivot is a riveted part, and it is not removed in normal takedown.

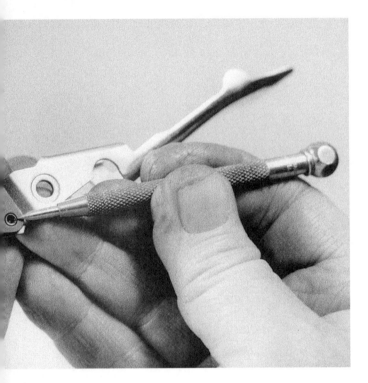

22. Move the safety to off-safe, restrain the hammer, pull the trigger, and ease the hammer down to the forward position. Depress the hammer slightly at lower front, and push out the hammer pivot toward the left.

23. Remove the hammer and its two-piece spring strut upward. The strut arms are easily detached from the hammer.

24. The hammer spring and plunger are contained in a cylindrical housing at the rear of the trigger group. The housing is retained by a roll-type cross pin. After removal of the pin, the housing, spring, and plunger are taken off rearward. If this unit is removed, control the spring.

25. Push out the grigger cross pin toward the right.

26. Remove the trigger assembly upward.

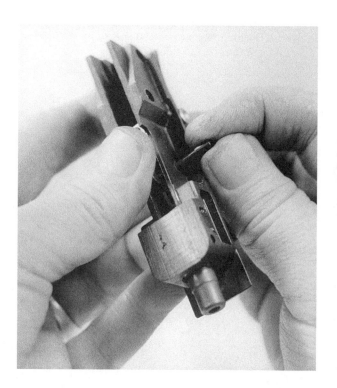

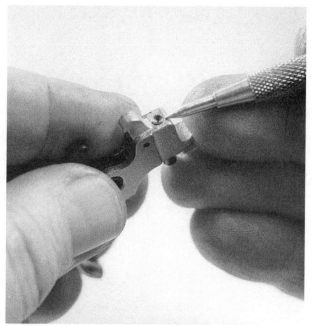

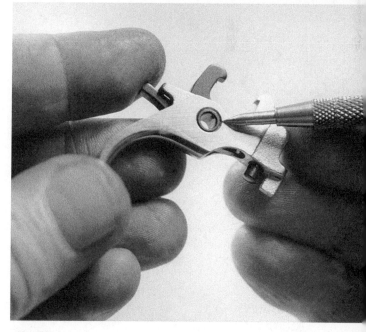

27. The trigger spring plunger is riveted at the top and removal should be only for repair purposes.

28. The secondary sear and its vertical plunger and spring at the front are retained by the trigger pivot sleeve. If the sleeve is pushed out, the plunger and spring will be released, so restrain them.

29. The carrier stop button and its coil spring are retained by a cross pin at the front of the trigger group. With the pin removed, the button and spring are taken out toward the front. The pin is staked on both sides, and removal should be only for repair.

30. A plunger and spring position retain the safety button on the right side of the trigger group. Use a small tool to depress the plunger upward, and push the safety out toward the left. Restrain the plunger and spring, as they will be released as the safety clears.

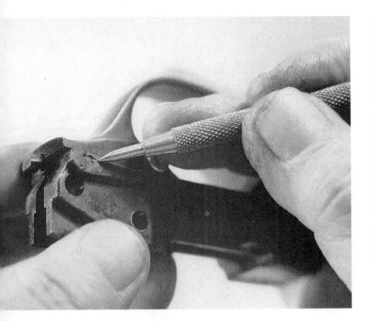

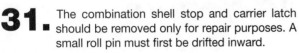

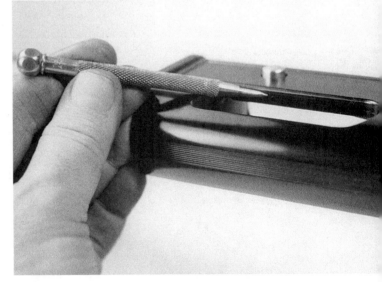

31. The combination shell stop and carrier latch should be removed only for repair purposes. A small roll pin must first be drifted inward.

32. After the roll cross pin has been drifted out inward, the vertical pin that pivots the shell stop and carrier latch is drifted out downward, using an aperture provided in the lower edge of the ejection port. The shell stop, latch, button, and spring are then removed inward. Again, this system should be removed only for repair.

33. Two screws retain the forend baseplate at the front of the receiver. The magazine tube is not routinely removable.

34. The rubber buttplate is retained by two Phillips screws. A 19mm socket is required for removal of the stock mounting nut. Removal of the stock will give access to the bolt spring housing. If the bolt spring and plunger are to be removed, use caution and control the spring.

Reassembly Tips:

1. When replacing the carrier spring system, do it in reverse of the takedown procedure. Engage the semi-circular attachment with its recess in the carrier, put the base on the rear tip of the spring guide, and push the base forward and then into its recess.

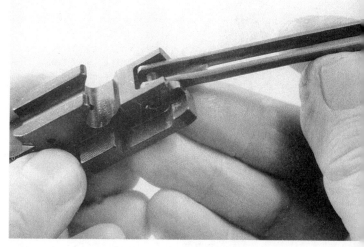

2. If the bolt slide strut has been removed, be sure it is reattached as shown.

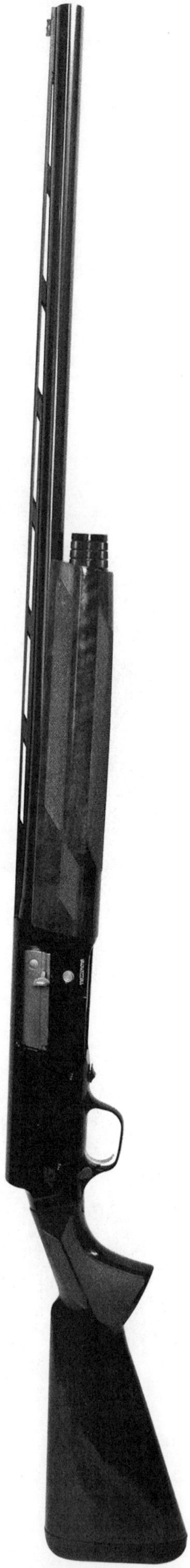

Browning A5

Data: Browning A5
Origin: Portugal
Manufacturer: Browning Arms Company, Morgan, Utah
Gauges: 12
Overall Length: 49.6 inches
Height: 7 inches
Barrel Length: 28 inches
Weight: 6 lbs. 13 oz.

The A5 shotgun is a step in the retro direction in cosmetics only. Designed to closely resemble the old Auto-5, the internals are much different, and it operates on what Browning calls a Kinematic Drive system, rather than the old recoil operation of the Auto-5. It is also significantly lighter weight than its cousin. Besides the field version seen here, three synthetic stocked versions were introduced in 2012, one black and the other two in camouflaged patterns.

Disassembly:

1. Remove the magazine cap from the forend.

2. Hold the bolt slightly pulled to the rear and pull the barrel and forend off the gun as a unit. The forend will pull off the barrel rearward.

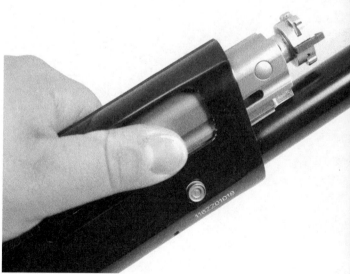

3. With the hammer cocked, pull the charging handle out to the right side to remove.

4. The bolt assembly can be pulled from the front of the receiver.

5. The two large torx screws on the left side of the receiver retain the ejector assembly (Picture A). The assembly consists of a large plate which holds the ejector and ejector spring (Picture B). There is no need to remove this assembly unless the ejector needs to be replaced.

6. Drive out the two trigger housing pins, one above the trigger and the other forward and above the trigger guard.

7. Depress the bolt latch button and pull the trigger housing from the receiver.

8. The bolt button and shell latch assembly can be removed by driving out this pin. Unless this needs to be replaced, it should be left installed as disassembly is likely to cosmetically damage the receiver.

9. Remove the buttpad by means of the two screws retaining it to the stock. The stock is held to the receiver by this nut and spacers. Remove them to free the stock for removal.

10. A spacer is present between the stock and the receiver. Remove this spacer.

11. Insert a small punch into the forward hole in the action tube to contain the spring. Drive out this spring pin to free the end bolt. Then unscrew the end bolt to remove it from the action tube.

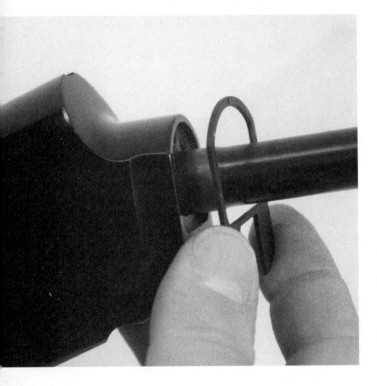

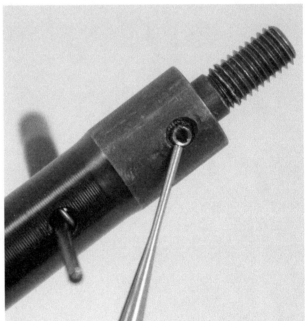

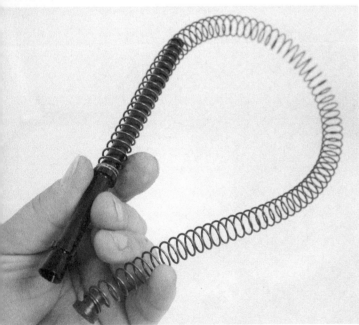

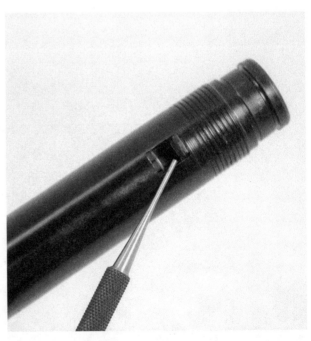

12. While containing the spring's plastic base and the spring, remove the punch securing the spring. Remove the spring, its base and the action tube plunger from the tube.

13. The magazine spring and follower can be removed by depressing this tab and pulling the plug out of the magazine tube. Contain the spring.

14. Push the firing pin into the bolt, then push out this pin from bottom to top. This will free the firing pin and spring. **Note**: Do not attempt to drive this pin out as it will only result in damage to the pin.

15. Pull out the bolt cam pin to the right

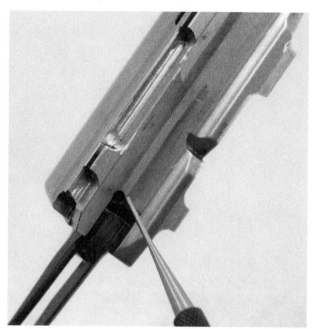

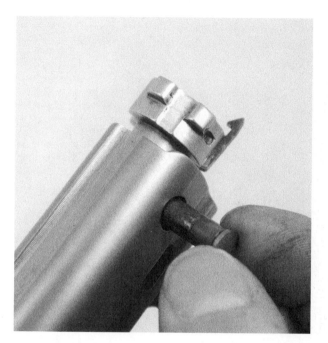

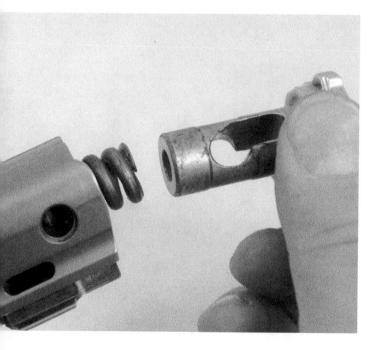

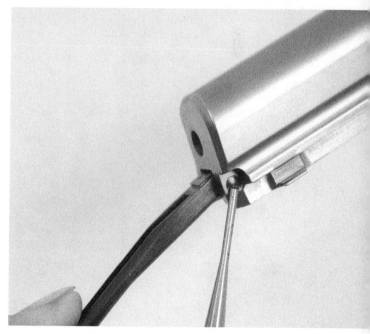

16. Pull the bolt head from the body. Behind the bolt is a large spring.

17. The link can be removed by driving out this pin.

18. The bolt handle detent and spring are retained by this small spring pin.

19. Unhook the carrier spring from the rear carrier and remove it from the trigger housing.

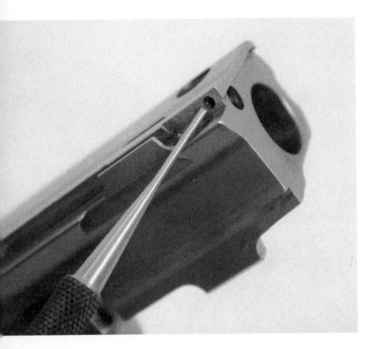

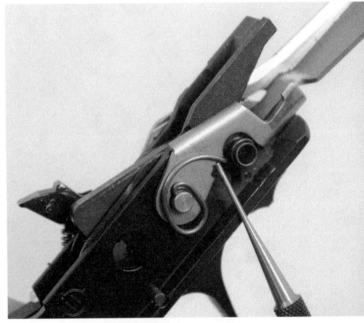

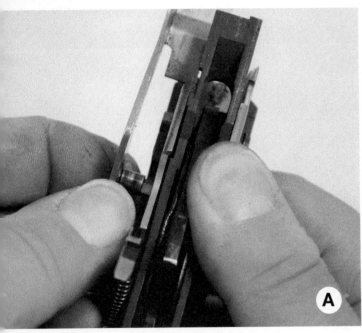

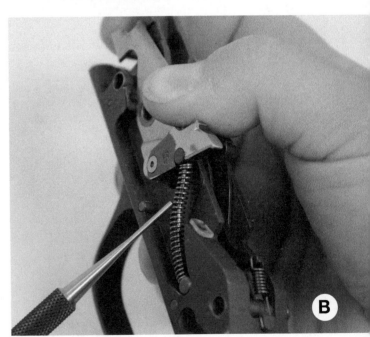

20. Pull the lifter out to the left (Picture A). This will free the rear carrier as well. The carrier dog spring and guide should be contained to prevent loss (Picture B).

21. The carrier dog is staked to the carrier and should not be removed.

22. Push out the rear trigger pin bushing.

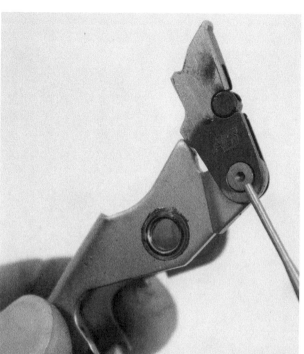

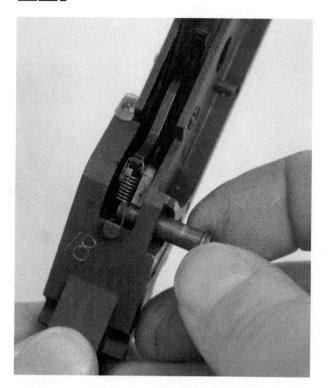

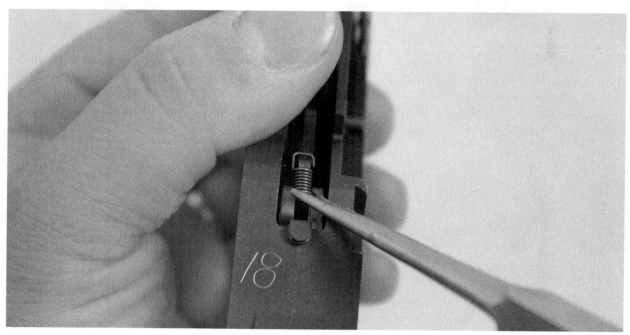

23. Detach the trigger/disconnector spring from the disconnector, and then from the trigger housing.

24. Remove the front trigger pin bushing to free the hammer. Then remove the hammer by pulling it from the front of the housing. Lift the disconnector to clear the way for the hammer bars.

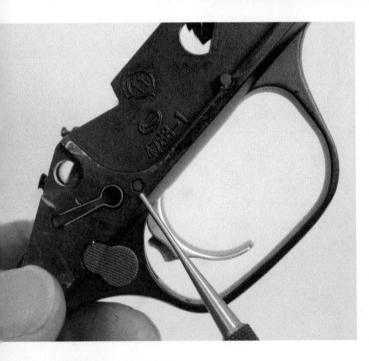

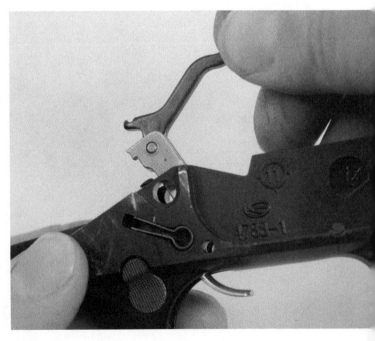

25. Push out the trigger pin.

26. Remove the trigger by pulling it up and out of the housing.

27. If necessary for repair, the trigger and disconnector can be separated by driving out this pin.

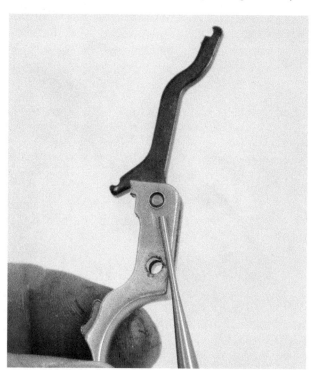

28. Push out the sear pin and pull the sear and sear spring forward and then up out of the receiver.

29. Push out this pin to free the carrier latch button and spring.

30. Remove this spring to free the safety detent. The safety button can then be removed from the housing.

31. This pin at the rear of the housing holds the hammer spring and plunger. Drive it out to free these parts. **Note**: The spring is compressed so contain it as the pin is removed.

32. The two synthetic buffers on the left side of the trigger housing (and the spongy pad inside the receiver) should be left alone, unless they need to be replaced.

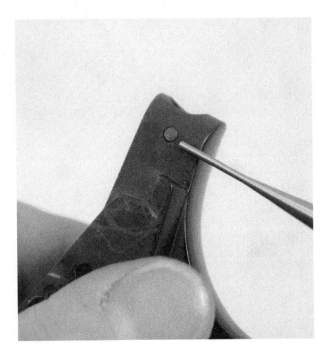

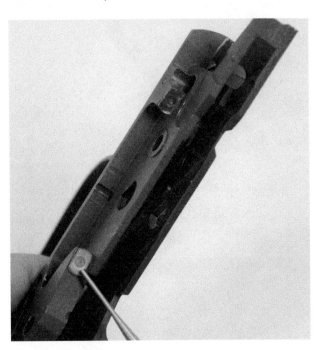

33. Do not remove the weld spring at the front of the forend unless it needs to be replaced.

Reassembly Tips:

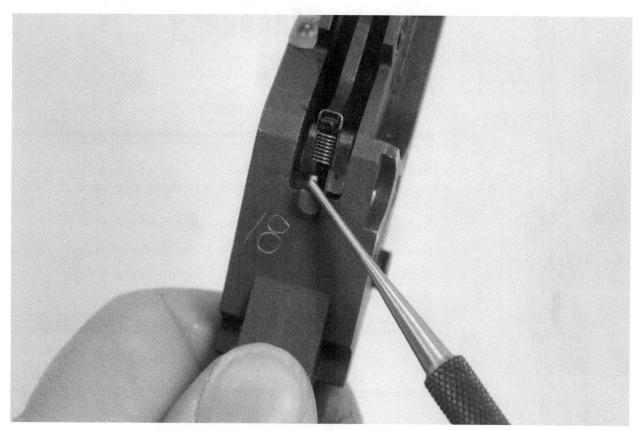

1. Reinstall the trigger/disconnector spring with the short loop forward, prior to reinstalling the rear housing pin bushing. This will keep the spring untensioned and make an easier install.

Browning Auto-5

Similar/Identical Pattern Guns:

The same basic assembly/disassembly steps for the Browning Auto-5 also apply to the following guns:

Remington Model 11	**Remington Model 11A**
Remington Model 11B	**Remington Model 11D**
Remington Model 11E	**Remington Model 11F**
Remington Model 11R	

Data:	Browning Auto-5
Origin:	Belgium and/or Japan
Manufacturer:	Fabrique Nationale, Herstal, for Browning, Morgan, Utah
Gauges:	12, 16, and 20
Magazine capacity:	4 rounds
Overall length:	47 inches
Barrel length:	24 to 30 inches
Weight:	6-1/8 to 8-1/4 pounds

Designed by the great John M. Browning just before the turn of the century, this fine gun was introduced in 1900. There have been tiny mechanical changes over the years, but the basic design is absolutely unchanged. At one time, both Remington and Savage made versions of the gun, during periods when the original Belgian model was not marketed in the U.S. The instructions will generally apply to the Remington Model 11s, but not to the Savage, which is mechanically different. In this revised edition, the Savage is covered separately.

Disassembly:

1. Pull back the operating handle to lock the bolt in the open position, and set the safety in the on-safe position. Depress the barrel slightly toward the rear, and unscrew and remove the magazine end cap. Take off the forend and barrel toward the front.

2. The ejector is mounted in a T-slot at the left rear of the barrel extension, and is retained by a riveted cross pin. In some models, it is solidly fixed, and in others it has an opening at the center and slides to the rear. In both cases, it should be removed only for repair. The riveted pin is driven out inward.

3. Remove the bronze friction piece and its attached spring toward the front.

4. Remove the compression ring toward the front. If the gun has been used with light loads, the ring will be found "stored" at the rear of the recoil spring.

5. Remove the recoil spring toward the front.

6. Hold the operating handle to restrain the bolt, depress the carrier latch button, and ease the bolt forward to the closed position. Remove the lock screw, then the stock screw, in the rear tip of the lower tang. It should be noted that for all screws on this gun, you will need screwdrivers with very thin blades. If necessary, alter some screwdrivers for this purpose. Remove the buttstock toward the rear. If it is very tight, bump the front of the comb with the heel of the hand or a rubber hammer.

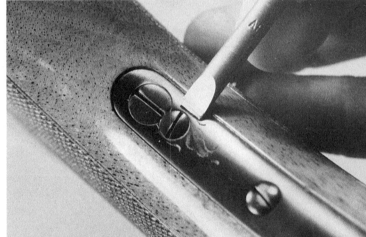

7. Remove the lock screw, then the main screw on the left side of the receiver, just above the front of the trigger housing.

8. Remove the lock screw, then the main screw on the left side at the lower rear of the receiver.

9. Remove the trigger group downward.

10. Remove the carrier spring from its post on the left side of the trigger housing. Note that on early guns, this spring will be mounted on a post inside the receiver, and must be detached at the front, then moved off its post inward for removal.

11. Move the safety to the off-safe position, tip the safety sear (arrow) forward, restrain the hammer, pull the trigger, and ease the hammer forward until its roller disengages from the tip of the hammer spring.

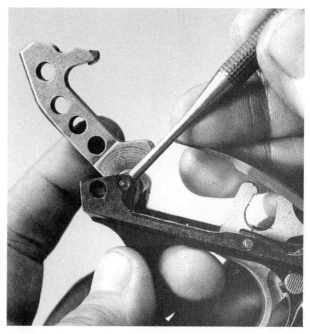

12. Drift out the hammer cross pin, and remove the hammer from the trigger housing.

13. Remove the hammer spring screw, located on the underside of the rear tang of the trigger housing. Note that the spring is not removed at this time.

14. Insert a small screwdriver at the front of the safety sear to depress the plunger and spring, and remove the safety sear toward the left. Caution: Keep the plunger under control, ease it out, and remove the plunger and spring upward.

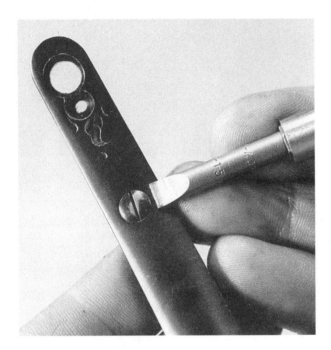

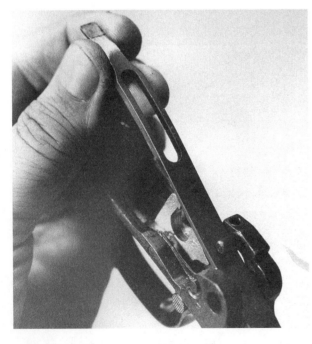

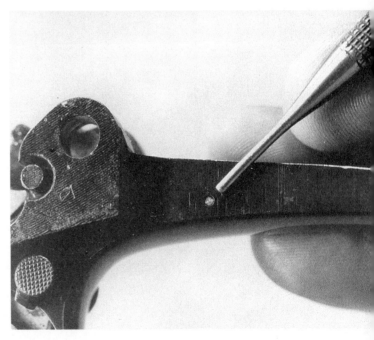

15. Lift the hammer spring at the front, and remove it upward and toward the front.

16. Push out the small cross pin in the rear tang of the trigger housing. Removal is easier if the trigger spring is slightly depressed in the vicinity of the pin.

17. Remove the trigger spring upward and toward the rear.

18. Invert the trigger housing over the palm of the hand, and move the safety to free the detent ball. If it does not drop out easily, tap the housing with a nylon hammer.

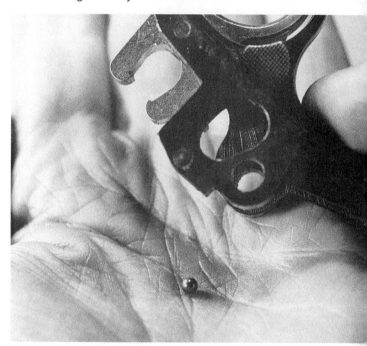

19. Drift out the trigger cross pin, and remove the trigger upward.

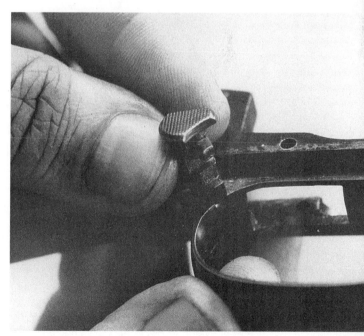

20. Remove the safety toward the right.

21. Remove the lock screw and the large carrier pivot screw on each side of the receiver.

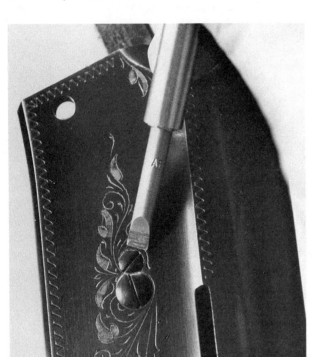

22. Remove the two sections of the carrier downward. Note that on early guns, the carrier will be a single part.

23. The dog and its plunger and spring are retained on the rear section of the carrier by a cross pin that is riveted in place, and this should be removed only for repair. If it is necessary, drift out the pin inward (toward the left), and be sure the carrier section is well supported.

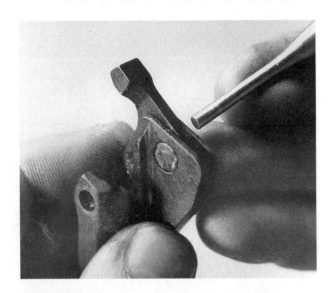

24. Restrain the bolt spring plug at the rear of its housing, push out the cross pin, and remove the plug, spring, and follower toward the rear. Caution: The spring is powerful and is under tension. Control it, and ease it out It is possible to also unscrew the housing (tube) from the rear tang of the receiver, but this is not advisable in normal takedown.

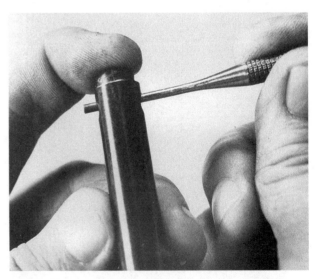

25. Move the bolt back to the position shown, until the locking block latch pin is aligned with the exit cut in the lower edge of the ejection port. Insert a drift punch through the access hole in the left side of the receiver, and push out the pin toward the right.

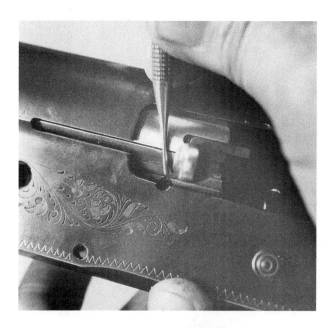

26. Removal of the pin will release the locking block latch from the bottom of the bolt. Remove the latch and its spring.

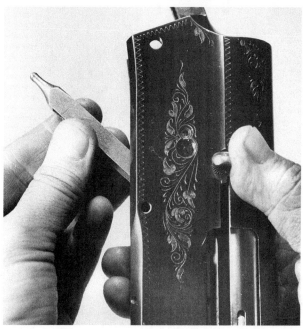

27. Move the bolt to the rear, swinging the link bar outward. Restrain the operating handle, and move the bolt forward, leaving the handle at the rear.

28. Swing the link bar back inside, and remove the bolt assembly toward the front.

29. Move the operating handle unit forward, and remove it from the ejection port.

30. Drift out the cross pin at the rear of the bolt toward the right, and remove the firing pin toward the rear.

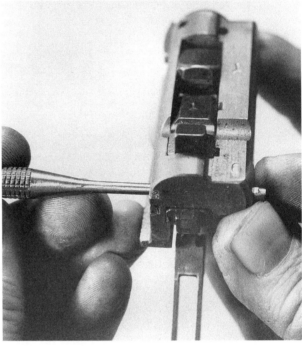

31. Push the front of the link bar upward, tipping the locking block out the top of the bolt, and remove the assembly upward. Drifting out the cross pin at the lower rear of the locking block will release the link bar for removal.

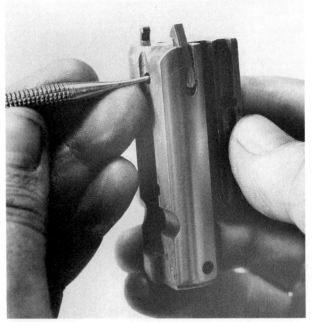

32. The extractors and their coil springs are retained on each side at the front of the bolt by vertical pins. Drift out the pins downward, and take off the extractors and springs toward each side.

33. Remove the magazine cut-off spring screw, located on the left side at the forward edge of the receiver, and take off the spring toward the front.

34. On early guns, the magazine cut-off, carrier latch, and shell stop are retained by vertical screws set in the lower edge of the receiver. In later guns, such as the one shown, these parts are retained by roll pins. For removal, the pins are drifted upward, and exit holes are provided inside the receiver. Use a roll pin punch to drift the magazine cut-off pin upward.

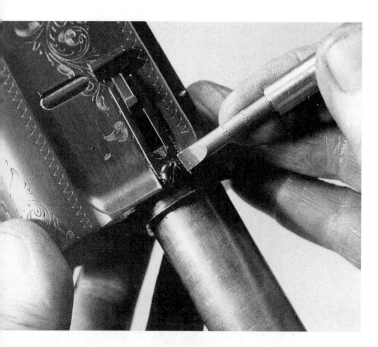

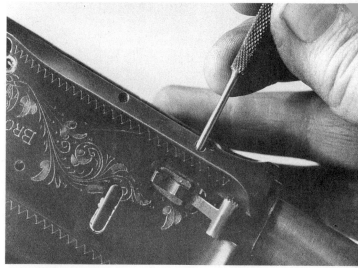

35. Remove the magazine cut-off toward the left.

36. Drift out the shell stop pin upward, and remove the shell stop and its spring from inside the receiver.

37. Drift out the carrier latch pin upward, and take out the latch and its release button from inside the receiver. Note that the carrier latch spring is riveted in place, and is not routinely removed.

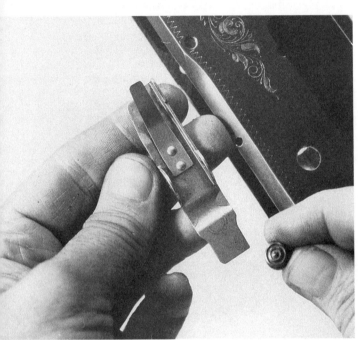

1. When replacing the pivot pins for the carrier latch, shell stop, and magazine cut-off, drive them in the same direction they were removed, upward. Take care that the parts are properly aligned before driving the pins into place. Insert a drift punch to insure alignment, then hold the parts in place with a fingertip while the pins are inserted. Be sure the pins are not driven too deeply, as their upper ends can enter the bolt track.

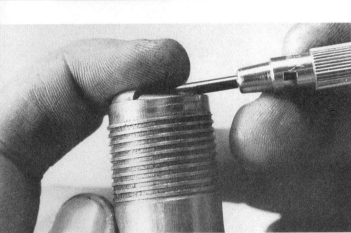

38. Insert a screwdriver in the open center of the magazine spring retainer, and pry the retainer out, moving the screwdriver to raise it equally around its edge. Caution: The magazine spring is under tension, so control the retainer and ease it out. Remove the spring and follower toward the front. Removal of the magazine cut-off spring screw will have freed the magazine tube, and it can be unscrewed from the receiver. These are tightly fitted, though, and are best left in place in normal takedown.

2. In the later guns that have the two-piece carrier, the parts may be difficult for the amateur. In this photo, the parts are shown in the proper position.

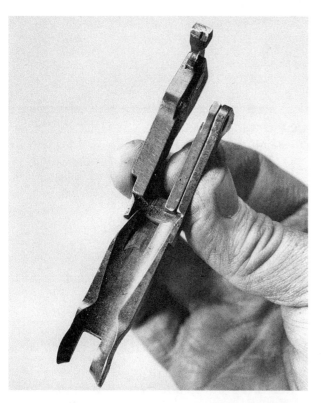

4. When installing the trigger group in the receiver, insert the group as shown, replacing the rear cross screw first. As the group is swung up into position for insertion of the front cross screw, use a tool at the rear to tip the safety sear forward, to insure that its upper arm enters the open track in the center of the link bar.

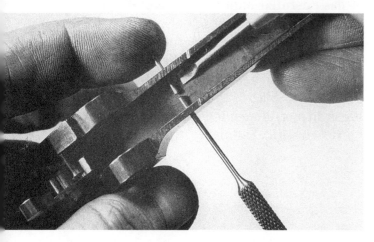

3. When installing the combination trigger and safety detent spring, use a tool to depress the spring at the cross pin location, and insert a drift punch to hold the spring down while putting in the cross pin. It will be necessary to depress the spring on the other side as the pin is inserted, and the end of the cross pin must also be depressed as it enters the hole on the other side of the tang.

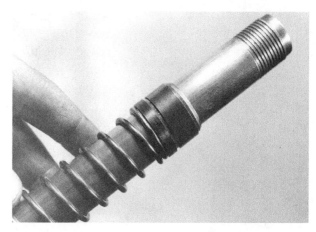

5. When replacing the compression ring (arrow) and friction piece at the front of the recoil spring, these parts should be in the position shown for medium to heavy loads, with the concave inner surface of the ring toward the front. For light loads, place the reversed ring at the rear of the spring, next to the receiver.

Browning B-2000

Data: Browning B-2000
Origin: Belgium
Manufacturer: Fabrique Nationale, Herstal, for Browning, Morgan, Utah
Gauges: 12 and 20
Magazine capacity: 4 rounds
Overall length: 46 inches (with 26-inch barrel)
Barrel length: 26 to 30 inches
Weight: 7-1/2 pounds

Introduced in 1975, this sleek autoloader was Browning's first entry in the field of gas-operated shotguns. While all guns of this type have operating systems that are somewhat similar, the B-2000 gas mechanism has some different features, including a valve that regulates the ported gas, allowing the use of a wide range of loads. For those who are accustomed to the large and simple parts of the venerable Auto-5, the takedown may have some surprises. There is an inter-dependence of small parts, and the amateur should proceed with caution.

Disassembly:

1. Pull back the operating handle to lock the bolt in the open position, and set the safety in the on-safe position. Unscrew the magazine end cap, and remove it. Take off the barrel and forend toward the front, and remove the forend from the barrel toward the rear.

2. Restrain the gas piston at the front of the magazine tube, and push out the gas piston bar toward either side. Caution: The piston is under spring pressure, so control it and ease it out.

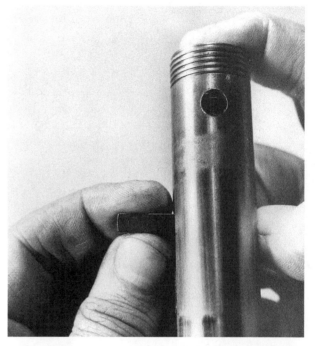

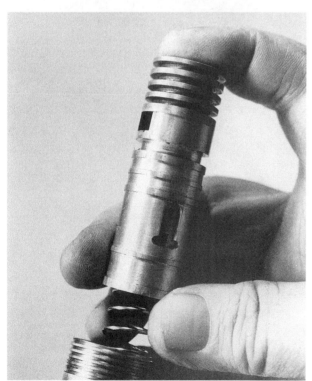

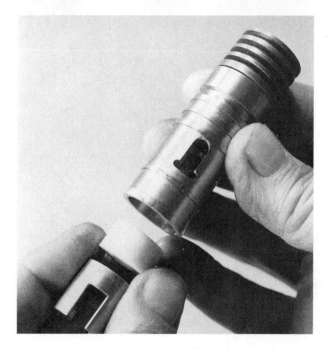

3. Slowly release the spring tension, and remove the gas piston assembly and its spring toward the front.

4. Remove the gas piston bar guide and the piston buffer from the rear of the piston.

5. Remove the gas cylinder plug from the front shaft of the gas piston valve.

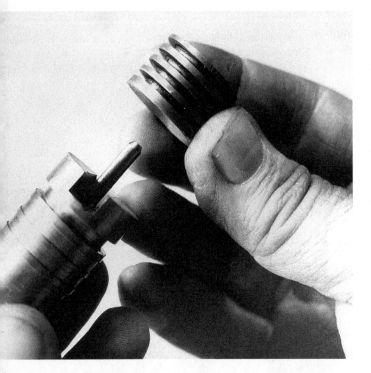

7. Restrain the bolt, operate the carrier latch, and ease the bolt forward to the closed position. With a non-marring tool, push out the trigger group retaining cross pin toward either side.

6. Remove the gas piston valve toward the rear.

8. Move the bolt about 1-1/2 inches toward the rear, depress the carrier latch, and move the guard unit a short distance toward the front. Tip the front of the trigger group slightly downward, ease the bolt back forward, and remove the trigger group from the bottom of the receiver.

9. Restrain the carrier, and push out the carrier pivot pin.

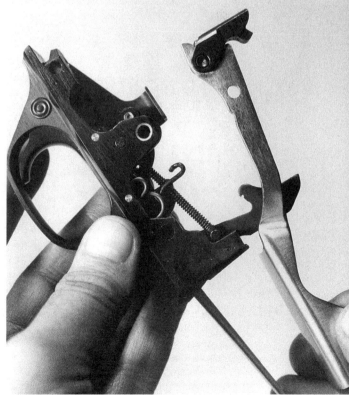

10. Remove the carrier upward. Note that the carrier dog and its plunger and spring are retained on the rear arm of the carrier by a cross pin that is heavily riveted in place, and removal is not advisable unless necessary for repair.

11. Remove the carrier spring from its recess on the right side of the trigger group.

12. Move the safety to the off-safe position, restrain the hammer, pull the trigger, and ease the hammer down to the fired position. Place a thumb on top of the twin hammer springs to restrain them, and push out the hammer pivot pin toward the left.

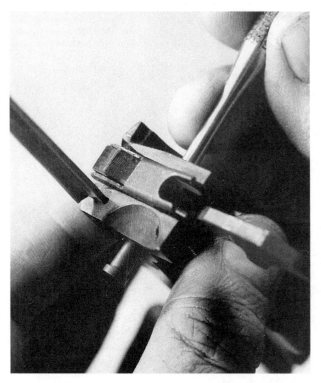

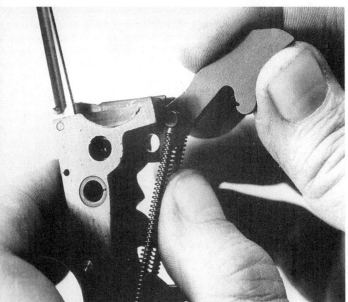

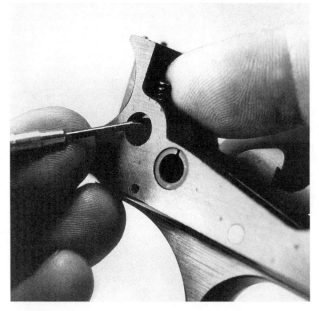

13. Move the hammer upward until its spring base pin climbs over the edge of the front projection of the guard unit, relieving the spring tension. Remove the hammer, springs, and guides upward. The spring system is easily removed from the hammer.

14. Removal of the hammer pivot pin will have freed the shell stop spring. Insert a small screwdriver to lift it out upward, and remove it.

15. Remove the cross pin that is the rear base for the twin hammer springs toward either side.

16. Drift out the small cross pin at the upper front of the trigger group, using a punch of very small diameter. Restrain the carrier latch assembly as the pin is removed.

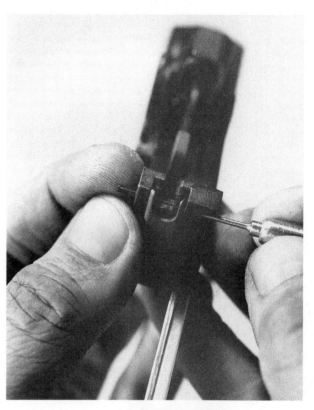

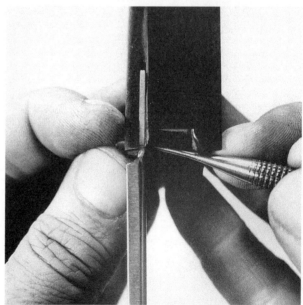

17. Remove the carrier latch assembly, and its spring and plunger, toward the front. The carrier latch trip can be separated from the latch by drifting out its small cross pin.

18. Removal of the carrier latch will give access to the shell stop pin. Use an angled punch at the front to push out the pin toward the left. The shell stop will not be freed for removal. See the next step.

19. Using a very small punch, drift the shell stop limit pin inward, and remove it from the carrier latch spring recess.

20. Remove the shell stop toward the front.

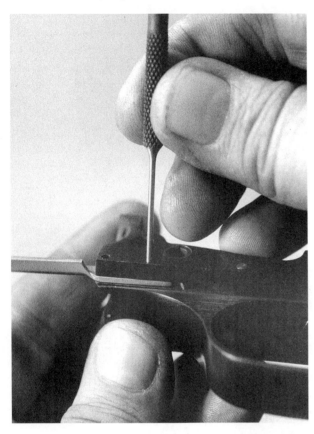

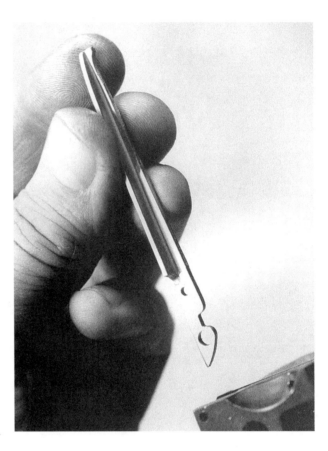

21. Drift the trigger shield cross pin toward the right, just far enough to clear the rear of the shield.

22. Remove the trigger shield upward.

23. Insert a screwdriver, angled from the rear, to pry the tip of the disconnector spring downward, out of its recess in the underside of the disconnector. Caution: Hold a fingertip on the left side to restrain the spring and plunger as it clears, and ease them off upward.

24. Push out the trigger pin, and remove the trigger and disconnector assembly upward. Drifting out the cross pin will allow separation of the disconnector from the trigger, but the pin is riveted in place, and should be removed only for repair.

25. Drift out the sear pin, and remove the sear upward.

26. Drift the roll pin at the rear of the housing further toward the right, and insert a small screwdriver from the left to lift the safety spring and its plunger out upward.

27. Remove the safety button toward either side.

28. Grip the action bar assembly, and move it slightly toward the rear. Grasp the operating handle firmly, and pull it straight out toward the right.

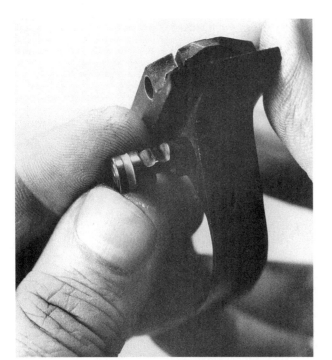

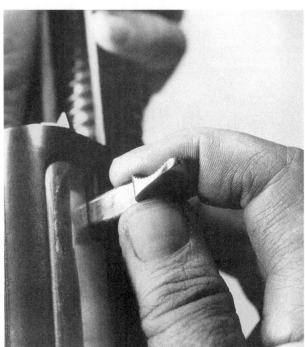

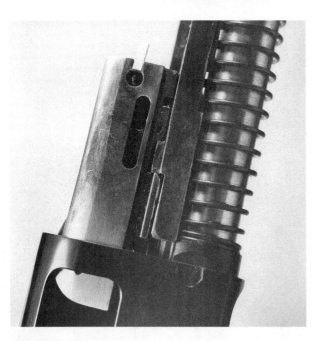

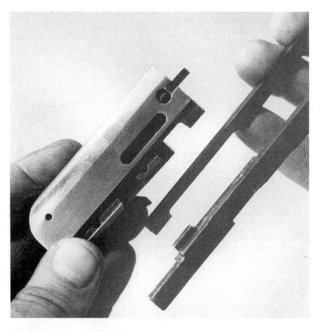

29. Insert a fingertip in the bottom of the receiver to depress the cartridge stop on the underside of the bolt, and slowly release the spring tension, moving the action bar and bolt assembly out toward the front.

30. Even after the bolt is moved out, the recoil spring is still under tension, so control it and ease it off the magazine tube. Detach the bolt from the action bars, tipping it toward the left to disengage it.

31. Remove the bolt slide from the underside of the bolt. Drifting out the cross pin in the slide will allow removal of the shell stop and its spring. Note that the spring is a torsion type, and is under tension, so restrain it as the pin is drifted out toward the right. The bolt handle retaining plunger and spring can also be removed by drifting out the cross pin at the front of the slide.

32. Drift out the cross pin at the upper rear of the bolt, and take out the firing pin bushing, firing pin, and return spring toward the rear.

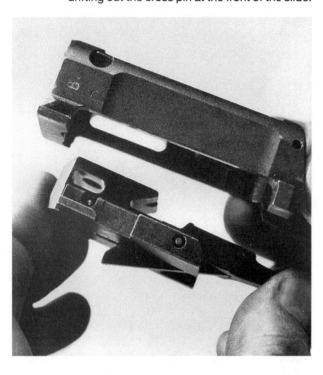

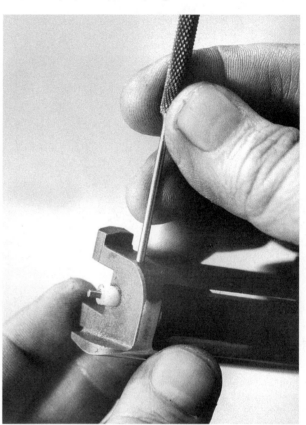

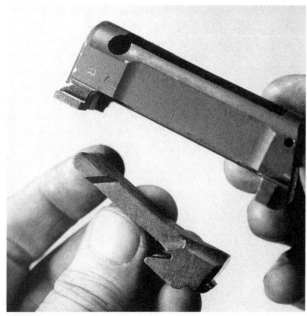

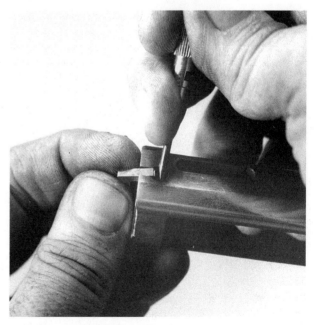

33. After the firing pin assembly is removed, take out the locking block downward.

34. Insert a small screwdriver between the extractor and its plunger, depress the plunger toward the rear, and lift the extractor out of its recess. Caution: Control the plunger, ease it out, and remove the plunger and spring toward the front.

35. The carrier release, which is tempered to be its own spring, lies in a recess on the inside of the right receiver wall, and is retained by a vertical pin at the rear. Use a roll pin punch to drift the pin upward (it is replaced in the same direction), and remove the carrier release.

36. Insert a tool from the front to restrain the magazine end piece, and push out the vertical pin in the magazine tube, just behind the gas piston area. Slowly release the spring tension, and remove the end piece, magazine spring, and follower toward the front.

37. Remove the buttplate, and use a B-Square stock tool or a long-shanked screwdriver to back out the stock bolt and its washer. Take off the stock toward the rear. Removal of the stock bolt will also free a nylon buffer, inside the rear of the receiver, and this can be pried out toward the front if necessary. A steel barrel guide is mounted inside the top of the receiver, staked in place, and this is not removed in normal takedown.

Reassembly Tips:

1. When driving the large roll pin at the rear of the trigger housing across toward the left, insert a tool to depress the top of the safety spring as the tip of the pin passes.

2. When replacing the hammer and hammer spring assembly, turn the rear spring base cross pin so the holes are oriented upward. Set the rear tips of the spring guides against the bar, and press the assembly downward until the tips enter the holes in the pin. Then, swing the assembly over toward the front to rest against the front shelf of the housing, holding it in place for reinsertion of the hammer pivot pin.

3. When reassembling the hammer pivot pin, insert a small tool on the left side to depress the shell stop spring as the tip of the pin passes.

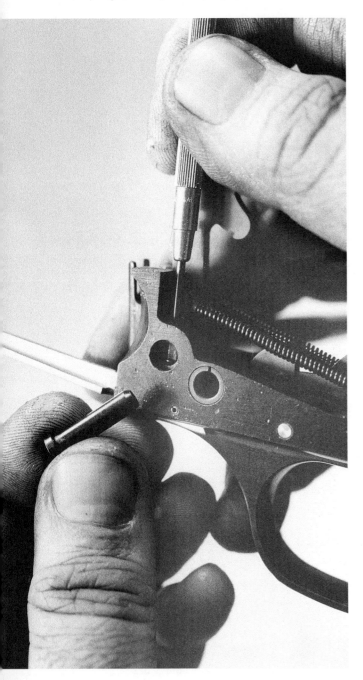

4. When reassembling the gas piston system, refer to steps 2 through 6 for the proper arrangement of these parts. When replacing the gas cylinder plug on the stem of the piston valve at the front, note that its concave surface goes toward the rear.

Browning BPS

Similar/Identical Pattern Guns:
10 Gauge Turkey & Camo Models
Waterfowl Camo
Game Gun Deer Special
Game Gun Turkey Special
Stalker
Micro

Data:	Browning BPS
Origin:	United States
Manufacturer:	Made in Japan for Browning, Morgan, Utah
Gauges:	10, 12, 20, 28, and .410
Magazine capacity:	4 rounds (12 gauge)
Overall length:	46-1/2 inches
Barrel length:	26 inches (others offered)
Weight:	7-1/2 pounds

Miroku of Japan has made the BPS for Browning since 1977. Some elements of its design are similar to the Ithaca Model 37, but the mechanical details and takedown are not the same. The BPS has been offered in numerous models, gauges, and barrel lengths. All are mechanically the same, and the instructions will apply.

Disassembly:

1. Cycle and close the action, and put the manual safety in on-safe position. Unscrew the magazine cap, and remove the barrel toward the front. NOTE: If you have one of the Game Gun versions, you must also remove the barrel-stabilizing lock washer and split ring before the barrel is taken off.

2. Use a suitable tool, such as a roll-pin drift or the Brownells tool shown, to push out the trigger-group cross pin.

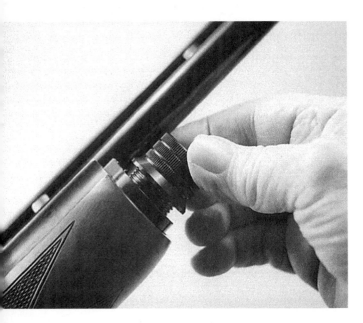

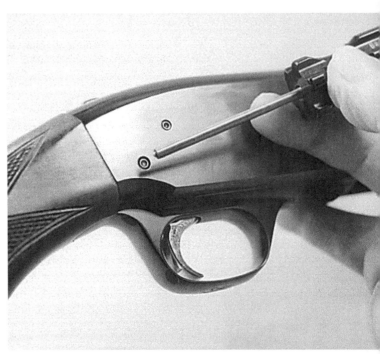

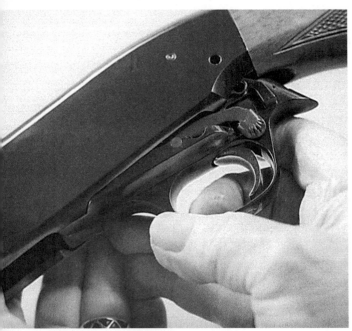

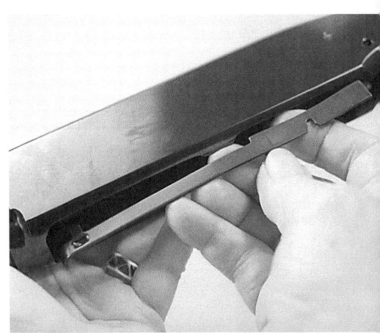

3. Tip the trigger group downward at the rear, and remove it downward and rearward.

4. As the trigger group is taken out, the shell stops on each side will be released for removal.

5. Turn the trigger group as shown, and depress the slide lock at the front. The slide-lock lever will fall off its post on the left side.

6. Restrain the hammer, pull the trigger, and ease the hammer forward to fired position. Keep the hammer under control. If it impacts the crosspiece, the slide lock can be damaged. If necessary for repair, the trigger-group cross-pin sleeve and its attached spring can be drifted out toward the right. However, it retains no parts, and can be left in place.

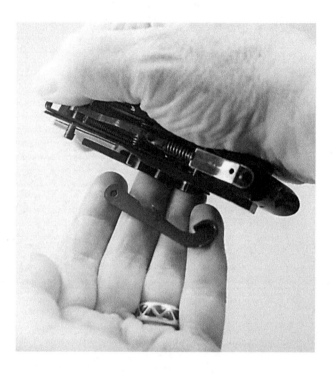

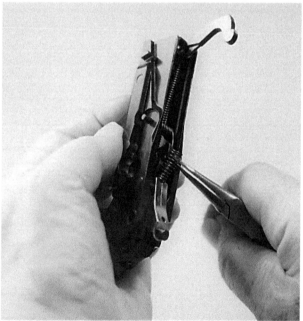

7. Using a suitable tool, detach, the sear spring from its stud on the sear, and remove it. The spring is slightly compressed, so control it.

8. Use a proper roll-pin punch to drift out the trigger-spring retaining cross pin. Block the hole at the rear as the punch is taken out, as the spring will be released.

9. Remove the trigger spring and plunger toward the rear. The plunger may not come out with the spring, but it can be easily pushed out after the trigger is removed.

10. Keep a finger on top to restrain the slide lock spring, and push the trigger cross pin slightly toward the left until the arm of the spring is released. Ease the spring arm over toward the front, releasing its tension. Caution: Control the spring.

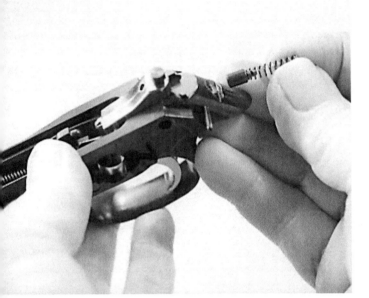

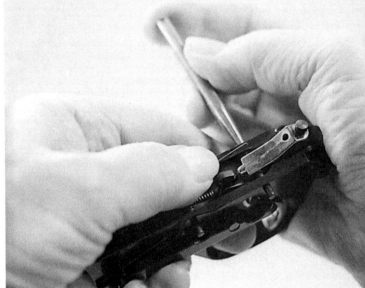

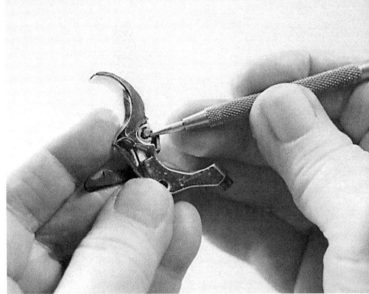

11. Push the trigger pin out toward the left, and remove the trigger upward. Because of the attached disconnector, the trigger will have to be turned slightly during removal.

12. The disconnector is retained on the trigger by a C-clip on the right side. If removal is not necessary for repair, it is best left in place.

13. Restrain the hammer, and push out the slide-lock cross pin toward either side.

14. Ease the hammer forward, move the slide-lock assembly forward, and take it off upward. The slide lock-spring is easily detached.

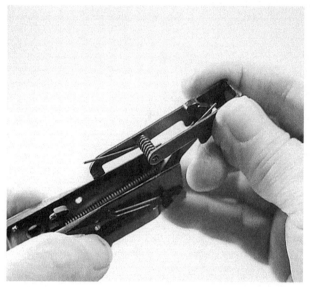

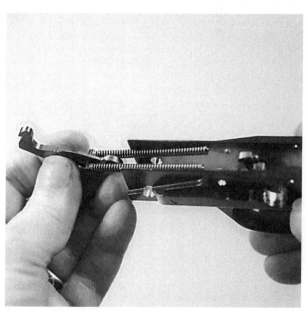

15. Restrain the hammer, and push out the hammer pin toward either side.

16. Remove the hammer assembly toward the front. The twin-hammer springs, spring guides, and the spring-base cross pin are easily detached from the hammer.

17. Push out the sear cross pin, and remove the sear upward.

18. Move the action slide to align the bolt with the trigger group recesses in the receiver, and lift the bolt slide piece at the rear for removal. Take out the action bar assembly toward the front. Separating the action bar from the forend wood requires a special tool for the retaining nut at the front, and it is best left in place except for repair.

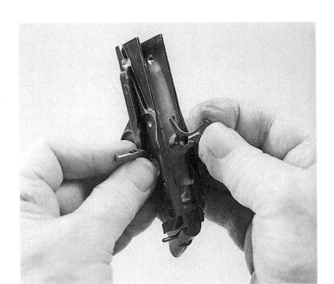

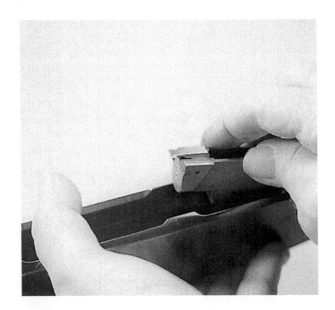

19. Remove the bolt from the receiver.

20. Drifting out this roll pin will allow removal of the locking block from the bolt.

21. The firing pin is retained by a vertical roll pin at the rear of the bolt.

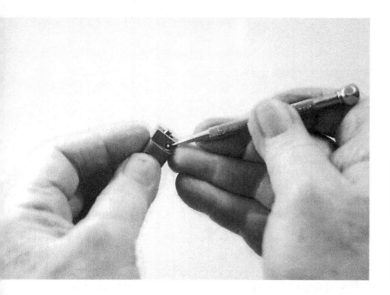

22. This roll pin retains the extractor and its coil spring. As the roll-pin drift is taken out, restrain the extractor

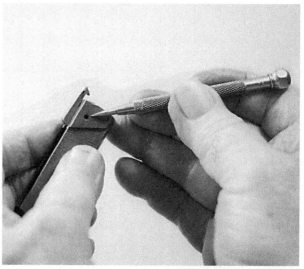

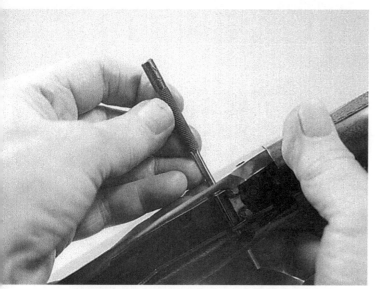

23. To keep the tool centered in the cross-pin depression, use a roll-pin punch to drift out the carrier pin. Use a 5/32 punch.

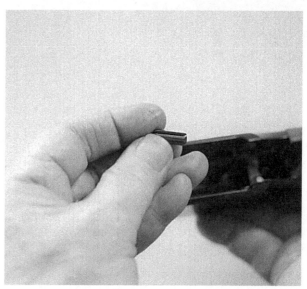

24. The carrier-pin retainer will be freed inside the receiver for removal.

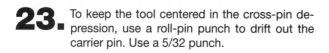

25. Remove the carrier.

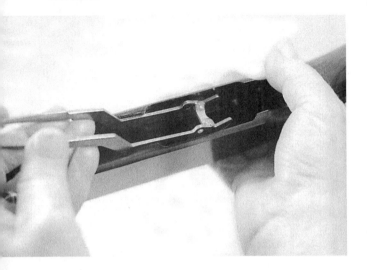

26. Given the precise mating of the manual safety post with the safety stud on the trigger, this system should not be disassembled routinely. It is retained by a 5/16-inch nut inside the receiver, and there is an adjustment screw inside the nut. The safety button and its plunger and spring are taken off upward. Again, amateur disassembly of this system is not recommended.

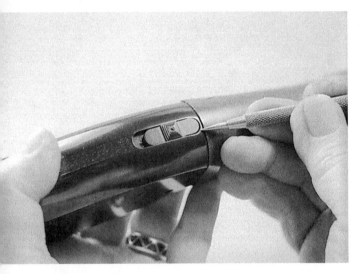

Some notes here on three other items, one of which could not be photographed inside the receiver: The rear continuation of the sighting rib on the top front of the receiver is internally retained by two vertical screws. The buttstock is retained by a through-bolt from the rear, accessible by removal of the buttplate. The magazine spring and follower can be removed by carefully prying out the retainer at the front of the magazine tube. Caution: Keep the retainer and spring under control.

Reassembly Tips:

1. When installing the sear cross pin, remember that the squared recesses on the pin must go toward the front, to mate with the hammer springs.

2. When installing the trigger cross pin, use a tool with a notched tip to depress the rear arm of the slide-lock spring to go beneath the pin.

3. Note that the sear spring has a slightly larger coil at one end, and that end goes at the front, to mate with the stud on the sear.

4. Before the trigger group is put back into the receiver, be sure the stepped ends of the hammer cross pin are turned to the position shown. Also, it will be necessary to hold the shell stops in their recesses in the receiver as the trigger group is moved into place.

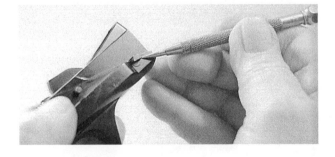

Browning Citori Skeet

Similar/Identical Pattern Guns:

The following basic assembly/disassembly steps for the Browning Citori Skeet can also be used for the following guns:

Browning Citori 325   **Browning Citori Field**

Browning Citori 425   **Browning Citori Hunter**

Browning Citori 625

Data: Browning Citori Skeet
Origin: Japan
Manufacturer: Browning Arms Company, Morgan, Utah
Gauges: 12, 20
Overall Length: 43 inches
Height: 7.25 inches
Barrel Length: 26 inches
Weight: 7 pounds

The Browning Citori was the successor to the long-lived Superposed. Significant changes were made and it spawned a large family of models for use in just about any contrived purpose. All the field, hunting, and sporting models are essentially the same internally. The later models in the 625 series added mechanically resetting triggers, replacing the inertia-operated older types. These steps will still greatly apply to the 625 as well as the original Citoris and their numbered competition offspring.

Disassembly:

1. Pull the forend latch while simultaneously pulling the forend and rotating it off of the barrels.

2. Press the top lever to open the action then rotate the barrels off of the receiver.

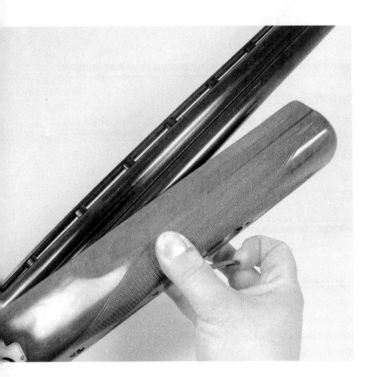

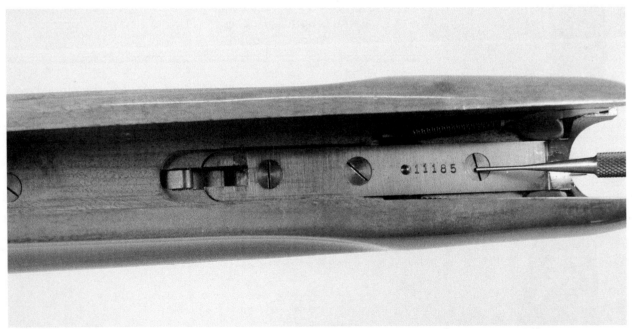

3. To remove the forend hardware, remove the four large thin slotted screws, then pull the hardware out of the back of the forend.

4. While controlling the ejector hammer's spring and guide rod, push the hammer forward. The guide rod will pop out of its recess below the hammer as it is over-rotated.

5. The ejector sears and springs are retained by these contoured and blended pins. Unless repair or replacement is necessary, removal is not recommended.

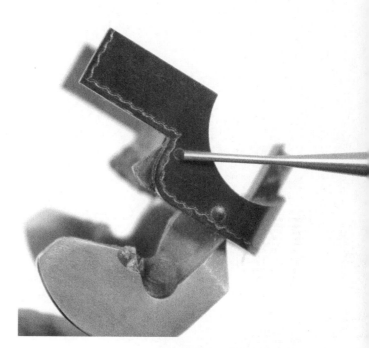

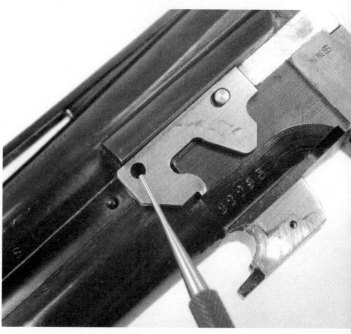

6. The ejector hammers can be removed by driving out this pin from right to left. The left end of the pin is splined.

7. Push the extractors fully extended. This will align this hole with a small slotted screw. Remove this screw to free the extractors. Each extractor is composed of two pieces, front and rear.

8. The cocking lever lifter and its spring can be removed by driving out this spring pin.

9. One of the forend screws, when threaded into the bottom of the latch housing can be used to gently pull the latch housing from the forend.

10. This screw retains the latch spring.

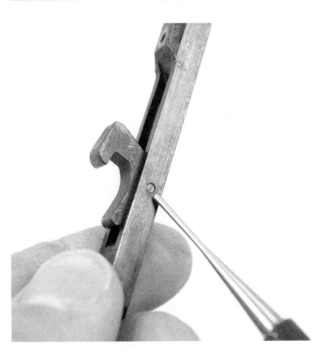

11. This pin when removed, will release the forend latch.

12. Remove the recoil pad, then use a long flat bladed screwdriver to remove the stock bolt from the buttstock.

13. Remove these two screws in the trigger guard tang. They are different. Then gently displace the trigger guard tang up from the stock by lifting up on the trigger guard.

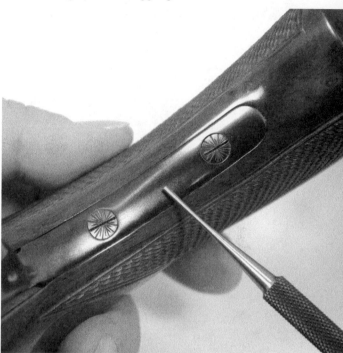

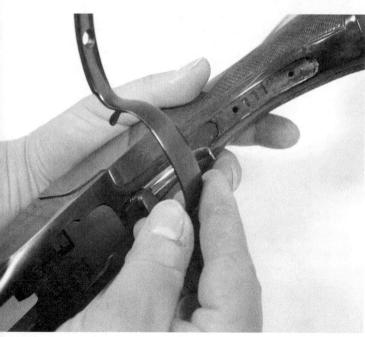

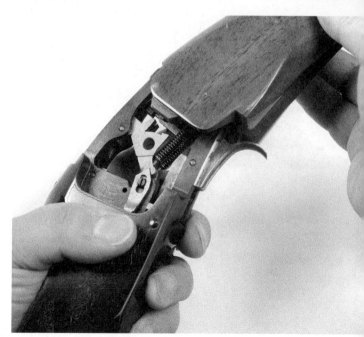

14. Rotate the trigger guard 90 degrees then lift it from the receiver.

15. Remove the buttstock.

16. Close the top lever by depressing the cocking lever in the front area of the receiver.

17. Release the hammers by pulling the trigger or lifting the sear pieces. Then remove the hammer springs and guide rods by slightly compressing them then pulling them out from behind the hammers.

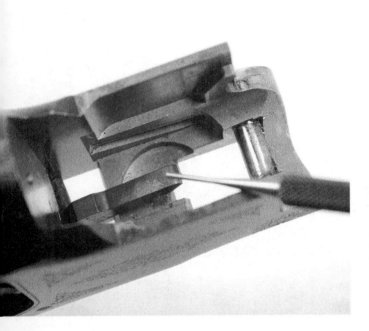

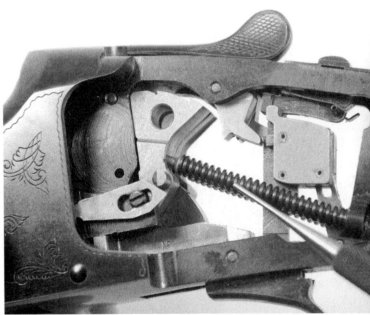

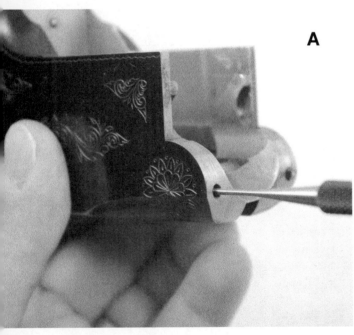

A

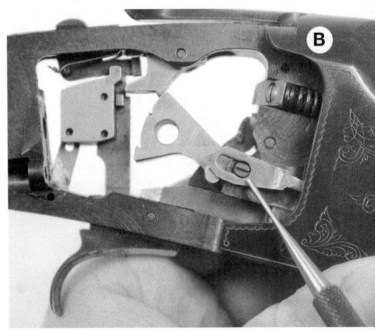

B

18. Rotate the hammers back until they stop. Then use a small punch to push the ejector trip rods from the front of the receiver (picture A). The rods should be pushed as far back into the receiver as they can go, thus aligning the hammer's retaining screw with the round section of the slot in the ejector trip rod's head (picture B). Remove this screw. The hammers can now be removed.

19. Remove the ejector trip rods through the back of the receiver.

20. Remove the top lever spring by dislodging it at one end and then pulling it out of the receiver. Control the spring.

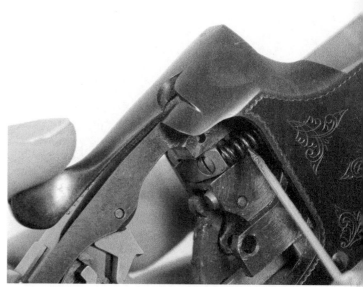

21. Drive out the splined firing pin retaining pins. The top pin should be driven out to the left and the bottom pin to the right. When the pins are removed, the bottom firing pin has a rebound spring.

22. Remove the top lever's spring seat by taking out this screw.

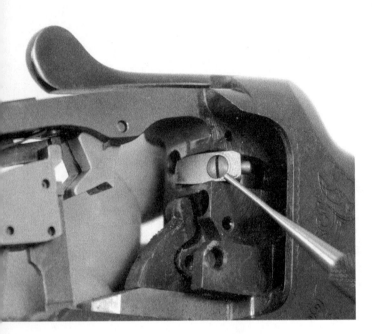

23. Drive out this large pin to free the cocking lever.

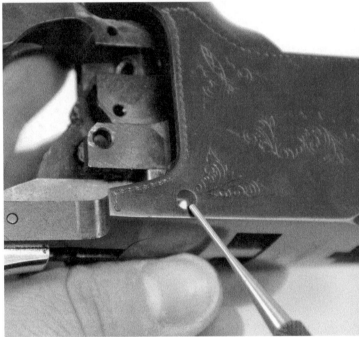

24. Gently drive out the two forward pins in the inertia block to free the trigger link from the block.

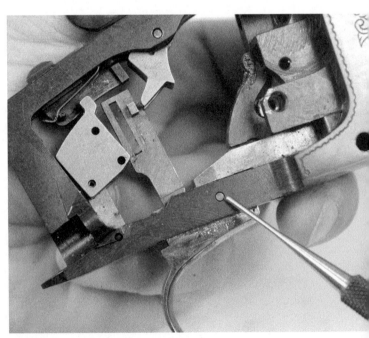

25. Drive out the splined trigger pin from right to left, then pull the trigger and link down through the trigger slot so that only the link remains in the receiver.

26. Drive out this pin which holds the inertia block arm. Then remove the inertia block assembly from the receiver.

27. With the trigger now floating, the cocking lever can be rotated down and then pulled up through the receiver front and removed from the receiver.

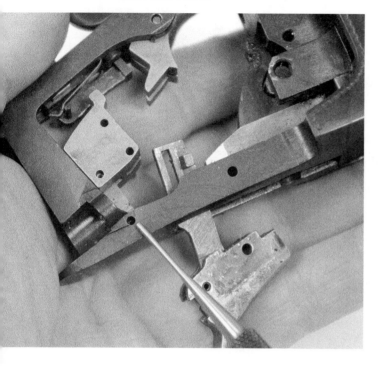

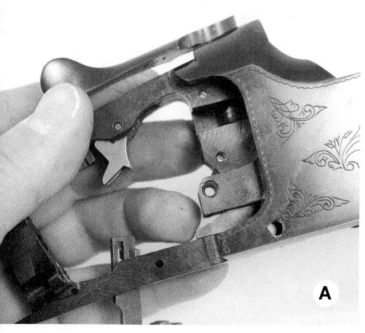

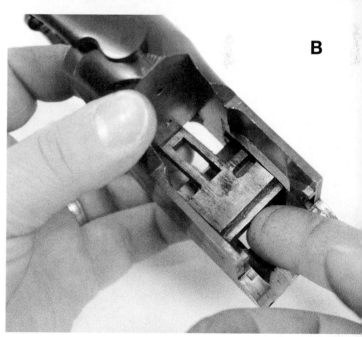

28. Lift the top lever until it stops. This will disengage it from the locking latch and the latch can be pushed forward (picture A) into the front of the receiver and removed (picture B).

29. Push the trigger up into the receiver and withdraw it to either side to remove it.

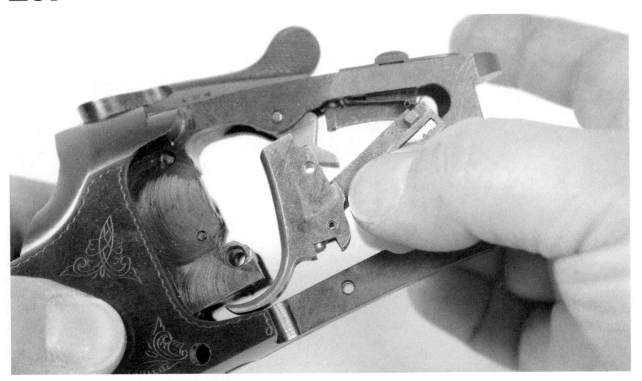

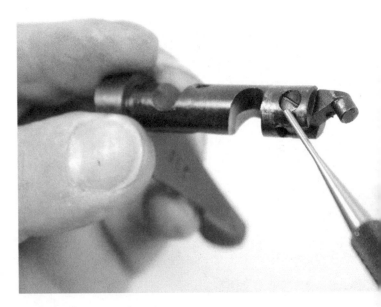

30. The camming arm on the bottom of the top lever will rotate down to clear the top lever's hole. Remove the top lever by pushing it up through the receiver and out the top.

31. The rotating camming arm can be removed from the top lever by taking out this screw.

32. Drive out this splined pin from right to left to remove the sears and the sear springs.

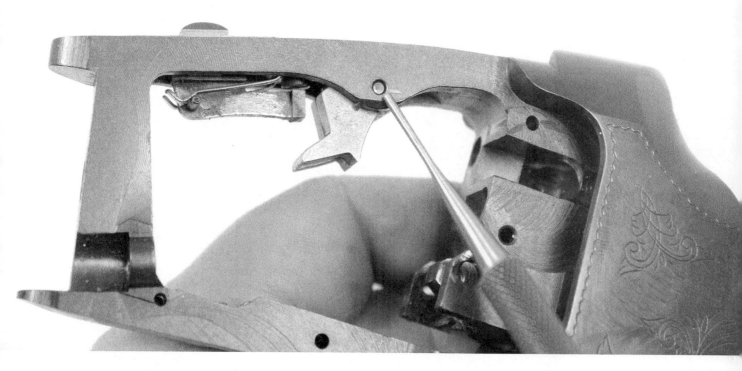

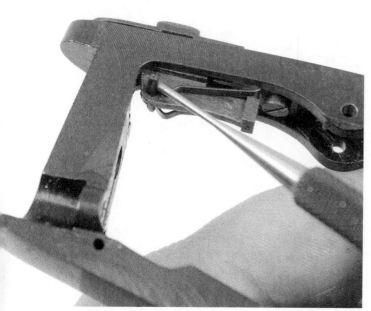

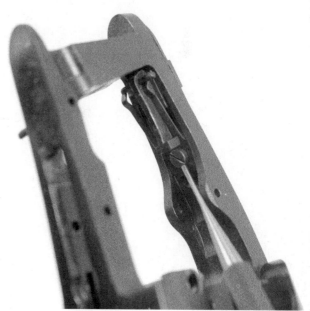

33. Drive out this pin to remove the safety/selector assembly. Once free of the receiver the safety button will separate from the selector arm. The safety arm can be removed by dropping down in to the receiver to clear its slot.

34. Remove this screw to take the safety spring from the receiver.

Reassembly Tips:

1. The inertia block stubs should be behind the nose of the selector as seen here or the trigger mechanism will be immobilized.

2. Note the difference between the top firing pin and the bottom pin, which has a spring.

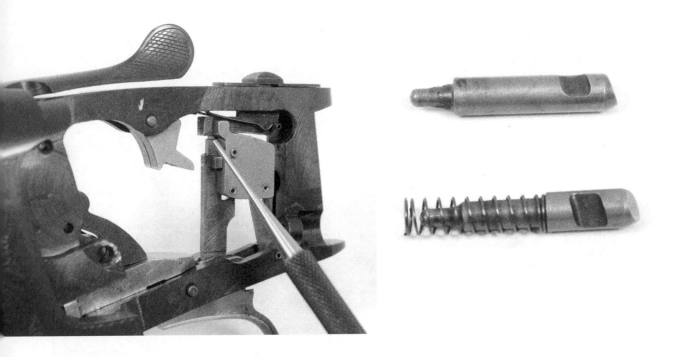

3. The four screws retaining the forend hardware are different. This is the order in which they are placed, with the forend in the background for reference.

Browning Cynergy Sporting

Similar/Identical Pattern Guns:

The same basic assembly/disassembly steps for the Browning Cynergy Sporting also apply to the following guns:

Cynergy Field

Cynergy Classic Sporting

Cynergy Feather

Cynergy Classic Trap

Data:	Browning Cynergy
Origin:	Miroku, Japan
Manufacturer:	Browning Arms Company, Morgan Utah
Gauges:	12, 20, 28, .410
Overall Length:	48 inches
Height:	7.5 inches
Barrel Length:	30 inches
Weight:	7 lbs. 15 oz.

The Cynergy is a new generation of Browning double barrel shotguns. The low receiver profile is a direct result of the internal arrangement of the receiver parts. Available in several models, mostly for sporting clays and trap competition, all the models are essentially the same as far as components go, including the hunting and field models. A couple units incorporate adjustable stock combs, but otherwise follow the pattern of the basic Sporting model seen here.

Disassembly:

1. With the safety on and the gun cocked, pull the forearm latch out and pull out on the forend to remove it from the barrel assembly.

2. Open the action using the top lever. Remove the barrel assembly by rotating it down and out of the receiver.

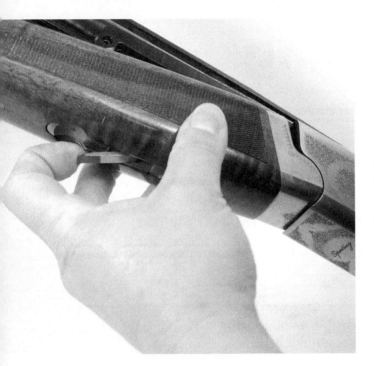

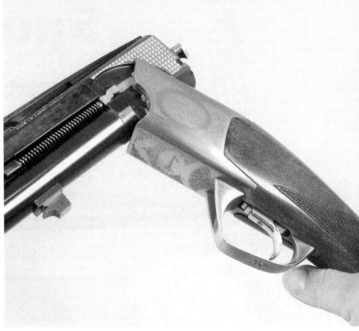

3. Remove the two wide screws in the forend hardware and lift the hardware assembly out of the forend. The nuts are splined and should not be removed unless replacement is warranted.

4. Remove this screw to take out the forend latch spring. Note the small set screw on the opposite end of the slot from the spring. This screw retains the tension screw beneath it and this screw and the set screw are adjusted at the factory and should not be fiddled with unless replacement or repair is necessary.

5. Drive out this pin to remove the forend latch.

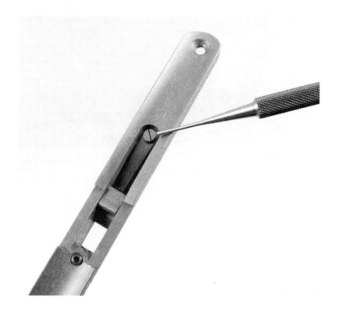

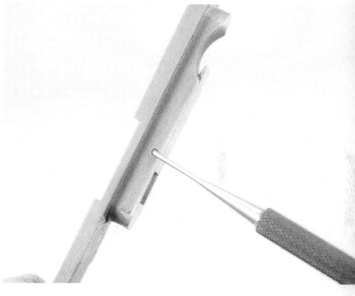

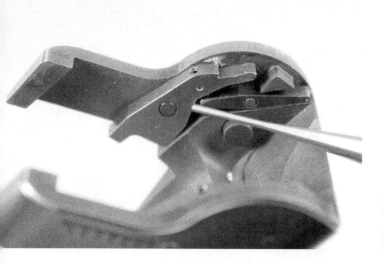

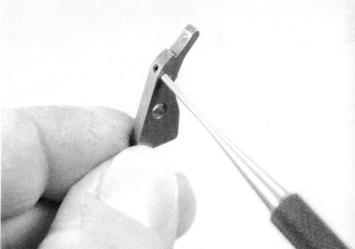

6. The ejector sear and sear link on either side can be lifted off of their pins. The easiest way to do this is to slightly depress the long straight sear link to relieve tension from the sear and then lift the sear off its pin followed by the sear link. The spring and detent under the sear arm should be controlled.

7. There is a small set screw in each ejector sear that is staked in. This should not be removed or adjusted.

8. These three pins are contoured and splined and should not be removed.

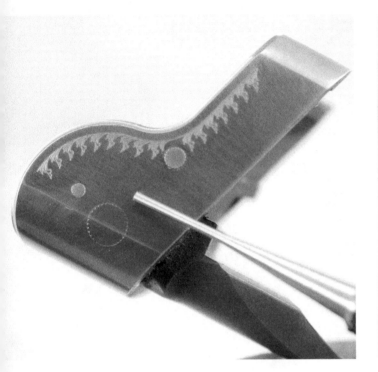

9. The forearm guide can be removed by the removal of the two screws which interpenetrate the rib between the barrels.

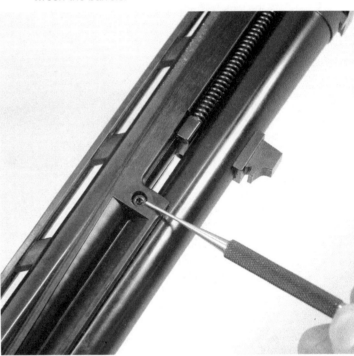

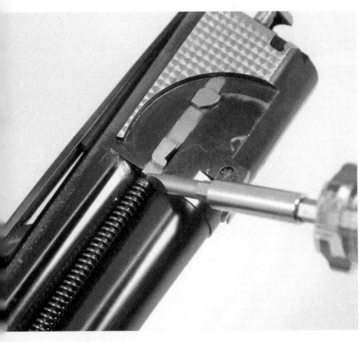

10. The ejector springs and guide rods can be lifted from the ejector and removed with a screwdriver.

11. Pull the bottom half of the ejector forward out of its slot.

12. This contoured pin can be punched out to separate the inner and outer pieces of the ejector. The piece with the extractor can be then pulled off to the rear, while the remaining piece can slide out to the front. This should not be done unless the extractor needs to be replaced.

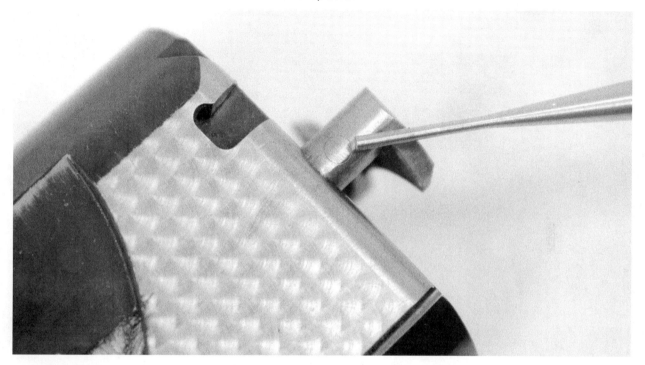

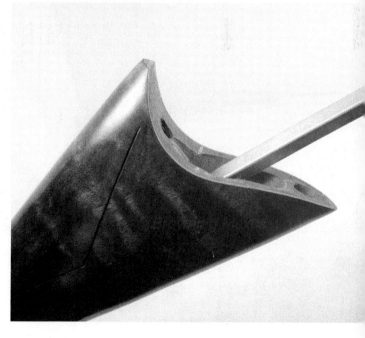

13. Remove the two stock screws to remove the buttpad.

14. The buttstock is retained by a large bolt, requiring a large flat bladed screwdriver to remove.

15. To remove the trigger guard, first take this set screw out, then pull the trigger guard slightly to the rear and then down off the receiver.

16. Depress this pin to close the top lever.

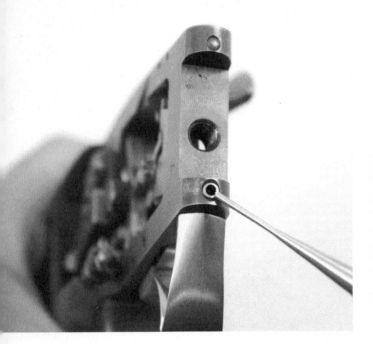

17. Remove this top lever spring by unscrewing the hex head socket screw above the rear of the spring. The spring guide and the spring can then be easily lifted out of the receiver. The spring is still under a considerable amount of tension and should be controlled.

18. Remove the locking pin screws.

19. Lift and pull to the rear the locking pins. The left pin will require slight rotation to clear the trigger disconnector arm which is attached to the top lever.

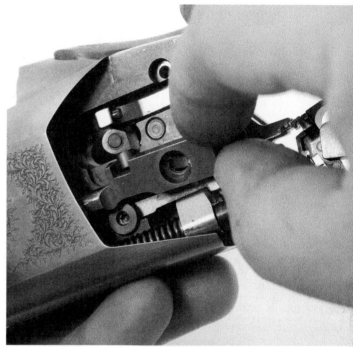

20. The small "E" clip retaining the rocker pin should now be removed.

21. Insert a paper clip between the sear link and the frame to prevent the strikers from falling when the rocker pin is removed.

22. Pull the rockers out to the rear. The trigger mechanism will have to be held back for the rockers to clear.

23. The trigger disconnector can now be pulled out to the rear.

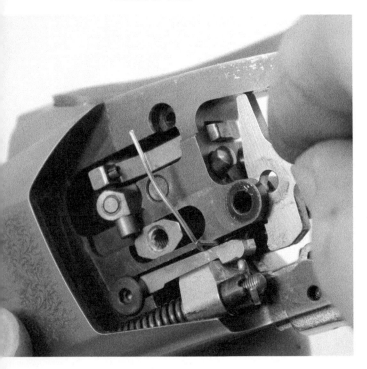

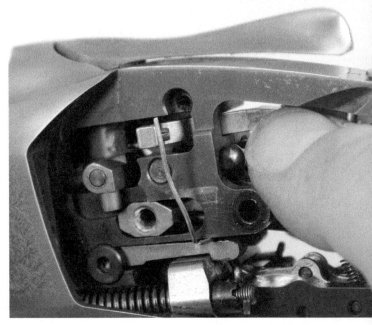

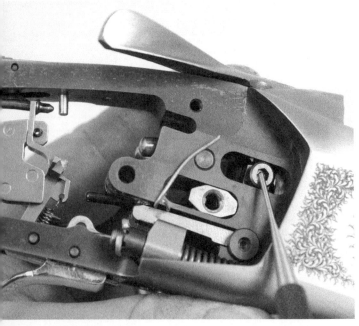

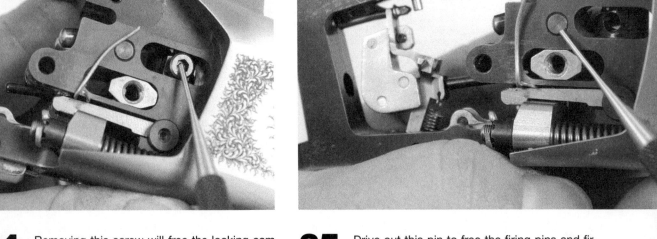

24. Removing this screw will free the locking cam on the left side and the top lever and the small top lever retainer (under the screw head) from the top lever.

25. Drive out this pin to free the firing pins and firing pin springs. It is splined and should be removed by driving it out to the left.

26. The top lever can now be removed by lifting it up and out of the receiver. Control the top lever retainer and spring as they are tensioned. Once the lever is out of the receiver the top lever disconnector will drop out of the its hole in the receiver.

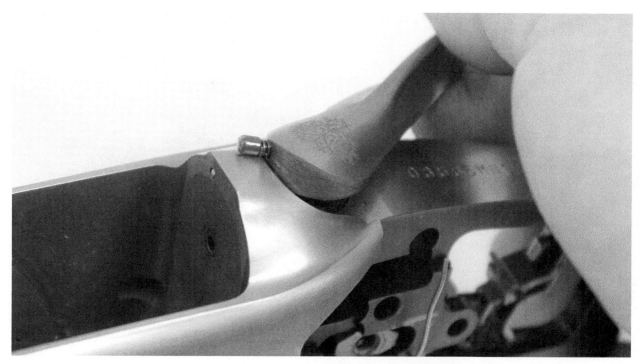

27. Drive out the roll pin holding the inertia mass to the trigger link and then remove the inertia mass from the receiver. Support the trigger link when driving out this pin, as the link's arms are easily broken.

28. Unhook the trigger spring from the trigger link then push out the spring's pin, which is directly below.

29. Push out the trigger pin to release the trigger, then the trigger can be removed from the bottom. The small pin in the top of the trigger unit retains the striker stop and spring.

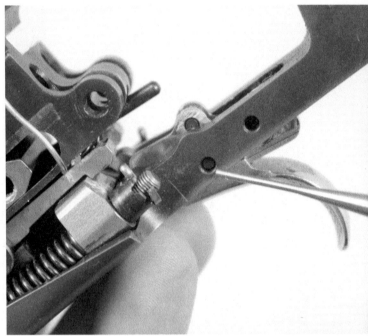

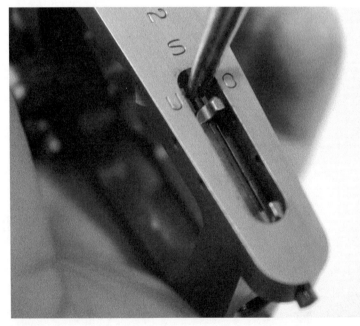

30. Push out these two pins to separate and remove the selector button from the selector.

31. The safety retaining pin can be pulled out to the rear using pliers. Take note that the detent ball and spring beneath the safety are quite compressed and can disappear if the pin is not removed carefully.

32. While supporting the strikers, pull out the previously inserted paper clips to release the sear link, which releases the strikers.

33. Remove the sear link screws. The sear links can then be pulled out to the side.

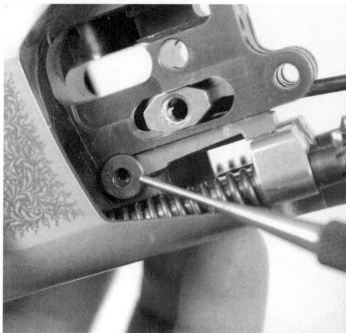

34. Remove the trigger link disconnect by taking out this set screw. The disconnect can then be removed to the rear and the locking pin cross member (which held the screw) can come out to either side.

35. To remove the striker assemblies, this cotter pin must be removed and the nut unscrewed off of the cocking lever rod. The striker will follow, then the spring. This should only be done if one of the components needs replacement.

36. The cocking pieces in the front of the receiver rotate in slots cut into the receiver and are linked to the cocking lever rods by a pin integral to the rods. If necessary for replacement, the rods (after striker assembly takedown) can be pushed forward through the receiver, taking the cocking levers with them.

Reassembly Tips:

1. The trigger link arms are quite fragile. As seen in this photo, the arm can snap off easily. When reinstalling the inertia mass and its retaining roll pin, ensure that the whole assembly is fully supported.

Browning Maxus

Data:	Browning Maxus Sporting Carbon Fiber
Origin:	Portugal
Manufacturer:	Browning Arms Company, Morgan, Utah
Gauges:	12
Magazine Capacity:	4 rounds
Overall Length:	51.25 inches
Height:	6.75 inches
Barrel Length:	30 inches
Weight:	7 pounds

The Maxus is a descendant of the Gold and Silver lines with some important refinements, mostly in the recoil suppression and gas systems. It is much quicker to disassemble for cleaning due to the quick detach lever on the handguard. This and the changes in the gas system justify a separate entry for the Maxus. It is available in a number of configurations for hunting and a variety of competition types.

Disassembly:

1. With the bolt locked back and the safety on "safe" depress the speed lock button while lifting the speed lock lever to disengage the forend. Pull the forend off the front of the shotgun. A large weld spring will remain in the handguard and can be removed by hand.

2. Pull the barrel from the front of the gun.

3. Pull the piston/sleeve assembly and the piston sleeve spring from the front of the magazine tube.

4. The piston sleeve and piston can be separated by pulling them apart by hand.

5. The piston assembly can be disassembled by unscrewing the large slotted ring at the rear of the assembly. However, it is best to avoid disassembly unless something needs to be replaced, as it is easily cleaned in assembly.

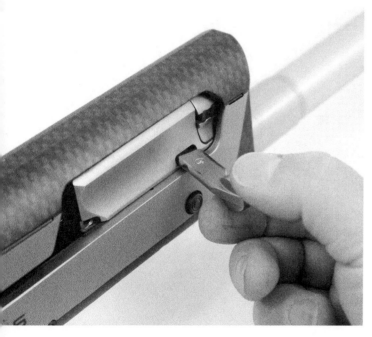

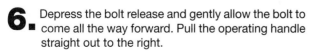

6. Depress the bolt release and gently allow the bolt to come all the way forward. Pull the operating handle straight out to the right.

7. Remove the bolt assembly by pulling it out of the front of the receiver. The bolt catch may need to be depressed for the bolt to clear. The bolt will easily lift out of the carrier.

8. The firing pin retaining pin bushing can be gently pried up off of the retaining pin with a small punch. The retaining pin can then be removed from the bolt to the right and the firing pin withdrawn to the rear of the bolt.

9. Drive out the extractor pin from top to bottom, then remove the extractor and extractor spring.

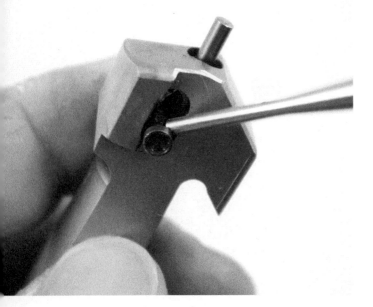

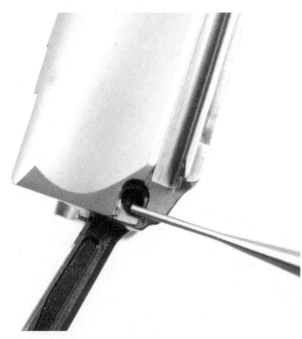

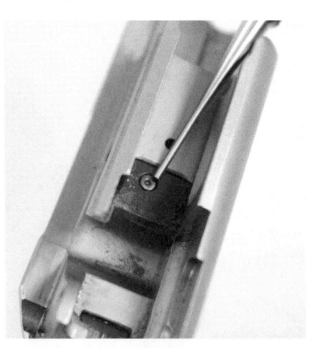

10. If necessary for repair, the link pin can be driven out from right to left. This will free the link and the detent and spring in front of it.

11. The bolt cam piece is not integral with the bolt carrier and is pinned in place in the carrier. The pin is staked and should not be removed unless the cam piece needs replacement.

12. This spring pin retains the operating handle detent and spring.

13. Push out these two pins to remove the fire control group.

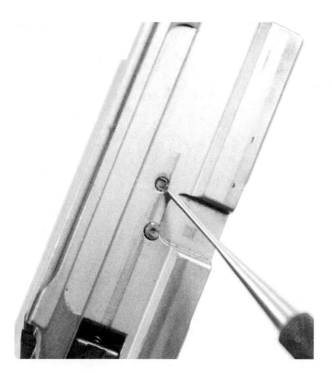

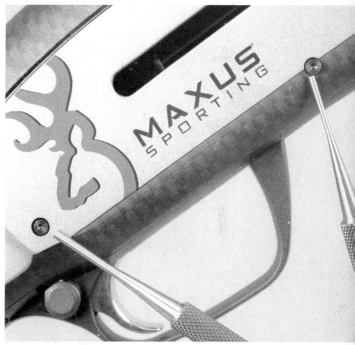

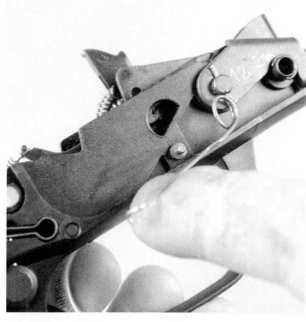

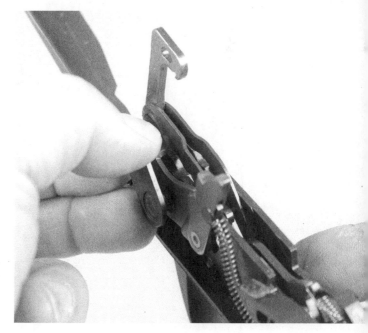

14. To disassemble the fire control group, first unlatch the front carrier spring from the group frame, then lifting the carrier assembly, pull the spring's short leg from the carrier pin.

15. Ensure that the hammer is forward, then pull to the left the front carrier assembly. This also frees the rear carrier assembly and the rear carrier spring and guides. Do this carefully to keep control of the spring and multiple parts.

16. Unhook the trigger/disconnector spring from the disconnector, then from the trigger guard.

17. Remove the trigger guard bushing.

18. Remove the hammer pin and pull the hammer from the housing.

19. Push out the trigger pin.

20. The trigger can now be pulled up and out of the housing.

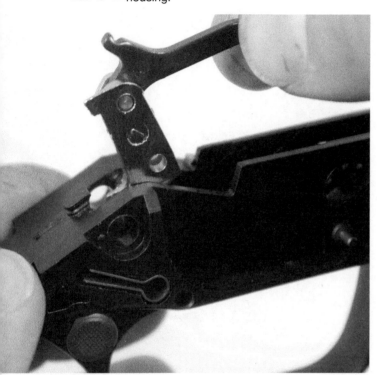

21. Remove the sear pin.

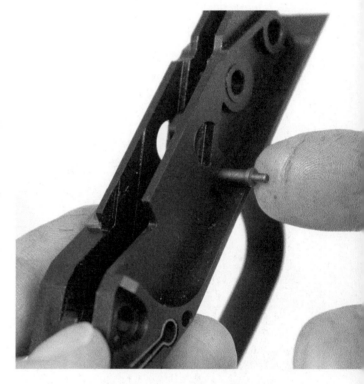

22. Lift the sear and sear spring from the trigger housing.

23. Push out this pin to release the hammer spring and detent. Control the spring as it is still compressed.

24. Remove this spring to relieve tension on the safety button. Once the spring has been removed the button can be easily taken out to either side and the safety detent will fall out of the bottom of the housing.

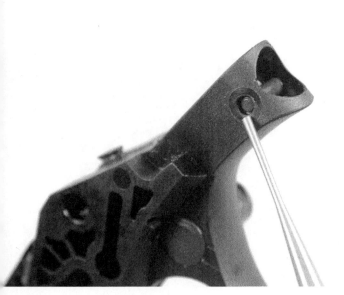

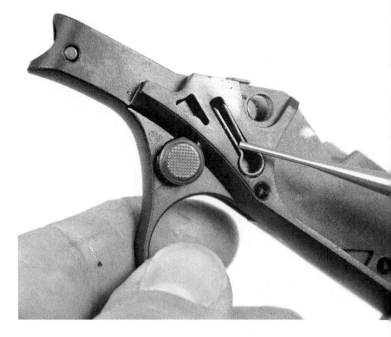

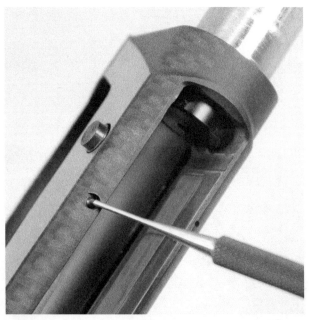

25. There are two synthetic pads on the left side of the housing that should be left unless replacement is needed.

26. This pin retains the shell latch/bolt release. It should be driven out from top to bottom. The assembly is composed of several parts and a spring which will separate upon removal from the receiver.

27. Remove the magazine plug with a screwdriver. Push the plug slightly in then turn 90 degrees. The plug will now fall from the magazine tube.

28. While depressing this small pin, begin turning the magazine tube retainer. With the retainer removed the magazine spring and follower can be pulled from the tube. The spring is still very compressed so control it.

29. The buttpad can be removed by unscrewing the two stock screws.

30. Pull any spacers present and the positioning plate from the stock.

31. Remove the stock bolt nut to remove the nut. Then remove the action spring support, the plate beneath the nut.

32. Remove the stock, then the stock spacer can be removed. Note the orientation.

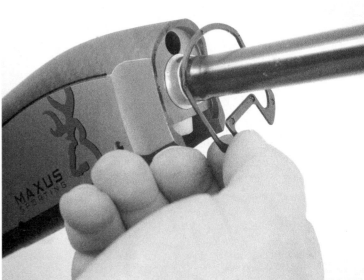

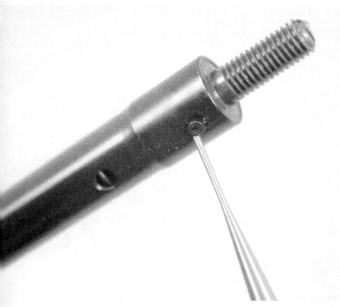

33. This roll pin retains the action spring retainer. Firmly retain the retainer when unscrewing the retainer piece or the action spring and detent will emerge from the action tube with great alacrity. Do not attempt to remove the action tube.

34. The synthetic bolt buffer and the spongy pad beneath the trigger group can be left alone unless they need to be replaced.

35. The ejector and spring can be removed by unscrewing this flat slotted screw, which also serves as the pin.

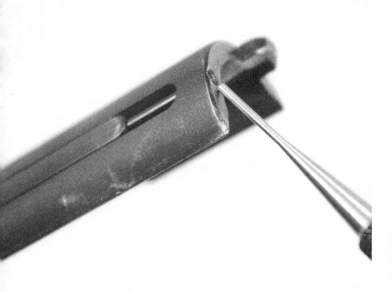

2. Note the orientation of the trigger/disconnector spring. The long leg goes to the rear.

Reassembly Tips:

1. When reinstalling the fire control, first install the trigger then slide the sear and sear spring under their rails in the housing. Next install the hammer over the sear. The disconnector can then be lowered and inserted under the sear, followed by the reinstallation of the trigger bushing.

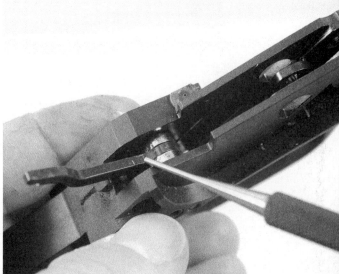

3. When reinstalling the bolt, depress the bolt release button.

Browning Superposed

Similar/Identical Pattern Guns:

The same basic assembly/disassembly steps for the Browning Superposed also apply to the following guns:

Browning Citori   **Browning Liege**

Browning ST-100   **Browning B-25**

Browning B-27   **Browning B-125**

Browning Lightning

Data: Browning Superposed Over/Under

Origin: Belgium

Manufacturer: Fabrique Nationale, Morgan, Utah

Gauges: 12, 20, 28, 410

Overall length: 46 inches (with 30-inch barrel)

Barrel length: 26-1/2 to 32 inches

Weight: 6-3/8 to 8 pounds

One of John M. Browning's last designs, the Superposed shotgun has been made since 1927, and is still in production. In 1974 a lower priced model called the Liege was introduced, and was made for about 2 years. A second moderately-priced version, the Citori, was offered in 1975, and is still in production. The internal mechanism of all the Browning over/under guns has enough similarity that portions of the instructions can be applied to each of them. The gun shown in the photos, however, is an early Superposed.

Disassembly:

1. Operate the forend latch by pushing the latch lever toward the rear, then pivoting the lever outward.

2. Slide the forend forward until it stops, and swing the cocking lever lifter out of its recess in the front underside of the receiver.

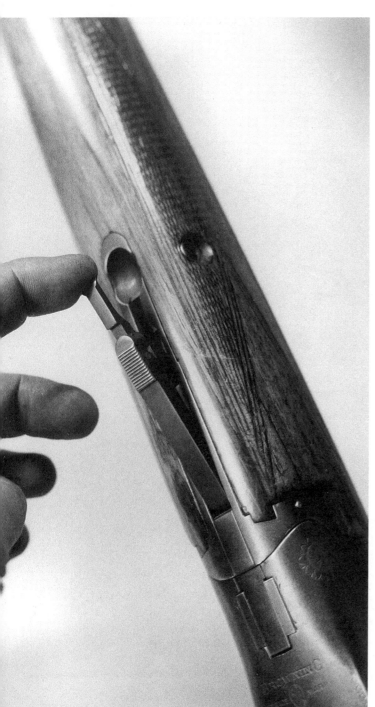

3. Operate the barrel latch, tip the barrels downward, then remove them toward the rear and upward.

4. Remove the cross screw on the left side near the lower edge of the forend.

5. Slide the forend wood forward until it clears the mechanism, and remove the wood downward.

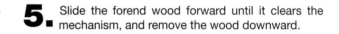

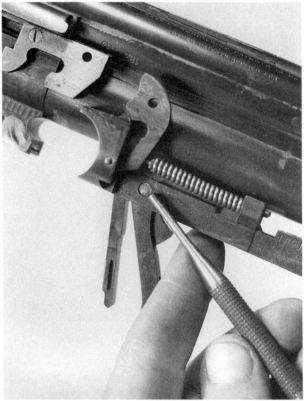

6. Drive out the large cross pin in the forend base, the pivot for the forend latch.

7. Remove the latch lever downward. Drifting out the cross pin at the front of the latch lever will allow removal of the lever release and its spring.

8. Slide the forend base mechanism forward until it stops, then remove it downward.

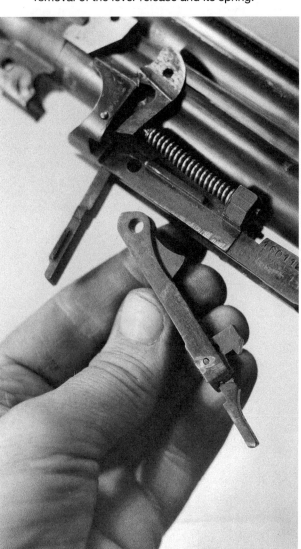

9. Pushing out the small cross pin near the large retaining pin will allow removal of the cocking lever lifter downward.

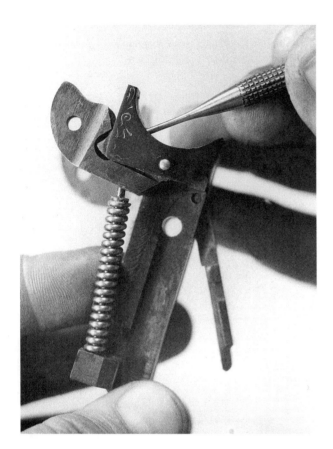

10. Trip the ejector hammer sears by inserting a tool in the slots in the rear face of the forend base, to allow the ejector hammers to snap toward the rear, relieving part of their spring tension.

11. Grip the tip of the ejector hammer spring plunger (guide) with sharp-nosed pliers, and tilt the pliers to lever the nose of the guide out of its depression on the back of the hammer. Caution: The spring is still under some tension, so control it and ease it out. Remove the spring and guide toward the rear, and repeat the operation on the other spring and guide.

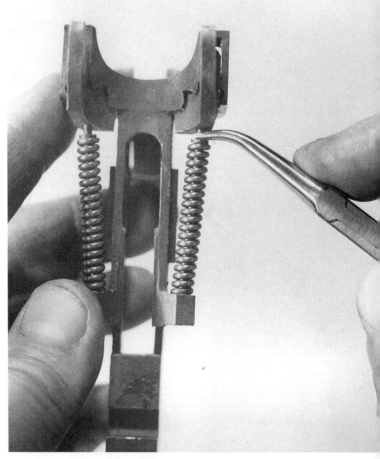

12. Drifting out the large cross pin at the rear of the forend base will release the ejector hammers for removal toward the front.

13. The ejector hammer sears are retained on each side by small pins in the upper wings of the forend base, and these pins are contoured on the outside to match the curve of the base. These are difficult to locate, and if possible should be left in place. If removal is necessary for repair, each pin must be driven out inward to release the sears and their springs.

14. Move the ejectors back until the hole in the side of each one aligns with the retaining screw. Back out the screws, and remove the ejectors toward the rear.

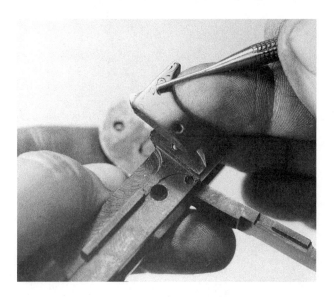

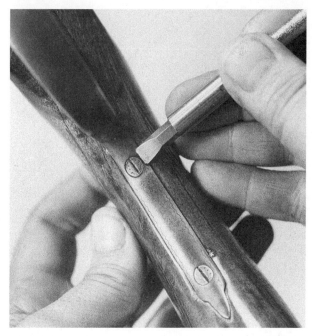

15. After the ejectors are removed, the ejector extensions can be slid out toward the rear. It is not necessary to remove the stop screws.

16. Remove the two screws in the rear tail of the trigger guard. The guard is not removed at this time.

17. Remove the buttplate, and use a B-Square stock tool or a long-shanked screwdriver to remove the stock mounting bolt, lock washer, and washer toward the rear. Take off the buttstock toward the rear.

18. Turn the trigger guard straight out to either side, and remove it downward.

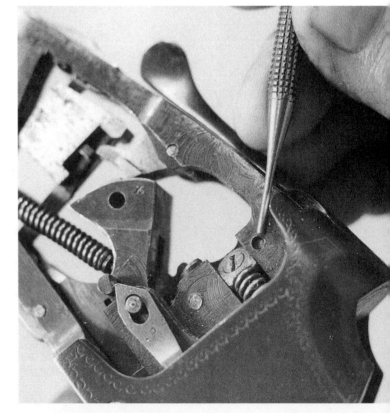

19. With the hammers in cocked position, it is possible to remove both firing pins without further disassembly. The upper firing pin is retained by a cross pin that is driven out toward the right, and the firing pin is removed toward the rear.

20. The cross pin that retains the lower firing pin is drifted out in the opposite direction, toward the left, and the lower firing pin and its return spring are taken out toward the rear. The upper firing pin has no spring.

21. Operate the trigger and intertia block to trip both sears, dropping the hammers to the fired position. Insert a tool behind each hammer spring guide, and lever them outward, disengaging the nose of the guide from the recess in the back of each hammer. Caution: These strong springs are under tension, so control them during removal.

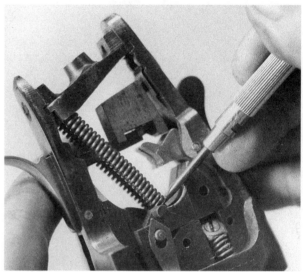

22. Drift out the trigger cross pin.

23. Move the trigger forward and downward, detaching the inertia block from the underlug of the safety button. Slide the trigger connector downward, detaching it from the inertia block. Restrain the inertia block spring and plunger, as these parts will be released as the connector is moved downward. The trigger is removed downward, and the inertia block toward the side. Drifting out the small cross pin in the trigger will allow removal of the trigger plunger and its spring toward the rear.

24. Use a tool to lift the front tab of the safety spring out of its recess, and rotate the spring straight out to either side. The spring is removed downward, and the safety button and small spacer block upward.

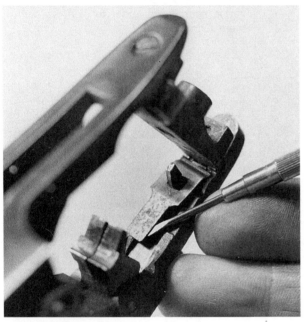

25. Drift out the cross pin at the top of the receiver, in the upper tang, and remove the sears and their springs downward and toward the rear.

26. Taking care not to damage the rear tips of the ejector trip rods, drift out the hammer pivot pin, and remove the hammers toward the rear.

27. Slide the ejector trip rods straight out toward the rear. Keep them separated, as they are not interchangeable.

28. Remove the barrel latch spring base screw, on the right side of the receiver, and take off the base and spring toward the rear.

29. Drift out the large cross pin near one lower edge of the receiver.

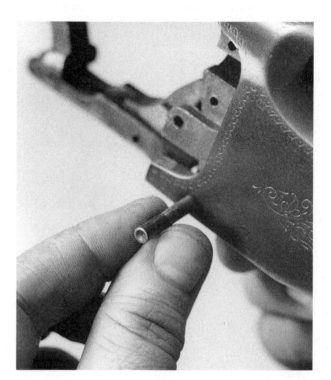

30. Remove the cocking lever downward and toward the rear. Remove the screws at the top and bottom of the insert at the rear of the receiver tangs, and slide the insert (arrow) out toward the right.

31. Insert a drift punch in the opening on the underside of the receiver, against the lower end of the barrel latch lever shaft, and tap it gently upward for removal.

Reassembly Tips:

32. The latch lever dog is retained in the lower end of the lever shaft by a cross screw that is contoured to match the curve of the shaft. Unless necessary for repair, the dog and screw should be left in place.

1. When replacing the small spacer block in the safety button slot, be sure it is installed between the two lower projections of the safety button, with the groove in the block at the rear and downward, as shown, to align with the spring cuts in the upper tang.

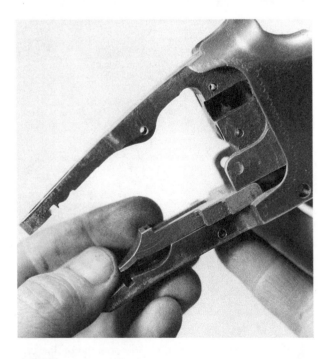

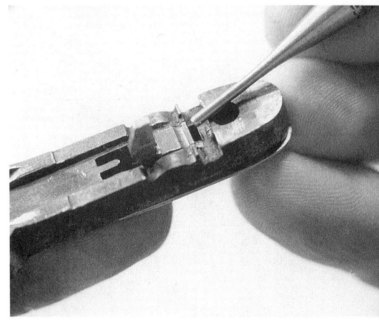

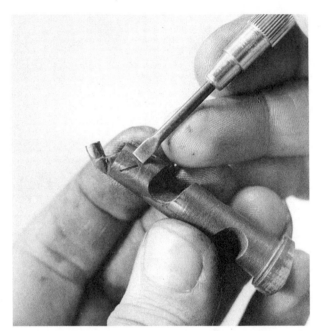

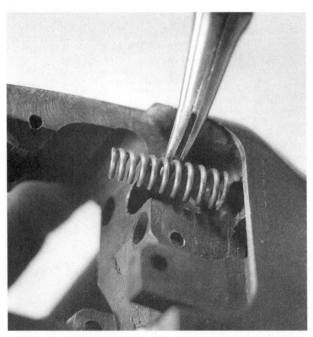

33. Move the barrel latch block straight out toward the rear. It may be tight, and may require nudging with a drift to free it.

2. When replacing the barrel latch spring, note that its larger end goes toward the front, with the smaller end engaging the stud on the spring base.

3. When replacing the barrel latch lever, move the barrel latch block to its normal protrusion at the front, and with the latch lever centered on the upper tang, tap the lever gently with a nylon hammer to seat the dog in its recess on the block. If the lever fails to move into place, use no extreme force. Move the locking block slightly until it is in proper alignment.

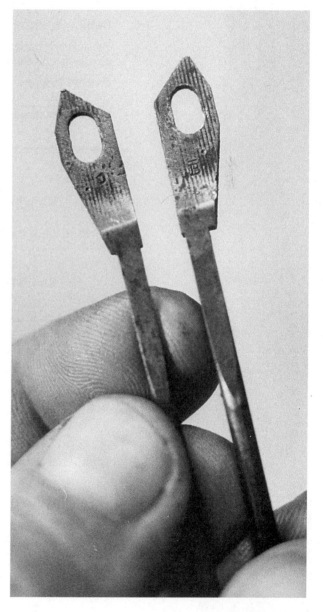

4. The ejector trip rods are usually marked for each side, the ones shown having a small "O" and "B" mark to signify "over" and "below." This is not always the case, though, and it's best to keep them separate during disassembly.

Citadel LE Pump

Similar/Identical Pattern Guns:

The following basic assembly/disassembly steps for the Citadel LE Pump can also be used for the following guns:

Escort Pump

Data:	Citadel LE Tactical Pump
Origin:	United States
Manufacturer:	APM, Meridian, Idaho
Gauges:	12
Magazine Capacity:	7 rounds
Overall Length:	42.25 inches
Height:	7.75 inches
Barrel Length:	22 inches
Weight:	6.35 lbs

Early 2012 saw the arrival of the Citadel line of law enforcement-themed shotguns. Three models were introduced. The first was a basic standard-stocked model which also came with a stockless pistol grip. The second traded the standard buttstock for a recoil-absorbing collapsible pistol grip stock, while the third mounted a recoil absorbing stock, fixed with a thumbhole design. An inexpensive shotgun, mounting an extended magazine, among other features, it is also manufactured domestically. This series is supplied by Legacy Sports International, as is the virtually identically constructed Escort series.

Disassembly:

1. With the hammer cocked and the safety on, unscrew and remove the magazine tube cap.

2. Pull the slide slightly to the rear then pull the barrel forward out of the receiver.

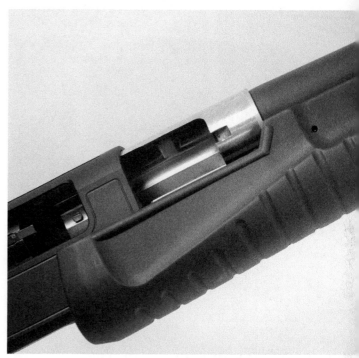

3. The slide and bolt and carrier assembly can be pulled straight forward out of the receiver.

4. Remove the bolt from the bolt carrier.

5. Depressing the firing pin will remove tension from the firing pin retaining pin, and the retaining pin can be pushed out of the bolt from top to bottom.

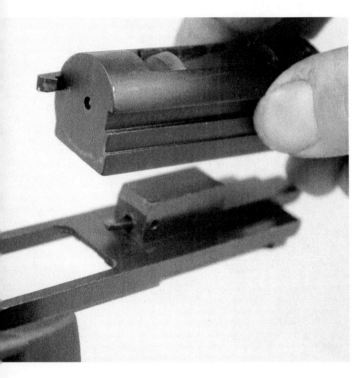

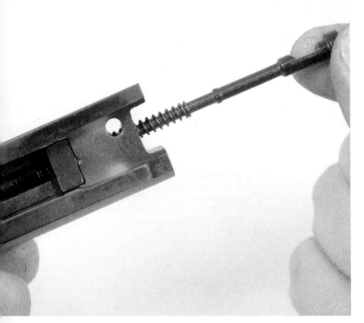

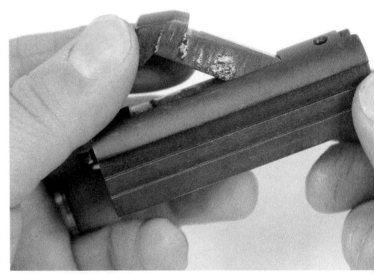

6. Pull the firing pin and firing pin spring out the back of the bolt.

7. Rotate the bolt locking block up and pull it out through the top of the bolt.

8. The extractor pin, which retains the extractor, extractor detent, and detent spring, is staked in and should not be removed unless replacement of one or more of the parts is necessary.

10. This pin holds the action bar to the forend, though it need not be removed unless the action bar needs to be replaced.

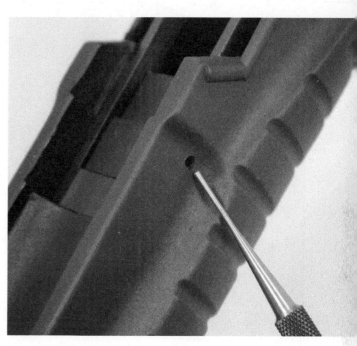

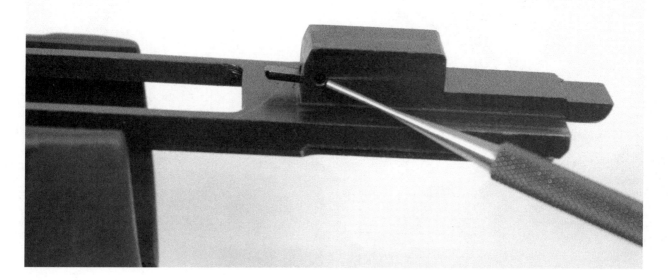

9. The action bar pin (and its spring), which helps unlock the bolt, can be removed by driving out this pin.

11. Push out the trigger plate retaining pins.

12. Remove the trigger assembly from the receiver.

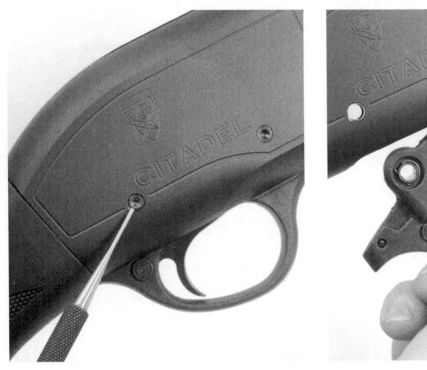

A

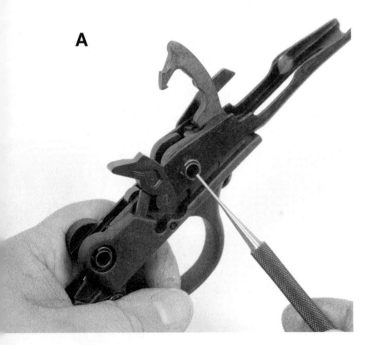

B

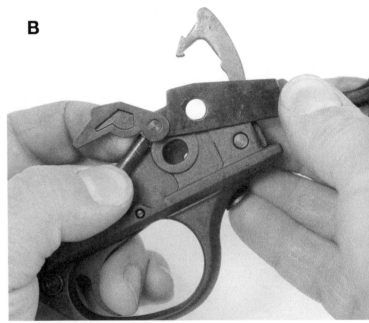

13. Push out this pin to remove the carrier assembly (Picture A). Then lift the carrier off the trigger housing while controlling the carrier spring guide and spring (Picture B).

14. Unseat the action bar control spring from its perch above the trigger. It can then be lifted off of its post and pulled to the rear to removed it from the trigger housing.

15. Using the hammer, compress the hammer spring slightly to release tension from the action bar control and lift the control off its post.

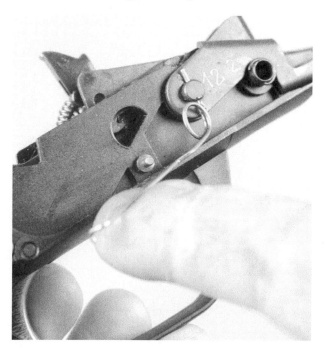

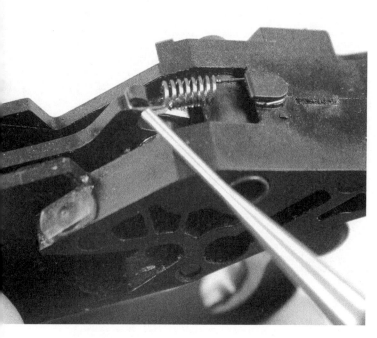

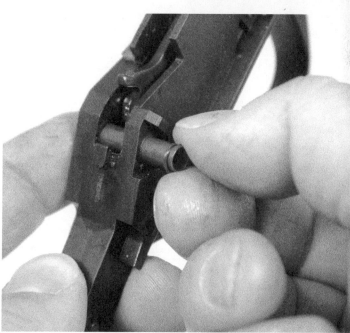

16. Push out the hammer pin. Control the hammer spring and spring guide as they are still compressed. Remove the hammer and the guide and spring.

17. Push out the rear carrier pin above the trigger. This will also free the trigger return spring.

18. Remove the trigger assembly by first pushing out this pin from right to left, and then lifting the trigger assembly out of the top of the trigger housing.

19. The disconnector and its spring and spring guide can be removed from the trigger by pulling it out to the right of the trigger assembly. Control the disconnector spring to prevent loss.

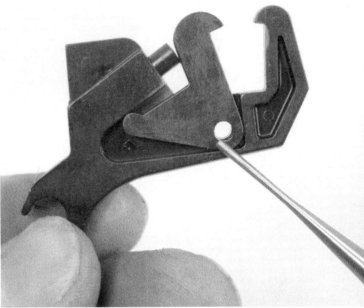

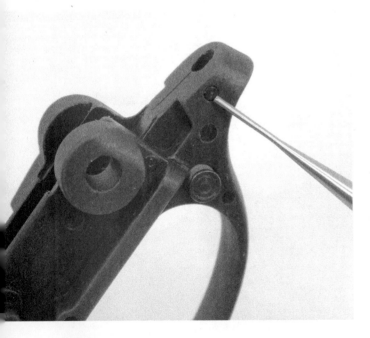

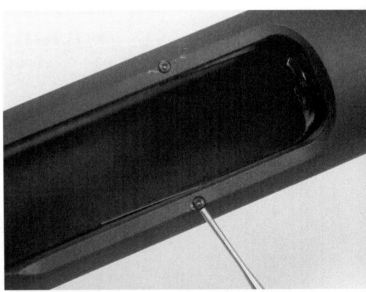

20. Press out this pin in the trigger tang to release the safety spring and detent. The safety button can now be pushed out to either side of the housing.

21. The shell latches can be removed by driving out the two pins on the bottom of the receiver up into the bolt way of the receiver. They are tensioned by two small plug springs on the inside of each receiver wall. However, unless these latches or their springs need to be replaced, such action is not recommended.

22. Use snap ring pliers to remove the springy magazine spring retainer from the mag tube. The spring is quite compressed, so control it, then remove the follower from the tube as well.

23. The magazine tube is threaded into the receiver and held there by a retaining ring. The magazine tube should not be removed unless damaged and needing replacement.

Reassembly Tips:

1. The hook on the trigger return spring should be facing forward.

CZ 712

Similar/Identical Pattern Guns:

The following basic assembly/disassembly steps for the CZ 712 can also be used for the following guns:

CZ 720

CZ 912

CZ 920

Data:	CZ 712
Origin:	Turkey
Manufacturer:	Huglu, Turkey
Gauges:	12
Magazine Capacity:	5 rounds
Overall Length:	49.5 inches
Height:	7 inches
Barrel Length:	26 inches
Weight:	7.3 pounds

The CZ 712 is a simple, light weight, yet well-constructed shotgun imported by CZ-USA. Available in several models including field, competition, youth, and shorter barreled utility types, an identical model is also produced in 20 gauge, the CZ 720. The very similar CZ912 and CZ 920 have a glossier, prettier appearance. Generally all will follow the takedown steps shown for the CZ 712. The only real exception is that the recoil spring in the CZ 912 and 920 is contained in the buttstock, rather than around the magazine tube, with the concurrent link added to the bolt carrier.

Disassembly:

1. Unscrew the magazine cap, then remove the forend by pulling it forward off the magazine tube.

2. Pull the bolt slightly to the rear then pull the barrel forward off the action.

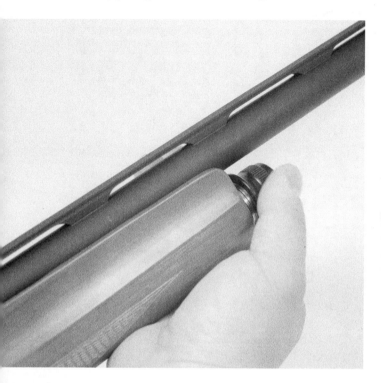

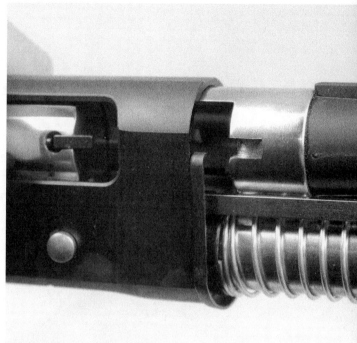

3. Remove the piston assembly from the barrel ring.

4. Only remove the gas seal from the barrel ring if it needs to be replaced. It resides in a groove near the front of the barrel ring.

5. Align the radius in the bolt body with the stem of the operating handle and pull the handle out to the right side. This will free the bolt carrier and action sleeve to spring forward out of the receiver, so control the entire assembly when removing the handle.

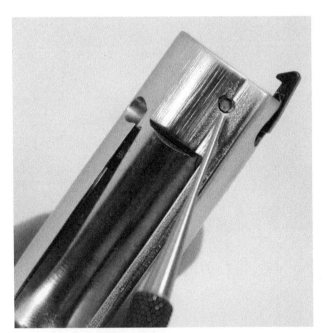

6. Pull the entire slide assembly off the magazine tube. Remove the action spring at this time as well. The bolt will separate on its own from the action bars as it is not retained, but only sits on a lip at the rear of the bar.

7. The extractor is held by this pin. It must be driven out from bottom to top.

8. The bolt lug is held in place by the firing pin and spring. To remove the firing pin and its spring, drive out this pin, again from bottom to top. This pin is also staked, so it would be advisable to leave it assembled unless replacement is necessary.

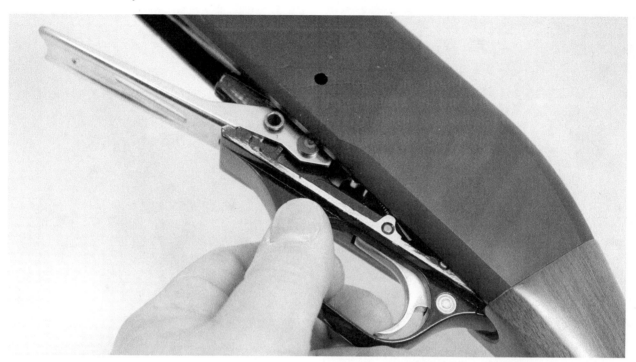

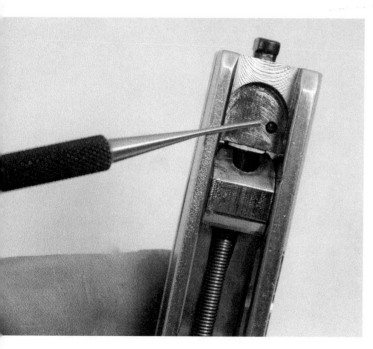

9. Drive out this trigger housing pin.

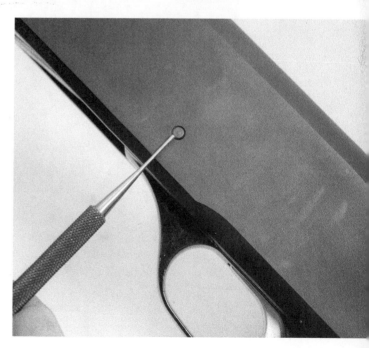

10. Remove the trigger housing by pulling forward and down on the trigger guard, while depressing the bolt release button.

11. Remove the carrier latch by driving out this pin.

12. The carrier latch can be detached from the bolt release button by driving out this small pin. Beneath the button is another spring. Control the assembly when separating the parts.

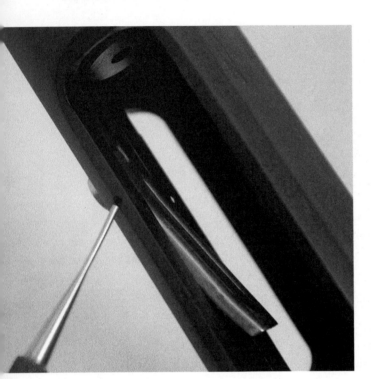

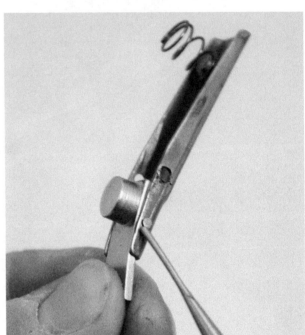

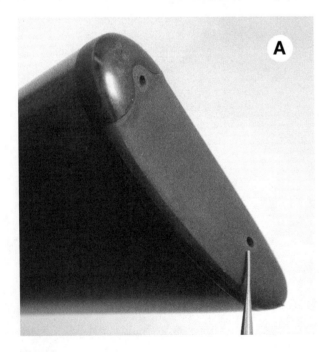
A

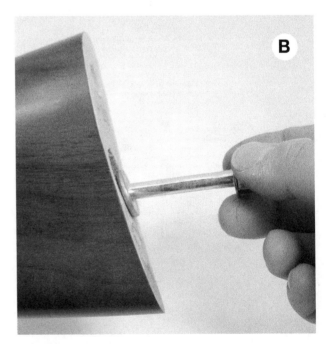
B

13. The stock can be removed by first pulling the buttpad held by two screws. The stock itself is retained by this long bolt.

14. With the hammer forward, remove the carrier dog plunger and spring by pulling slightly to the rear to clear the dog then off to the side.

15. Remove the small spring clip on the right side of the trigger housing bushing/hammer pivot.

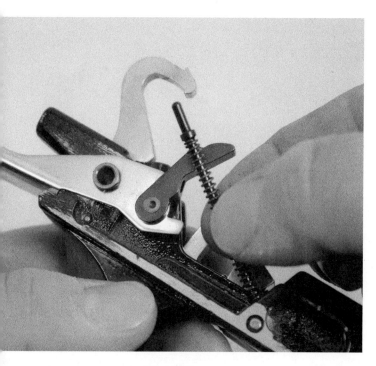

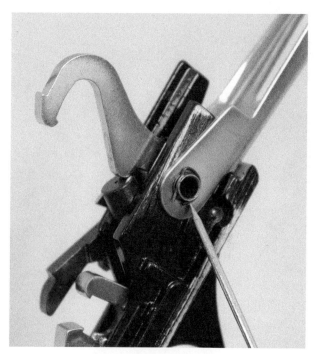

16. Push out the trigger housing bushing from right to left. The hammer spring is compressed and should be controlled as the hammer pin is removed. This will free the carrier assembly, hammer, and the hammer spring and plunger from the housing.

17. This pin retains the carrier plunger and spring.

18. Drive out the trigger pin.

19. Pull the trigger assembly forward and up to remove it from the housing.

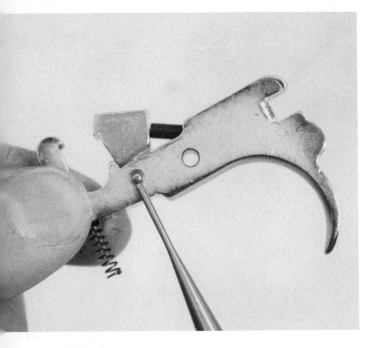

20. The disconnector can be separated from the trigger assembly by driving out this pin. The plunger and spring are compressed so control the assembly when removing.

21. This pin acts as a trigger stop and need not be removed.

22. This pin retains the safety plunger and spring. Driving it out and removing those parts will allow the safety button to be pushed out to either side of the housing.

23. To remove the magazine plug, depress in the center of the plug into the magazine tube while lifting the retainer by the protruding flange. This will upset the flanged wing and allow its removal, followed by the plug.

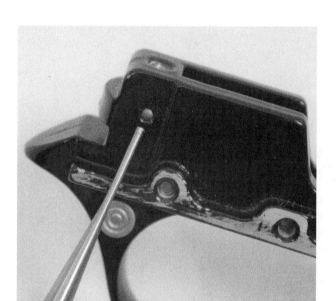

24. This disc has no flanges but can be removed by prying it from the magazine tube. The magazine spring and follower can then be removed. However, this will damage the disc and repeated removals will require the disc to be replaced.

Reassembly Tips:

1. Ensure that the trigger return spring is seated in its hole seat on the floor of the trigger housing. This is facilitated by placing a small amount of grease in the trigger's spring hole to hold the spring in place, then inserting the trigger back into the housing. Then use a small punch or probe to nudge the spring into the housing's spring seat.

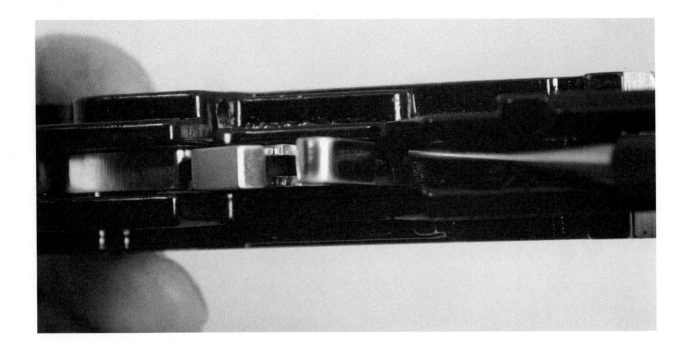

CZ Canvasback

Similar/Identical Pattern Guns:

The following basic assembly/disassembly steps for the CZ Canvasback can also be used for the following guns:

CZ Redhead

CZ Mallard

Data:	CZ Canvasback 103D
Origin:	Turkey
Manufacturer:	CZ
Gauges:	12, 20
Overall Length:	43 inches
Height:	7.5 inches
Barrel Length:	28 inches
Weight:	7.3 pounds

The Canvasback is the basic model of over/under shotguns offered by CZ. Its brothers in the over/under line are all somewhat similar, certainly the Mallard and Redhead types. The Mallard has double triggers and the Redhead auto-ejectors, but these items should pose no issue as the rest of the guns are very closely alike.

Disassembly:

1. Lift the forend latch and lift the forend off of the barrels.

2. Open the action and rotate the barrels off the receiver.

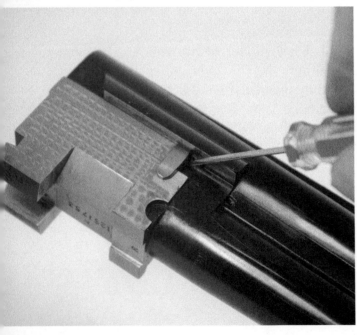

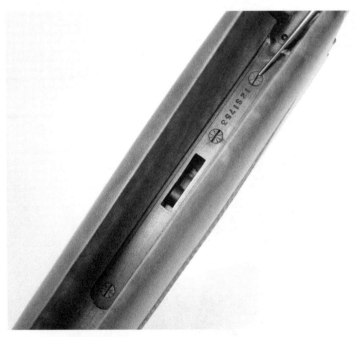

3. To remove the extractor, insert a small screwdriver beneath the front of the right side extractor arm. Gently lift the right side up and push the extractor back off the rear of the monoblock.

4. Remove the three screws holding the forend metal to the forend and lift the forend metal out of the forend piece. The latch assembly will separate from the larger metal piece.

5. This pin holds the latch into its body piece. The long flat spring is held beneath the latch and slides into a slot on the body.

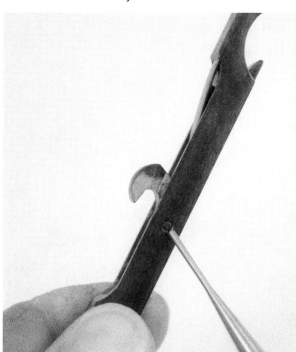

6. Remove the screw at the rear of the trigger guard.

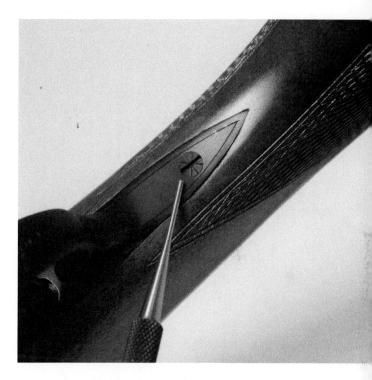

7. Remove the buttpad by taking out these two screws.

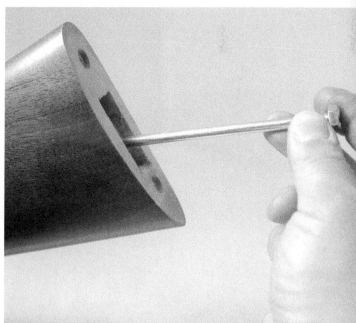

8. The buttstock is held by a large bolt. Remove it. Then pull off the buttstock.

9. Unscrew the trigger guard and remove it from the receiver.

11. Pull back on the hammer spring guide rods to clear the hammers and remove the guide rods and springs to the sides.

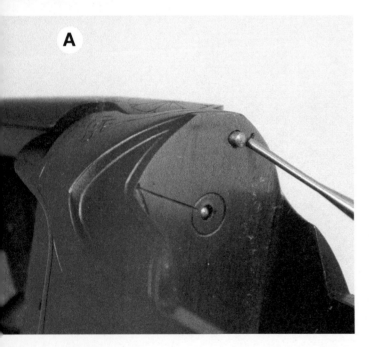

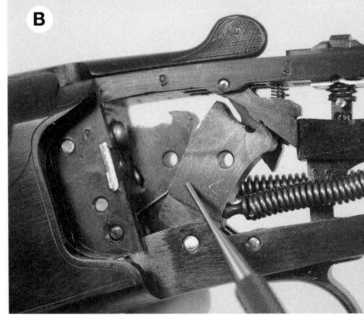

10. Close the top lever by depressing the small pin at the top front of the receiver (Picture A). Then drop the hammers to relieve most of the tension on the hammer springs (Picture B).

12. Drive out the sear pin to free the sears and the sear springs.

13. Drive out the hammer pin to free the hammers.

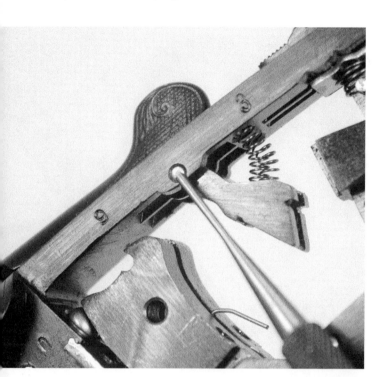

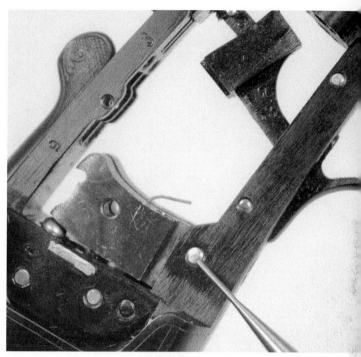

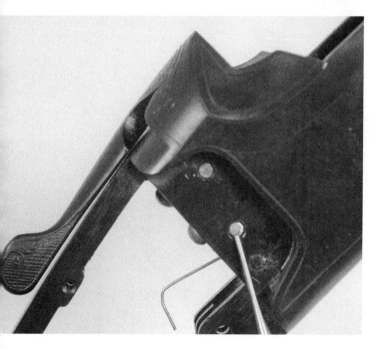

14. Drive out these two pins to free the firing pins and firing pin springs.

15. Remove the screw just to the rear of the safety Then remove the similar screw behind the trigger to remove the hammer spring seat. The hammer spring seat can be removed to the left or right.

16. Remove the pin behind the trigger and the rear trigger return spring.

17. Drive out the trigger pivot pin to remove the front trigger return spring and release the trigger assembly. The trigger assembly can be lifted up and then out to the side of the receiver.

 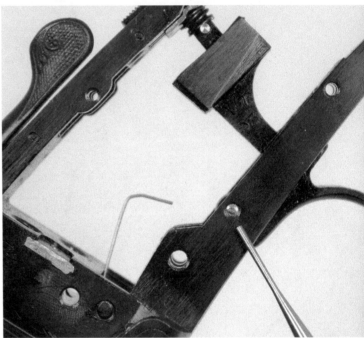

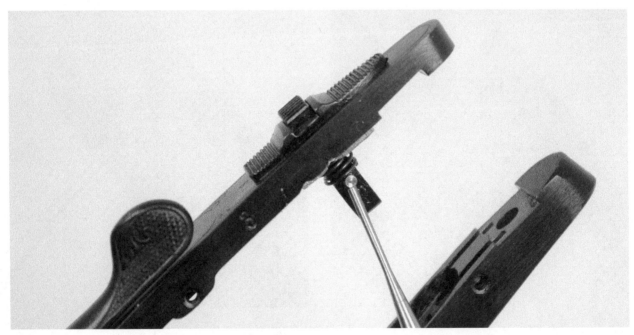

18. Drive out the safety retaining pin. This will free the spring and detent plate above it. The safety button and selector can then be removed out of the top of the receiver. The small detent in the safety button is staked in place.

19. Drive out the roller pin to free the roller and its spring (Picture A). This will also release the bottom tang to be pulled from the bottom of the receiver (Picture B).

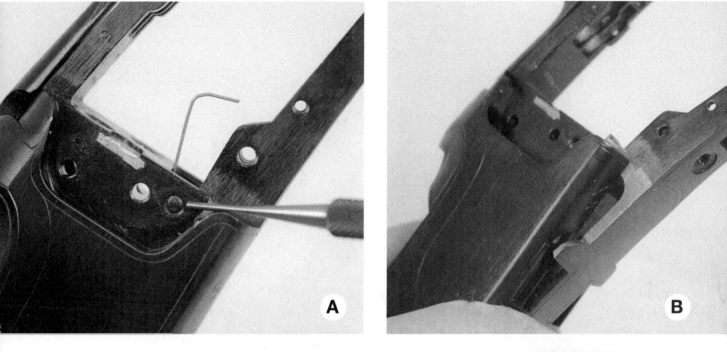

20. Pull the cocking arm from the receiver to the rear.

21. Drive out the top lever spring retainer to the left to expose and then remove the spring and detent.

22. Depress the top lever safety pin while simultaneously lifting the top lever out of the receiver. Contain the spring and detent in the front of the lever as it is removed. Then push the safety pin out to the rear.

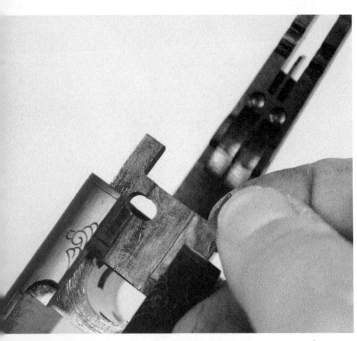

23. Remove the locking block to the rear.

24. The trigger and selector cannot be separated without damaging the components.

Reassembly Tips:

1. The screw holes in the hammer spring plate are off center to the front of the plate. Ensure the thin wall of the plate is forward.

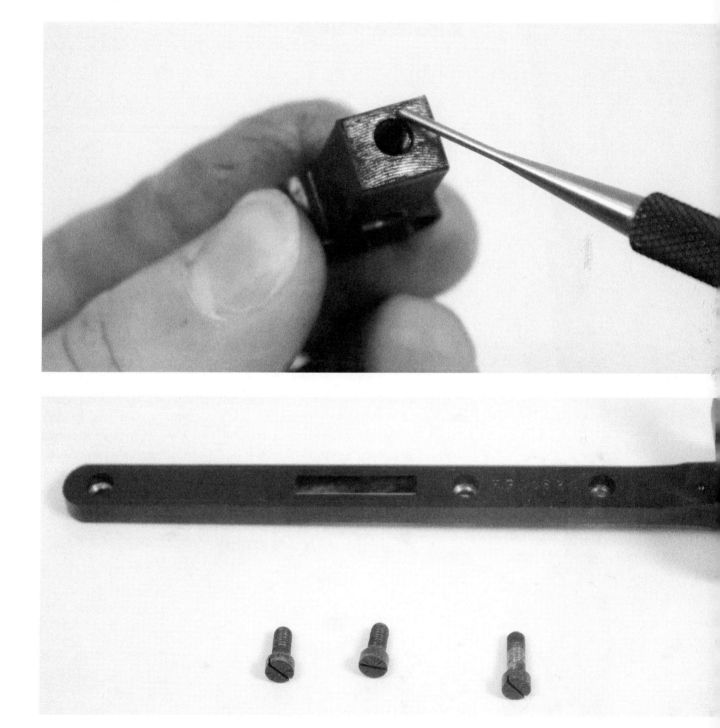

2. The forend screws are of different sizes. See them here in relation to the forend metal.

EAA Baikal IZH-18

Data:	EAA Baikal IZH-18
Origin:	Russia
Manufacturer:	Izhevsky Mechanichesky Zavod, Izhevsk, Russia
Gauges:	12, 16, 20, and .410
Overall length:	44-1/2 inches
Barrel length:	28-1/2 inches (others offered)
Weight:	6.4to 6.6 pounds

European American Armory began importing this fine little single-shot in 1998. Modestly priced, it has excellent workmanship and some outstanding features. Two of these are a selective ejector and a decocking system. Two versions are offered - a plain gun, and the one shown here, with a ventilated rib and a plated receiver.

Disassembly:

1. Open and close the action to cock the internal hammer. Put the manual safety in on-safe position. Pull the forend latch lever outward, and tip the forend away from the barrel for removal. Operate the barrel latch, and separate the barrel unit from the receiver.

2. The two rear Phillips screws in the forend retain the forend iron, and it is taken out rearward. Note that the rear screw has a separate escutcheon.

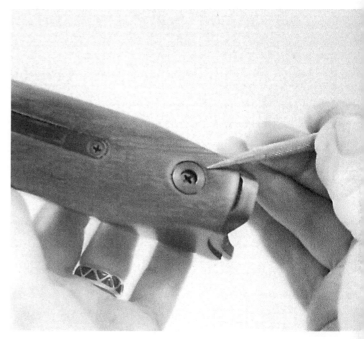

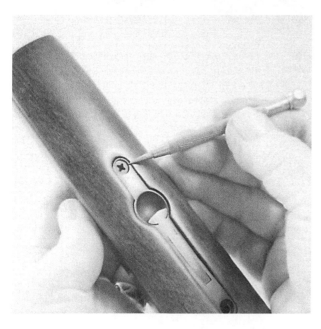

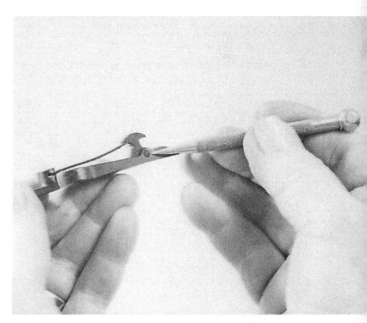

3. Taking out the front screw will allow removal of the forend latch. Note that this screw is threaded into an oblong washer on the inside. The three forend screws are not identical so keep them separate for reassembly.

4. The forend latch is retained by a cross pin. The blade-type spring is staked in place, and should be removed only for repair.

5. The ejector sear is pivoted and retained by a cross pin. Caution: The plunger and coil spring will be released, so control them.

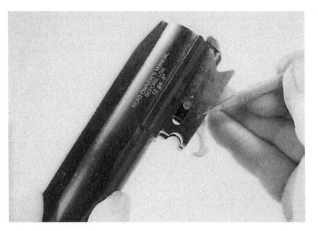

7. Insert a finger or tool to depress the cocking lever detent, and allow the lever to move downward.

9. Take out the two slotted screws at the rear, and remove the recoil pad. The stock mounting bolt is a slotted screw, and it is only about two inches inside, so a regular large screwdriver can be used. Remove the buttstock toward the rear.

6. The ejector should be removed only if necessary for repair. Drifting out the small retaining pin and the larger cocking pin will allow the ejector to be taken out toward the rear. Caution: Control the spring.

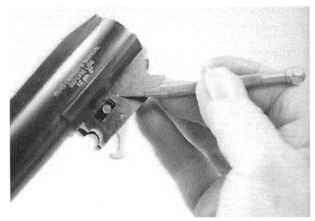

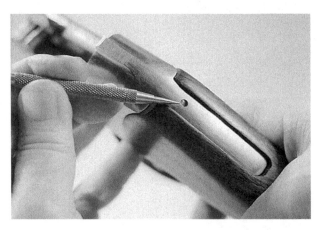

8. Move the safety to off-safe position. Depress the cocking lever just far enough that resistance is felt, pull the trigger and slowly release the cocking lever. This operation will uncock the hammer, and the indicator will retract into the upper tang, as shown.

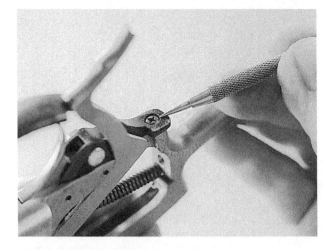

10. Remove the small Phillips screw at the rear of the trigger guard.

11. Turn the trigger guard out toward the left, and remove it downward.

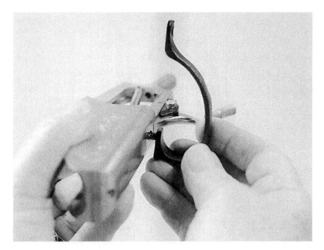

12. Depress the cocking lever to re-cock the hammer, and insert a small tool through the cross-hole in the hammer spring guide. Pull the trigger and ease the hammer down to fired position.

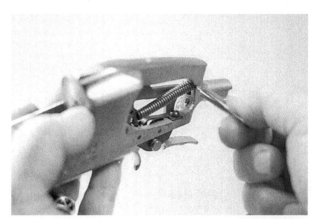

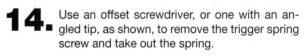

13. Be sure the hammer is all the way forward. Lift the front of the hammer spring and guide assembly, then tilt the front outward for removal. If necessary for repair, you can use locking pliers and a slightly-opened vise to remove the tool and release the spring. If this is done - Caution! The spring is fully compressed.

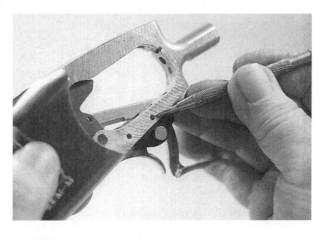

14. Use an offset screwdriver, or one with an angled tip, as shown, to remove the trigger spring screw and take out the spring.

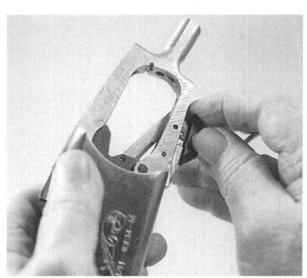

15. Drift out the safety housing cross pin.

16. Remove the safety housing downward.

17. If necessary for repair, insert a small tool on the right side just above the cross piece to depress the safety detent plunger. The cross piece can then be removed. Caution: Control the plunger and spring.

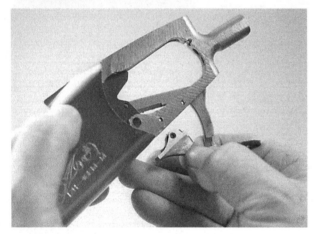

18. Drift out the trigger cross pin.

19. Remove the trigger downward.

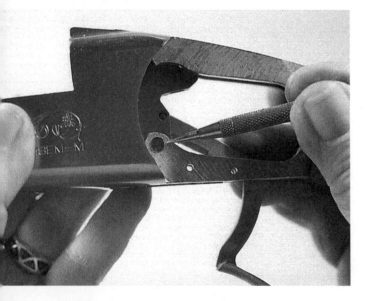

20. The sear is also pivoted and retained by the trigger cross pin, and it can now be lifted out of its recess in the top of the trigger. Note its orientation for reassembly.

21. Drift out the hammer cross pin.

22. Invert the receiver to take out the hammer, as the indicator and its spring will be freed as the hammer is removed. Move the hammer rearward, turn it to the position shown, and take it out to the side.

23. Remove the cocking indicator and its spring.

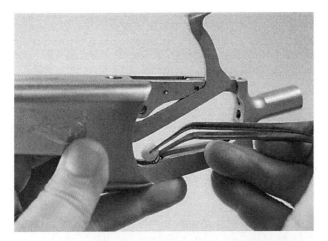

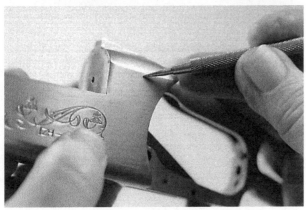

25. If firing pin replacement is necessary for repair, the firing pin and its coil return spring are retained by this cross pin, and they are taken out rearward. This pin is finished-over, and the finish will be marred.

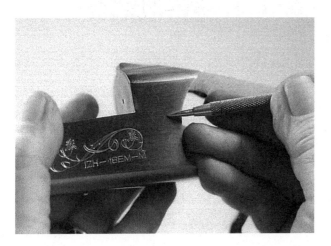

27. This finished-over cross pin pivots and retains the cocking lever, and the lever is taken out toward the rear. In normal takedown, this system is left in place.

24. Removal of the Phillips screw at the front of the receiver will allow the bottom plate to be taken out. This will give access to the cross pin that retains the barrel latch detent and its coil spring. However, the plate is tightly fitted and finished-over, and some marring will be inevitable. The plate should be removed only for repair.

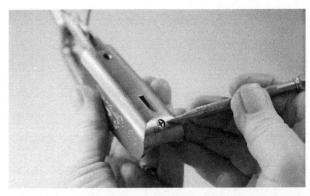

26. If the combination cocking and barrel latch lever has to be removed for repair, this finished-over cross pin retains the coil spring that powers the lever. Again, the finish will be marred. Control the spring.

Reassembly Tips:

1. When installing the cocking indicator and its spring, remember that it goes into its recess in the upper tang at a slight rearward angle.

2. When installing the sear and trigger, insert a tool from the opposite side to align the sear as the cross pin is drifted back in. Or, a slave pin can be used.

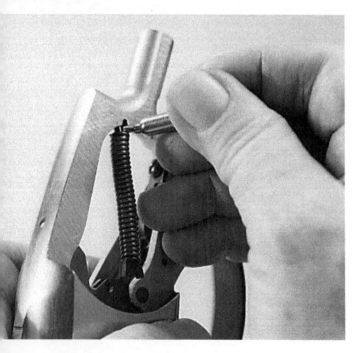

3. Insert the rear tip of the hammer spring guide first, then swing the front into position to engage the hammer.

EAA Baikal IZH-27

Data:	EAA Baikal IZH-27
Origin:	Russia
Manufacturer:	Izhevsky Mechanichesky Zavod, Izhevsk, Russia
Gauges:	12, 16, 20, 28, and .410
Overall length:	45 inches
Barrel length:	28 (others offered)
Weight:	7.7 pounds

This nicely-made over/under was introduced by European American Armory in 1999. Its good balance and relatively low price have made it quite popular. As with most over/under guns, it is somewhat more complicated than other types of shotguns. The amateur should approach total takedown with caution.

Disassembly:

1. Open and close the action to cock the internal hammers. Pull the forend latch lever outward, and tip the forend downward for removal. Operate the barrel latch, tip the barrel unit downward, and remove it upward.

2. The ejector sears are pivoted and retained by small screws. As the screws are removed, the coil sear springs will be released, so control them.

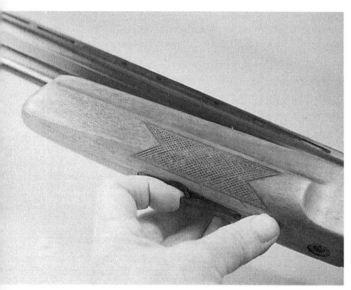

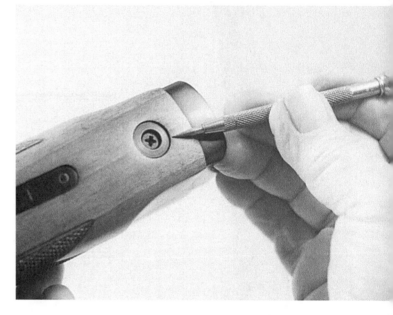

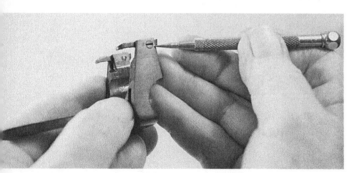

3. The forend iron is retained by two screws, on the inside and outside. The outside screw has an escutcheon, which may come off with the screw. Remove both screws, and take out the forend iron toward the rear.

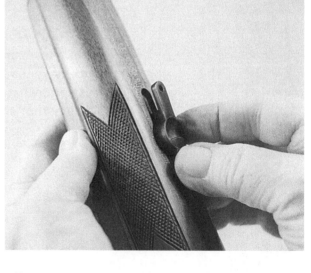

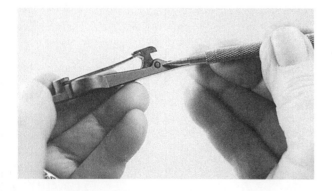

4. Remove the forward inside screw, and push the forend latch assembly outward for removal. Note that this screw has a small washer, and take care that it is not lost. The three forend screws are not identical, so keep them separate for reassembly.

5. Drifting out this cross pin will free the forend latch lever. The blade-type spring is staked in place in its slot, and is removed only for repair.

6. Restrain the ejector at the rear- (Caution: The spring is very strong.) and lift the front of the ejector very slightly, just enough to free it for rearward movement.

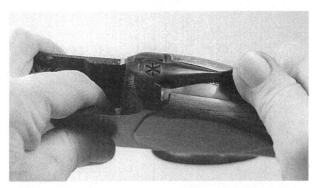

8. Restrain the barrel latch lever, and use a tool or fingertip inside the receiver to trip the latch detent. Allow the lever to move back to center.

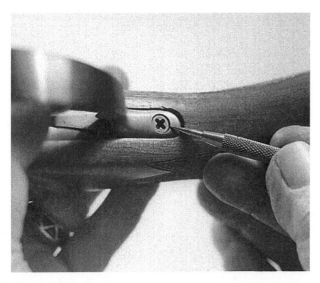

7. When the ejector has moved far enough to the rear to clear its dovetailed portion, it can be lifted off. The plunger and coil spring can then be removed. Repeat this operation for the other ejector.

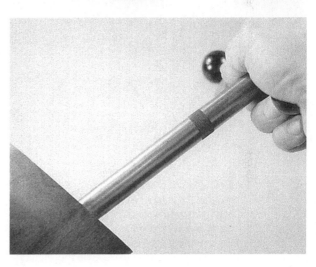

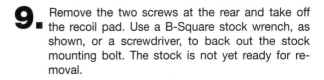

9. Remove the two screws at the rear and take off the recoil pad. Use a B-Square stock wrench, as shown, or a screwdriver, to back out the stock mounting bolt. The stock is not yet ready for removal.

10. Remove the small Phillips wood screw at the rear of the trigger guard, and take off the buttstock toward the rear.

11. Unscrew the trigger guard (counter-clockwise, bottom view) and remove it.

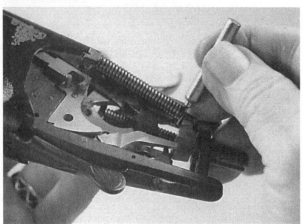

12. Insert a slim tool (or a piece of wire) through the cross-hole in the hammer spring guide at the rear. Do this on the right side first, as the right one is the first to fire. Move the safety to off-safe position, and pull the trigger to drop the hammer to fired position. If it doesn't go all the way forward, push it there.

13. Tilt the guide and the trapped spring outward at the front, and remove it. It is possible, using locking pliers and a slightly-opened vise, to take off the spring. If you do this - Caution: The spring is fully compressed. Repeat these two steps to remove the other spring. To release the left hammer, it may be necessary to manually move the sear upward.

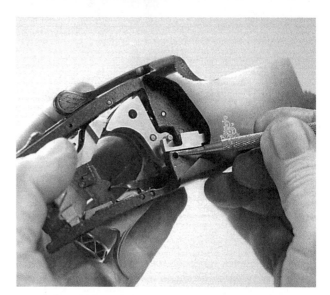

14. Drift the hammer pivot pin toward the left until it clears the right hammer.

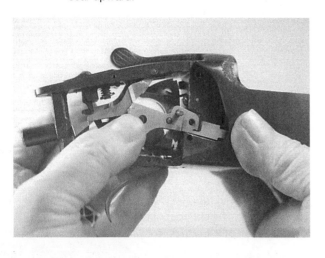

15. Tip the hammer back, and lift it at the front to clear its side pin from the recess in the cooking rod, freeing it for removal.

16. The cocking rod can now be taken out toward the rear. After drifting the hammer pivot the rest of the way out, repeat these steps to remove the left hammer and cocking rod. Keep the parts for each side separate for reassembly.

17. The upper and lower firing pins are now accessible for removal. The retaining cross pins are drifted out, and the firing pins and their coil return springs are taken out toward the rear. Control the parts during removal, as the springs are partially compressed and these small parts are easily lost. If removal is not necessary for repair, leave them in place. If the firing pins are removed, note that they are not interchangeable.

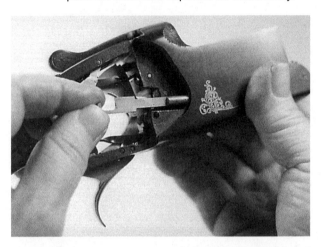

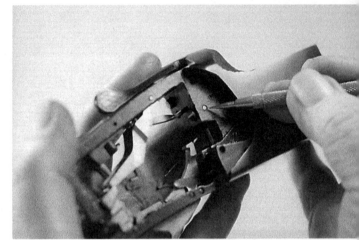

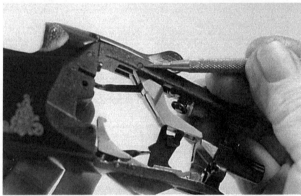

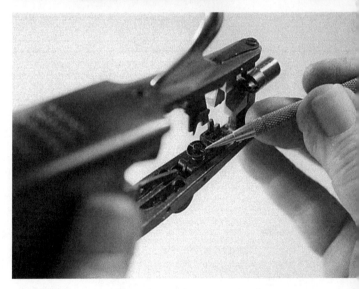

18. The sears are retained in the top of the receiver by a cross pin. Drift the pin across in intervals, to release one at a time. Control the spring during removal.

19. The manual safety system should be removed only for repair. To take it out, you must depress the flanged washer on the button shaft, and push out the small cross pin. The button must be held against a firm surface during this operation. Caution: The detent spring will be fully compressed, so control the washer.

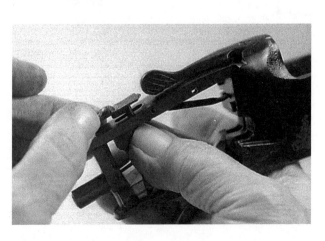

20. Remove the safety button upward.

21. The internal safety block is retained at the front by a cross pin that passes through the semicircular detent lever. The detent lever pivots on a riveted cross pin in the block, and it is not routinely removed. The same applies to the sear contact levers at the rear, and their small coil springs. Remove only for repair.

22. The automatic safety-set bar can now be taken out rearward.

23. Drift out the cross pin that pivots and retains the hammer interceptor. Caution: Control the spring, as the interceptor is removed.

24. Drift the trigger cross pin toward the left, just far enough to clear the action-open cam bar.

25. Remove the cam bar (disconnector).

26. Drift the trigger pin out, move the trigger forward, and remove it downward.

27. If necessary for repair, the small cross pin in the trigger can be drifted out to free the trigger lever assembly. If this is done, control the small vertical coil spring at the rear. The stop lever at the top and its coil spring are retained by a riveted pin, and it is not routinely removed.

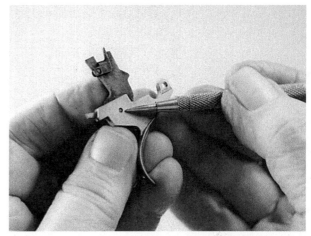

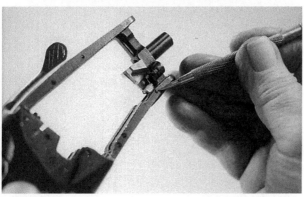

28. The inertia block at the rear of the receiver is pivoted and retained by a cross pin. Caution: A small torsion type wire spring at its center will be released, so control it. Remove this system only for repair.

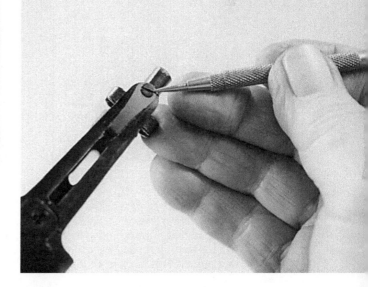

29. The trigger rebound spring is retained at the rear by a small screw. Remove it only for repair.

30. Use a properly fitted screwdriver to avoid marring, and remove the large screw on the underside of the receiver.

31. Use a non-marring tool on the inside front edge of the bottom plate to tip it outward for removal.

32. The barrel latch detent and its coil spring are retained in the bottom plate by a cross pin. Control the spring during removal.

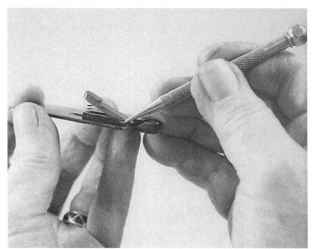

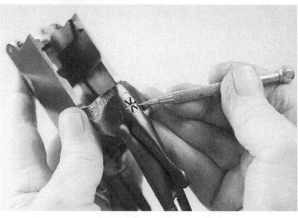

33. The barrel latch system should be disassembled only for repair purposes. The large screw that retains the top lever is contoured and finished-over, and removal would inevitably mar the finish. If absolutely necessary, the screw is removed and the lever is taken off upward.

34. After removal of the top lever, the vertical shaft is drifted out downward. Caution: Control the very powerful locking block spring. Also note that in several over/under designs, the shaft is relieved for passage of the firing pins, so it would be wise to remove them before this operation. After the shaft is drifted out, the locking block can be taken out toward the rear. Again, in normal takedown, this entire system is best left in place.

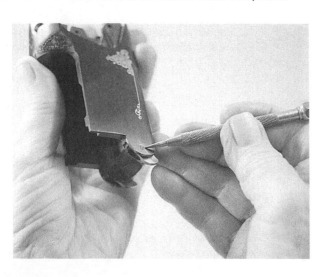

35. The cocking rod levers are pivoted and retained at the front of the receiver by pins that are semi-riveted in place. If they have to be removed, the pins are drifted outward. The sear-trip plungers for the ejectors are retained by the main barrel pivot pin, which is pinned at its center and finished-over on each side. This system is not routinely removable.

Reassembly Tips:

1. The safety system retainer is shown here outside the gun and without the spring, for illustration purposes. Note that the flanged rim of the washer retains the small cross pin.

2. When installing the hammer spring units, be sure the concave tip of the upper arm of the guide is aligned with the cross pin in the hammer. To cock the hammer, insert a drift in the hole near the top and lever it rearward. Leave the hammers cocked, for reassembly of the barrel unit and the forend

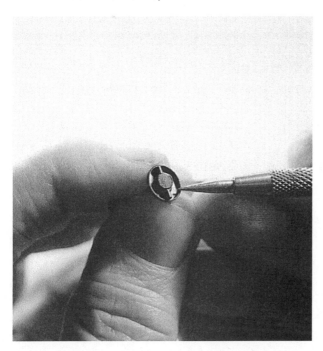

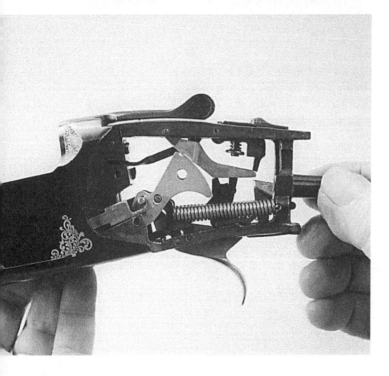

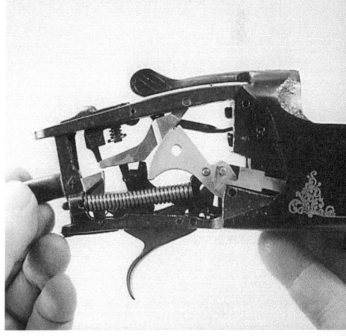

3. As a reassembly aid, here are views of both sides of the receiver, with all parts in their proper places.

Franchi Model 48AL

Similar/Identical Pattern Guns:

The same basic assembly/disassembly steps for the Franchi Model 48AL also apply to the following guns:

Colt Standard Auto	**Colt Custom Auto**
Franchi Dynamic	**Franchi Dynamic 12 Skeet**
Franchi Dynamic 12 Slug	**Franchi Eldorado**
Franchi Hunter	

Data:	Franchi Model 48AL
Origin:	Italy
Manufacturer:	Luigi Franchi, S.p.A. Brescia
Gauges:	12, 20
Magazine Capacity:	5 rounds
Overall length:	43 inches (with 24-inch barrel)
Barrel length:	24, 26, 28 & 30 inches
Weight:	5.2 to 7-1/2 pounds

The original Franchi autoloader has been imported into the U.S. since around 1950. It has been called the Model 48AL, and also simply the Standard Model. Very early guns will have a few small mechanical differences, but nothing that would cause difficulty in takedown. These instructions, however, do not apply to the current gas-operated Franchi guns.
Superposed.

Disassembly:

1. Lock the action open, and set the safety in on-safe position. Push the barrel slightly rearward, and unscrew and remove the magazine end cap.

2. Ease the barrel and forend forward. Remove the forend toward the front.

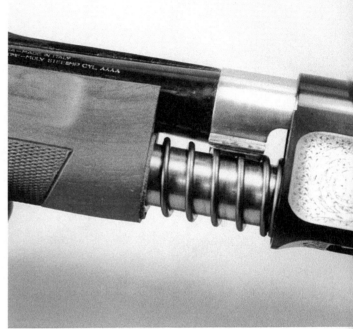

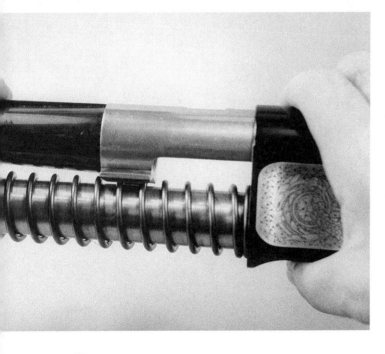

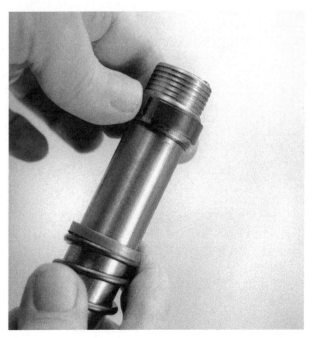

3. Remove the barrel toward the front.

4. Remove the friction piece from the magazine tube.

5. Remove the compression ring and the recoil spring.

6. If the magazine spring and follower need to be removed, gently pry out the circular keeper at the end of the magazine tube. **Caution: Control the spring and ease it out.**

7. Restrain the bolt, depress the carrier latch button, and ease the bolt to forward position. Push out the two trigger group retaining pins.

8. Remove the trigger group downward.

9. Insert a tool to depress the bolt spring plunger rearward, and swing the bolt spring strut outward.

10. Move the bolt handle to the rear, freeing it from the bolt.

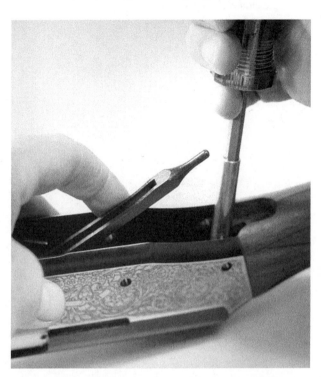

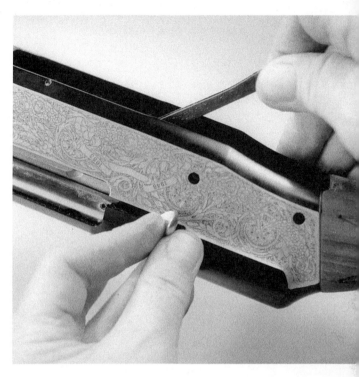

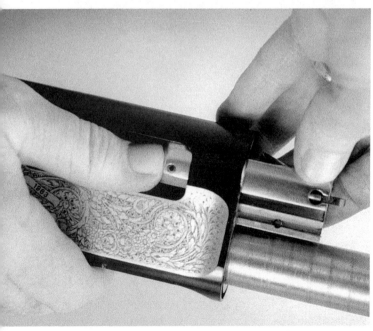

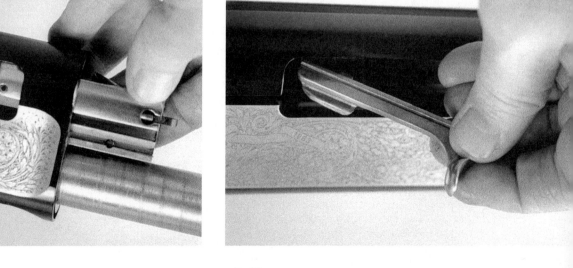

11. Remove the bolt assembly toward the front.

12. Remove the bolt handle through the ejection port.

13. Remove the buttplate screws and take off the buttplate. Use a large screwdriver to take out the stock mounting bolt. Beneath the bolt head are a lock washer and a bearing plate. Remove the buttstock toward the rear.

14. The bolt spring and its plunger can be removed by unscrewing this threaded plug at the rear of the spring housing. Caution: Control the powerful spring, and ease it out.

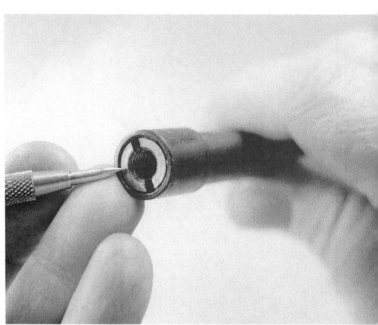

15. The carrier latch and its button and spring are pivoted and retained by a vertical pin in the left side of the receiver. The pin is retained by a tiny spring clip in a slot, just inside the lower edge of the receiver. Removal of the clip will require a small L-shaped tool like the one shown, and the clip is taken out rearward. The pin is then pushed out upward to free the parts. Unless repair is necessary, this system is best left in place.

16. On the right side of the receiver, the shell stop and its spring have much the same arrangement, and the same instructions and advice apply.

17. The firing pin and its return spring are retained by a roll-type cross pin at the rear of the bolt.

18. Note that the firing pin return spring is very short and quite small. Take care that it is not lost.

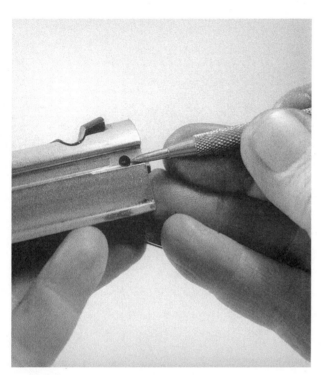

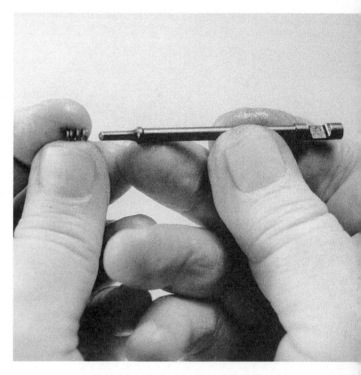

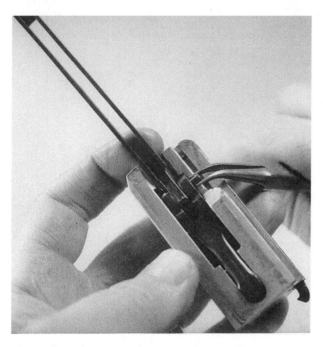

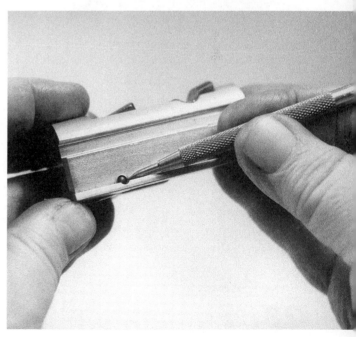

19. The pivot of the bolt spring strut can be moved out by tapping the bolt with a nylon hammer. It is then removed, and the strut is taken off rearward.

20. The locking block lever is retained by a cross pin that is drifted out toward the right. As the pin is removed, control the strong lever spring, and ease it out.

21. Remove the locking block lever and its spring.

22. Turn the locking block upward until its guide rib on the right side clears its track, and remove it.

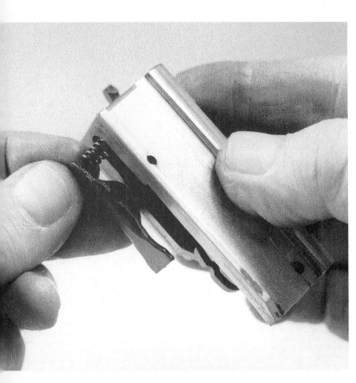

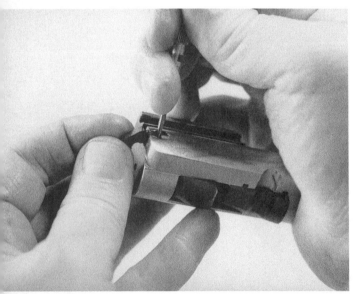

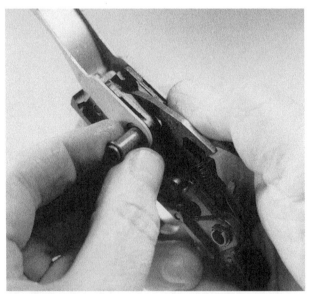

23. Insert a tool between the extractor and its plunger. Push the plunger toward the rear, and tip the extractor out toward the front. Caution: Control the plunger and spring.

24. Restrain the carrier plunger and spring on the right side, and push out and remove the front cross pin sleeve, which is also the carrier pivot. Note that on very early Franchi guns, the carrier spring system is almost exactly the same as the one used on the SKB autoloader, covered elsewhere in this book.

25. Release the spring tension slowly, and remove the carrier upward. The carrier dog pivot is a riveted part, and it is not routinely removed.

26. Remove the carrier plunger and spring.

27. Move the safety to the off-safe position, and depress the auto safety lever forward. Restrain the hammer, pull the trigger, and ease the hammer down to the forward position. Push out the small upper pin at the rear of the trigger group.

28. Restrain the lower arms of the auto safety spring, and the manual safety spring, and push out the small lower cross pin at the rear of the trigger group.

29. Remove the safety plunger and spring toward the rear.

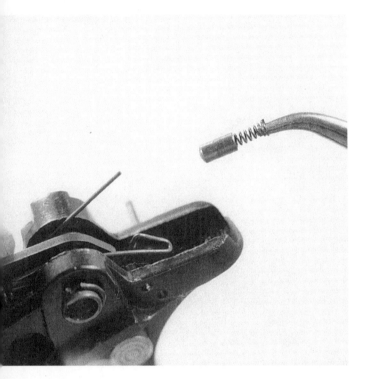

30. Remove the safety button toward either side.

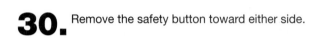
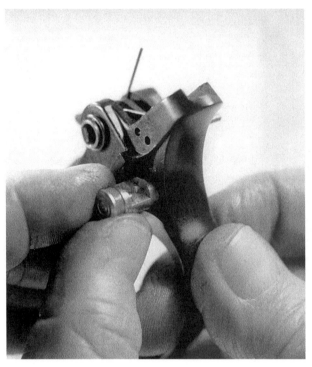

31. Remove the rear cross pin sleeve that is also the pivot for the auto safety and its spring.

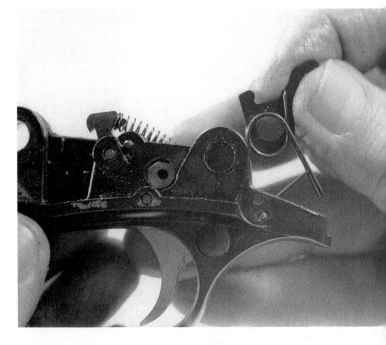

32. Remove the auto safety and its spring upward and toward the rear.

33. Unhook the combination sear and trigger lever spring from its post on the sear, and remove it.

34. Push out the sear pin toward the left, and take out the sear upward.

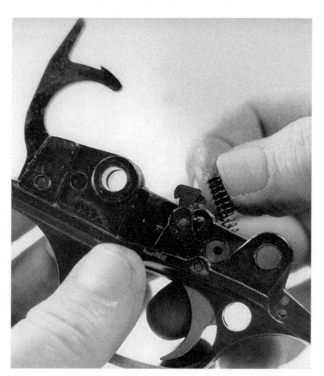

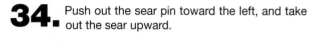

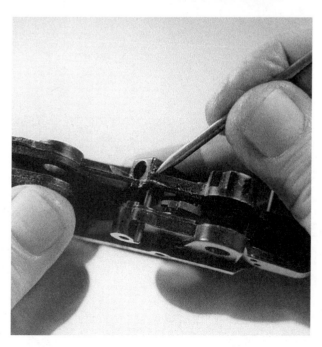

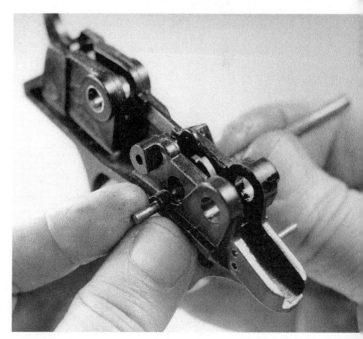

35. Nudge the sear limit pin leftward until it can be grasped with pliers and taken out.

36. Push out the trigger pin toward the left.

37. The trigger can now be moved upward to the point shown, giving access to the lever cross pin. The cross pin can be pushed out toward the right, and the lever is taken off upward. The trigger can be removed only if the adjustment screw is taken out. This screw is set and sealed at the factory, and it should not be disturbed unless necessary for repair.

38. Restrain the hammer against the tension of its spring, and drift out the hammer pivot toward the left. Ease the hammer, plunger, and spring out upward.

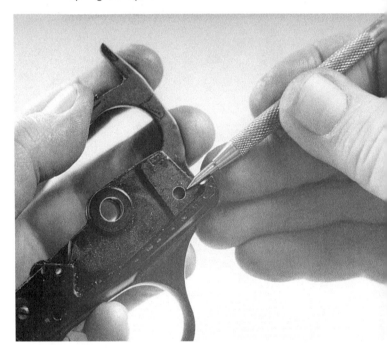

Reassembly Tips:

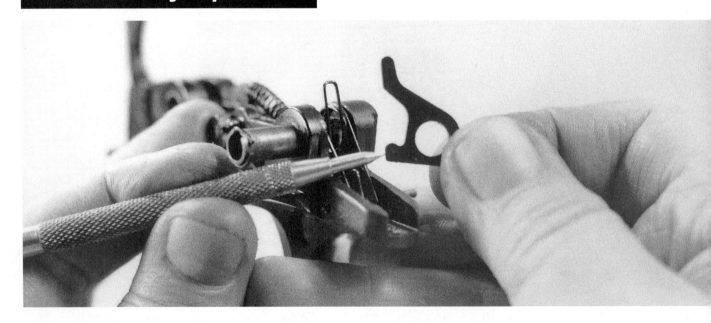

1. When the auto safety is reinstalled, be sure its lower front projection goes beneath the rear lower edge of the trigger lever.

2. When replacing the pins at the rear of the trigger group, use slim pliers to position the left arm of the auto safety spring. Its lower loop will hold the manual safety spring in place. Put the upper cross pin in first, from the left, moving the right arm of the spring behind the pin as it is pushed across. Depress the spring arms again as the lower pin is installed.

3. When reattaching the bolt spring strut to the locking block, be sure it is installed in the orientation shown.

When replacing the trigger group, it is necessary to slightly retract the bolt to insure that the auto safety is properly engaged.

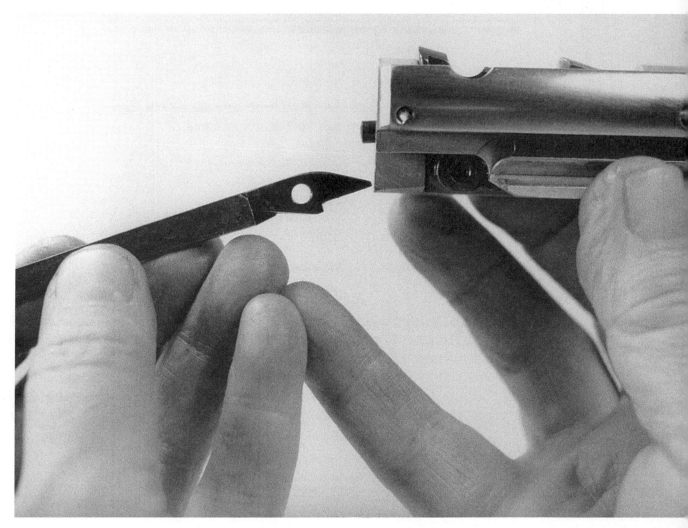

Harrington & Richardson Topper

Similar/Identical Pattern Guns:

The same basic assembly/disassembly steps for the Harrington & Richardson Topper also apply to the following guns:

H & R Model 48	H & R Model 088
H & R Model 058	H & R Model 099
H & R Model 098	H & R Model 162
H & R Model 158	H & R Model 188
H & R Model 176	H & R Model 258
H & R Model 198	H & R Model 590
H & R Model 490	H & R Model 490 Greenwing
NEF "Mini-Pardner"	NEF "Handi-Gun"
NEF "Pardner"	

Data: Harrington & Richardson Topper
Origin: United States
Manufacturer: Harrington & Richardson
Gardner, Massachusetts
Gauges: 12, 16, 20, and 410
Overall length: 43 inches (with 28-inch barrel)
Barrel length: 26 to 36 inches
Weight: 5 to 6-1/2 pounds

The Model 158 used here is one of a long line of H&R single-barrel guns, named in 1946 the "Topper." Introduced in 1962, the Model 158 designation was changed to Model 58 from 1975 through 1979, and was later called the Model 058. Several sub-models have also been offered, including youth models with shorter stocks and barrels. The mechanical changes have been so slight over this period that the instructions will generally apply. They will also apply generally to the later guns by New England Firearms, and their successor, H&R 1871, Inc.

Disassembly:

1. Remove the large screw on the underside of the forend, and take off the forend downward and toward the front.

2. Removal of the two screws at the rear of the forend will allow the forend spacer to be taken off.

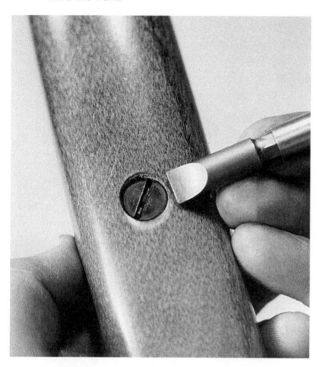

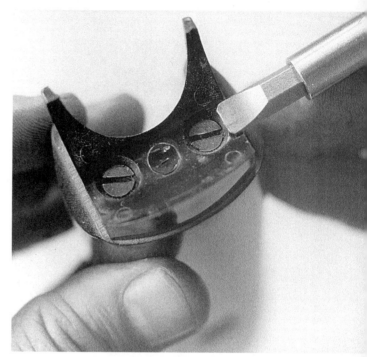

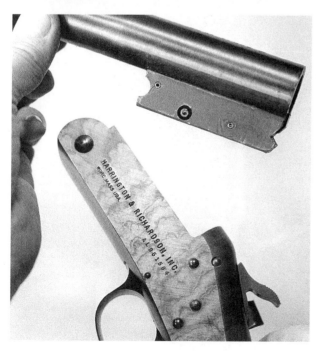

3. Operate the barrel latch, tip the barrel unit down beyond its normal open position, and remove the barrel upward.

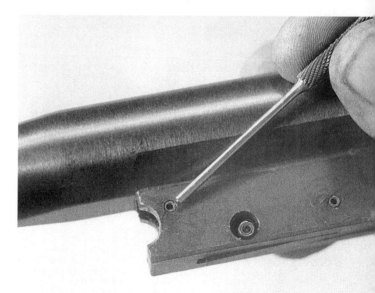

4. Insert a screwdriver above the large roll pin in the oversized hole in the barrel underlug, and lever the pin downward, releasing the ejector to snap to the open position. Drift out the small cross pin at the upper front of the underlug, and take out the ejector spring toward the front. The spring will have some tension, so control it and ease it out.

5. Drift out the small cross pin near the lower edge of the underlug, and the large cross pin in the over-sized hole, and remove the ejector catch and its coil spring downward. Remove the ejector toward the rear.

6. Remove the buttplate, and use a long-shanked screwdriver or a socket wrench of suitable size to back out the stock bolt. Remove the bolt, washer, and stock toward the rear.

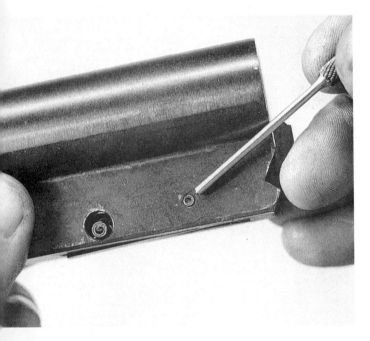

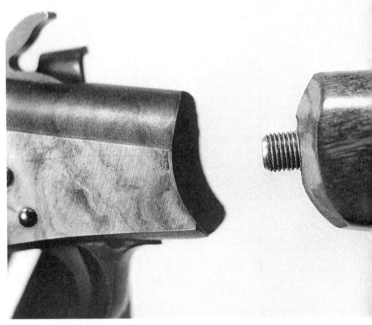

7. Drift out the small cross pin at the front of the trigger guard. If the pins are as originally installed, they should all be drifted out toward the left, as one end is slightly enlarged and ridged for tight seating. There is always the possibility that someone has reversed the pins, so check before driving them out.

8. Drift out the trigger cross pin toward the left.

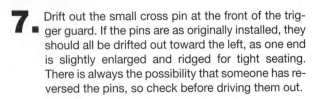

9. Remove the trigger assembly downward.

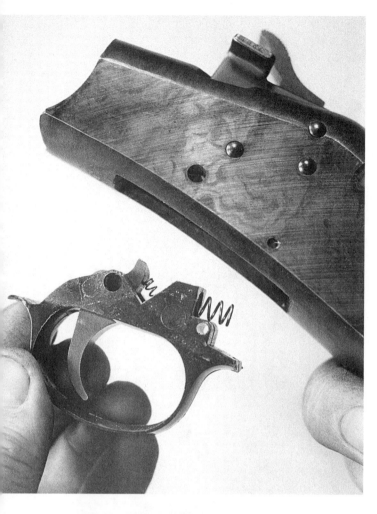

10. The trigger, trigger spring, and barrel latch spring are easily removed from the guard unit.

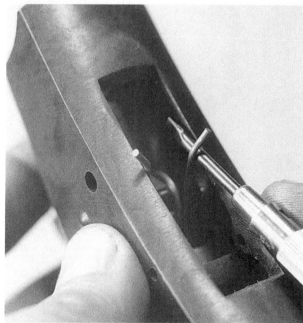

11. Insert a screwdriver into the bottom of the receiver, and nudge the tails of the hammer spring from the inside edges of the receiver, allowing them to rotate downward.

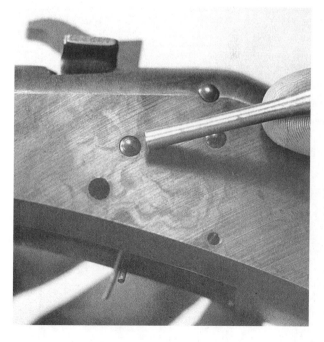

12. Drift out the hammer cross pin toward the left.

13. Remove the hammer spring downward.

14. Remove the hammer downward.

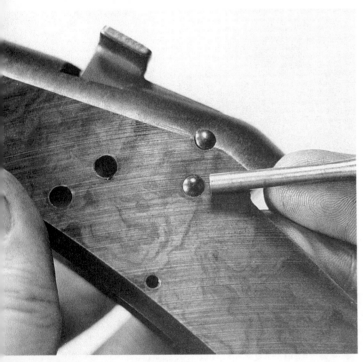

15. Drift out the barrel latch cross pin toward the left.

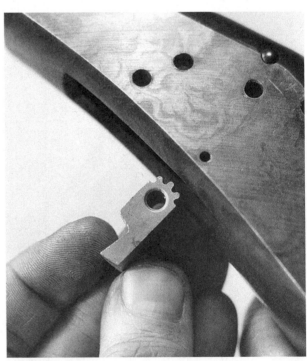

16. Remove the barrel latch block downward.

17. Drift out the upper cross pin toward the left.

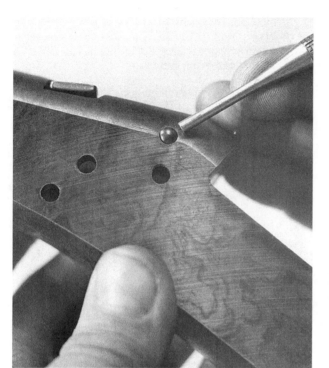

18. Remove the barrel latch lever upward.

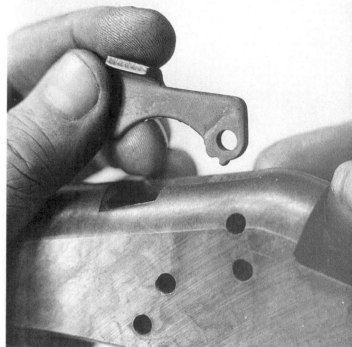

19. Remove the firing pin and its return spring toward the rear.

Reassembly Tips:

1. When replacing the barrel latch block, be sure the ratchet teeth on its upper edge engage the lobes on the lower edge of the latch lever, as shown, to give the latch block the proper arc. The latch lever and block are shown assembled outside the receiver, on their respective pins, for illustration purposes only.

2. When replacing the trigger assembly, use a slave pin to hold the trigger in place until the guard is back in the receiver and the original pin is driven into place. When installing the guard unit, insert the forward end first, being sure that the barrel latch spring engages the back of the latch block, then tip the rear of the unit into place.

High Standard Supermatic

Similar/Identical Pattern Guns:

The same basic assembly/disassembly steps for the High Standard Supermatic also apply to the following guns:

Sears Model 60   **Sears Model 66**

Western Auto 420   **Western Auto 425**

Data:	High Standard Supermatic Auto
Origin:	United States
Manufacturer:	High Standard Mfg. Corp. Hamden, Connecticut
Gauges:	12, and 20
Magazine capacity:	4 rounds
Overall length:	47-3/4 inches (with 28-inch barrel)
Barrel length:	22 to 30 inches
Weight:	7-1/2 (12 gauge)

Marketed under the name "Supermatic," this gun was made by the High Standard company from 1960 to 1976. In addition to their own brand, High Standard also made the gun on contract for large sales firms such as Sears, Roebuck & Company. One of the main design points was a gas control system that automatically adjusted to shells of different power. Early guns have slight differences in the mechanism, especially in the area of the operating handle and gas piston connector. Otherwise, the instructions will apply.

Disassembly:

1. Cycle the action to cock the internal hammer, returning the bolt to the forward position. Set the safety in the on-safe position. Push out the two cross pins at the lower rear of the receiver.

2. Remove the trigger assembly downward.

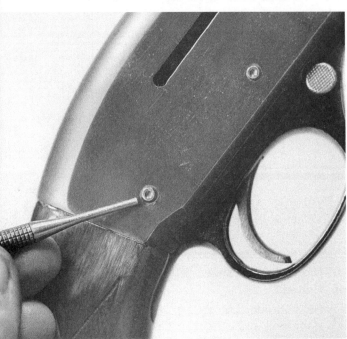

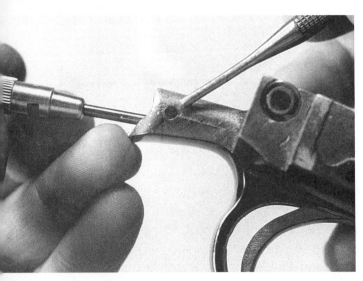

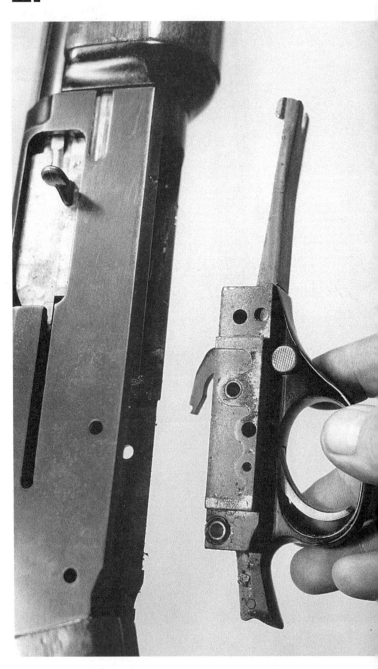

3. Move the safety to the off-safe position, restrain the hammer, and pull the trigger, easing the hammer down to the fired position. Push out the cross pin at the rear of the trigger housing, and remove the hammer spring and its plunger toward the rear. Caution: The spring is under tension, so control it. Removal of the pin can be made easier by inserting a screwdriver at the rear to slightly compress the spring.

4. The carrier pivot is also the front cross pin sleeve. Push the pivot slightly toward the left, just enough to allow the carrier actuator spring to be detached from the end of the pivot/sleeve.

5. With the pivot extended slightly toward the left, unhook the spring from its left tip, then remove the pivot sleeve from the housing. The spring is not removed at this time.

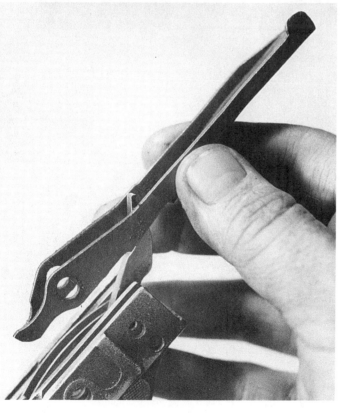

6. Remove the carrier upward and toward the front, and take out the carrier plunger and spring upward.

7. Turn the actuator spring to free its rear tip from the actuator stud, and remove the spring forward and toward the left.

8. Push out the hammer pivot toward the left.

9. Remove the hammer upward. As the hammer clears, the two hammer struts will detach from the cross pin in the hammer, and the cross pin is also easily removed.

10. Push out the carrier actuator pin toward the left.

11. Remove the carrier actuator upward.

12. Push out the trigger cross pin toward the left.

13. Remove the secondary sear from the top of the trigger.

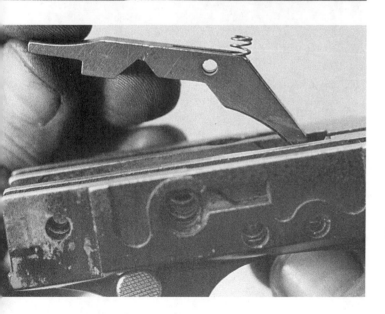

14. Remove the trigger from the top of the trigger housing. The sear spring is easily removed from the top of the trigger. Remove the trigger spring and plunger from the floor of the housing, upward.

15. Position the safety exactly half-way between its two normal stations in the housing, and give it one-quarter turn counter-clockwise (right side view), then push it out toward the left. Caution: As the safety clears the center, its plunger and spring will be released inside the housing, so control them and ease them out

16. Push out the rear cross pin sleeve toward the right.

17. Remove the large screw at the front of the forend cap, and take off the cap toward the front. Remove the forend toward the front.

18. Use a large screwdriver to unscrew the magazine end cap. Caution: The magazine spring is under tension. Control it and ease it out. Remove the magazine spring and follower toward the front.

19. Insert a large diameter drift punch through the holes in the end of the magazine tube, and unscrew the tube from the receiver, counter-clockwise (front view).

20. As soon as the tube clears its threads at the rear, pull it out toward the front, while holding onto the recoil spring. When the tube is out, the spring is easily detached and removed.

21. With the piston in the forward position, squeeze the connecting bars together slightly, and remove the forend base downward.

22. Move the bolt to the rear until the locking slide aligns with the exit cuts in the receiver, and lift the front of the slide, to free it from the locking block. Remove the slide from the bottom of the receiver. Pressing the bolt toward the rear will make this operation easier.

23. Move the operating handle forward to the ejection port and remove it.

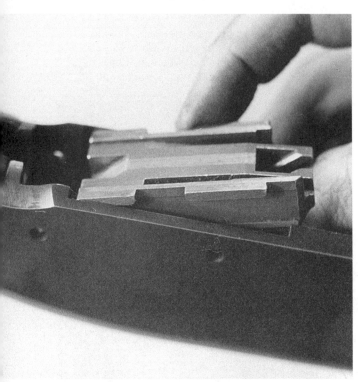

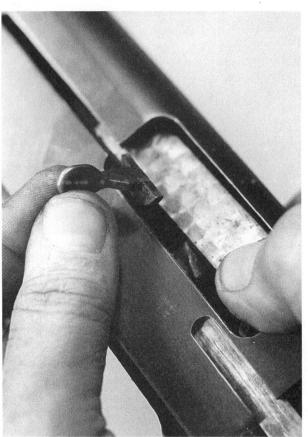

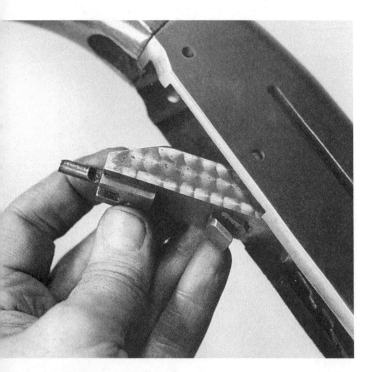

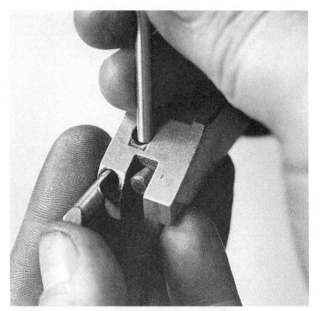

24. Move the bolt back toward the rear, and remove it.

25. A single large vertical pin in the bolt retains the ejector and its spring, and the firing pin and its return spring. Drift the retaining pin out downward, and remove the ejector, firing pin, and their springs toward the rear.

26. Removal of the firing pin will free the locking block to be taken out upward.

27. The extractor is retained by a vertical pin that must be driven out upward. Only a portion of the pin is accessible on the underside of the bolt, so a very small drift punch must be used to start it. The pin can then be removed at the top with smooth-jawed pliers, and the extractor and its coil spring can be taken off toward the right.

28. Tip the rear end of the gas piston outward, away from the barrel, and it will disengage from the connector bars for removal.

29. The connector bar unit can be sprung toward the side to clear the barrel loop, and is then pulled out toward the front. In normal disassembly, this unit is best left in place.

30. The shell stop and carrier latch are retained in the sides of the receiver by vertical pins, and the pins are held in place by spring clips set in narrow slots inside the lower edge of the receiver. Use a small tool to slide the spring clips off toward the rear, as shown.

31. Holes are provided at the top, inside, to allow the pins to be nudged downward for removal. The hole on the right side is accessible through the ejection port with a straight tool, but the one on the left will require a curved or L-shaped tool. When the pins are out, the shell stop, carrier latch, and their springs are taken out inward.

32. Remove the buttplate, and use a B-Square stock tool or a long-shanked screwdriver to back out the stock mounting bolt. Take off the bolt, its washers, and the buttstock toward the rear.

Reassembly Tips:

1. When replacing the trigger assembly, use a slave pin to hold the parts in place while inserting the cross pin.

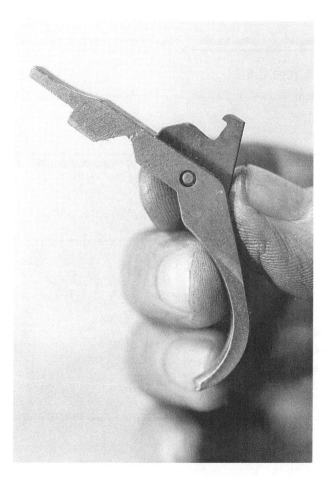

2. When properly installed, the carrier actuator spring will be as shown.

When replacing the bolt and bolt slide, remember that the operating handle must be put in before the slide is lowered into position. Be sure that all of these parts are properly aligned before installing the slide.

Ithaca Model 37

Similar/Identical Pattern Guns:

The same basic assembly/disassembly steps for the Ithaca Model 37 also apply to the following gun:

Ithaca Model 87

Data:	Ithaca Model 37
Origin:	United States
Manufacturer:	Ithaca Gun Company, Ithaca, New York
Gauges:	12, 16, and 20
Magazine Capacity:	4 rounds
Overall length:	45 inches (with 26-inch barrel)
Barrel length:	26 to 30 inches
Weight:	5-3/4 to 6-1/2 pounds

The model designation is the same as the year of its introduction, and this gun has a mechanism that is totally unlike all other slide-action shotguns made today. Its completely closed receiver and bottom ejection make it ideal for use in bad weather, and these same features make it ideal for the left-handed shooter. A left-handed safety is also available. The Model 37 is a simple gun with a minimum of parts, and takedown and reassembly are quite easy, even for the amateur. In 1987, the reorganized Ithaca Acquisition Co. changed the designation to Model 87, but there were no major mechanical changes, and the instructions will apply.

Disassembly:

1. Operate the slide latch and open the action. Set the safety in the on-safe position, and turn the magazine end cap clockwise (front view) until it stops. Note that on early guns, made before 1954, there is a pull-out pin in the end cap for added leverage.

2. Rotate the barrel one-quarter turn counter-clockwise (front view), and remove the barrel toward the front.

3. After the barrel is removed, the magazine end cap can be unscrewed and taken off. Caution: The magazine spring will be released as the end cap is removed, so control it and ease it out. Take out the spring and follower toward the front. Removal of the cross screw in the magazine yoke will allow it to be moved off the end of the magazine tube.

4. Move the bolt forward to the closed position, and insert a small screwdriver through the loading port on the underside of the receiver, engaging its blade in the groove in the slide bar pin, located on the underside of the slide piece. Move the pin toward the right, and take off the forend and action slide assembly toward the front.

5. With a small steel plate of proper dimensions, unscrew the forend cap nut, and remove the action slide tube and bar assembly toward the rear.

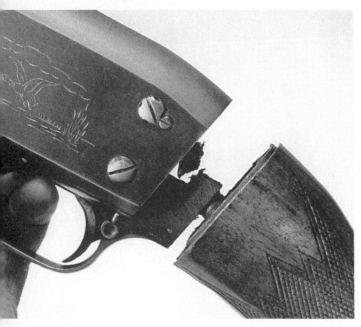

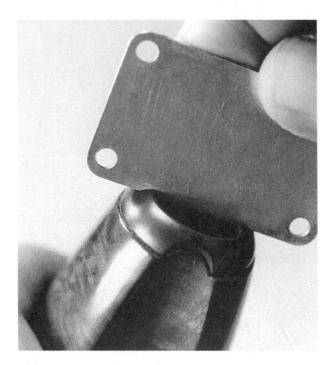

6. Remove the buttplate, and use a B-Square stock tool or a long-shanked screwdriver to back out the stock bolt. Take off the bolt, its washers, and the buttstock toward the rear.

7. Remove the large cross screw at the lower rear of the receiver.

8. Release the safety, and pull the trigger to drop the hammer to the fired position. Slide the trigger housing toward the rear until its side rails clear, then move it downward for removal.

9. As the trigger housing is removed, the right shell stop will be released inside the receiver, and can be taken out downward.

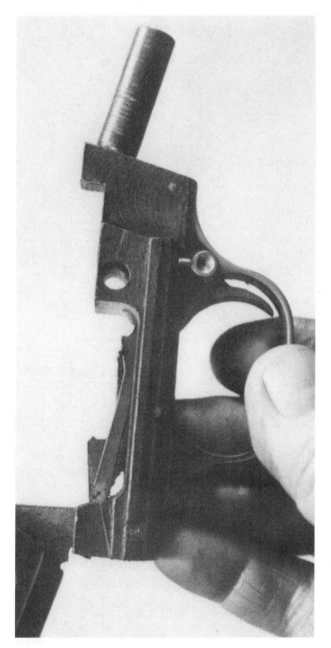

10. Remove the lock screw and the main carrier pivot screw on each side of the receiver.

11. Move the bolt assembly to the rear, and remove the carrier from the rear of the receiver.

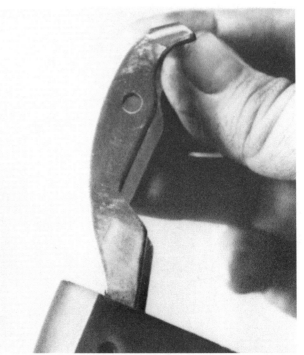

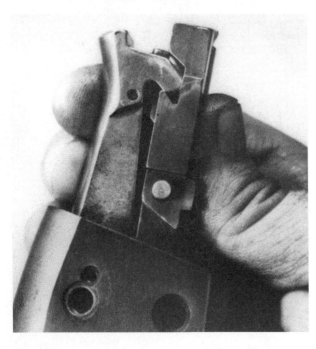

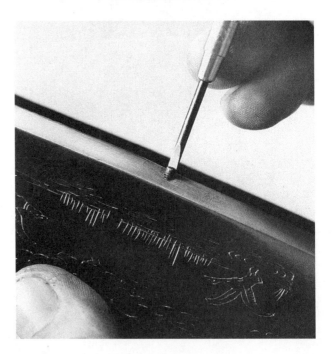

12. Remove the bolt and slide piece toward the rear

13. The left shell stop is retained inside the left wall of the receiver by a small vertical screw. Back out the screw downward.

14. Remove the left shell stop and its coil spring from inside the receiver.

15. With the hammer in the fired position, insert a tool at the lower rear of the trigger housing to slightly depress and restrain the hammer spring cap, and push out the retaining cross pin toward the right. Caution: The spring is powerful, and under tension even when at rest, so control the spring cap and ease it out.

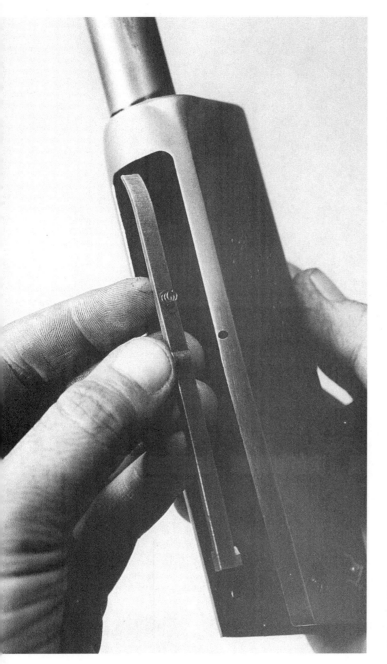

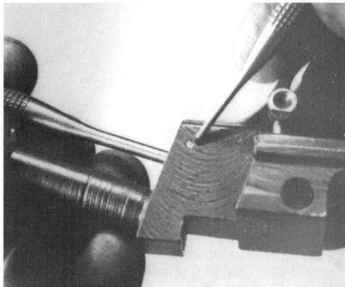

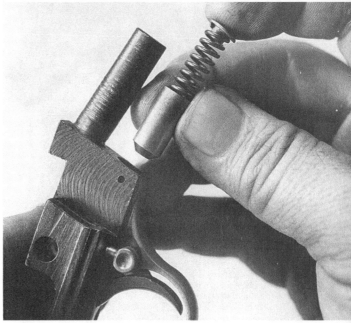

16. Remove the hammer spring cap, spring, and follower toward the rear.

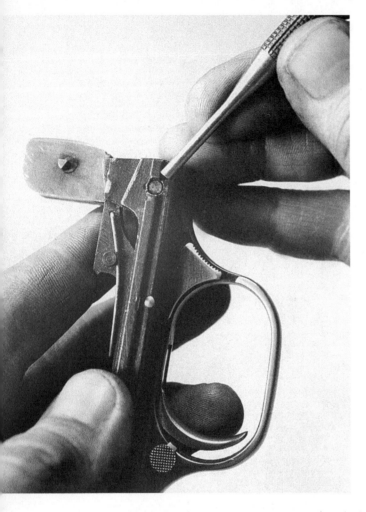

17. Push out the hammer cross pin toward the left.

18. Remove the hammer upward. If necessary, the hammer strut can be removed by drifting out its cross pin.

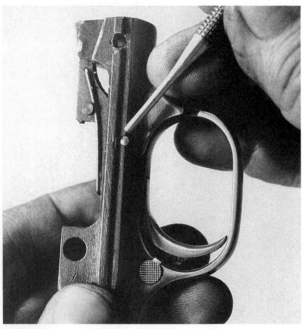

19. Push the trigger cross pin about half-way out toward the left.

20. Remove the slide latch upward and toward the rear, and take out the latch spring from its recess on the right side of the housing.

21. The slide latch release spring can be removed by flexing it slightly and snapping it off its post toward the right.

22. Drift the trigger pin out toward the left, and remove the trigger upward. Take out the trigger spring from its recess in the housing.

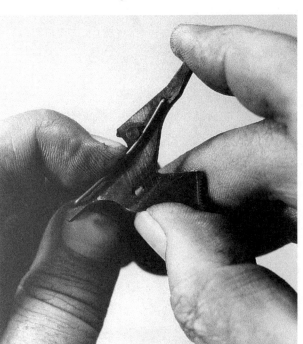

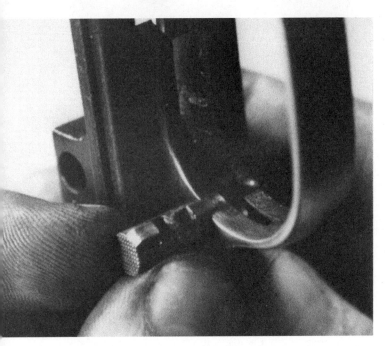

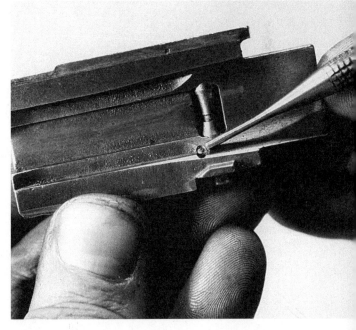

23. Push the safety button out toward the right, and remove the safety plunger and spring downward.

24. Detach the action slide piece from the bottom of the bolt. Drifting out the vertical pin in the slide piece will release the slide bar pin and its spring for removal toward the left.

25. Drift out the cross pin at the rear of the bolt, and remove the firing pin and its return spring toward the rear.

26. Drift out the cross pin at the lower front of the bolt, and remove the lower extractor and its spring downward.

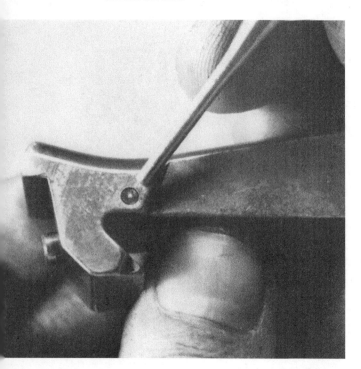

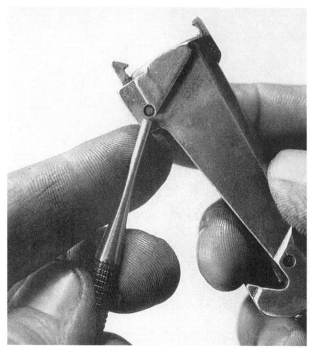

27. A special tool is required for removal of the top extractor, and this can be made by heating and bending the tip of a small screwdriver to give it an "L" shape. Insert the tool at the rear of the extractor, depress the plunger toward the rear, and lift the extractor out of its recess. Slowly release the spring tension, and remove the plunger and spring toward the front.

Reassembly Tips:

1. If the left shell stop has been installed prior to replacement of the bolt and bolt slide in the receiver, it will be necessary to depress the front of the shell stop to clear its rear upper projection for passage of the bolt assembly.

2. When installing the carrier, move the bolt all the way to the rear, insert the carrier until it stops, then move the carrier and bolt together back toward the front to align the carrier pivot holes.

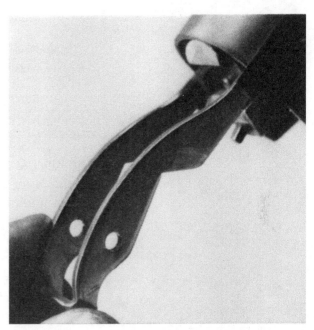

3. When replacing the hammer spring plunger, it will be necessary to lift the hammer strut to insure that its rear tip engages the cup at the front of the plunger, as shown.

4. When replacing the hammer spring cap, depress the cap and insert a drift punch to retain the cap while the pin is replaced.

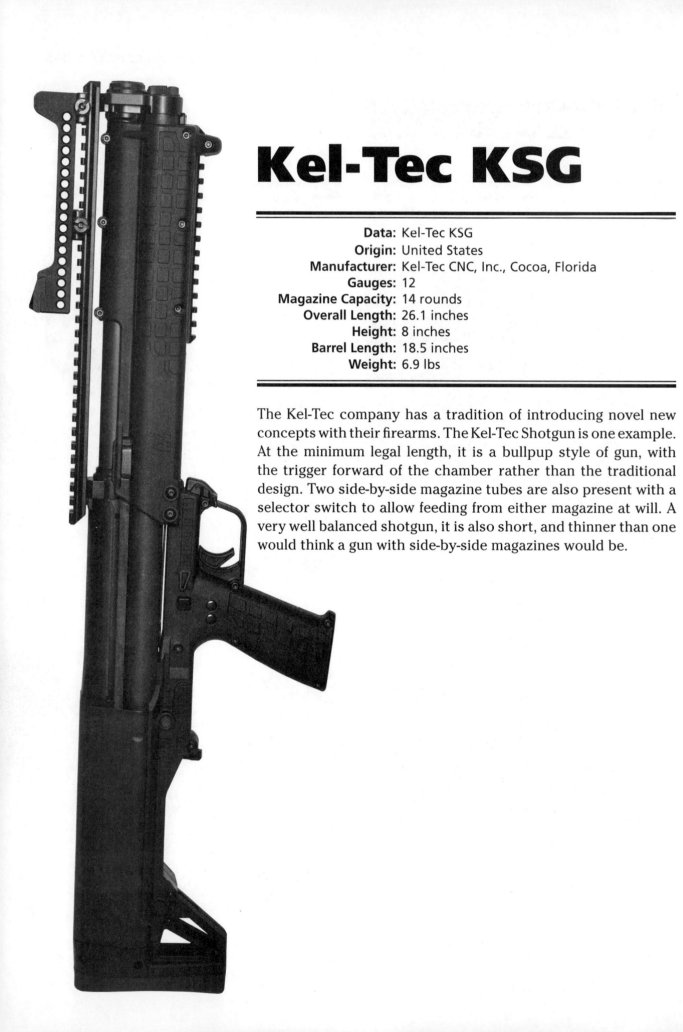

Kel-Tec KSG

Data: Kel-Tec KSG
Origin: United States
Manufacturer: Kel-Tec CNC, Inc., Cocoa, Florida
Gauges: 12
Magazine Capacity: 14 rounds
Overall Length: 26.1 inches
Height: 8 inches
Barrel Length: 18.5 inches
Weight: 6.9 lbs

The Kel-Tec company has a tradition of introducing novel new concepts with their firearms. The Kel-Tec Shotgun is one example. At the minimum legal length, it is a bullpup style of gun, with the trigger forward of the chamber rather than the traditional design. Two side-by-side magazine tubes are also present with a selector switch to allow feeding from either magazine at will. A very well balanced shotgun, it is also short, and thinner than one would think a gun with side-by-side magazines would be.

Disassembly:

1. With the hammer cocked, the magazine selector in the center position, the safety on "safe," and the slide forward, push out the two rear assembly pins. These pins can be stored in the two holes in the pistol grip.

2. Lift the rear of the grip assembly, rotating it forward, and pull the assembly off the receiver.

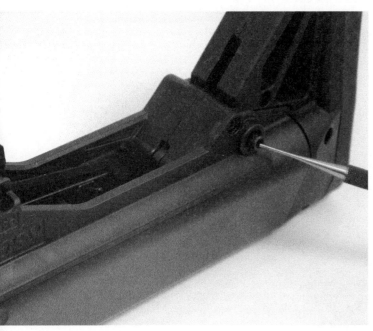

3. Grasp the stock and pull it out to the rear.

4. Holding the KSG upside down, pull the slide to the rear. The bolt assembly will drop into the top of the receiver and can be pulled out.

5. Jointly unscrew the magazine bolts until both are fully disengaged from their threads. This may require alternating quarter turns of the magazine bolts.

7. The barrel and slide assembly can now be pulled from the receiver and magazine assembly.

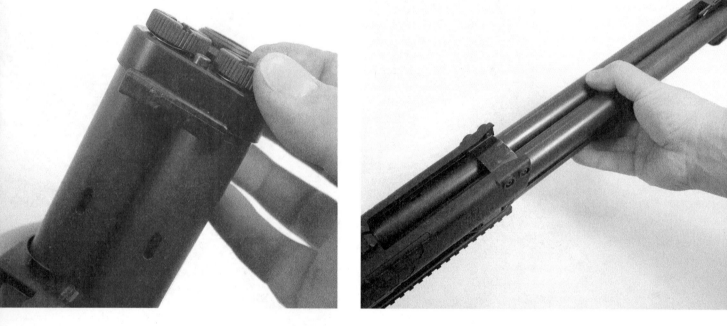

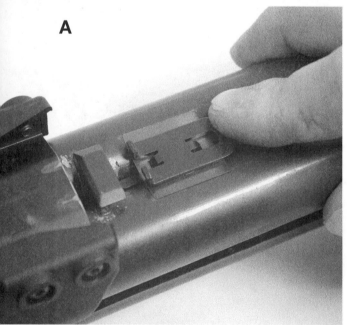

A

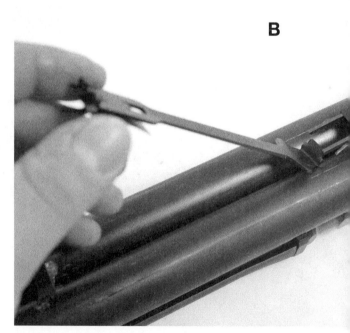

B

6. With the forend forward, push down on this link to allow the forend to slide over it (Picture A). Lift the link out from under the cartridge stops and remove (Picture B).

8. There are five socket screws in the stock unit. Remove these screws to access the lifter. The lifter rotates on two lifter axes, these spuds indicated on either side of the stock assembly. Unless the lifter needs to be replaced, there should be no need to disassemble the stock assembly.

9. Drift out the lock button's spring pin. The lock button can then be removed from the action lock.

10. Remove the eight socket screws that hold the grip assembly together. Note that the two rearmost screws are of differing lengths than the foremost six screws.

11. Slowly work apart the two halves of the grip assembly. All of the internal parts should stay attached to the left half of the grip assembly

12. Lift the slide lock off its pin. The slide lock spring is retained by both halves of the grip and will likely fall or spring free when the halves are parted. Control the spring. The slide lock axis pin can also be removed at this time.

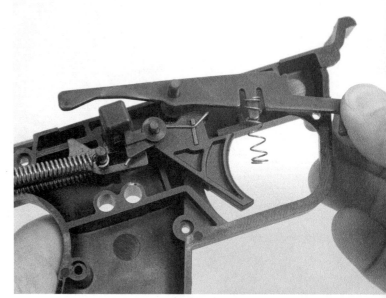

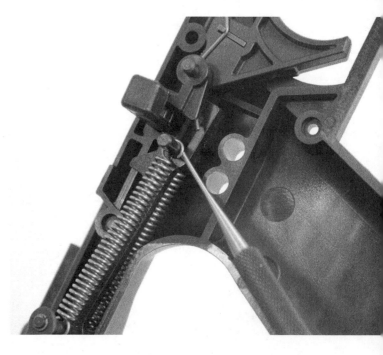

13. Lift the hammer from its axis pin at the rear of the grip assembly.

14. Lift the top (right) hammer spring from the sear bar pin to release tension. While not under a great deal of tension when the hammer is down,   it should still be controlled.

15. Remove the sear bar pin. It may be necessary to use pliers, since the bottom (left) hammer spring is still pulling on the pin.

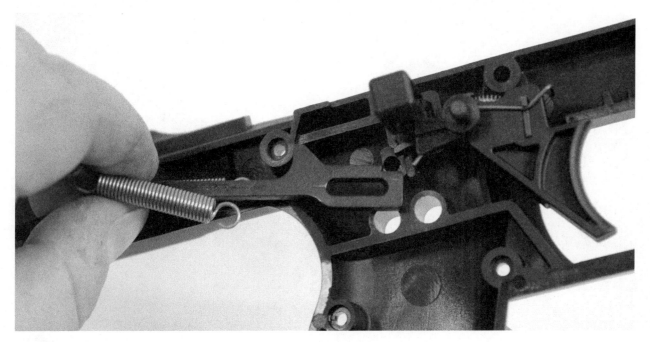

16. The hammer and sear bar assembly can now be removed.

17. There is no need to further disassembly the hammer and sear bar assembly unless replacement or repair is warranted. The two hammer bar pins retain the bars with small spring clips. Removing these clips will allow the entire assembly to be taken apart.

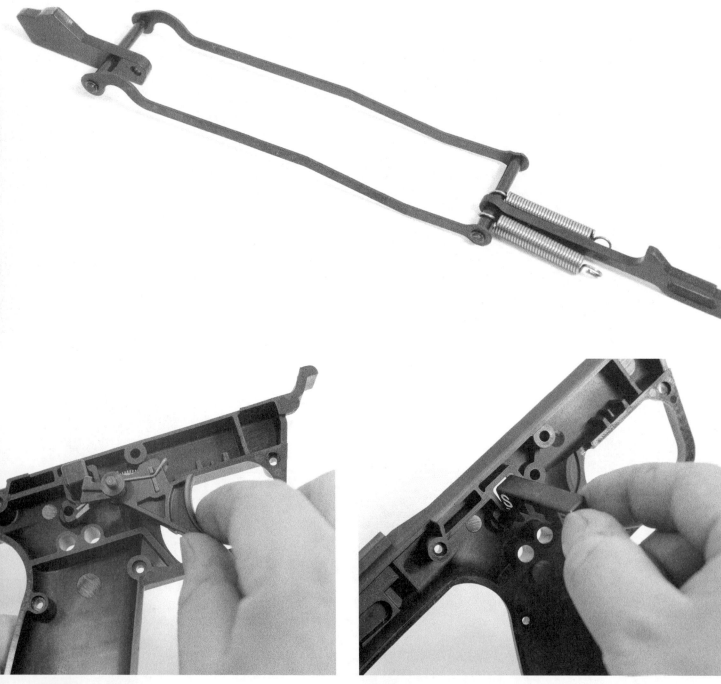

18. The trigger assembly can now be removed In total from the grip.

19. The safety can now be removed from the grip.

20. Remove the safety snap from the trigger axis pin.

21. Push the trigger axis pin left until it is flush with the trigger spring's right side coil. Then remove the trigger spring by lifting the right side coil off the pin. Follow this up by doing the same procedure to the left side coil of the trigger spring.

22. Fully remove the trigger axis pin to free the sear. The sear spring is powerful, so control it, and there is a spring guide inside the sear spring which should not be misplaced. The metal sear catch embedded in the top of the trigger should not be removed.

23. If necessary, the magazine springs and followers can be removed by unscrewing the two magazine plugs.

24. Remove this socket screw to release the magazine selector. There is a small brass washer under this screw. Do not lose it.

25. Push out this pin to remove the selector catch.

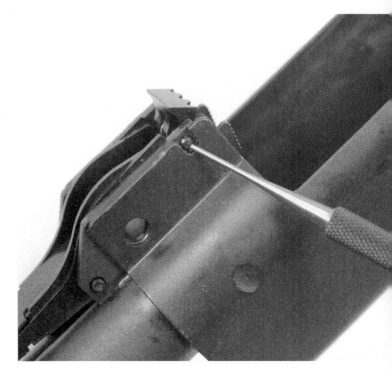

26. Push out the cartridge stop dowel pin to release the stops and spring.

27. This is the cartridge stop assembly, with all four catches and the spring. The four catches are each unique and proper orientation should be observed.

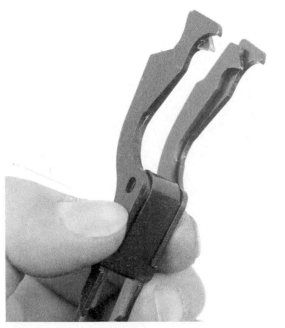

28. If necessary, to remove the Picatinny rail, unscrew the two button head screws on the rail's top. These screws are retained with thread locking compound and are tightly retained. Beneath the rail and rearward of the sight base is the recoil pad.

29. Remove the six socket screws on the handguard forend, three above and three below. The two forend halves can then be spread and pushed around and off the barrel.

30. The bolt carrier legs can be lifted from the forend here.

31. The socket screw in the muzzle plate retains the pump buffer which rests at the bottom rear of the plate.

32. If necessary, the magazine bolts can be removed using a split-ring pliers to remove the split-rings on the rear side of the muzzle plate. Only do this if replacement is necessary.

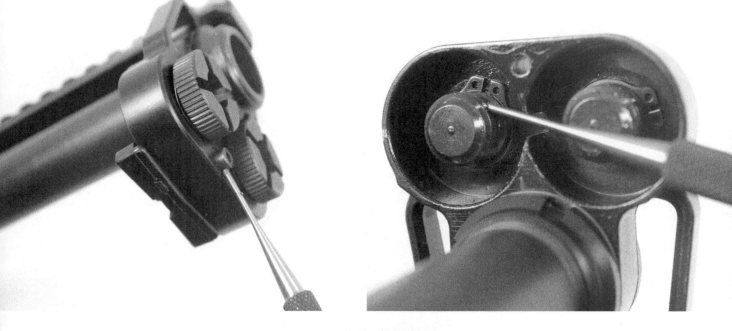

33. The sight base and the muzzle plate are held to the barrel by means of three barrel rings. One retains the rear sight base, and two sandwich the muzzle plate. Unless barrel bore work or barrel replacement is to be done, there is no need to remove these rings or the sight base and muzzle plate, as these rings are heavily torqued and are retained with thread locker.

34. Pushing out this pin will free the firing pin which can then be drawn out of the bolt to the rear.

35. Pushing out this pin will free the extractor and extractor spring. Note the spring orientation when removing.

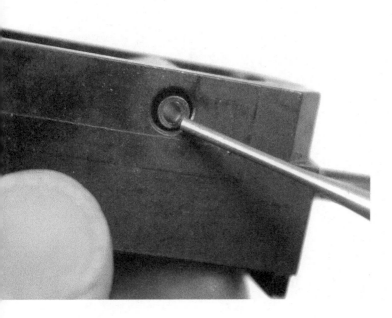

36. Pushing out this large roll pin will release the bolt lock to fall from the bolt.

Reassembly Tips:

1. When reinstalling the trigger assembly, the left leg of the trigger spring must rest against the back of this boss on the left side grip. Simply place the leg of the spring then compress and insert the trigger axis pin into its hole, then push the entire assembly into the left grip.

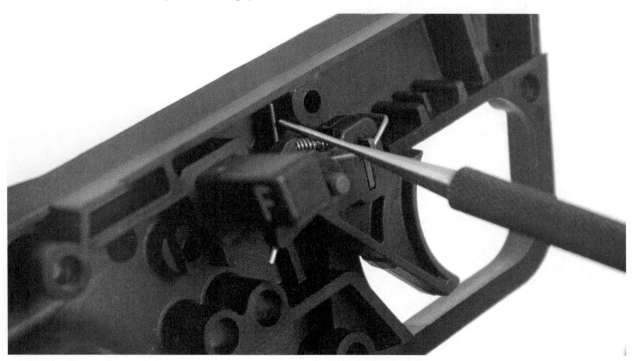

2. There should be no gap between the barrel extension and the receiver when reassembled.

Marlin Model 26

Similar/Identical Pattern Guns:

The same basic assembly/disassembly steps for the Marlin Model 26 also apply to the following guns:

Model 1898	Model 24
Model 17	Model 30
Model 19	Model 42
Model 21	Model 49

Data:	Marlin Model 26
Origin:	United States
Manufacturer:	Marlin Fire Arms Co., New Haven, Connecticut
Gauges:	12, 16, and 20
Magazinre Capacity:	5 rounds
Overall length:	49 inches
Barrel length:	30 inches (others offered)
Weight:	7-1/8 pounds

Designed by Lewis L. Hepburn, the Marlin slide-action was a better and stronger gun than its main competitor, the Winchester of 1897. Most of the Marlins were "takedown" types, with the barrel unit being easily removable from the receiver. The Model 26, shown here, had a fixed barrel. The "takedown" types have a little lever that is aligned with a recess in the action slide, allowing it to move forward out of the receiver. The barrel unit is then turned for removal.

Disassembly:

1. Remove the stock retaining screw.

2. Remove the buttstock toward the rear. It may be tight, and may require bumping with a rubber mallet to start it.

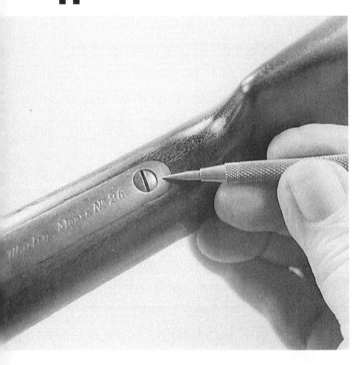

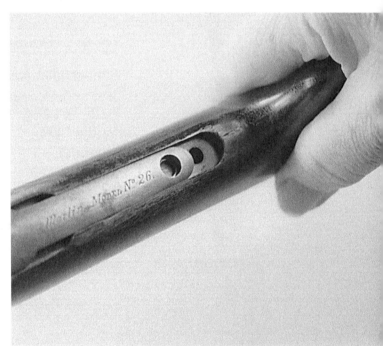

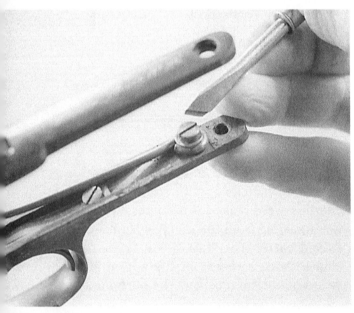

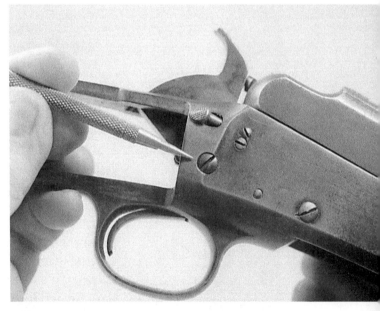

3. In this particular gun, the hammer spring has been replaced with a round-wire type. Normally, the spring will be a blade type. Use an offset or angle-tip screwdriver to loosen or remove the spring mounting screw. You can swing the spring to the side, or remove it.

4. Remove the hammer pivot screw.

5. Tip the hammer forward to clear its rear upper edge, and remove it upward.

6. Remove the screws on both sides of the receiver at the front of the trigger guard.

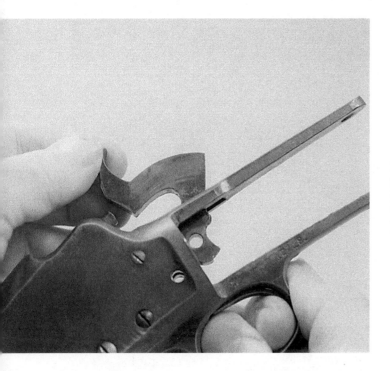

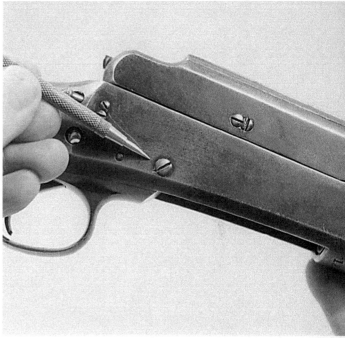

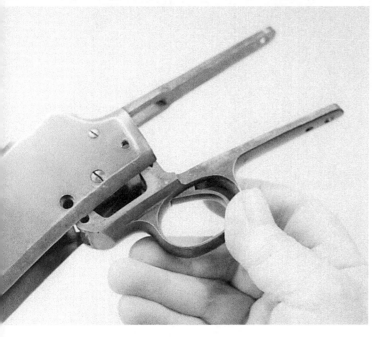

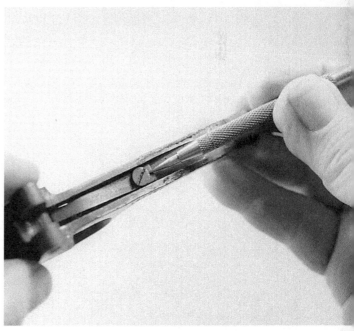

7. Remove the trigger guard unit downward. It may require a tap with a nylon mallet to loosen it.

8. Removal of this screw will allow the trigger spring to be taken out upward.

9. Drift out the cross pin, and remove the trigger upward.

10. Remove the screw that pivots and retains the hang-fire safety. (Note: Marlin parts lists call this the "recoil block." Its function was to keep the action closed in case of a hang-fire with early shells.)

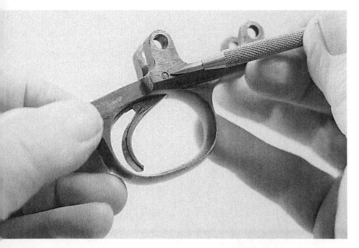

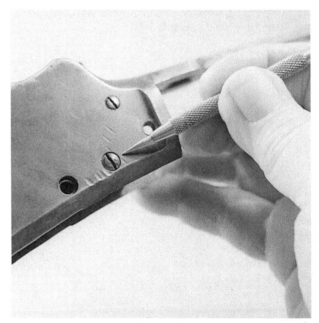

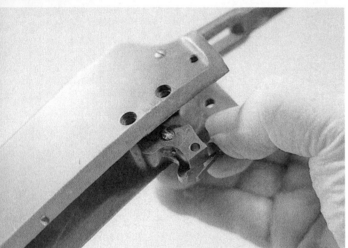

11. Remove the hang-fire safety or "recoil block." Its blade spring is staked in place, and is removed only for repair.

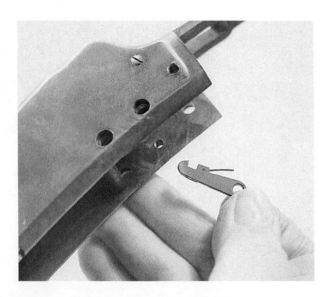

12. The release plunger and its coil spring are retained in the safety by an angled pin. Remove this system only for repair.

13. Take out the hang-fire safety catch lever. Its blade spring is staked in place, and is removed only for repair.

14. Remove the carrier pivot screw.

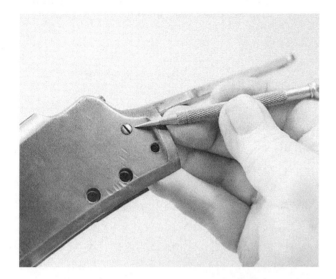

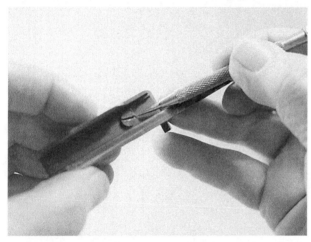

16. The secondary shell stop is retained in the carrier by this screw.

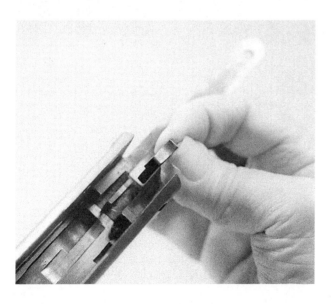

15. Lift the carrier at the rear, and move it rearward for removal.

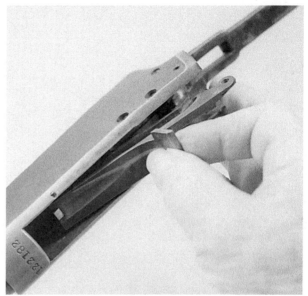

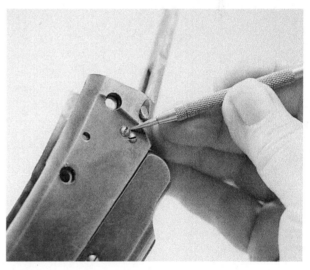

17. Remove the safety-sear screw. Restrain the safety-sear as the screw is taken out.

18. Remove the safety-sear. Its staked-in blade spring is removed only for repair.

19. The bolt release button can be taken out toward the rear by removing this screw.

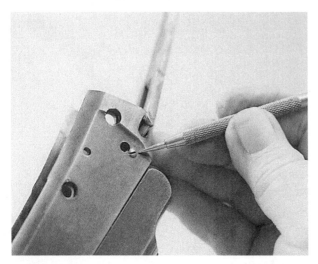

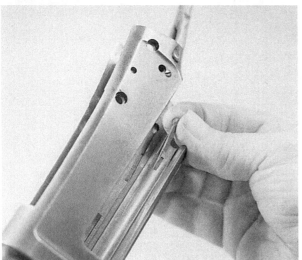

20. Depress the firing pin to release the bolt lock, and use the action slide to move the bolt all the way to the rear. Disengage the bolt from the action slide, and tip it outward for removal.

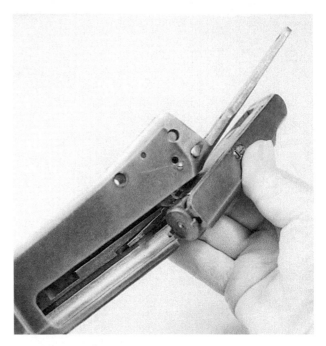

21. Remove the ejector from its recess inside the receiver. Remove its staked blade-type spring only for repair.

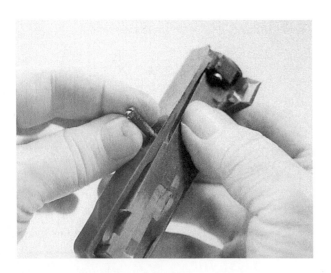

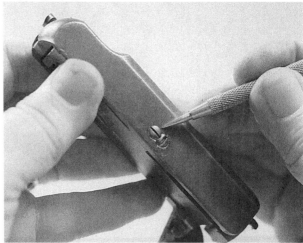

22. Remove the lock screw on the right side of the bolt. Note that the screw-slotted part beside it is not a screw, it is a cross pin.

23. Push the front of the locking block inward, to relieve the tension of its positioning plunger and spring. Drift out the locking block cross pin toward the right.

24. Remove the locking block from the bolt.

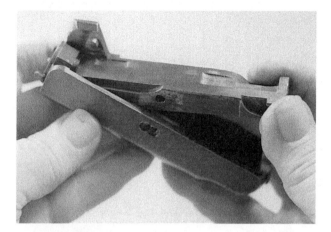

25. The firing pin and its spring can be taken out toward the rear by drifting out this vertical pin downward. If this is done, use a non-marring drift.

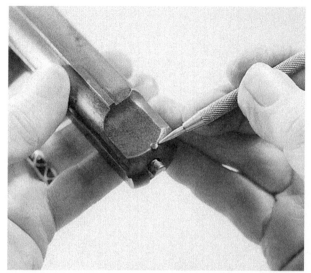

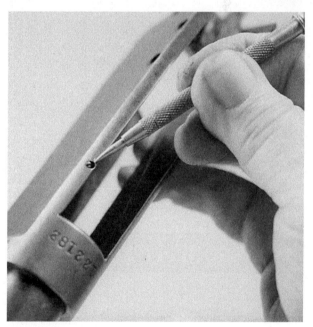

26. The left extractor and its coil spring can be removed by drifting out this pin upward. The pin retaining the right extractor and its blade-type spring is drifted out downward, and the right extractor is removed toward the front. Remove the spring only for repair. If the pin is drifted all the way out, the bolt lock tension plunger and its coil spring will be released for removal. Control the plunger and spring as the pin is drifted out.

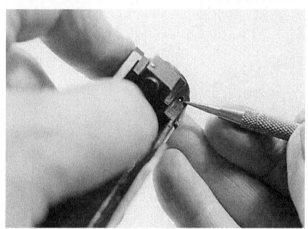

27. This tiny vertical screw pivots and retains the primary shell stop inside the receiver. The shell stop is powered by a blade spring, staked in place. Remove it only for repair.

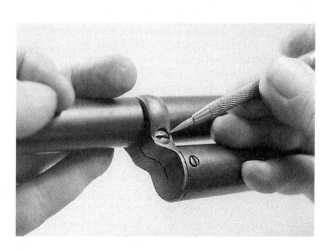

28. Remove the cross screw from the magazine tube hanger.

29. Remove the cross screw at the front of the magazine tube. If the tube plug on the hanger is loose, the magazine spring will push it out, so control it.

30. If the hanger and plug are tight, use a non-marring tool to nudge it forward. Remove the hanger, magazine spring, and magazine follower.

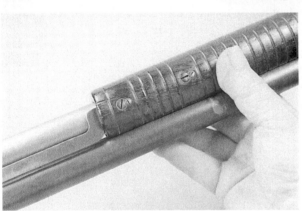

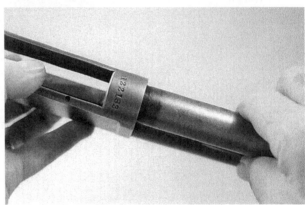

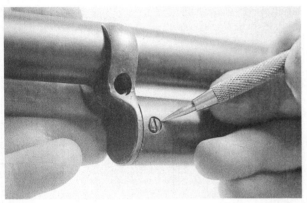

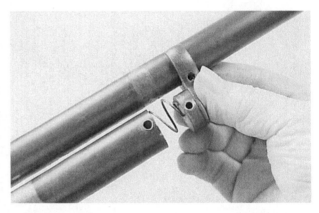

31. Remove the action slide toward the front. Taking out the two lock screws and the two mounting screws will allow the action slide to be removed from the wood handle.

32. Unscrew (counter-clockwise, front view) the magazine tube and remove it from the receiver.

Reassembly Tips:

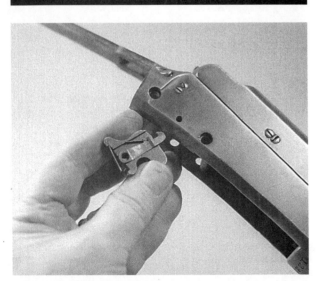

1. When installing the hang-fire safety, it is best to set the catch-lever in its recess on the side of the safety before insertion. Note that the hook at its top goes toward the rear, as shown. As the cross-screw is put in, use a drift on the opposite side to align the lever hole.

Marlin Model 55

Similar/Identical Pattern Guns:

The same basic assembly/disassembly steps for the Marlin Model 55 also apply to the following guns:

Glenfield Model 50	**Marlin Model 55S**
Marlin Model 55 Super Goose	**Marlin Model 5510**
Marlin/Glenfield Model 55-G	**Marlin Model 55-G**
Marlin Model 55 Hunter	**Marlin Model 55 Swamp Gun**

Data:	Marlin Model 55
Origin:	United States
Manufacturer:	Marlin Firearms Company North Haven, Connecticut
Gauges:	10, and 12
Magazine Capacity:	2 rounds
Overall length:	46-1/2 inches (with 26-inch barrel)
Barrel length:	26 to 36 inches
Weight:	7-1/2 to 10-1/2 pounds

Originally offered in 1950 in 12-, 16-, and 20-gauge, the Model 55 is now available only in 12-gauge as the "Goose Gun," and in 10-gauge as the "SuperGoose." The Marlin/Glenfield Model 50 is mechanically the same, and the instructions will apply to that gun as well. As with most bolt-action shotguns, the mechanism is relatively simple, and takedown and reassembly are not difficult, with the possible exception of the safety system. This gun was made in 10-gauge from 1976 to 1985 as the Model 5510.

Disassembly:

1. Remove the magazine. Open the bolt, pull the trigger and hold it to the rear, and remove the bolt from the rear of the receiver.

2. Grip the front portion of the bolt, and turn the bolt handle clockwise (rear view) to drop the striker to the fired position, as shown.

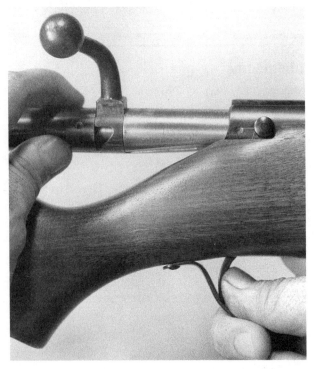

3. Use a roll-pin punch to drift out the roll cross pin near the forward edge of the rear section of the bolt. Note that the striker spring is still under some tension, so control the rear section when the pin is drifted out and the punch removed.

4. Remove the rear section, and take out the striker spring and its guide from inside it.

5. Remove the striker (firing pin) from the forward section, toward the rear.

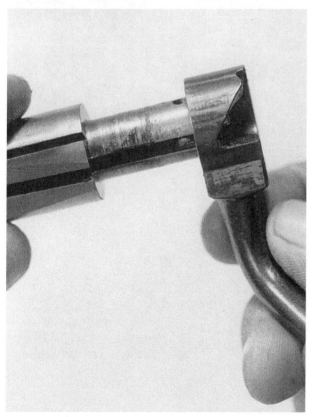

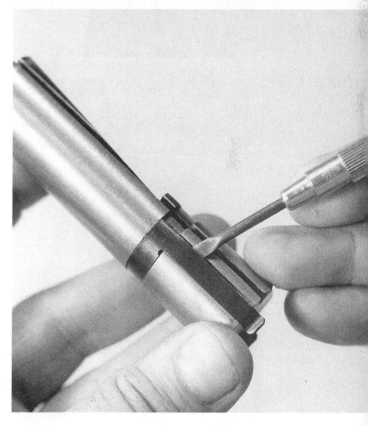

6. Remove the bolt handle unit toward the rear.

7. Insert a small screwdriver at the front of the left extractor arm, and slide it toward the rear until it can lever the arm outward just enough to clear its recess. Pivot the extractor unit over toward the right, and take it off.

8. Back out the stock mounting bolt, located in the forward tip of the magazine plate on the underside, and separate the action from the stock. Note that the magazine catch must be moved to clear as the action is taken out upward.

9. Removal of the two small wood screws at the front and rear of the trigger guard will allow the guard/ magazine plate to be taken off downward.

10. Drifting out the large roll cross pin at the lower rear of the trigger housing will allow removal of the trigger and the combination trigger and sear spring downward. Note that the trigger/ magazine housing is welded to the receiver, and is not removable.

11. After the trigger and the spring are removed, drifting out the upper roll cross pin will release the sear for removal downward and toward the rear.

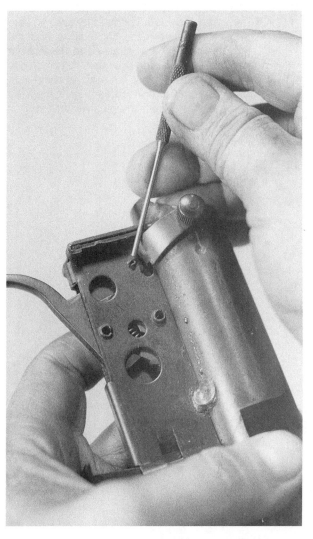

12. Drifting out the small pin at the upper rear of the trigger housing will allow removal of the safety-lever toward the right and upward, and the safety blade and blade spacer downward and toward the front.

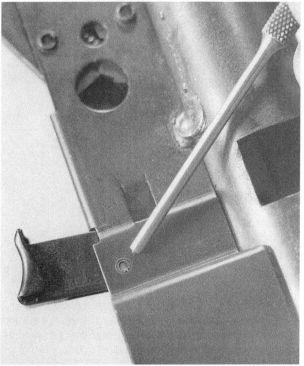

13. Drifting out the roll cross pin behind the magazine well will allow removal of the magazine catch downward. The magazine catch spring is a tempered arm of the catch, and is not removable.

14. The barrel is threaded into the receiver at the front, and there is a spring-steel spacer plate or washer between the barrel collar and the receiver. The collar is attached to the front of the magazine housing by a small roll cross pin. In normal disassembly, the barrel is best left in place. If removal is necessary, care must be taken not to deform the receiver and trigger/magazine housing.

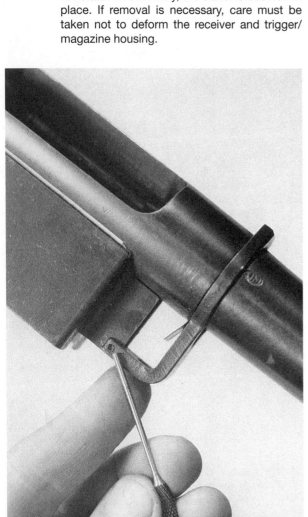

Reassembly Tips:

1. When replacing the safety system, note that the spacer goes on the right side of the safety-lever, and the blade goes on the left. Be sure the parts are aligned properly before inserting the cross pin.

2. When replacing the combination sear and trigger spring, note that it angles upward toward the front, and should be visible in the large hole on the right side of the housing, as shown.

3. Before replacing the rear section of the bolt, be sure the striker is in the full forward position, as shown, and take care that the holes in the rear section, front section, and striker are aligned before replacing the cross pin.

4. Before the bolt can be reinserted in the receiver, the striker must be in the cocked position, as shown. Grip the front of the bolt, and turn the bolt handle counterclockwise (rear view), until the striker lug is on its detent notch.

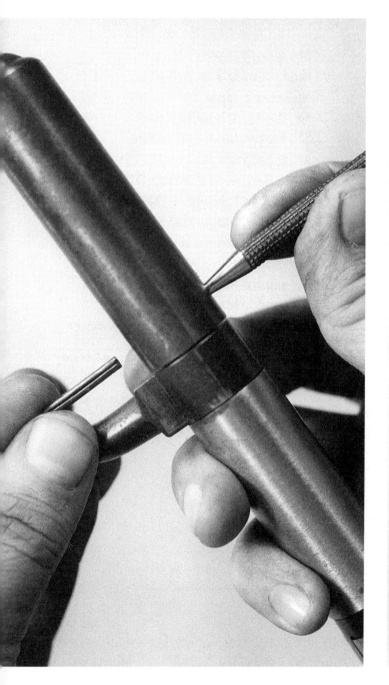

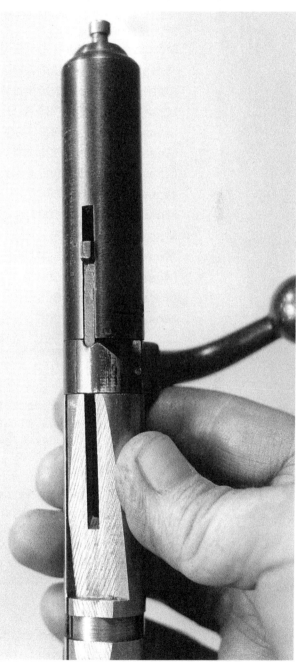

Mossberg Model 500

Similar/Identical Pattern Guns:

The same basic assembly/disassembly steps for the Mossberg Model 500 also apply to the following guns:

Mossberg Model 500 AGVD	Mossberg Model 500 AHT
Mossberg Model 500 AHTD	Mossberg Model 500 ALD
Mossberg Model 500 ALDR	Mossberg Model 500 ALMR
Mossberg Model 500 ALS	Mossberg Model 500 APR
Mossberg Model 500 ASG	Mossberg Model 500 ATP6
Mossberg Model 500 ATP8	Mossberg Model 500 ATP8-SP
Mossberg Model 500 CLD	Mossberg Model 500 CLDR
Mossberg Model 500 CLS	Mossberg Model 500 500E
Mossberg Model 500 EGV	Mossberg Model 500 EL
Mossberg Model 500 ELR	Mossberg Model 500 ETV
Mossberg Model 500 Medallion	Mossberg Model 500 Security Series
Mossberg Model 500 Trophy Slugster	Mossberg Model 500 Mariner
Mossberg Model 500 590	Mossberg Model 590 Mariner
Mossberg Model 500 600E	New Haven Model 600 AST Slugster

Data: Mossberg Model 500
Origin: United States
Manufacturer: O.F. Mossberg & Sons, North Haven, Connecticut
Gauges: 12, 16, 20, and 410
Magazine Capacity: 4 rounds
Overall length: 48 inches (with 28-inch barrel)
Barrel length: 18-1/2 to 32 inches
Weight: 6 to 7-1/4 pounds

Since its introduction in 1961, the Model 500 has been offered in a wide variety of sub-models, ranging from a full trap-type gun with a high rib and Monte Carlo stock to the "Slugster," a hunting version available with an 18 1/2-inch barrel. The Model 500 series of guns is still in production, and variations have been made for several large retail firms bearing their brand names. All of these guns are mechanically identical, and the instructions will apply.

Disassembly:

1. Open the action, and unscrew the takedown knob, located at the front of the forend, until it stops. Remove the barrel toward the front.

2. If necessary, the knob can be removed by inserting a tool inside the rear of the barrel loop to immobilize the C-clip. The knob can then be unscrewed and taken off toward the front.

3. Move the bolt back to its forward position, and push out the cross pin at the lower rear of the receiver.

4. Remove the trigger housing downward.

5. Removal of the trigger group will release the right and left shell stops for detachment from their recesses inside the receiver. The left shell stop will usually fall free as the trigger housing is removed, and can be taken out downward.

6. Move the right shell stop inward, withdrawing its post from the wall of the receiver, and take it out downward.

7. Restrain the hammer, pull the trigger, and ease the hammer down to the fired position. Insert a tool at the rear of the housing to slightly depress the hammer spring, and push out the cross pin at the rear of the housing. The spring is under some tension, so control it. Remove the hammer spring and follower toward the rear.

8. Remove the hammer strut toward the rear.

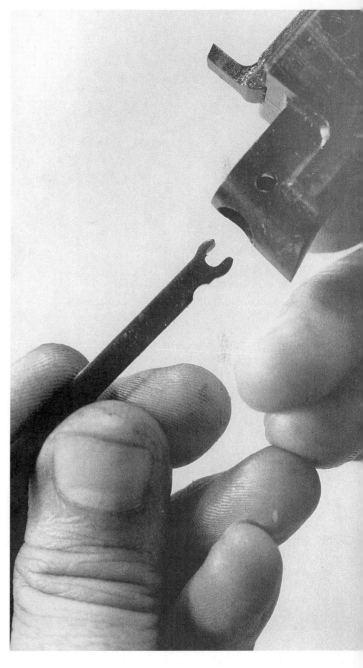

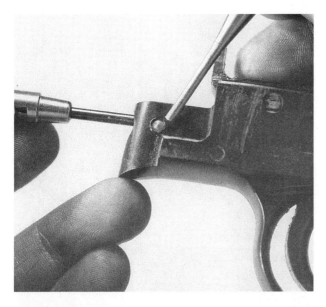

9. Push out the trigger pin.

10. Remove the trigger and its spring upward, disengaging it from the rear tip of the disconnector.

11. Push out the hammer pivot toward the left.

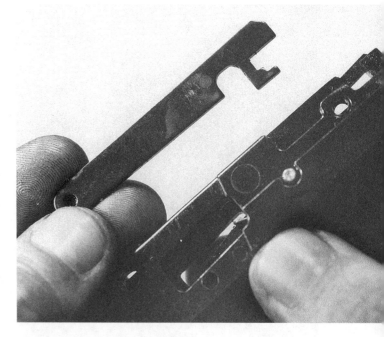

12. Remove the hammer upward. Note that the two cross pins in the hammer are bearing pins, and their removal is not necessary in normal disassembly.

13. Move the disconnector toward the rear, then remove it upward.

14. Push out the slide latch pivot pin toward the left.

15. Remove the combination disconnector and slide latch spring upward.

16. Lift the slide latch at the front, swing it over toward the right and remove it from the housing, along with its attached release spring.

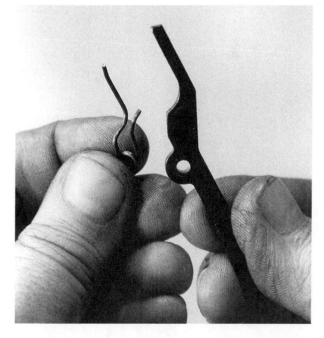

17. The slide latch release spring is easily detached from the front of the slide latch.

18. Pushing out the small cross pin at the front of the trigger housing will release the sear and its torsion spring for removal upward and toward the rear. The spring is under tension, so restrain it as the pin is removed.

19. Move the bolt and slide assembly toward the rear until the sides of the slide piece align with the exit cuts on the inside of the receiver. Lift the slide piece at the front, disengaging it from the bolt, and remove it from the bottom of the receiver. Move the forend and slide bar assembly out toward the front and remove it. (Note: This applies to late guns only. See step 24.)

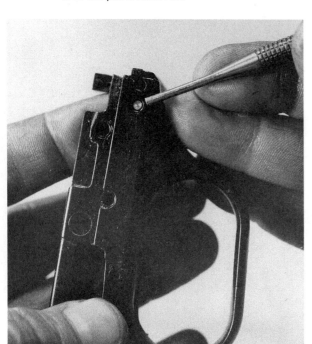

20. Remove the bolt from the front of the receiver.

21. Swing the carrier out, squeeze the rear arms of the carrier to move the pivot studs out of their holes in the receiver, and remove the carrier. Note that the safety must be in the on-safe position (pushed to the rear) during this operation, to clear the arms of the carrier.

22. Insert a screwdriver through the ejection port, and remove the large screw that retains the ejector. Remove the ejector toward the right.

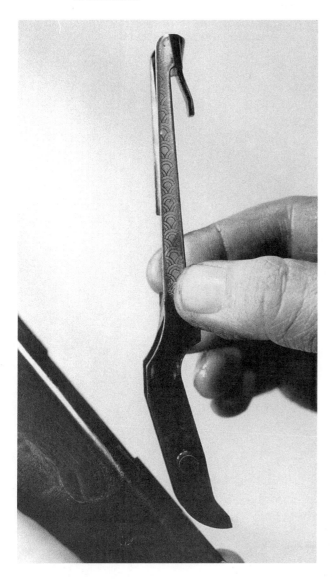

23. Back out the screw in the center of the safety button. Remove the safety button, the detent ball, and detent spring upward, and take out the safety block from inside the receiver.

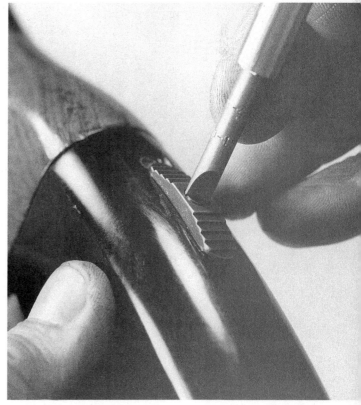

24. The magazine spring and follower can be removed only by taking off the magazine tube, which is threaded into the receiver. A large screw slot is provided at the front of the tube, and a tool can be made from steel plate to fit the curve of the slot. Note that if the gun is an early one, removal of the magazine tube will be necessary before the action slide can be taken off, as the earlier versions have a stop ring on the tube.

25. Remove the buttplate, and use a B-Square stock tool or a long-shanked screwdriver to back out the stock bolt. Remove the bolt, washer, and stock toward the rear.

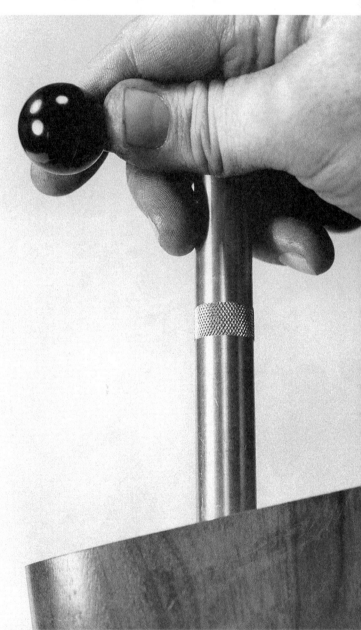

26. Use a small piece of steel plate of the proper size and thickness to fit the notches in the front of the slide tube nut, and unscrew the nut counter-clockwise (front view). Slide the tube and slide bar assembly out toward the rear.

27. The firing pin is retained in the bolt by a vertical pin on the left side at the rear, and the pin is drifted out upward. Remove the firing pin toward the rear.

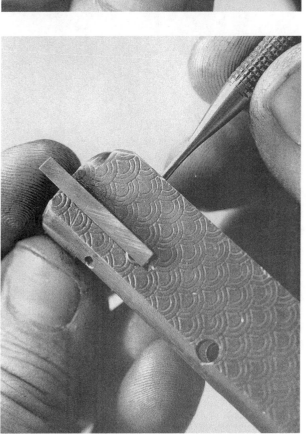

28. Drift out the locking block cross pin, and remove the locking block from the bolt. Note that the cross pin is splined at the center for tight seating, and a firm support will be required when driving it out.

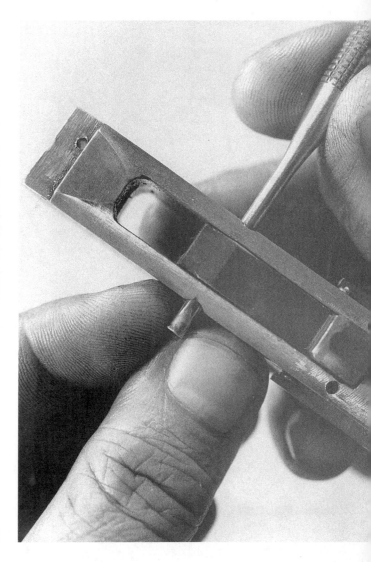

29. The extractors are retained on each side of the bolt by vertical pins which are driven out upward, and the extractors and their coil springs are taken off toward each side. Keep them separate, as they are not interchangeable.

Reassembly Tips:

1. When installed inside the front of the trigger housing, the sear and its spring must be assembled as shown (the cross pin has been temporarily inserted for purposes of illustration). Remember that before the hammer is installed, the sear must be lifted to the vertical position.

2. This top view of the trigger housing, before installation of the hammer, trigger, and disconnector, shows the proper engagement of the two torsion springs with the slide latch.

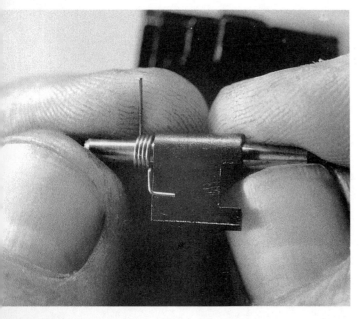

3. When replacing the safety block inside the receiver, note that it must be installed with its lower projection at the rear, as shown. (The safety button has been temporarily attached for purpose of illustration.)

Mossberg Model 695

Data:	Mossberg Model 695
Origin:	United States
Manufacturer:	O.F. Mossberg & Sons, North Haven, Connecticut
Gauges:	12 only
Magazine Capacity:	2 rounds
Overall length:	42-1/2 inches
Barrel length:	22 inches
Weight:	7-1/2 pounds

Introduced in 1996, the Model 695 "Slugster" is notable for having a fully rifled barrel that is also ported to reduce recoil. It also has a set of good open sights, and is drilled and tapped for scope mounts. In an emergency, regular shotshells could be fired in it, but the patterning would be erratic. It was designed for hunting with slug loads.

Disassembly:

1. Remove the magazine. Open the bolt, keep the trigger depressed, and remove the bolt toward the rear. Back out the takedown screw, and separate the action from the stock. The screw is retained in the stock by a spring washer, and is not routinely removed. If necessary, the recoil pad can be taken off by removing its retaining screws.

2. Remove the large screw at the front of the trigger group. Take care that the lock-washer is not lost.

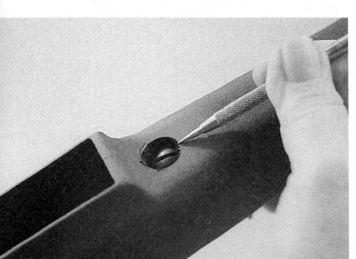

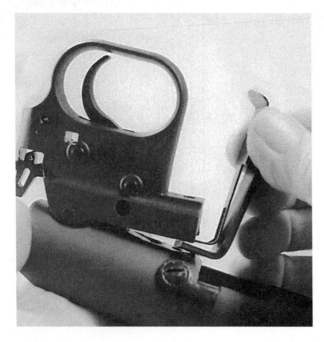

3. Remove the magazine guide and magazine catch toward the front.

4. Remove the C-clip from the trigger group cross pin. As with all C-clips, take care not to lose it.

5. Push out and remove the pin toward the left.

6. Remove the trigger group downward. The sear and its spring will likely stay in the receiver, and can be lifted out.

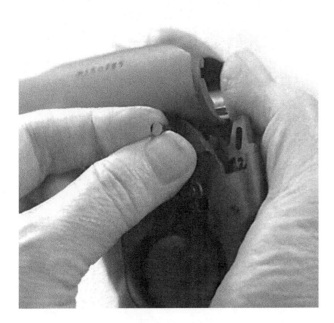

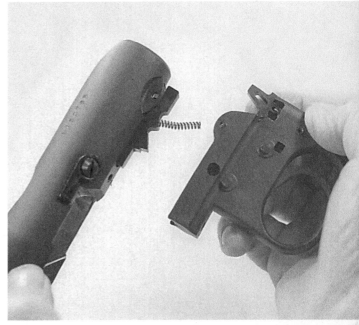

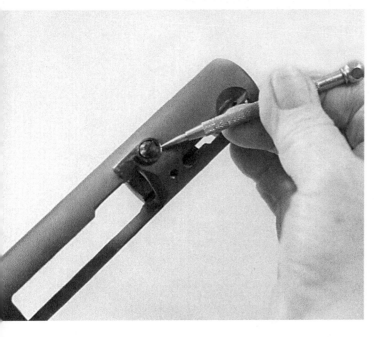

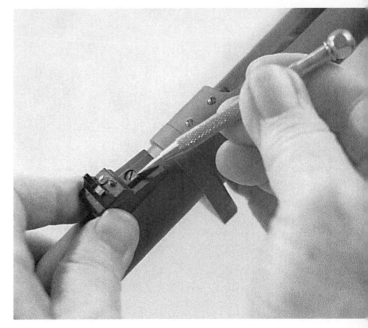

7. The ejector can be removed from the receiver by taking out its mounting screw.

8. Loosening the smaller vertical adjustment screw will allow the rear sight to be moved upward and off its base. This will expose the base retaining screw. The front sight is not routinely removable from the barrel.

9. Use a small tool to unhook the trigger spring from its hole in the back of the trigger. It will have to be turned as it comes out, to clear.

10. Remove the C-clip from the end of the trigger pin.

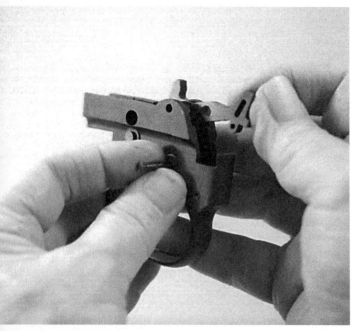

11. Remove the trigger pin toward the left. Remove the trigger upward.

12. Using a proper roll-pin drift to push out this cross pin will release the trigger spring for removal upward. If removal is not necessary for repair, it is best left in place.

13. Remove the C-clip from the sear-trip cross pin.

14. Push the sear-trip pin toward the left, and remove it.

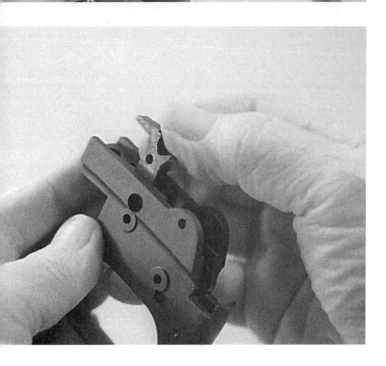

15. Remove the sear-trip upward.

16. Remove the sear-trip plunger and spring.

17. The extractors are retained on each side of the bolt by vertical pins. Drift the pins out upward, and remove the extractors and their small coil springs toward each side. Note that the extractors, springs, and pins are not identical, so keep them separate if both are removed.

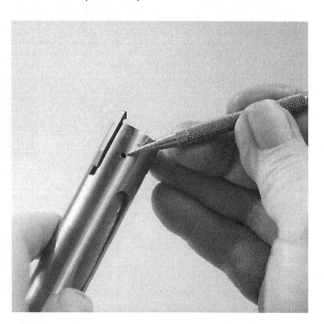

18. Depress the bolt index plunger toward the rear, and turn the front section of the bolt clockwise (front view).

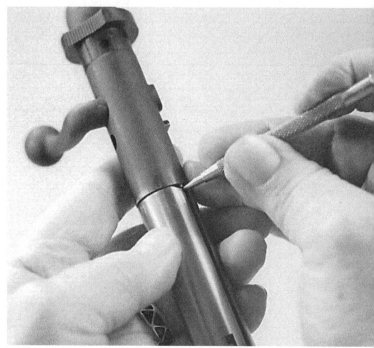

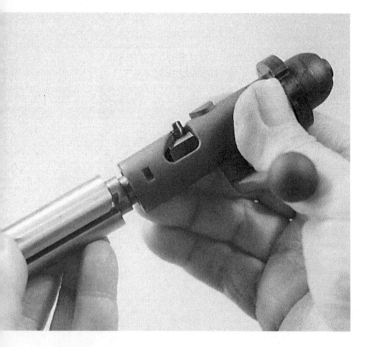

19. When it reaches the position shown, the front section can be removed toward the front.

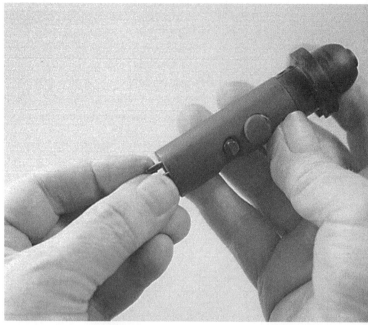

20. Remove the index plunger and its spring from the rear section of the bolt. Use a small hooked tool to pull out the spring.

21. Press the firing pin point against a solid surface and depress it slightly rearward. Turn the cocking lug to the left (rear view) and ease the striker down to fired position. This is not part of disassembly; it's to prevent it from being inadvertently tripped and pinching the fingers during further operations. It is possible to align the cocking lug/sear lug with an access hole and drive it out, releasing the striker/firing pin unit and its spring, but this is not recommended. If this system needs repair, it must be returned to the factory.

22. The safety system should be disassembled only for repair. To remove the safety knob, you must use spring-ring pliers. Install the .045-inch tips, and spread the ring only enough to clear one side and tip it off. Do not attempt to slide it straight off, or the ring will be damaged. This operation is best done with the bolt body held in a padded vise.

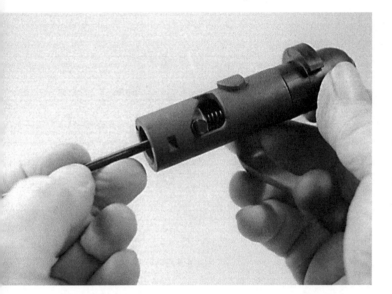

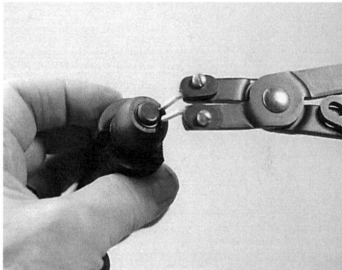

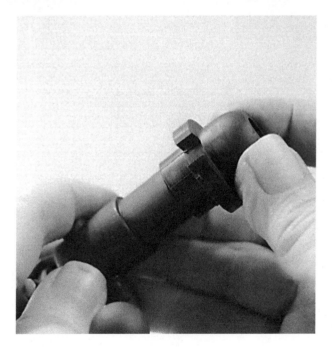

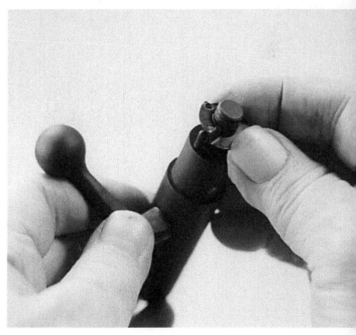

23. Remove the safety knob toward the rear.

24. Remove the safety detent plate toward the rear.

25. Remove the safety detent plunger and spring. Use a small hooked tool to pull out the spring.

26. The magazine can be disassembled for cleaning by pushing down the front of the follower until its rear end will clear the feed lips. The follower and its attached spring are then taken out upward.

Reassembly Tips:

1. ▪ When installing the safety detent plunger, note that its rounded end must go outward, to the rear.

2. ▪ When re-attaching the trigger spring, be sure its "hook" is inserted all the way through the hole in the trigger.

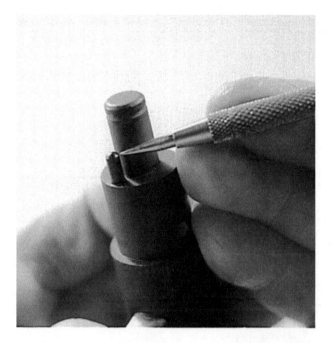

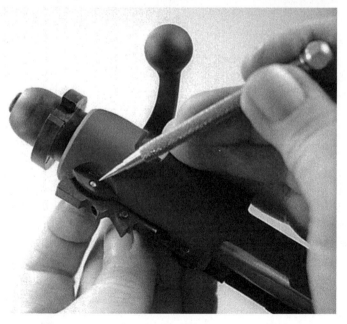

3. ▪ When installing the trigger group, use a short "slave pin" to hold the sear in place for reinsertion of the group cross pin. Put the bolt in to keep the sear in position. Be sure the sear spring enters its well in the trigger.

Mossberg Model 9200

Similar/Identical Pattern Guns:

The same basic assembly/disassembly steps for the Mossberg Model 9200 also apply to the following guns:

Model 9200 Viking　　　　**Bantam**

Crown Grade　　　　　　　**Custom Grade**

Special Hunter

Data:	Mossberg Model 9200
Origin:	United States
Manufacturer:	O.F. Mossberg & Sons, North Haven, Connecticut
Gauges:	12 only
Magazine Capacity:	4 rounds
Overall length:	44-1/2 inches
Barrel length:	24 inches (others offered)
Weight:	7-1/2 pounds

The Model 9200, introduced in 1992, was a slight re-design of the Mossberg Model 5500. Some of the instructions can also be applied to that gun. It should be noted that on several Mossberg shotguns, including this one, the manual safety systems cannot be disassembled easily. If repair is necessary, it is intended to be factory done. The company would likely wish it otherwise, but this is a legal protection.

Disassembly:

1. Cycle the action to cock the internal hammer, leaving the bolt in closed (forward) position. Set the manual safety in on-safe position. Unscrew the forend cap, and remove the forend toward the front.

2. Remove the gas cylinder cover.

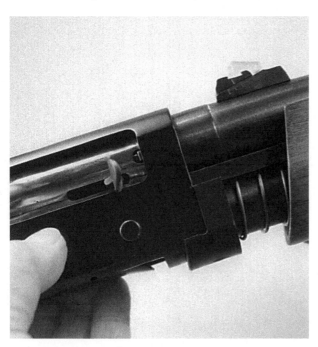

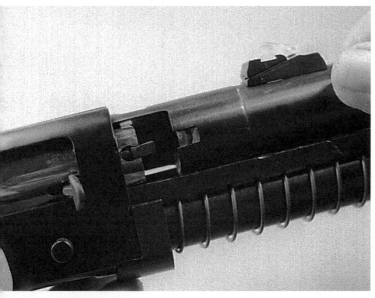

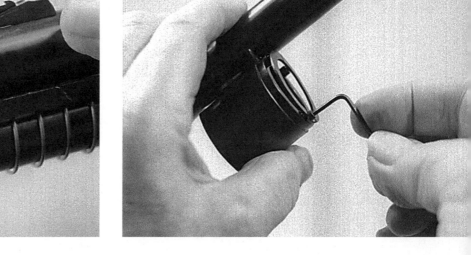

3. Remove the barrel toward the front. On this rifled-barrel version, the front sight blade can be moved sideways out of its dovetail by loosening the small Allen screw at the front. The rear sight base can be taken off by sliding the vertical adjustment plate off to expose the mounting screw.

4. The valve ball spring can be removed by taking out this Allen screw. This screw is tightly installed, and removal should be done only for repair purposes.

5. Use a magnet to lift out the two valve balls and prevent the loss of these small parts. Again, this system should be disassembled only for repair purposes.

6. Remove the O-ring and the forward seal ring.

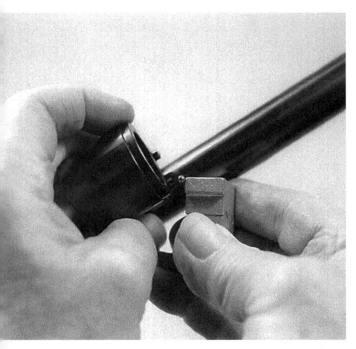

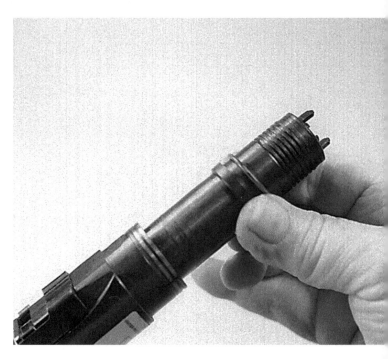

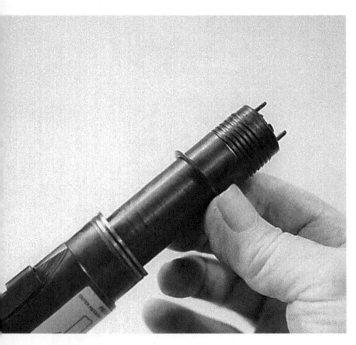

7. Remove the inner seal ring.

8. Move the action slide slightly to the rear, and remove the bolt handle. Control the action slide, as the spring, will tend to push it forward.

9. Ease the action slide forward until the bolt is clear of the receiver, and lift off the bolt.

10. Remove the action slide assembly.

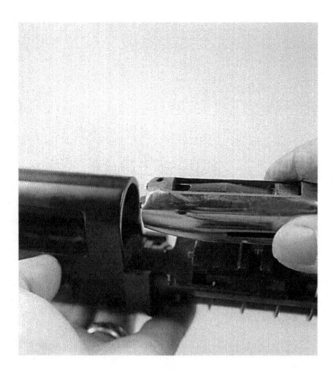

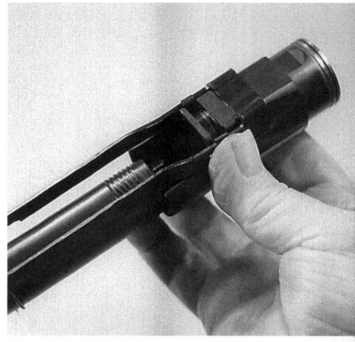

11. The outer piston ring should be removed only for repair. If necessary, it can be spread very slightly at its cut and taken off the front of the inertia weight.

12. Again, if necessary, the ends of the action bar spring retainer can be slightly compressed inward, and the action bar can be separated from the inertia weight.

13. This cross pin in the bolt base on the action bar retains the buffer plunger, coil spring, and bolt handle plunger. The spring is compressed, so control it, if this pin is drifted out.

14. Remove the action spring and the inertia weight buffer from the magazine tube. The magazine tube is not routinely removable.

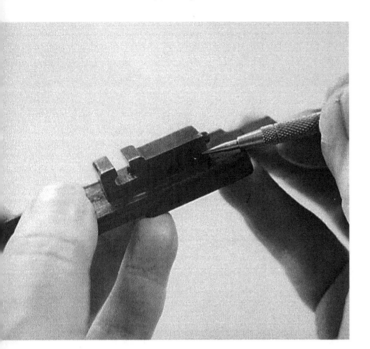

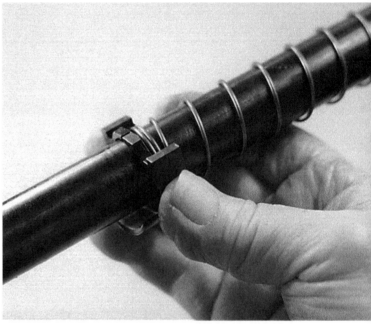

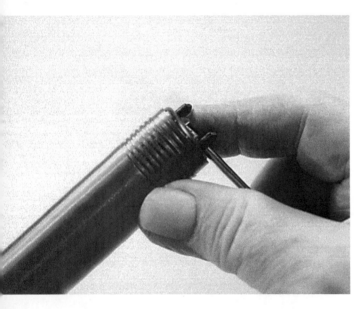

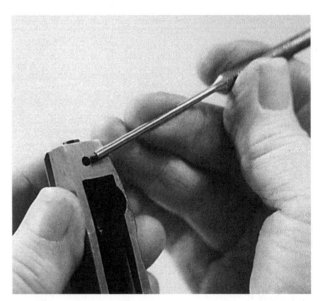

15. To remove the magazine spring, follower, and the forend cap detent, insert a tool to pry out the spring retainer, using alternate angles. Caution: The magazine spring will be released, so control the retainer. Wear eye protection.

16. Use a proper roll-pin drift to remove the firing pin retaining pin upward. Control the firing pin as the drift is withdrawn, and take out the firing pin and its spring toward the rear. This will free the locking block for removal from the bottom of the bolt.

17. Insert a sharp tool, such as a small screwdriver, between the extractor and its plunger. Depress the plunger rearward, and lift out the extractor. Ease the plunger and spring out for removal. Caution: Keep the plunger and spring under control. This operation is best done with the bolt in a padded vise.

18. Use a small drift, or the special Brownells tool shown, to push out the two trigger assembly retaining cross pins.

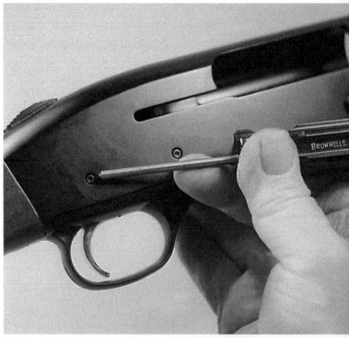

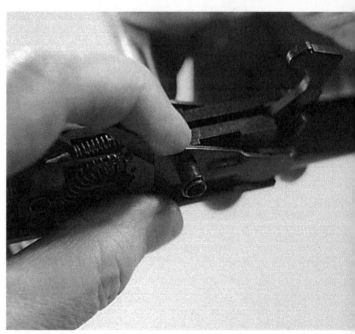

19. Remove the trigger assembly. Restrain the hammer, pull the trigger, and ease the hammer down to the fired position.

20. Restrain the carrier, and push out the carrier pivot toward the right. The cross-pin spring clip can be left in place on the pivot/sleeve.

21. Remove the carrier assembly from the trigger housing.

22. The carrier dog, or "pawl," is easily taken off by pushing out its pivot. The spring strut is retained on the carrier dog by a small roll pin.

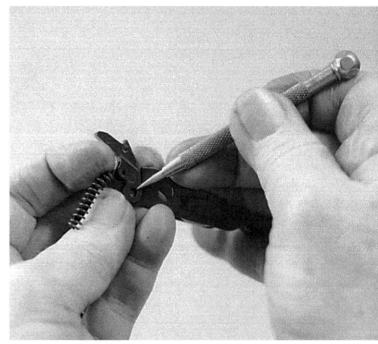

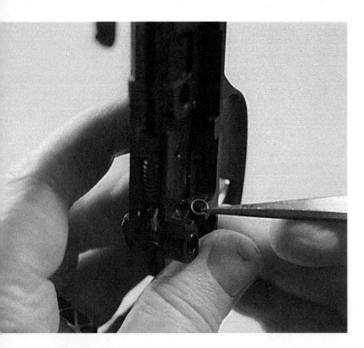

23. In the carrier spring recess on the right side of the trigger housing there is a small ring washer that keeps the spring end level. Take care that it isn't lost.

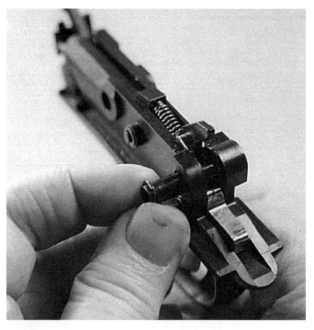

24. The rear cross-pin sleeve is easily taken out toward the left.

25. Depress the disconnector, and insert a tool (slim pliers are being used here) to detach the sear and trigger spring from its stud on the disconnector. Remove the spring rearward, pulling it off its stud on the sear.

26. It is not necessary to remove the C-clip from the trigger cross pin. Just push the pin out toward the left.

27. Remove the trigger and the attached disconnector upward. If necessary for repairs the stop pin and disconnector pivot can be drifted out of the trigger.

28. Push out the sear pin toward the left, and remove the sear upward.

29. Push out the hammer cross pin, and remove the hammer upward.

30. Removal of the hammer pin will also release the guideplate for removal. The guide plate pin is best left in place. It retains no part.

31. Insert a small tool to lift the hammer spring and follower for removal.

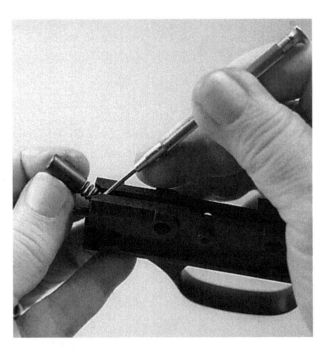

32. The shell stops are pivoted and retained by vertical pins in each side of the receiver. The pins are retained by spring clips in slots, and the clips are slid off the posts rearward. A dental tool, shown, or something similar, will be needed. Take care that the small spring clips are not lost.

33. If buttstock removal is necessary, it is retained by a through-bolt from the rear, accessible by taking off the recoil pad. Use a B-square stock tool or a long, large screwdriver. With the stock removed, two Allen screws will be visible at the rear of the receiver. These are not routinely taken out. They retain the bolt-buffer assembly, and the manual safety system is involved.

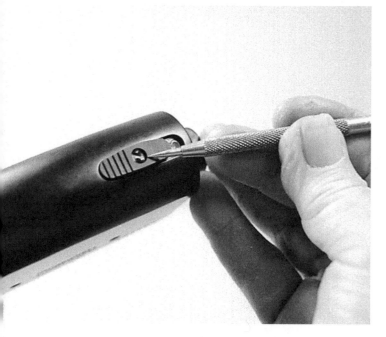

34. Note that the manual safety is installed with a "one-way" screw. It is intended that any disassembly of this system be done by returning the receiver to the factory.

Reassembly Tips:

1. When installing the combination sear/trigger/disconnector spring, remember that the smaller end of the spring goes on the sear stud, toward the front.

2. As the bolt and action slide are being moved back into the receiver some resistance may be felt as the system encounters the shell stops. USE NO FORCE. Turn the action slide slightly from side to side, keeping rearward pressure, and it will move into place.

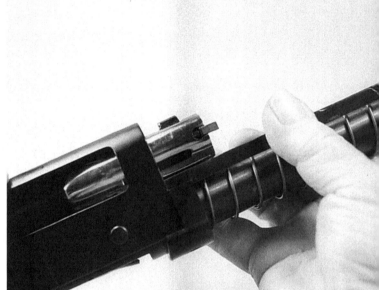

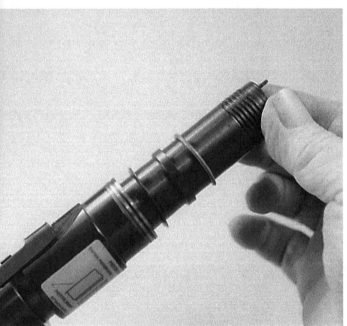

3. Install the three rings as shown, with the two steel rings having their beveled sides toward the rear.

Mossberg SA-20

Data: Mossberg SA-20
Origin: Turkey
Manufacturer: Kayhan Armsan, Turkey
Gauges: 20
Magazine Capacity: 5 rounds
Overall Length: 43.5 inches
Height: 6.75 inches
Barrel Length: 24 inches
Weight: 5.6 pounds

The SA-20 is a lightweight inexpensive semi auto manufactured in Turkey for Mossberg and imported by Mossberg International. Several versions are extant, including two tactical versions with and without pistol grip, and two field versions-full sized and the Bantam model covered here. They are all mechanically the same, save the different stock arrangement on the pistol grip tactical model, and have certain other cosmetic features that differ.

Disassembly:

1. Unscrew the magazine cap, then remove the forend by pulling it forward off the magazine tube.

2. Pull the bolt slightly to the rear then pull the barrel forward off the action.

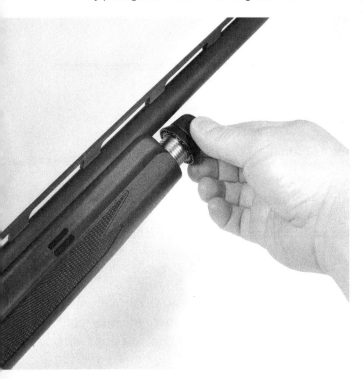

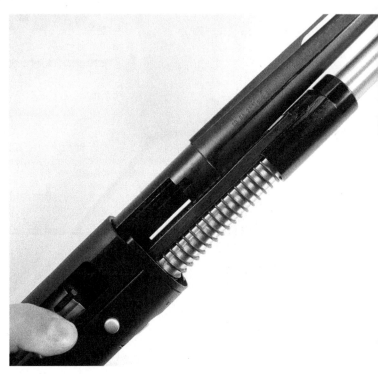

3. Remove the piston assembly from the barrel ring.

4. Only remove the gas seal from the barrel ring if it needs to be replaced. It resides in a groove near the front of the barrel ring.

5. Align the radius in the bolt body with the stem of the operating handle and pull the handle out to the right side. This will free the bolt carrier and action sleeve to spring forward out of the receiver, so control the entire assembly when removing the handle. Then pull the entire assembly off the magazine tube. Remove the action spring at this time as well.

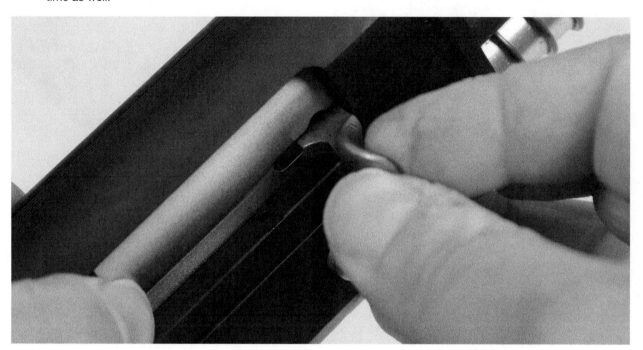

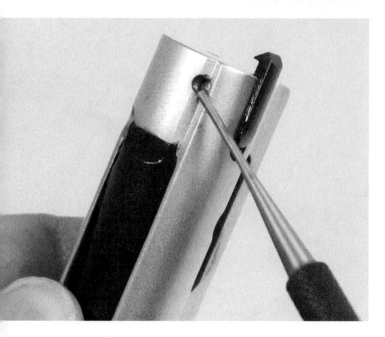

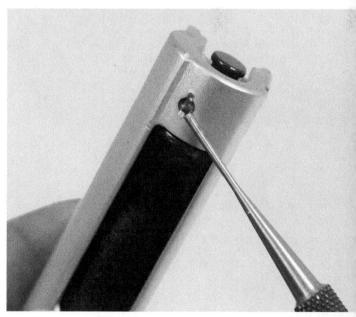

6. The extractor is held by this staked pin. It must be driven out from bottom to top.

7. The bolt lug is held in place by the firing pin and spring. To remove the firing pin and its spring, drive out this pin, again from bottom to top. This pin is also staked, so it would be advisable to leave it assembled unless replacement is necessary.

8. Drive out this trigger housing pin.

9. Remove the trigger housing by pulling forward and down on the trigger guard, while depressing the bolt release button.

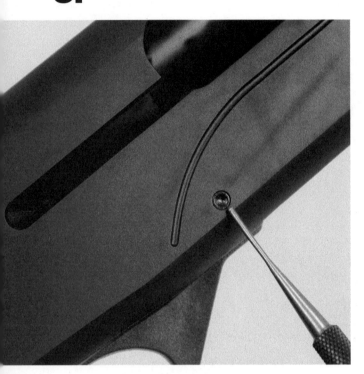

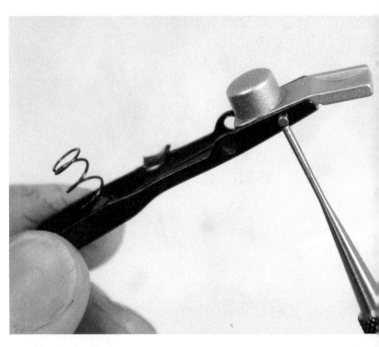

10. Remove the carrier latch by driving out this pin.

11. The carrier latch can be separated from the bolt release button by driving out this small pin. Beneath the button is a small stiff spring. Control the assembly when separating the parts.

12. The stock can be removed by first pulling the buttpad held by two screws. The stock itself is retained by this long bolt.

14. Push out the trigger housing bushing/hammer pin from right to left, as the left end has a small retaining spring clip. The hammer spring is compressed and should be controlled as the hammer pin is removed.

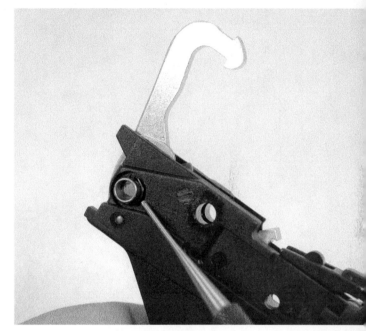

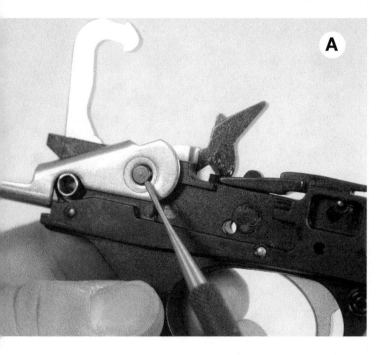

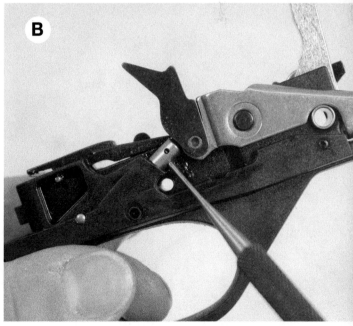

13. With the hammer forward, push out the carrier pin (Picture A). The carrier will come off the housing forward and the carrier's spring and plunger must be controlled as the assembly is removed as they are highly compressed (Picture B).

15. The hammer can now be removed, as well as the small hammer spring plunger stop to its left. Remove the hammer spring and plunger from the housing.

16. This pin acts as a hammer stop and should there be need to replace it, it can be driven out to either direction.

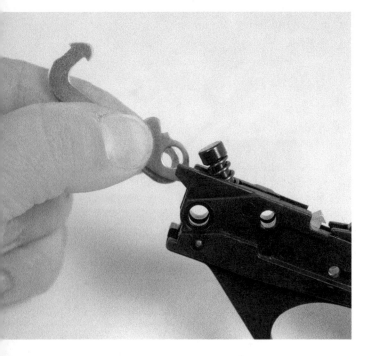

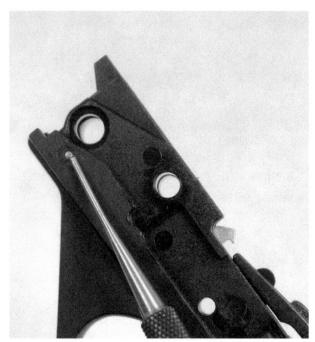

17. This pin holds the disconnector arm. Drive out the pin to free the arm and spring.

18. Drive out the trigger pin.

19. Pull the trigger assembly forward and up to remove it from the housing.

20. The disconnector can be separated from the trigger assembly by driving out this pin. The pin to the rear of the disconnector pin is acts as a disconnector stop.

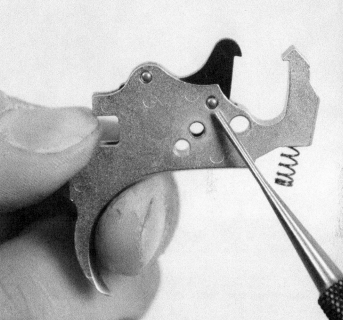

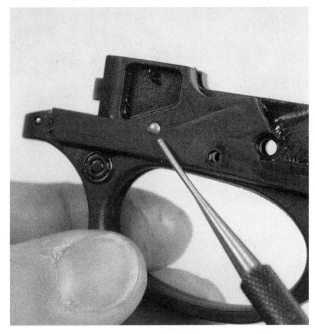

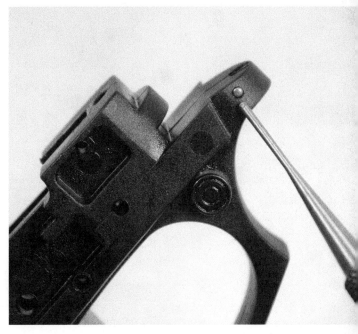

21. This pin acts as a trigger stop and need not be removed.

22. This pin retains the safety plunger and spring. Driving it out and removing those parts will allow the safety button to be pushed out to either side of the housing.

22. This pin retains the safety plunger and spring. Driving it out and removing those parts will allow the safety button to be pushed out to either side of the housing.

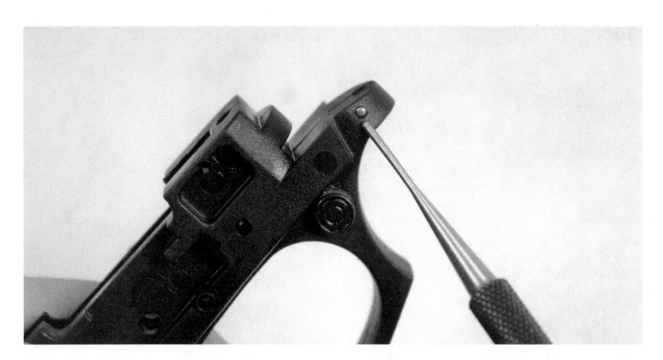

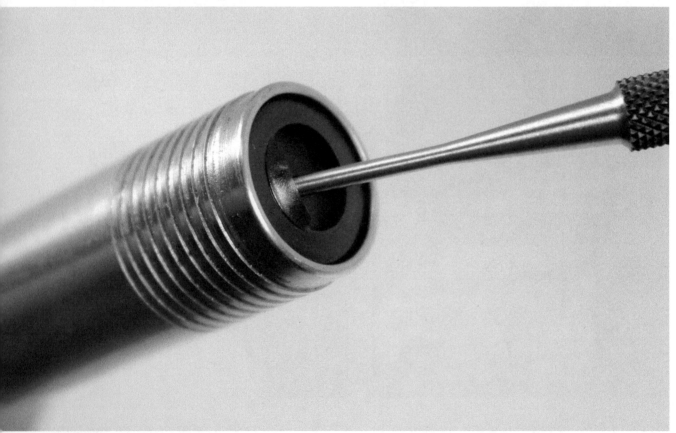

23. To remove the magazine plug, depress in the center of the plug into the magazine tube while lifting the retainer by the protruding flange. This will upset the flanged wing and allow its removal, followed by the plug.

Reassembly Tips:

1. When reinstalling the trigger housing, be sure to place the rear lip of the housing into the receiver and rotate the front into place. It is necessary to depress the bolt release button to prevent damage to the carrier latch.

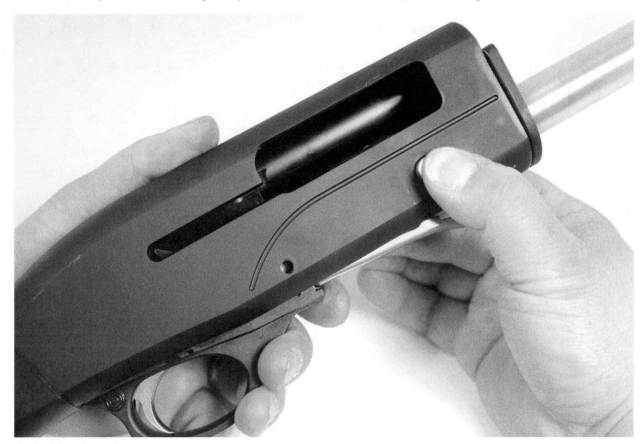

Mossberg Silver Reserve Over/Under

Similar/Identical Pattern Guns:

The following basic assembly/disassembly steps for the Silver Reserve O/U can also be used for the following guns:

Mossberg Onyx Reserve O/U

Data:	Mossberg Silver Reserve
Origin:	Turkey
Manufacturer:	Mossberg International, North Haven, CT
Gauges:	12, 20, 28, .410
Overall Length:	46 inches
Height:	7.25 inches
Barrel Length:	28 inches
Weight:	7 lbs. 11 oz.

The Silver Reserve shotguns are a series of low cost import guns available through Mossberg International. Several different versions are imported in the over/under style, such as the field model seen here, sporting models, and a bantam youth sized model. The higher priced, higher featured, prettier version, the Onyx Reserve, is functionally similar. Most models are fitted with extractors and some with ejectors, but there is otherwise little difference among the entire Reserve series of Over/Unders. A side-by-side set can also be purchased, but these steps do not apply to that pattern of shotgun.

Disassembly:

1. Pull out on the forearm latch to disengage the forearm. Pull the forearm from the barrels.

2. Push the top lever to open the action, then rotate the barrels off of the receiver.

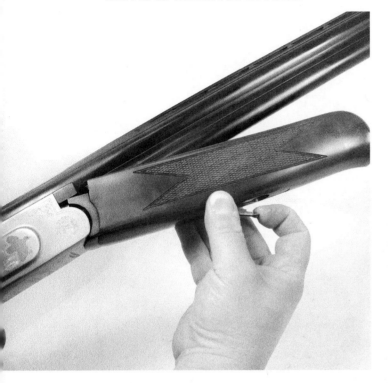

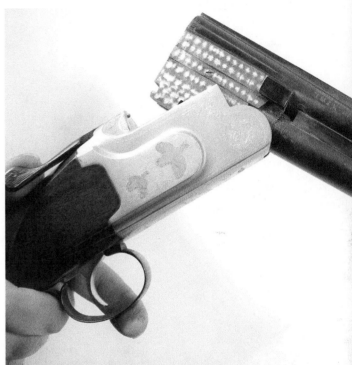

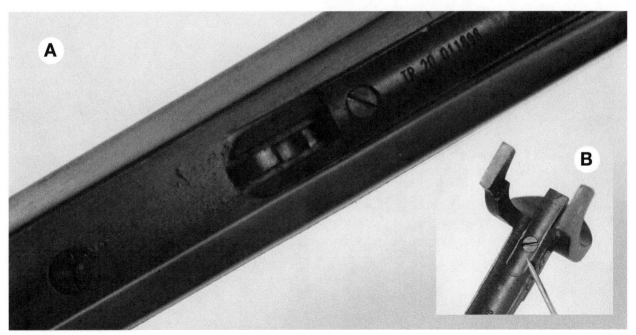

3. Remove the center screw in the handguard to take out the forend hardware (seen here on the right picture A). The rear screw holds the forearm bolt and need not be removed unless it needs to be replaced, seen in picture B.

4. Push out this pin to free the forend latch. The spring is retained under a hook on the other end of the latch housing.

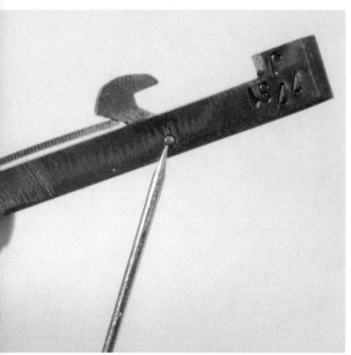

6. The stock is retained by a bolt. Remove the bolt, then pull the stock from the receiver.

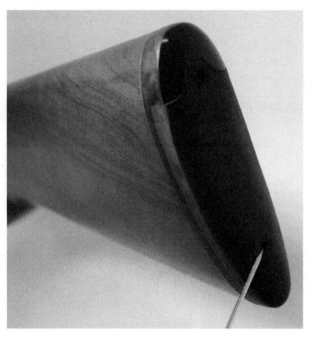

5. Remove the buttpad screws and the then the buttpad.

7. Close the top lever by depressing the top lever lock pin.

8. With the hammers forward, remove the hammer springs and guide rods. Control them as there is still compression present.

9. Drive out this pin and remove the hammers to the rear.

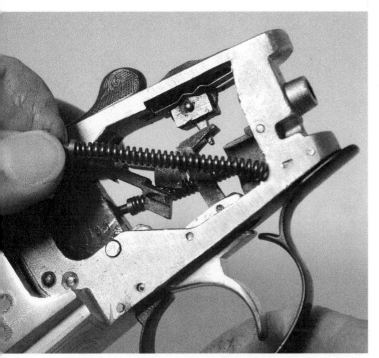

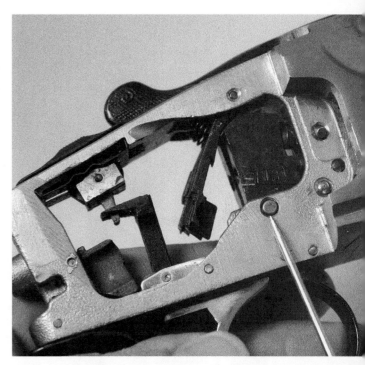

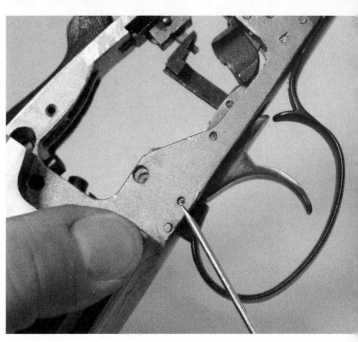

10. Drive out this pin to remove the sears and sear springs.

11. Drive out the front trigger guard pin.

12. Drive out the rear trigger guard pin, then remove the trigger guard.

13. Drive out this pin to remove the receiver under cover. There is a tab at the front of the under cover that, with the pin, holds the cover in place.

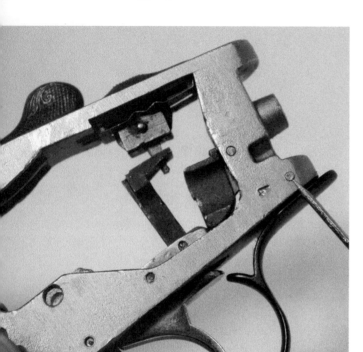

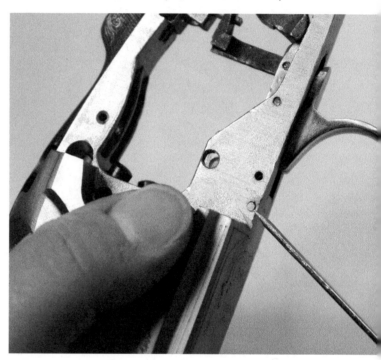

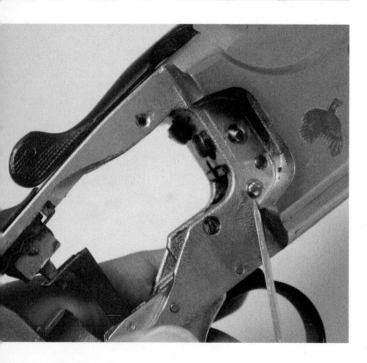

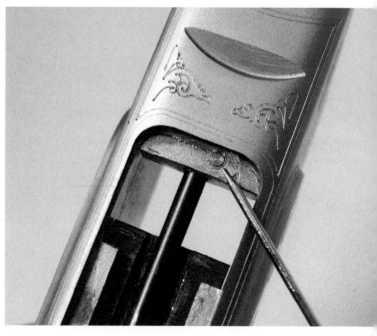

14. Drive out this pin to remove the cocking lever and spring. The parts may be pulled from the bottom of the receiver.

15. Drive out this pin. The cocking rod may now be pushed out the front of the receiver.

16. To remove the firing pins and springs, this pin must be pushed out from left to right.

17. Drive out this pin. It retains the top lever in the receiver.

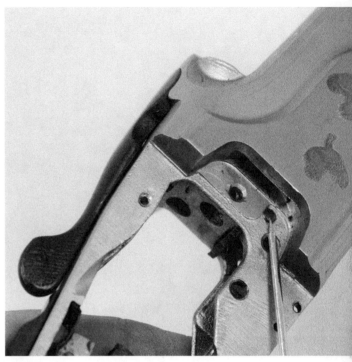

18. Pull out the retaining plate to the rear.

19. Turn this "screw" head (top lever tube) counterclockwise. It will cam up the top lever for removal. It encapsulates the top lever spring and can be eased out of its hole (Picture A). The top lever locking detent and spring will also be exposed at this time and should be controlled as the top lever tube is turned or it will be expelled from the top lever (Picture B).

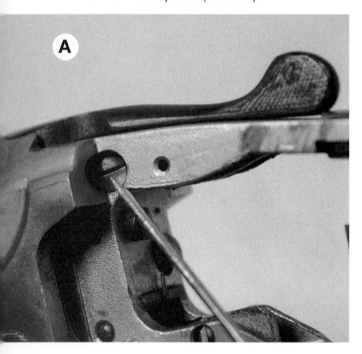

A

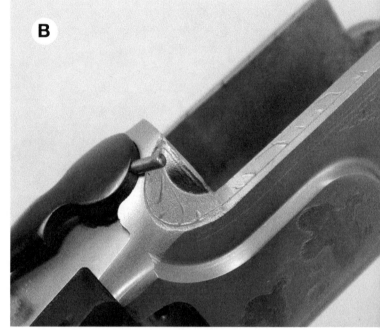

B

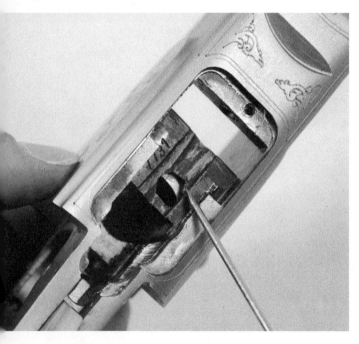

20. Push the blocker plate forward into the gap of the receiver and remove down.

21. Drive out this pin to remove the floating block.

22. Drive out this pin to disassemble the safety mechanism. The button itself should be lifted out first, followed by the pointed lower block, then the spring.

23. Drive out the trigger pin and remove the trigger and link out through the bottom.

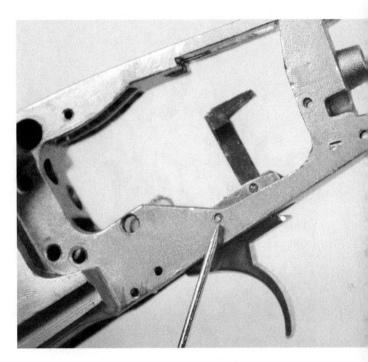

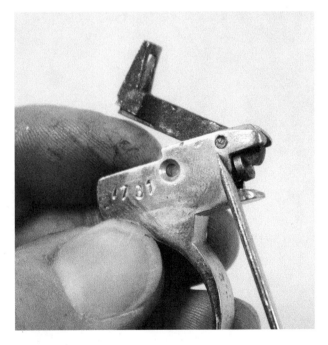

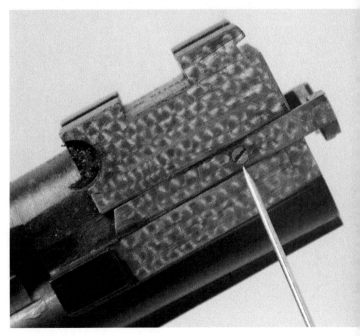

24. The link can be removed from the trigger by driving out this pin. The spring and plunger will also be freed. Control the spring and plunger.

25. Removing this screw will free the extractor to be removed to the rear of the barrel assembly.

Reassembly Tips:

1. The little tab on the safety spring goes to the front.

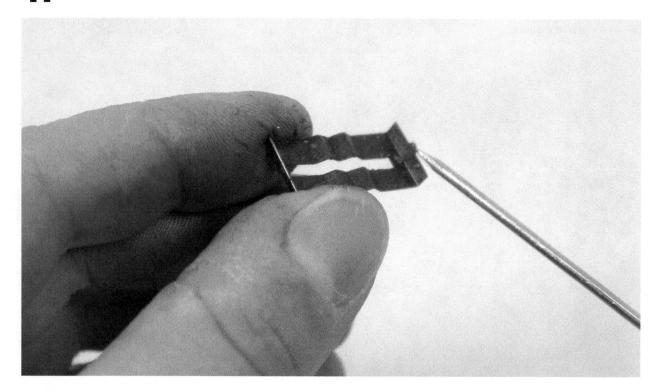

Mossberg Silver Reserve Side by Side

Similar/Identical Pattern Guns:

The following basic assembly/disassembly steps for the Silver Reserve SxS can also be used for the following guns:

Mossberg Onyx Reserve SxS

Data:	Mossberg Silver Reserve
Origin:	Turkey
Manufacturer:	Mossberg International, North Haven, CT
Gauges:	12, 20, 28, .410
Overall Length:	46 inches
Height:	7.25 inches
Barrel Length:	28 inches
Weight:	7 lbs. 11 oz.

This is the side-by-side counterpart to Mossberg International's Silver Reserve Over/Under. The black Onyx Reserve has a like takedown procedure. They are mid-price range shotguns for well under a thousand dollars, thus filling a niche between the low end $400 guns and the higher end $1000 on up guns.

Disassembly:

1. Depress the forend latch button to free the forend, then remove it from the barrels.

2. Remove this screw and pull the extractors rearward off the barrels.

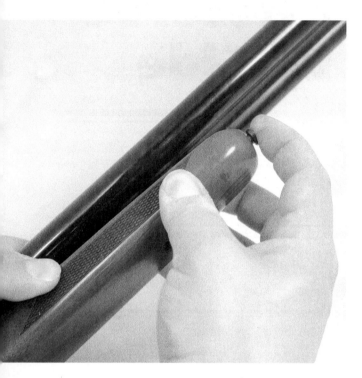

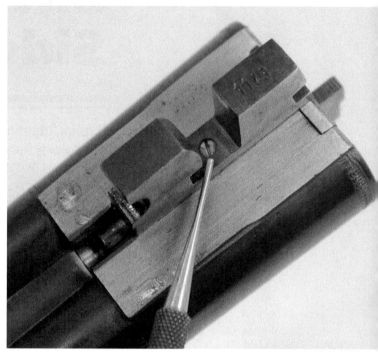

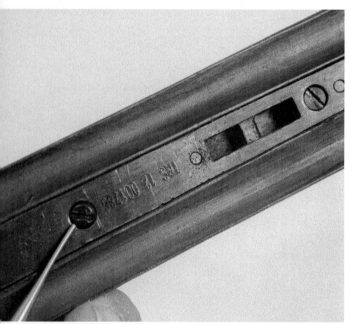

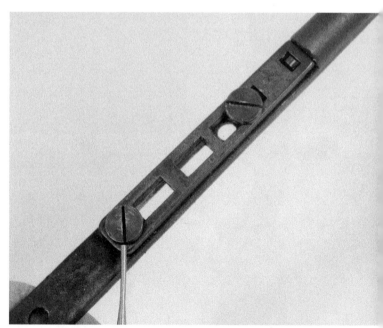

3. These two screws, the front a machine screw and the rear a wood screw, hold the forend metal to the forend.

4. These two large flat screws hold the forend latch bar to the forend metal. Remove these screws while holding the latch button depressed. Then lift the bar off the button's shaft. The button and spring can then be pulled from the front of the forend.

5. This spring pin retains the extractor cam.

6. Remove the buttpad by unscrewing the two buttpad screws.

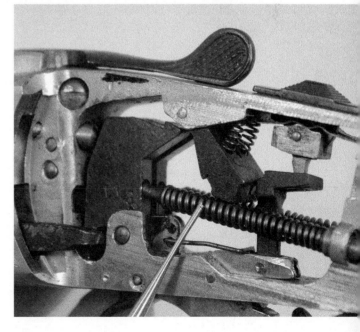

7. The stock is held to the receiver by a large bolt. Remove the bolt and pull the stock from the receiver.

8. With the hammers forward, remove the hammer springs and guides. Pull the forward ends back and then out to the side to clear the hammers.

9. Drive out this pin to remove the sears.

10. Drive out this pin to remove the hammers.

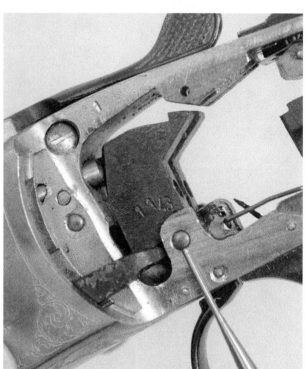

11. Push out the front trigger guard pin.

12. Push out the rear trigger guard pin and pull the trigger guard down off the receiver.

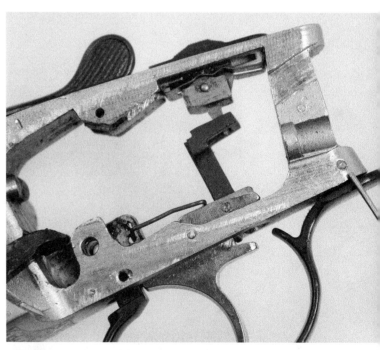

13. Remove the trigger spring by pushing the forward end to the right to dislodge it, then "threading" the spring around and out.

14. Push out the safety retaining pin to free the selector link to be removed down. The safety button can then be pulled up and out and the safety spring can be pulled down and to the side.

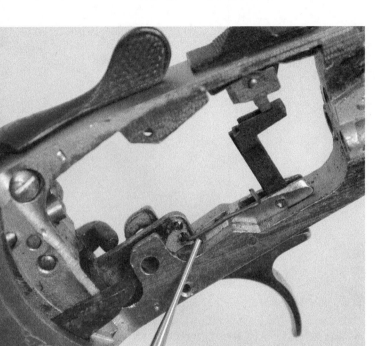

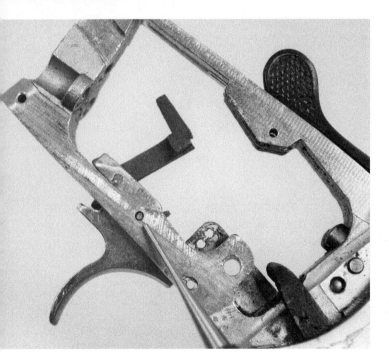

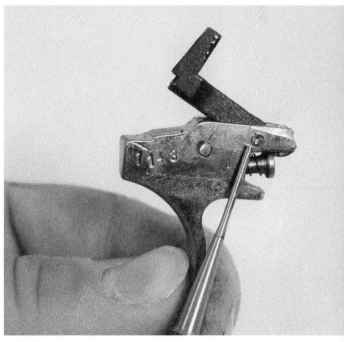

15. Drive out this pin to remove the trigger. Pull the trigger down through the bottom of the receiver.

16. The trigger assembly can be disassembled by driving out this staked pin. However there is no need unless repair is necessary.

17. Drive out this pin (which is actually two small pins, one on either side) to remove the cocking levers. The cocking levers will pull out of the receiver to the rear.

18. Drive out this pin to remove the firing pins and springs.

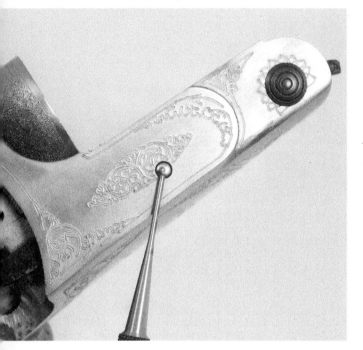

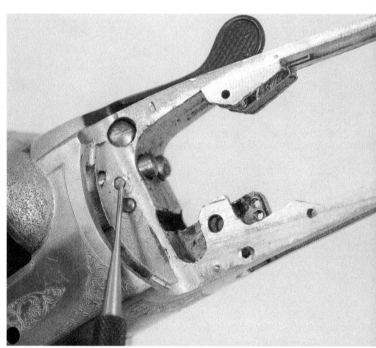

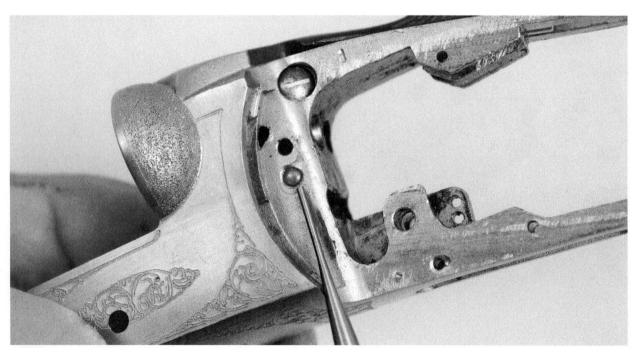

19. While holding the top lever centrally, drive out this pin, which is the top lever retaining pin.

20. Removing the top lever retaining pin will allow the lever to move to the left of centerline of the receiver. This will provide clearance for the top lever spring and follower to jump out of the receiver. Control them as the top lever is slowly released.

21. Pull the top lever up and out of the receiver.

22. Remove the barrel latch plate from the receiver by pulling it out to the rear.

Reassembly Tips:

23. These are hinge pin covers. Do not remove them or the hinge pin unless the pin needs replacement.

1. Reinstalling the top lever retaining pin is simplified by using a punch to hold the top lever and its spring and plunger in place. Drive the punch out with the installation of the pin.

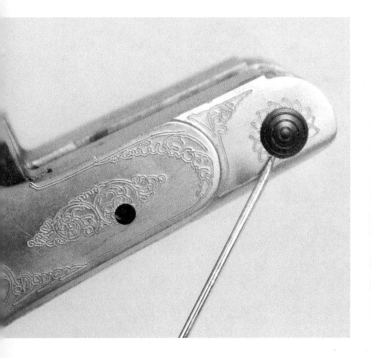

Parker Double

Similar/Identical Pattern Guns:

The same basic assembly/disassembly steps for the Parker Double also apply to the following guns:

**Parker Reproductions Double   Remington Parker AHE
Winchester Parker**

Data:	Parker Double
Origin:	United States
Manufacturer:	Parker Brothers, Meriden, Connecticut
Gauges:	10, 12, 16, 20, 28, and 410
Overall length:	43-1/2 inches (with 28-inch barrel)
Barrel length:	26 to 32 inches
Weight:	7 to 9 pounds

From the first external hammer gun of 1868, the Parker has been known for its quality and reliability. The serious Parker collectors have pursued the breed so avidly that these shotguns are now almost too valuable to shoot. The internal hammer version was introduced in 1889, and was made until about 1939, the last 5 years under Remington auspices. There are slight variations in the mechanism among the many options that were offered, but the basic action was unchanged, and the instructions will apply to the entire line. This includes the excellent Parker Reproductions guns that were made in Japan from 1984 to 1989.

Disassembly:

1. Open and close the action to cock the hammers. Pull the forend latch lever outward, and remove the forend downward and toward the front. Some models have a plunger-and-roller system instead of the lever, and with these, the forend is simply tipped away from the barrel at the front and removed.

2. Operate the barrel latch lever, tip the barrels open beyond their usual stop point, and remove the barrels upward.

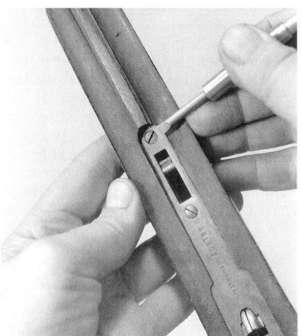

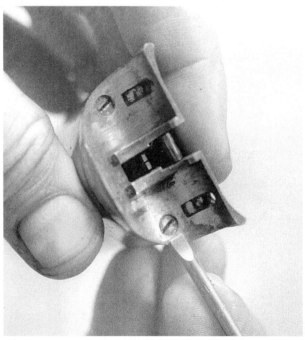

3. Remove the two wood screws on the inside top of the forend piece. If the forend has a steel tip inlay, backing out the small screw at the front will allow the tip to be removed.

4. Remove the two small screws at the rear of the forend iron, in the pivot curve.

5. Remove the forend iron assembly toward the rear.

6. Insert a small-diameter drift punch in the forward screw hole, from the top, and nudge the forend latch lever assembly out downward. Work slowly and carefully, taking care not to chip the wood around its recess.

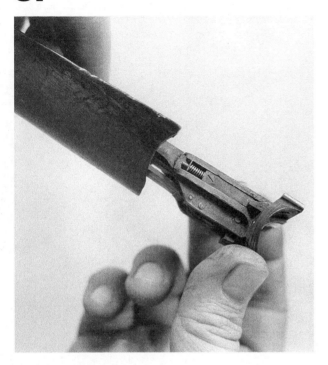

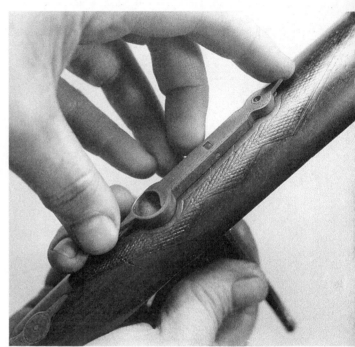

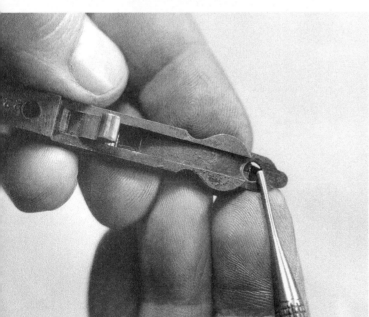

7. The forend latch lever spring is dovetail-mounted on the inside of the latch plate, and is pushed out toward the front for removal. The latch lever is retained by a cross pin, and the lever is taken out downward.

8. Push the rear tips of the ejector hammer sears downward to trip the hammers to the rear position, as shown, before disassembling the mechanism.

9. Drifting out the small cross pin on the underside of the forend iron at the front of the mechanism will release the ejector hammer springs and their cover for removal. Caution: The springs are under tension. Control them, and ease them out. The next pin toward the rear, a slightly larger pin, is the pivot for the ejector hammer sears, and the large cross pin at the rear pivots and retains the ejector hammers. The sears are taken out forward and downward, and the hammers are removed upward. After the hammers are taken out, the cocking plate can be removed toward the front.

10. To remove the ejector sear control bars on each side, insert a screwdriver under the front edge of the spring base, tip its front outward, and remove the base plate toward the front. Back out the small screw on the side of each bar, and the bar, spring, and guide can be slid out toward the front.

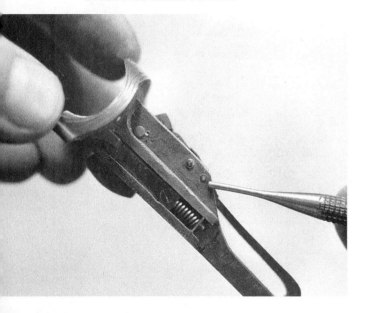

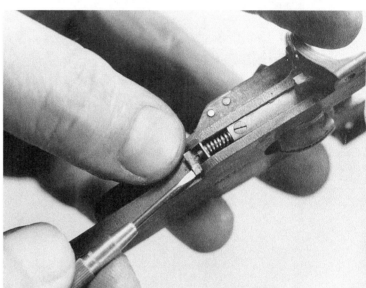

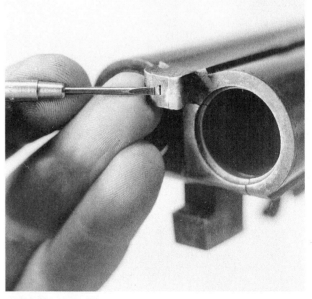

11. Remove the large screw on the left side of the barrel underlug, and take off the cocking hook downward, and its spring and plunger toward the rear.

12. Removal of the tiny screw in the top rear extension of the barrel rib will allow a small plate to be slid upward, and the ejectors can then be taken out toward the rear.

13. Remove the screw in the rear tail of the trigger guard, move the tail out of its recess in the stock, and rotate the guard counter-clockwise (bottom view) to unscrew it from the receiver.

14. With the barrel latch lever locked in open position, remove the large screw at the center of the upper tang. After the screw is removed, insert a tool in the slot in the breech face and depress the trip to return the lever to the center position.

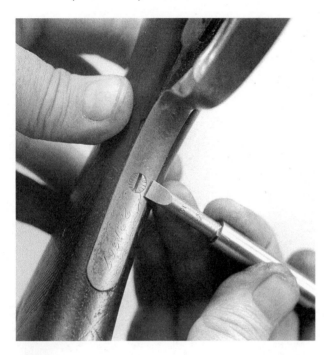

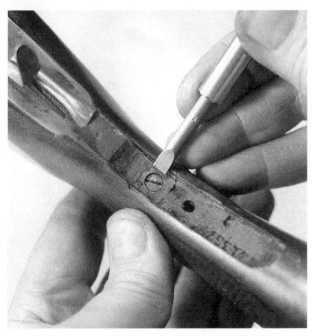
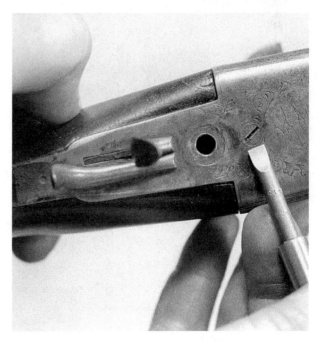

15. Remove the vertical screw on the underside at the rear tip of the trigger plate.

16. Remove the three screws on the underside of the receiver, forward of the triggers.

17. After the screws are removed, insert a brass or nylon drift punch from the top to nudge the trigger plate off downward. The cocking slide will likely come off with the trigger plate.

18. After the trigger plate is removed, move the stock carefully toward the rear, tipping it downward to clear the internal mechanism.

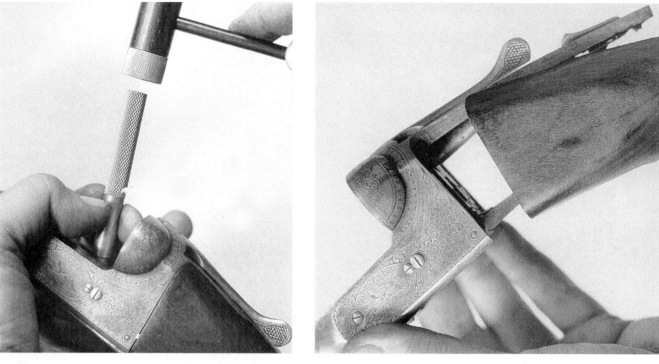

19. Tap the safety lever from below to raise its housing upward out of the stock. When the housing is out, drifting out the cross pin will release the lever for removal.

20. Use a screwdriver wide enough to contact both notches, and unscrew the screw sheath from the top of the stock. The automatic safety pin can now be pushed out of the stock toward the front.

21. Remove the small vertical screw behind the triggers to release the double spring for removal.

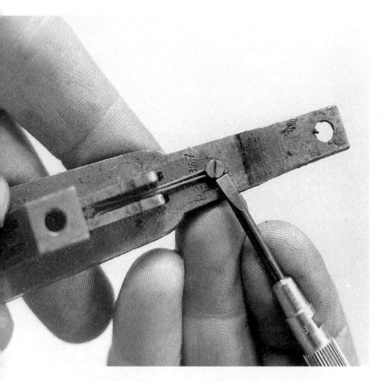

22. A cross screw retains the triggers at the front of the block on the inside of the trigger plate.

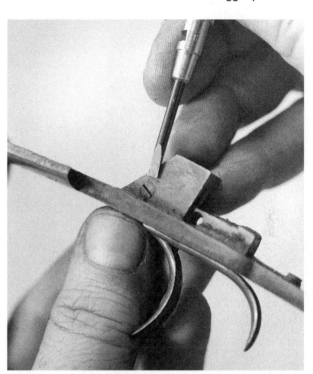

23. Remove the small screw on the right side of the trigger plate, just to the rear of the front lobe, and move the unhooking slide out toward the front, along with its spring and plunger.

24. Lift the barrel latch trip, along with its plunger and spring, out of its recess in the bottom of the receiver. This unit will occasionally come out when the trigger plate is removed, so take care that it isn't lost.

25. Remove the two small screws, one on each side, in the forward flat of the receiver. These are the cover screws for the cocking crank pin, which is not removed at this time.

26. Push the sear tails upward to drop the hammers, and drift out the cross pin that pivots and retains the sears. Remove the sears downward.

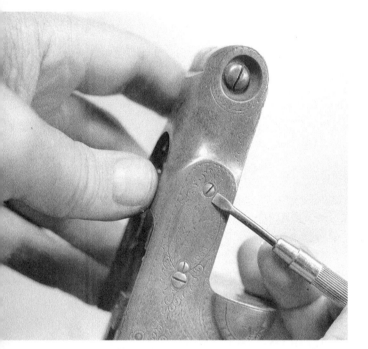

27. After the sears are removed, the dual sear spring is slid out toward the rear.

28. Remove the lock screw, then back out the hammer pivot screw on each side. While the screws are being taken out, exert pressure on the back of the hammers to ease removal.

29. Remove the hammers toward the rear. Drifting out the cross pin in each hammer will release the hammer strut for removal.

30. Remove the hammer springs and their plungers toward the rear.

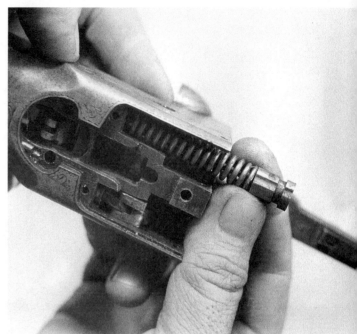

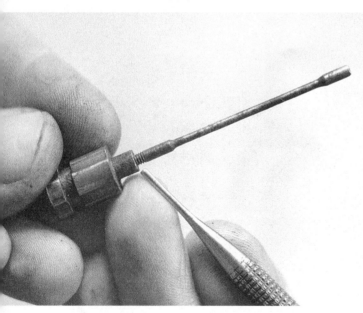

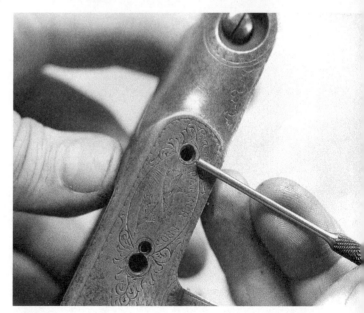

31. Note that the ejector control pin is screwed into the front of each hammer spring plunger, and its depth controls the degree of protrusion at the front of the receiver. These pins are best not disturbed in normal disassembly.

32. After the hammers and hammer springs have been removed, insert a long-shanked punch into one of the screw holes cleared in step #25, and push out the cocking crank pin toward either side. Remove the cocking crank from the receiver.

33. Push out the small cross pin in the lower projection of the safety button. Remove the safety spring downward, and the safety button upward.

34. Tip the barrel latch lever spring housing out of its recess on the underside of the upper tang, and remove the housing, spring, and plunger toward the rear.

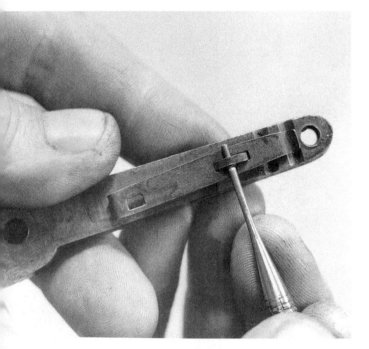

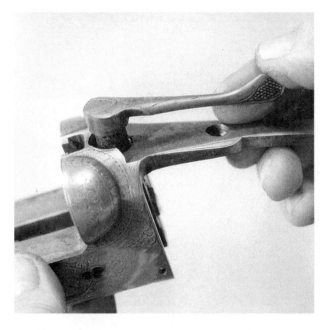

35. Remove the small screw on the left side of the receiver, just above the left hammer recess.

36. Remove the barrel latch lever upward. If the lever is tight, do not exert any pressure on the rear tail. If necessary, it can be nudged by inserting a drift into the spring plunger opening.

37. Slide the barrel latch block straight out toward the rear.

38. On the Parker shown, the unhooking pin and its spring are retained by a vertical pin which is driven out upward to release the pin and spring. This was originally a vertical screw, removed upward. The unhooking pin and its spring are taken out toward the front.

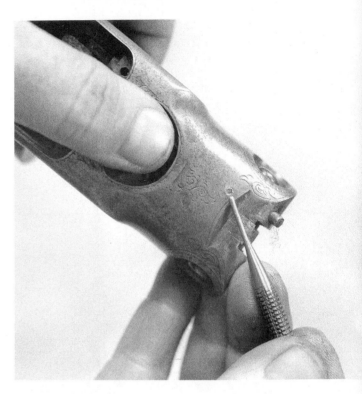

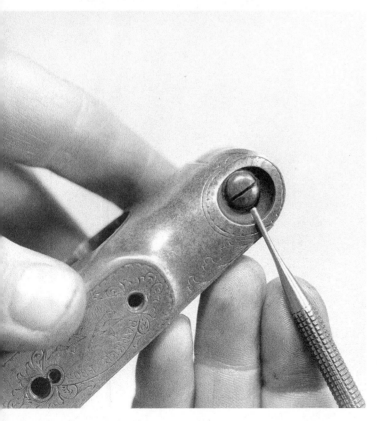

39. The barrel pivot cover screw can be removed, and the barrel pivot pushed out toward the right, but in normal disassembly this system is best left in place. Removal of the pivot will free the ejector actuator ("joint roll"), if necessary for repair.

Reassembly Tips:

1. When replacing the hammer springs, use a tool to depress the follower, and insert a drift into the hole provided on each side to retain the follower while the hammer is installed. Caution: Take care not to dislodge the drift from the hole during this operation, as the hammer springs are powerful.

2. When replacing the cocking slide on the underside of the receiver, be sure the opening in its forward end engages the lower lobes of the cocking crank, as shown.

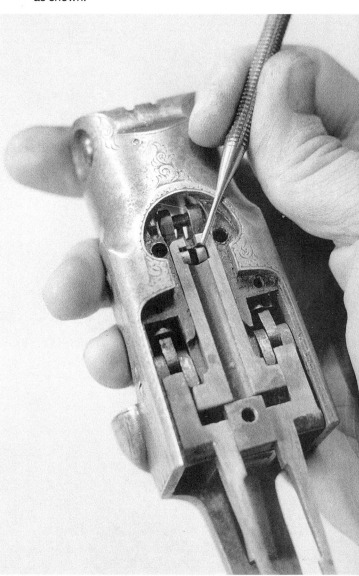

When replacing the stock, be sure the upper extension of the safety lever engages its slot in the safety spring. To check this, with the stock held against the upper tang, move the safety, and see that the lever changes position.

When replacing the forend latch lever assembly, be sure the rear extension of the lever engages inside its recess in the latch tumbler.

Remington Model 870

Similar/Identical Pattern Guns:

The same basic assembly/disassembly steps for the Reimington Model 870 also apply to the following guns:

Remington Model 870 LT-20	**Remington Model 870ADL**
Remington Model 870AP	**Remington Model 870BDL**
Remington Model 870D	**Remington Model 870DL**
Remington Model 870F	**Remington Model 870SA**
Remington Model 870SF	**Remington Model 870 SP**
Remington Model 870TB	**Remington Sportsman Pump**

Data: Remington Model 870
Origin: United States
Manufacturer: Remington Arms Company
Gauges: 12, 16, and 20
Magazine capacity: 4 rounds
Overall length: 48-1/2 inches (with 28-inch barrel)
Barrel length: 26 to 30 inches
Weight: 6-1/4 to 7-1/2 pounds

Introduced in 1950 to replace the Model 31, the Remington 870 has been made in a wide variety of sub-models, but all have the same basic mechanism. The trigger group design is particularly notable, having made its first appearance in the Model 11-48 autoloader, and used with only slight variation in every Remington rifle and shotgun (auto or slide action) made since. The Model 870 is a simple and reliable gun, and is still in production today.

Disassembly:

1. Open the action, and unscrew the magazine cap and remove it. Pull the barrel straight out toward the front.

2. Insert a screwdriver to pry the magazine spring retainer from inside the front of the magazine tube. Move the screwdriver to pry the retainer in equal increments, to avoid warping it. Caution: The magazine spring is under tension, so control the retainer and ease it out Remove the spring and follower toward the front.

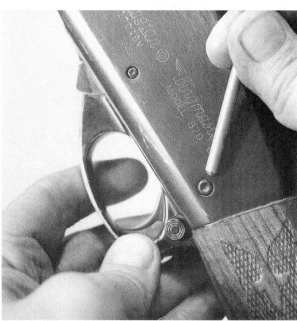

3. Move the action slide back to the front, bringing the bolt to the closed position, and set the safety in the on-safe position. Push out the large and small cross pins at the lower edge of the receiver toward either side.

4. Remove the trigger group downward, tilting it slightly as it emerges to clear the arm of the slide lock on the left side.

5. Restrain the carrier by resting a thumb on the carrier dog, and push out the carrier pivot, which is also the front cross pin sleeve.

6. Slowly release the tension of the carrier spring, and remove the carrier upward and toward the front. Remove the carrier spring and plunger from the right side of the trigger housing. Note that the carrier dog and its washer/plate are retained on the right rear wing of the carrier by a cross pin that is riveted in place. If removal is necessary for repair, be sure the wing of the carrier is well supported.

7. Move the safety to the off-safe position, restrain the hammer, pull the trigger, and ease the hammer down to the fired position. Keeping the trigger pulled to the rear, push out the rear cross pin sleeve toward the left and remove it.

8. Removal of the rear cross pin sleeve will allow the top of the trigger to move to the rear beyond its normal position, easing the tension of the combination sear and trigger spring. This spring is now easily detached from its studs on the sear and trigger and is removed upward.

9. Drift out the trigger cross pin.

11. The sear cross pin is accessible by angling a drift punch on the right side into the top of the carrier spring hole, and the sear pin is nudged out toward the left for removal with smooth-jawed pliers. The sear is then removed upward.

10. Remove the trigger and its attached connectors upward. It will be necessary to tilt the trigger slightly to clear the left connector arm past the shelf on the housing. The cross pin that retains the connectors on the trigger is riveted in place, and should be removed only for repair. If removal is necessary, be sure the top of the trigger is supported firmly, and take care not to deform the upper extension of the trigger.

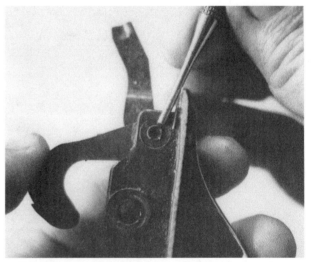

12. The hammer pivot is also the pivot and retainer for the slide latch/disconnector, and the pin is riveted on the right side over a washer which is set into a recess. Unless absolutely necessary for repair, this system should be left in place. If it must be removed, be sure the assembly is well supported on the left side when driving out the cross pin, and take care not to deform the slide latch. Use a drift that will enter the depression at the center of the cross pin. While driving out the pin, restrain the hammer spring plunger, as the spring will be released as the pin clears the slide latch. When the pin is out, ease the spring out slowly, and remove the plunger, spring, hammer, slide latch, and the round-wire slide latch spring.

13. Push out the small cross pin at the rear of the housing, and remove the safety spring upward, along with the safety detent ball, if it can be shaken out. Remove the safety button toward either side. If the ball can't be taken out upward, wait until the button is removed, then use a small tool to push the ball downward, for removal through the button tunnel. Take care that the small ball isn't lost.

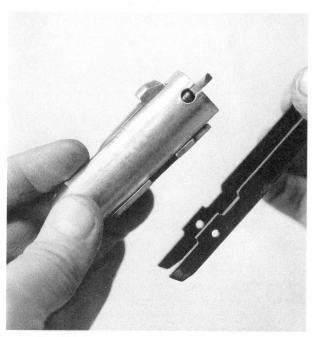

14. Insert a fingertip through the underside of the receiver to depress the left shell stop, and move the bolt and slide assembly out toward the front.

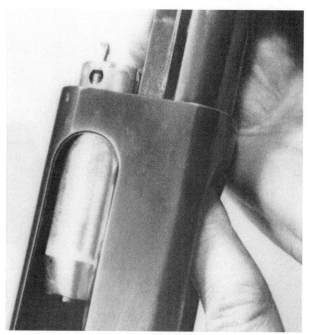

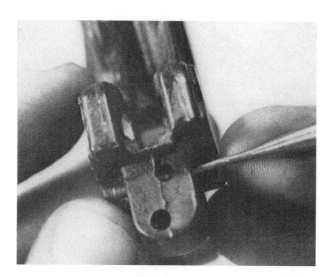

15. As soon as the slide bars are clear of the receiver, the bolt and locking slide are easily detached from the bars.

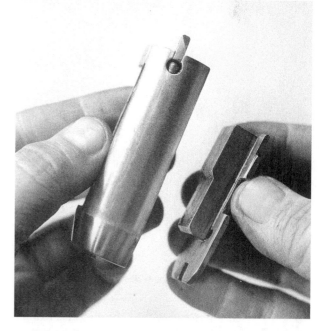

16. The locking slide is easily removed from the bottom of the bolt.

17. Drift out the vertical pin at the rear of the bolt downward, and remove the firing pin and its return spring toward the rear.

18. Remove the locking block downward.

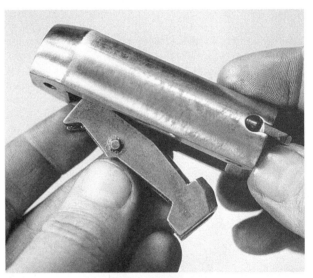

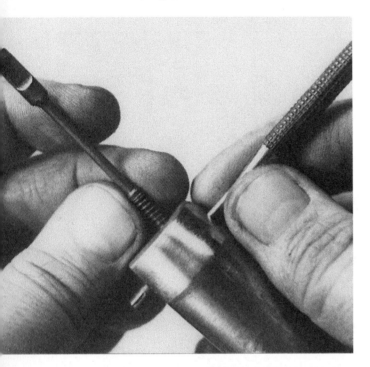

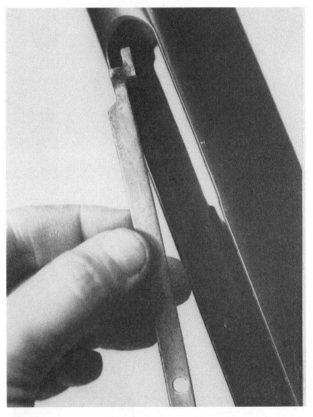

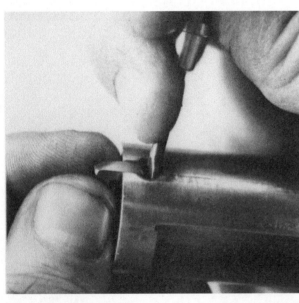

19. Insert a small screwdriver between the extractor and its plunger, depress the plunger toward the rear, and remove the extractor from its recess. Caution: Control the plunger, and ease out the plunger and spring for removal toward the front.

20. The right and left shell stops are lightly staked in their shallow recesses at the rear, and can usually be freed by inserting a tool beneath the rear tail of each one and prying them gently inward. If the stakes are particularly heavy, angle a drift punch into the cross pin holes from inside the receiver, and nudge them slightly toward the rear to clear the stakes. Keep the right and left shell stops separate, as they are not interchangeable.

21. The ejector and its housing are attached to the inside left wall of the receiver by two riveted pins, through to the outside, and this assembly should not be disturbed unless necessary for repair. If replacement is necessary, this is a job for a competent gunsmith, or the factory.

22. Removal of the action slide assembly from the forend is much easier with a B-Square wrench made especially for this purpose. If the wrench is not available, a section of steel plate cut to the right dimensions can be used. The forend tube nut is unscrewed counter-clockwise (front view), and the tube and action bar assembly is taken out of the forend toward the rear.

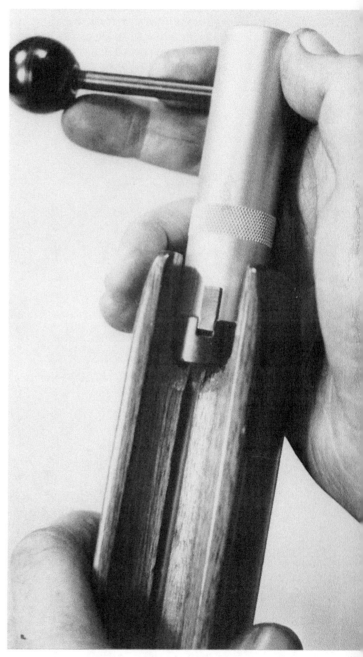

23. Remove the buttplate, and use a B-Square Model 870 stock tool or a long-shanked screwdriver to back out the stock mounting bolt. Remove the bolt, lock washer, and washer toward the rear. Take off the buttstock toward the rear, and remove the stock bearing plate from the rear of the receiver.

Reassembly Tips:

1. When replacing the shell stops, the upper extensions at the front must be inserted first, then the rear of the parts moved into the recesses on each side. Note that the stop with the recessed section goes on the left side. Temporarily inserting the front trigger group cross pin will help to hold the stops in alignment as they are re-staked in place. This can be done with an angled punch, but is much easier if a B-Square Remington staking tool is used, as shown.

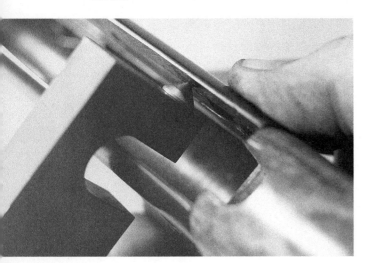

2. When replacing the trigger assembly in the housing, be sure the forward tip of the left connector is above the rear tail of the slide latch, as shown.

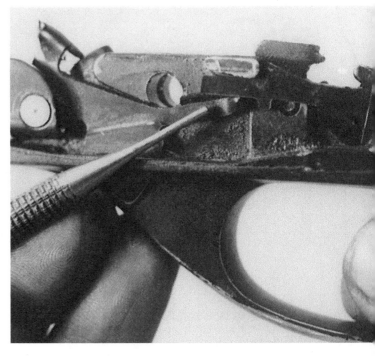

3. When replacing the carrier assembly, be sure the step at the rear of the carrier dog engages the top of the carrier spring plunger, as shown.

When replacing the bolt and slide assembly in the receiver, you must depress the shell stops in sequence as the assembly is moved toward the rear. Depress the right, then the left shell stop, in that order.

Remington Model 887

Similar/Identical Pattern Guns:

The following basic assembly/disassembly steps for the Remington 887 Nitro Mag can also be used for the following guns:

Remington 887 Nitro Mag
Tactical

Data:	Remington 887 Nitro Mag
Origin:	United States
Manufacturer:	Remington Arms Company, Ilion, NY
Gauges:	12
Overall Length:	48 inches
Height:	7.25 inches
Barrel Length:	28 inches
Weight:	7.4 pounds

Remington decided to create a weather-impermeable gun in the 887. Even the barrel is sheathed in polymer, leaving only the bore readily exposed to the elements. The sheathing even wraps around the muzzle to cover the inside of the barrel under the choke tubes. The Tactical model incorporates a much shorter barrel, optic rail, accessory rail on the magazine tube, and extended choke.

Disassembly:

1. With the slide pulled slightly to the rear, unscrew the magazine cap and remove the cap and the barrel.

3. The forend tube assembly and action bars can be separated from the forend for repair by removing this notched tube nut.

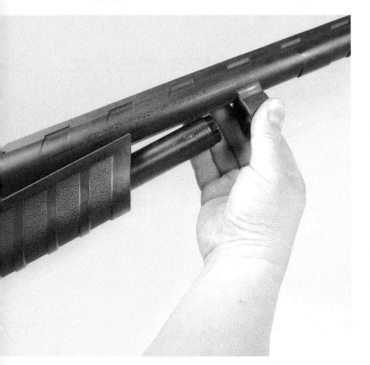

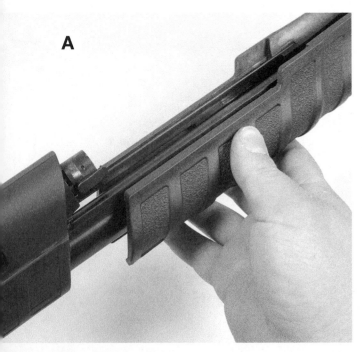

A

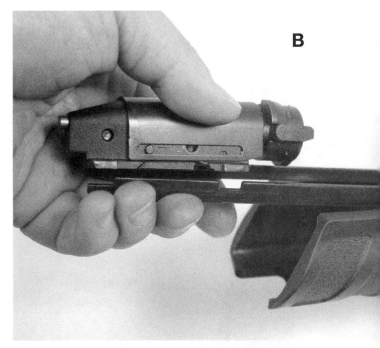

B

2. With the barrel removed, slide the forend assembly fully forward and off the magazine tube (Picture A). The bolt assembly will follow and will fall off of the action bars (Picture B) as it is retained only by the receiver walls.

4. Lift this tab to remove the ejection port cover from the bolt bolt assembly. It will lift over the top and lift its slot off of the small nub on the right side of the bolt.

5. Drive out the rear pin of the bolt assembly in the direction of its spline, to free the firing pin to be removed from the rear of the bolt.

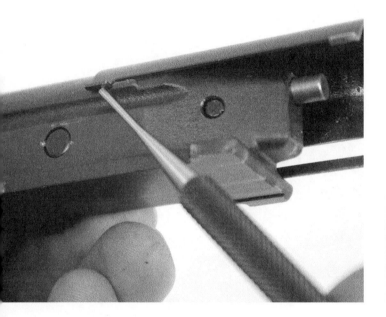

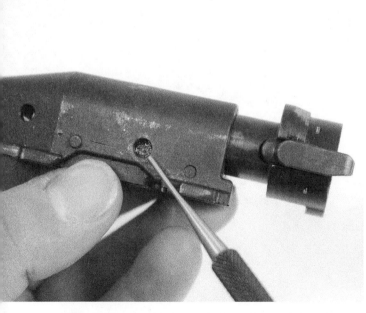

6. Drive out this large pin from right to left to free the bolt head. The bolt head will easily be removed from the front of the bolt body.

7. Drive out this pin to remove the extractor and spring.

8. Depress the magazine spring retainer and rotate it 90 degrees to align its channels and remove it from the magazine tube (Picture A). The spring behind it is compressed, so control it on its way out. Invert the magazine tube to remove the follower, which will also need to have its assembly channels aligned to exit the tube (Picture B).

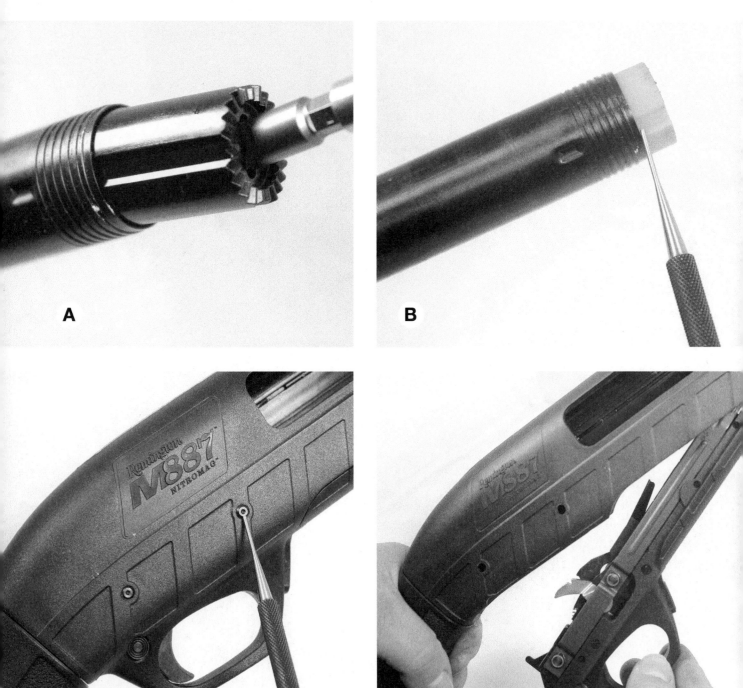

A

B

9. Drive out the two trigger plate pins. The front pin is slightly longer than the rear.

10. Remove the trigger plate assembly from the receiver by pulling it down at the rear and rotating it forward and out.

11. This long pin retains the ejector and ejector spring, which sit just to the rear of the pin. The pin is staked in place and should not be removed unless replacement is necessary.

12. To remove the buttpad, remove these two stock screws and pull the pad off the rear of the stock.

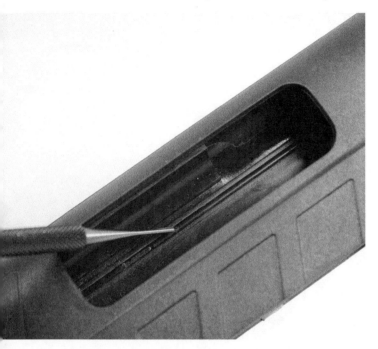

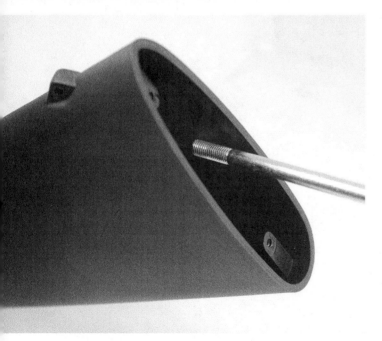

13. This long bolt retains the buttstock. Remove it to take the stock off the receiver.

14. With the hammer forward, remove the small spring clip from the rear trigger plate bushing. Then push this bushing out to the left.

15. As the rear bushing is removed the action bar lock spring on the left of the plate, under some tension, will be freed, as will the disconnector right behind it (Picture A). Furthermore, as the bushing is removed, the space allows the trigger top to move rearward and the tension is removed from the sear spring (Picture B). Remove it at this time.

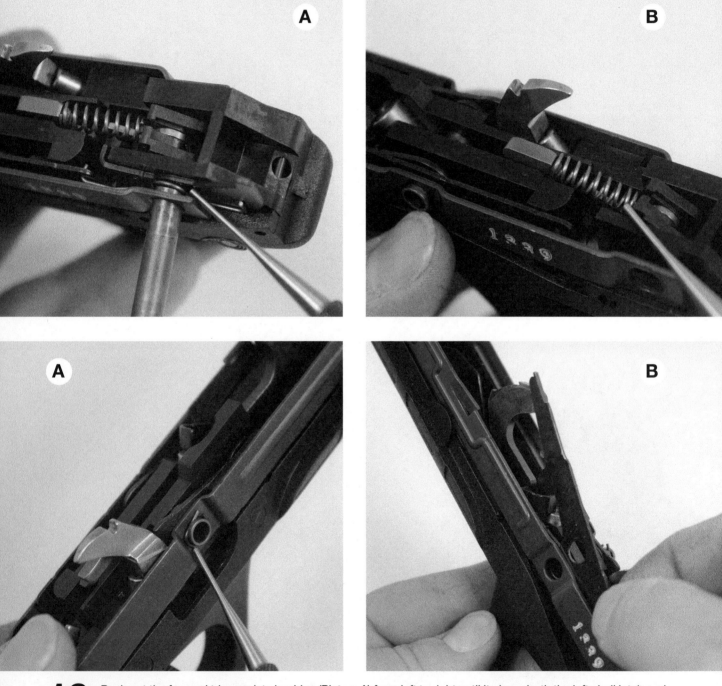

16. Push out the forward trigger plate bushing (Picture A) from left to right until it clears both the left shell latch and action bar lock. One end will have another spring clip. Then lift the lock up from behind the shell latch (Picture B). Then the left shell latch will follow.

17. Completely remove the front trigger plate bushing. This will allow the carrier to be removed forward and down. Control the carrier dog follower and spring as they will emerge with speed.

18. Lift and remove the right shell latch from the trigger plate.

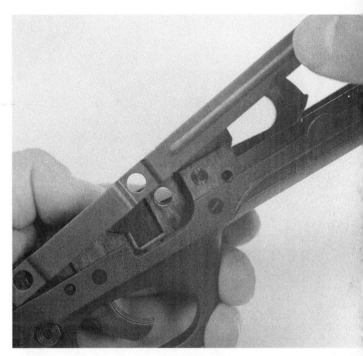

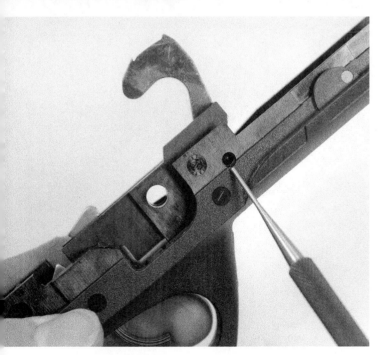

19. Drive out the hammer pivot pin to remove the hammer and action bar lock release. This will also free the hammer spring and follower, which are still slightly compressed.

20. Drive out the trigger pin and remove the trigger up through the receiver.

21. This pin retains the connector in the trigger.

22. Push out this pin to free the safety spring and detent ball. The safety button can now be removed to either side of the trigger plate.

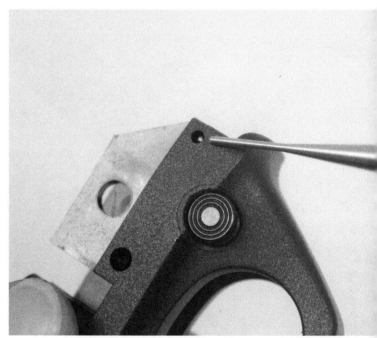

Reassembly Tips:

1. Remember that the firing pin retaining pin is spline and should be replaced in the same orientation as which it was removed.

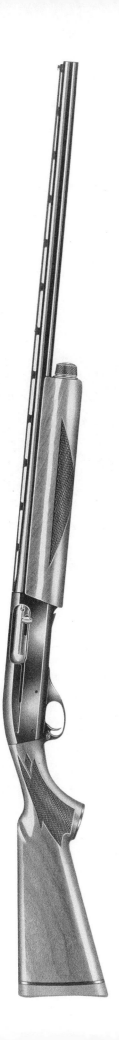

Remington Model 11-87

Data:	Remington Model 11-87
Origin:	United States
Manufacturer:	Remington Arms Company, Llion, New York
Gauges:	12
Magazine Capacity:	4 rounds
Overall length:	46 inches (with 26-inch barrel)
Barrel length:	26, 28 & 30 inches
Weight:	8-1/4 pounds

In 1987, Remington slightly redesigned the Model 1100, and the result was the Model 11-87. One of the main changes was a pressure-compensating gas system that would handle the lightest and heaviest loads without adjustment. While the mechanism of the Model 11-87 is very much like the Model 1100, there are a few important differences.

Disassembly:

1. Lock the action open, and set the safety in on-safe position. Unscrew and remove the magazine end cap.

2. Remove the forend toward the front.

3. Remove the gas cylinder collar.

4. Remove the barrel toward the front.

5. The gas cylinder spring is not removed in normal takedown.

6. Remove the rubber gas seal ring, and the piston and piston seal ring toward the front.

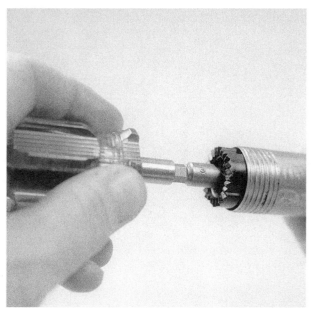

7. To remove the magazine spring and follower, use a screwdriver in the slot in the end piece to depress the end piece about an inch, turn it 90 degrees in either direction, and ease it out. Control the compressed spring,

8. Restrain the bolt, push the carrier latch, and ease the bolt to the forward position. Grip the bolt handle firmly, and pull it out toward the right.

9. Depress the latch and push the carrier inward. Depress the feed latch, on the right side inside the receiver. Move the bolt and action bar assembly out toward the front. The bolt is easily detached from the action bar.

10. The sleeve at the front is not normally removed from the action bar assembly. The forend support can be sprung off the action bar, if necessary for repair. The slide block buffer is retained at the rear of the action bar by a cross pin that is drifted out toward the left. Removal of the pin will release the three parts of the buffer, a strong coil spring (control it), and the ball that retains the cocking handle.

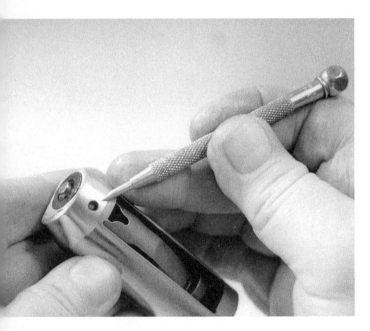

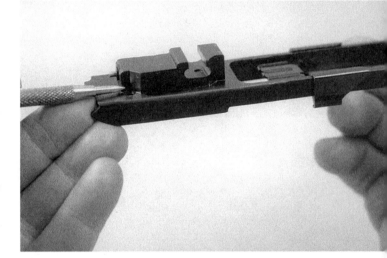

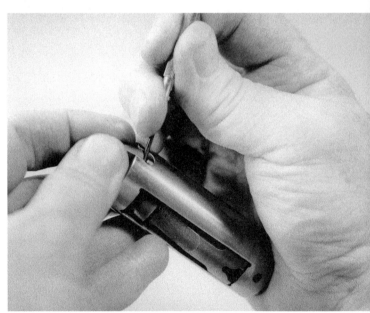

11. The firing pin and its return spring are retained at the rear of the bolt by a vertical pin that is drifted out downward. Removal of the firing pin and its spring will allow the locking block to be taken out downward.

12. To remove the extractor, insert a small tool between the extractor and its plunger, and depress the plunger toward the rear. Tip the extractor out toward the front. Caution: Control the plunger and spring.

13. Push out the two trigger group retaining cross pins.

14. Remove the trigger group downward, turning it slightly to clear the disconnector arm.

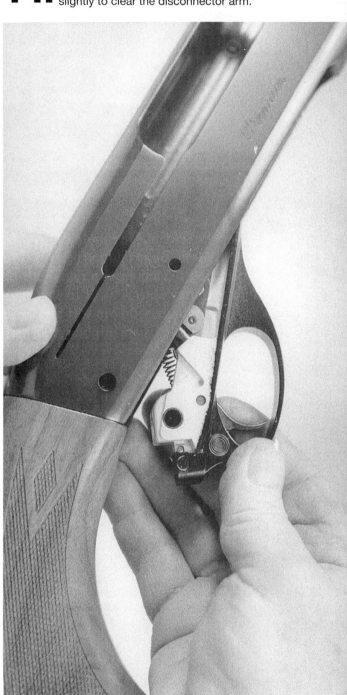

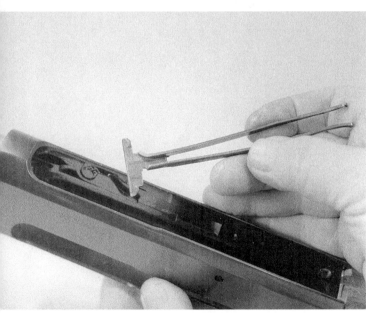

15. Move the bolt spring link forward until its rear tips spring out of the spring plunger. Swing the ends out and turn the link for removal.

16. The secondary shell stop ("feed latch"), located inside the receiver on the right side, is factory-staked in place. It should be removed only for repair.

17. Inside the left receiver wall, the primary shell stop ("interceptor latch") is mounted on a fixed post, and retained by a two-hole spring clip. If necessary for repair, the clip can be pried off. The torsion spring for the stop, located just to the rear, is factory-staked in place. Again, removal should be only for repair.

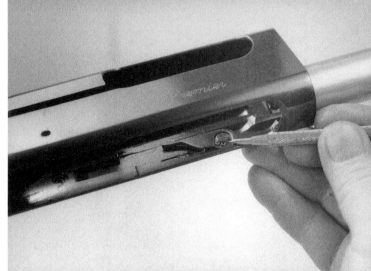

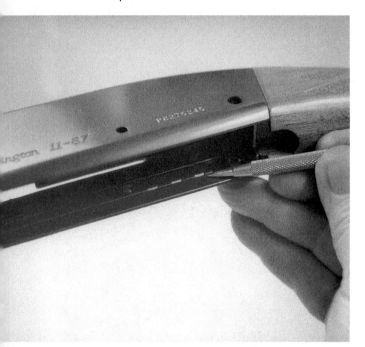

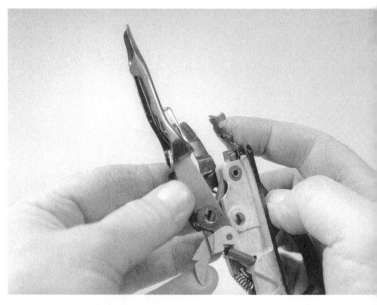

18. Remove the spring ring from the right tip of the front cross pin sleeve, which is also the carrier pivot. Control the carrier spring tension, and push the sleeve out toward the left.

19. Trip the carrier release, and ease the carrier latch over toward the front. Remove the carrier upward. The carrier dog and its spacer plate have a riveted pivot, and are not removed. The carrier release and its spring also have a riveted cross pin.

20. Remove the carrier plunger and spring.

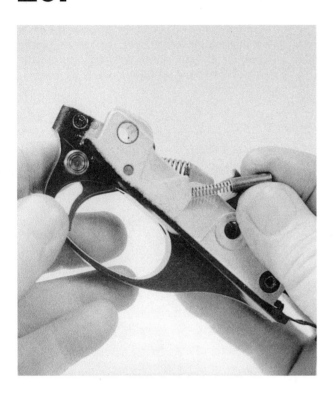

21. Move the safety to off-safe position, restrain the hammer, pull the trigger, and ease the hammer to the forward position. Pull the trigger slightly, and push out and remove the rear cross pin sleeve toward the left.

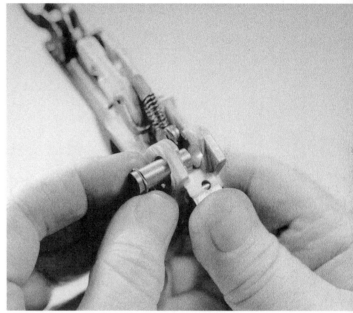

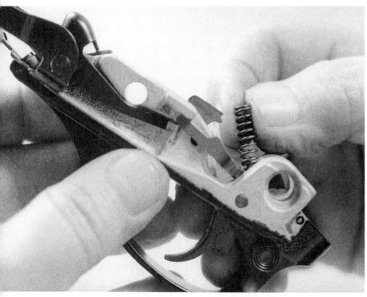

22. The top of the trigger will now move further rearward, easing the tension of the combination sear and trigger spring. Unhook the spring from its stud on the back of the sear, and remove it.

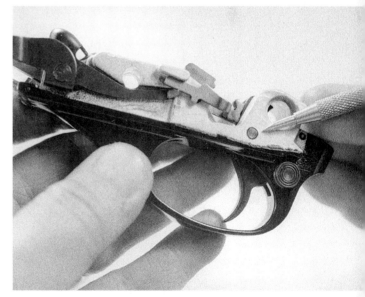

23. Drift out the trigger cross pin toward the left. The direction is important, as the pin is splined at its left tip.

24. Push the hammer back slightly to unspring the disconnector, and remove the trigger assembly upward. The trigger connector arms have a riveted pivot, and they are not removed.

25. There is an access hole on the right side at the mouth of the recess for the carrier plunger and spring, exposing the right tip of the sear cross pin for drifting out leftward. However, the pin is staked on the left side, so removal should be only for repair purposes. After the pin is out, the sear is taken out upward.

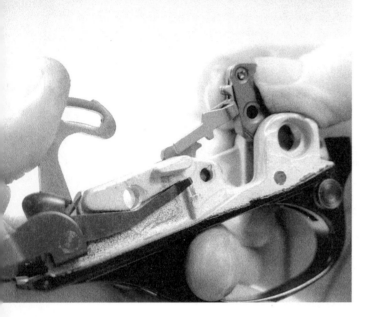

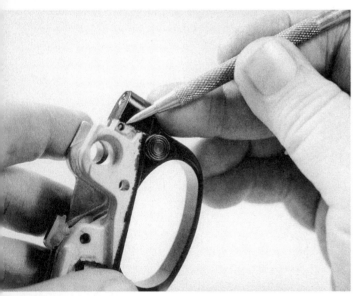

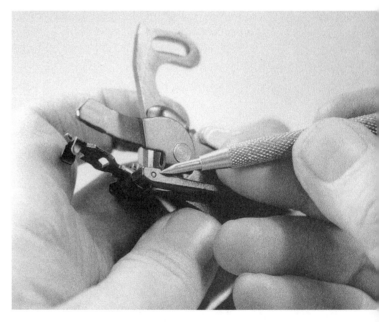

26. Drifted out toward the right, this cross pin will free the safety spring and plunger. Cover the hole on top at the rear to arrest the spring when the pin is removed. With the spring and plunger out, the safety button can be taken out toward either side.

27. The carrier latch is pivoted and retained by a slim cross pin at the front of the trigger group. The plunger and spring behind the latch must be controlled as the pin is pushed out. This is a powerful spring, so be careful.

28. The hammer and disconnector are pivoted and retained by a cross pin that is heavily riveted over a steel washer on the right side. If the pin is driven out, the hammer spring and plunger will be released, and must be controlled. Actually, with the possibility of damage to the disconnector, this portion of disassembly should be handled by the factory or a repair station.

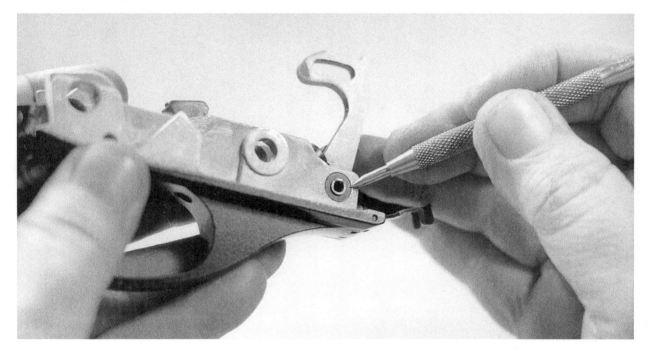

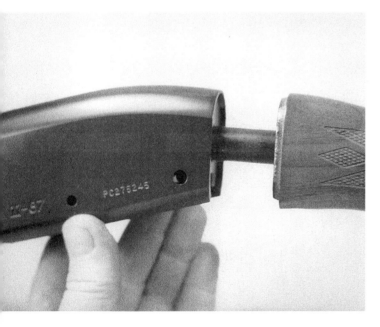

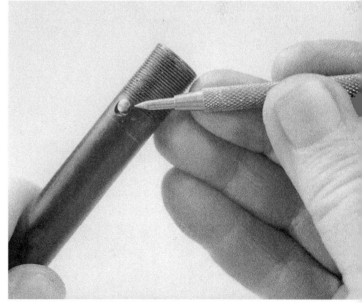

29. The recoil pad is retained by two Phillips screws, and a very large regular screwdriver is used to remove the stock nut. Remove the nut and lock washer, and take off the buttstock toward the rear. Remove the stock bearing plate.

30. Use a tool to slightly depress the internal plug from the rear, and push out the plug retaining cross pin. Caution: Control the bolt spring, and ease it out, along with the plunger, toward the rear.

Reassembly Tips:

1. When replacing the trigger, remember that its splined cross pin must be driven in toward the right. Also, be sure the left connector arm of the trigger is installed above the tail of the disconnector, as shown.

2. If there is difficulty in installing the carrier plunger and spring, it may be that the sear pin is protruding into the recess. Just push it gently back toward the left.

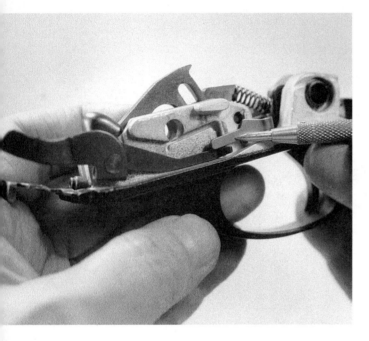

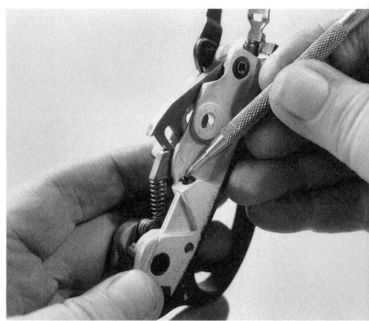

3. As the carrier is installed, the latch must be turned up to vertical position and held there until the carrier pivot is in place.

As the bolt and action bar assembly are reinstalled, it will be necessary to again depress the shell stop as the bolt enters the receiver.

Remington Model 1100

Similar/Identical Pattern Guns:

The same basic assembly/disassembly steps for the Remington Model 1100 also apply to the following guns:

Remington Model 1100D	Remington Model 1100F
Remington Model 1100SA	Remington Model 1100SB
Remington Model 1100SF	Remington Model 1100TB
Remington Model 1100 LT-20	Remington Sportsman Auto

Data:	Remington Model 1100
Origin:	United States
Manufacturer:	Remington Arms Company Bridgeport, Connecticut
Gauges:	12, 16, 20, 28, and 410
Magazine Capacity:	4 rounds
Overall length:	48 inches (with 28-inch barrel)
Barrel length:	22 to 30 inches
Weight:	6-1/2 to 7-3/4 pounds

Replacing the Model 58 and Model 878 in 1963, the Model 1100 rapidly became one of the most popular gas-operated autoloaders. Originally offered in the larger gauges only, it became available in 28 and 410 chamberings in 1970. A wide variety of options in barrel lengths, chokes, and ribs are offered. All of the variations are mechanically the same, and the instructions will apply.

Disassembly:

1. Pull back the operating handle to lock the bolt in the open position, and unscrew and remove the magazine cap. Take off the forend and barrel, in that order, toward the front.

2. Move the rubber gas seal ring out of its shallow recess on the magazine tube, and slide it off toward the front.

3. Remove the gas piston and the piston seal ring toward the front.

4. Restrain the bolt, depress the carrier latch, and ease the bolt forward to the closed position. Push out the large and small cross pins at the lower rear of the receiver toward either side.

5. Remove the trigger group downward, turning it slightly as it is moved out to clear the disconnector on the left side.

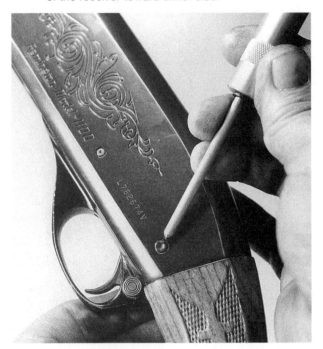

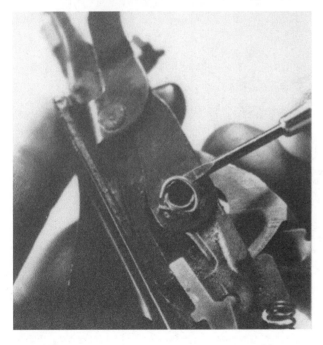

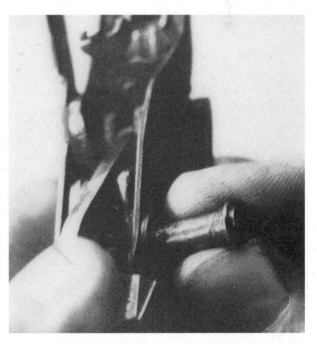

6. If both retaining clips are present on the front cross pin sleeve, remove one of them.

7. Restrain the carrier, and push out the pivot/sleeve and remove it.

8. Ease off the carrier spring tension, removing the carrier upward and toward the front. Caution: As the carrier is removed, restrain the carrier latch, as its powerful spring will force it over toward the front.

9. Slowly release the tension of the carrier latch spring, allowing the latch to pivot over forward while restraining the spring plunger. Remove the plunger and spring toward the front.

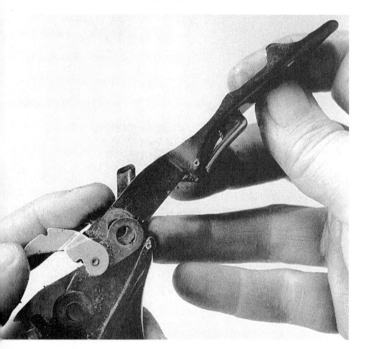

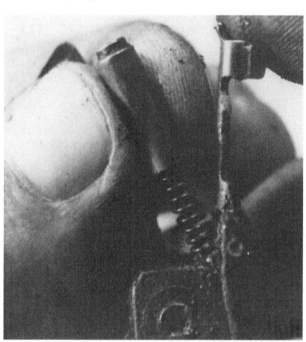

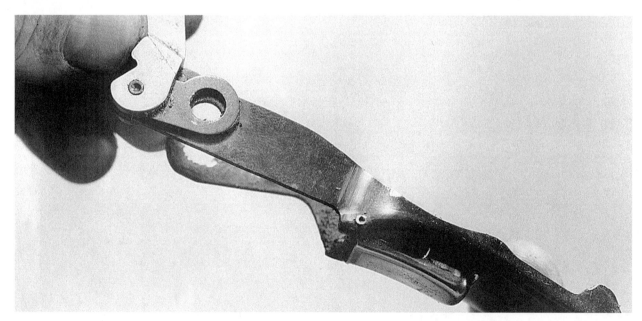

10. Remove the carrier spring and plunger from their hole on the right side of the housing. The carrier dog and its washer/plate are retained on the right rear wing of the carder by a cross pin that is riveted in place, and this is not removed in normal takedown. if removal is necessary for repair, be sure the wing is well supported, and drive out the pin toward the left. The pin that retains the carrier release button is also riveted, and the same advice applies.

11. The carrier latch is cross pinned at the front of the trigger group, The pin is of very small diameter, and is very near the edge of the alloy trigger housing, so take care when drifting it out, to avoid damage to the housing and the loops on the latch.

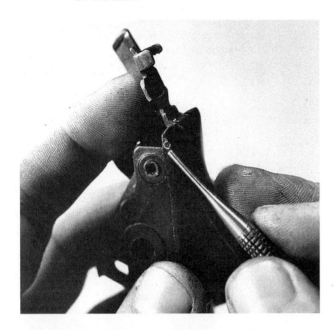

12. Restrain the hammer, pull the trigger, and ease the hammer down to the fired position. Keep the trigger pulled to the rear, and push out the rear cross pin sleeve toward the left.

13. Removal of the rear cross pin sleeve will allow the top of the trigger to move to the rear beyond its normal position, relieving the tension of the combination sear and trigger spring. The spring can now be detached from its studs on the sear and trigger and is removed upward.

14. Drift out the trigger pin toward the left, and remove the trigger upward, turning it slightly to clear its connector arm past the shelf on the housing. The connectors are cross pinned to the top of the trigger, and the pin is riveted in place. If removal is necessary for repair, be sure the top of the trigger is well supported, and drive the pin out toward the right.

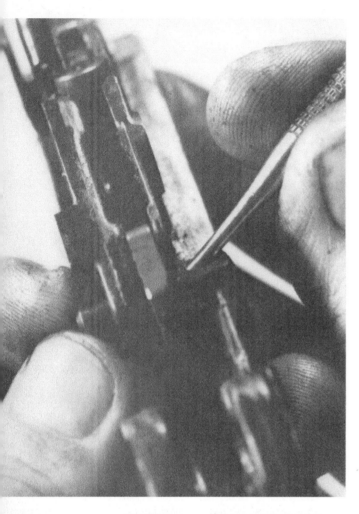

15. The sear cross pin is accessible by angling a drift punch into the top of the carrier spring hole on the right side. Nudge the pin toward the left, and remove it with smooth-jawed pliers. Remove the sear upward.

16. The hammer and disconnector are retained by a cross pin that is riveted over a recessed washer on the right side of the housing. If removal is necessary for repair, be sure the disconnector is supported firmly on the left side. Use a drift punch small enough to enter the depression on the right tip of the pin, and restrain the hammer spring plunger, as it will be released as the pin clears the disconnector.

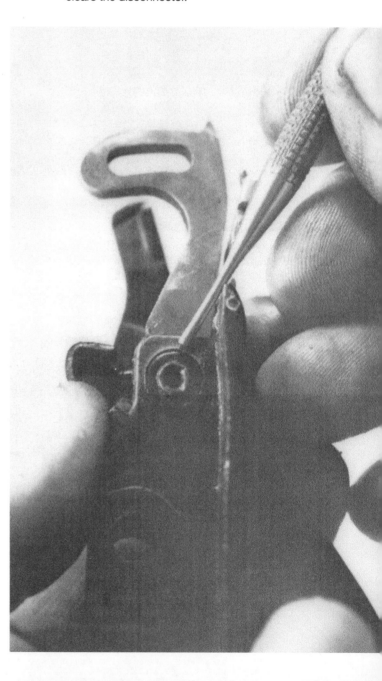

17. Push out the small cross pin at the upper rear of the housing, and remove the safety spring upward, along with the detent ball, if possible. Push out the safety button toward either side. If the ball can't be removed upward, wait until the button is taken out, and insert a drift punch to push the ball downward into the button tunnel for removal.

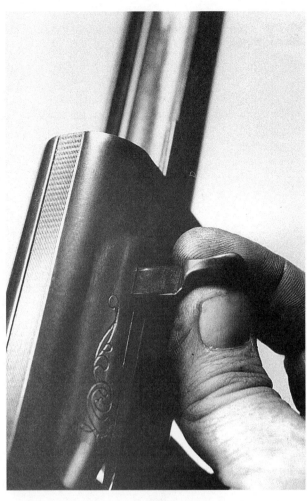

18. Grip the operating handle firmly, and pull it straight out toward the right.

19. Use a fingertip inside the receiver to depress the right shell stop, and remove the bolt and slide assembly toward the front.

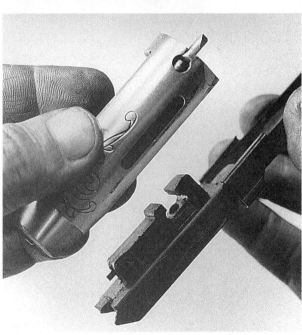

20. After the assembly is taken out, the bolt can be lifted off the rear of the action bar assembly.

21. The forend support and the action bar sleeve are not removed in normal takedown, but both can be sprung off the action bar assembly if necessary. The slide block buffer at the rear can be taken out by drifting out its cross pin, and the operating handle retaining ball and spring can be removed by depressing the ball and sliding the retaining plate out toward the side.

22. Drift the vertical pin at the rear of the bolt out downward.

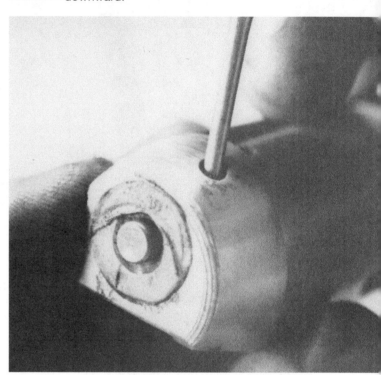

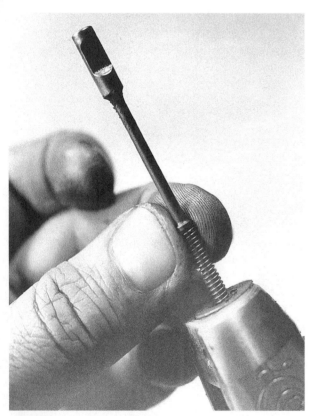

23. Remove the firing pin and its return spring toward the rear.

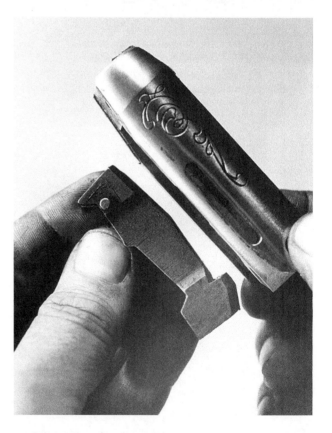

24. Remove the locking block downward.

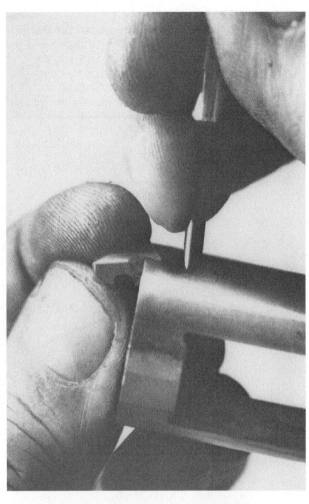

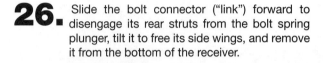

25. Insert a small screwdriver between the extractor and its plunger, depress the plunger toward the rear, and lift the extractor out of its recess. Control the plunger and spring, ease them out, and remove them toward the front.

26. Slide the bolt connector ("link") forward to disengage its rear struts from the bolt spring plunger, tilt it to free its side wings, and remove it from the bottom of the receiver.

27. The left shell stop ("interceptor") is retained on a post inside the receiver wall by a snap ring. Spread the ring just enough to remove it, and detach the shell stop from the post. The spring for this part is staked in place on the receiver wall, and is removed only for repair.

28. The right shell stop lies in a shallow recess inside the receiver, and is lightly staked in place at the rear. If the staking is light enough, the stop can be removed by prying it gently out of its recess at the rear. If the staking is too tight for this, angle a drift punch in the cross pin hole, and nudge the shell stop toward the rear, swaging the staking out of the shell stop recess.

29. Insert a screwdriver in the open end of the magazine spring retainer, and pry it out toward the front. Move the screwdriver as this is done, to raise the retainer equally around its edges. The magazine spring is under tension, so control it, and ease it out. Remove the spring and follower toward the front.

30. Remove the buttplate, and use a B-Square Model 1100 stock wrench or a large, wide screwdriver to back out and remove the stock retaining nut, along with its lock washer and washer. Take off the stock and stock bearing plate toward the rear.

31. Insert a tool at the rear to restrain the bolt spring plug, and push out the retaining cross pin. Caution: The spring is under tension, so control it and ease it out. Remove the plug, spring, and follower toward the rear.

Reassembly Tips:

1. When re-staking the right shell stop, it's best to use a B-Square staking tool, as shown. This can also be done by angling a punch into the receiver. The front trigger group cross pin can be temporarily inserted to help in holding the shell stop in place during re-staking.

2. When replacing the trigger assembly, be sure the left connector arm is installed with its forward tip above the rear tail of the disconnector, as shown.

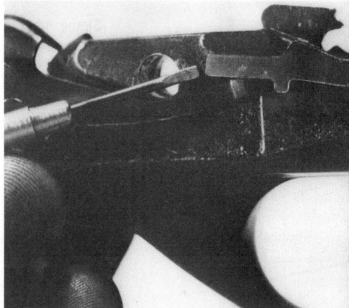

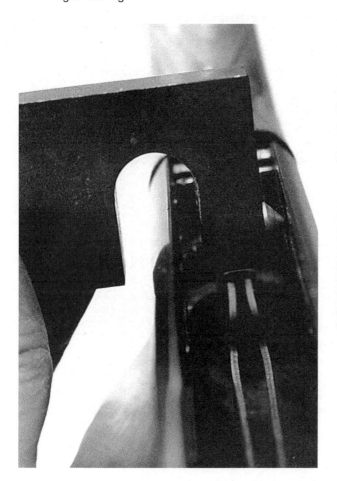

Remington Versa Max

Similar/Identical Pattern Guns:

The following basic assembly/disassembly steps for the Remington Versa Max can also be used for the following guns:

Remington Versa Max Tactical

Remington Versa Max Waterfowl

Data:	Remington Versa Max Synthetic
Origin:	United States
Manufacturer:	Remington Arms Company, Ilion, NY
Gauges:	12
Magazine Capacity:	3 rounds
Overall Length:	49.9 inches
Height:	7.5 inches
Barrel Length:	28 inches
Weight:	7.7 pounds

Remington's Versa Max auto-loading shotgun is a deviation from the usual Remington line, not using the common fire control group so famous for the company. Capable of self-regulating from the lightest 2 ¾ loads to the fastest 3 1/2" loads, it is a versatile gun. The Tactical model incorporates an extended choke, optic rail, and extended magazine tube, but is otherwise identical to the field models, existing in black synthetic and hunting camouflage.

Disassembly:

1. With the action open and the safety on, remove the magazine cap.

2. Remove the handguard and then the barrel from the receiver.

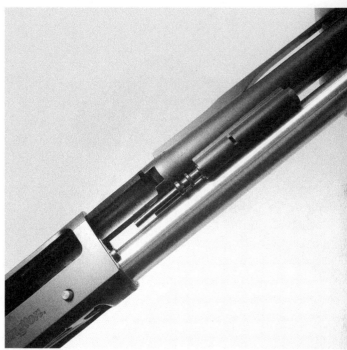

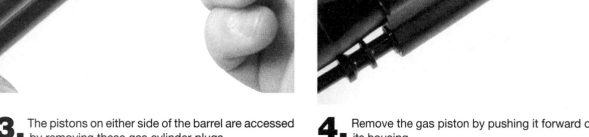

3. The pistons on either side of the barrel are accessed by removing these gas cylinder plugs.

4. Remove the gas piston by pushing it forward out of its housing.

5. The ejector and spring may be removed from the back of the barrel extension by removing this set screw.

7. Allow the bolt to slide forward. Depress the bolt into the bolt carrier until the charging handle can be removed.

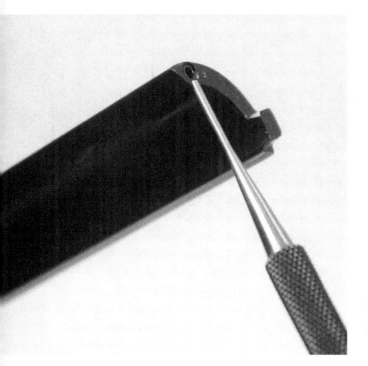

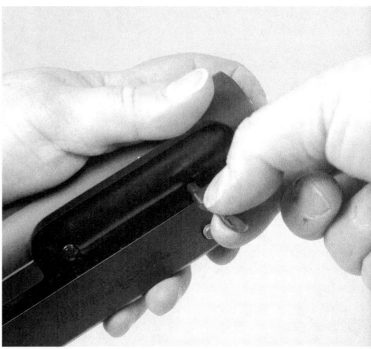

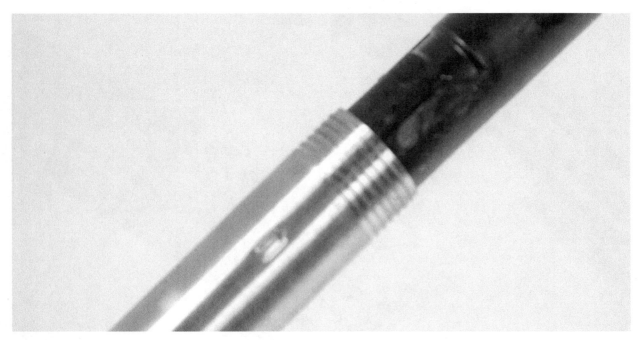

6. Remove the magazine retainer by pushing it in and then rotating it approximately 90 degrees to release it from the tube by its channels. Remove the retainer, magazine spring, and follower carefully as the spring is compressed. The follower also has channels that need to be aligned with the mag tube projections for removal.

8. Pull the bolt assembly forward out of the receiver.

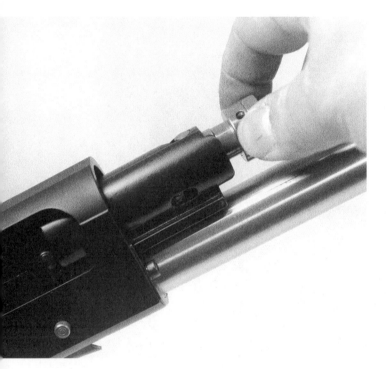

9. Pull the firing pin retaining pin and withdraw the firing pin and return spring from the back of the bolt body.

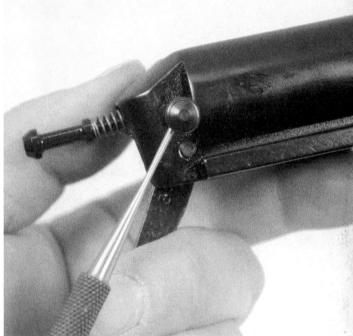

10. The cam pin should drop from the bolt head when it is inverted. Then pull the bolt head from the bolt body.

11. The link assembly can be separated from the bolt body by driving out this pin.

12. Drive out the trigger plate pin to remove the trigger group.

14. Unhook the feed latch release spring from the latch release.

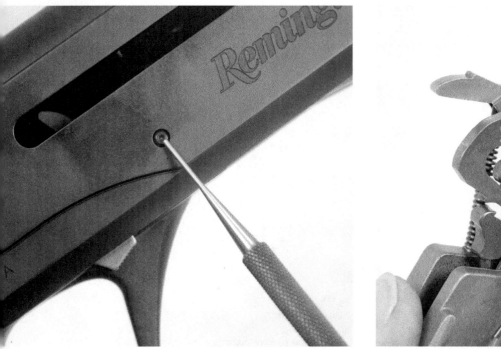

13. Pull the trigger group down and to the rear to remove it from the receiver.

15. Remove the carrier dog pivot strut and spring from the left side of the trigger group by pulling the end slightly to the rear and then forward to the left side of the trigger group. The spring is under some compression, but this can be done with the fingers.

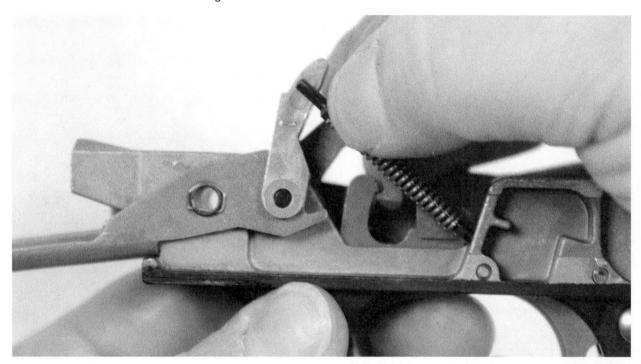

16. Remove this clip spring from the carrier pivot tube.

17. With the hammer forward, pull out the carrier pivot tube. This will free the carrier assembly, hammer and plunger and spring, and the feed latch.

18. This small pin holds the carrier dog to the carrier. It is retained only by the trigger housing wall. Do not lose it.

19. Push this trigger pin out slightly to free the feed latch release spring, then push it out the rest of the way to the left.

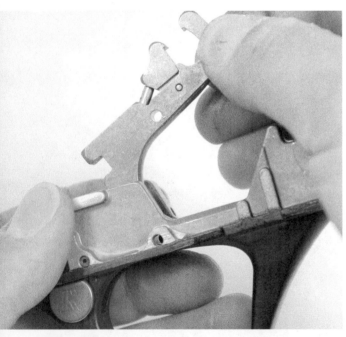

20. Pull the trigger up and out of the trigger group.

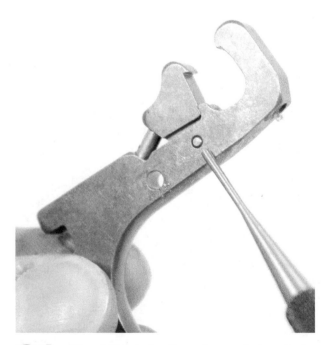

21. The disconnector, its spring, and plunger can be removed by driving out this pin.

22. The safety button can be removed by first driving out this pin. The safety detent and spring will come out of the hole in the top of the housing. The safety button can be removed toward the larger of the two ends of the button. The remaining small pin is a trigger stop pin and need not be removed.

23. Drive out this roll pin from top to bottom to allow the feed latch to be removed. The latch is tensioned by two springs beneath it.

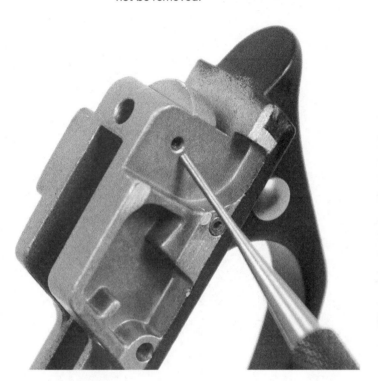

24. Remove the butt pad by means of the two screws retaining it to the buttstock.

25. Remove the stock bolt and washer.

26. The buttstock can now be removed from the receiver by pulling it to the rear (Picture A). Inside the stock is a multi-holed plate used to set cast and drop. It can be removed by pulling it out of the rear of the stock (Picture B).

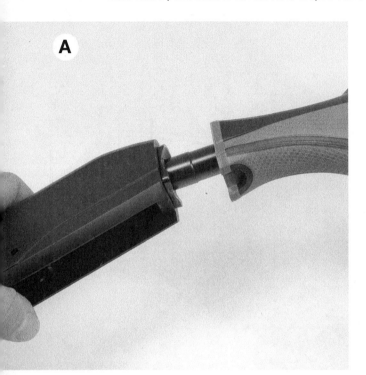

A

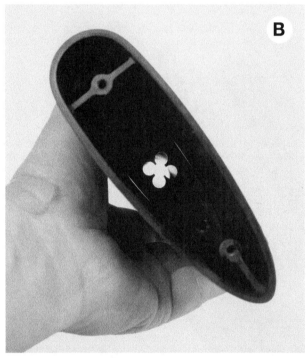

B

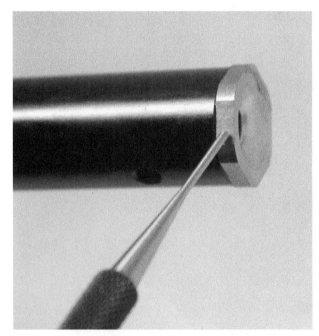

27. The concave pivot block can be removed at this time as well.

28. The action spring and follower can be removed by unscrewing this bolt from the action spring tube. The spring is highly compressed.

29. There is a snap ring which restricts forward movement of the action spring follower. The action spring tube must be removed to access this snap ring, however, do not remove the tube unless it or the ring needs to be replaced.

Reassembly Tips:

1. When reassembling the link to the bolt body, the numbers on the link should not be upside down but legibly upright to indicate proper assembly.

2. Align the indicator on the cam pin toward the rear when reassembling the bolt.

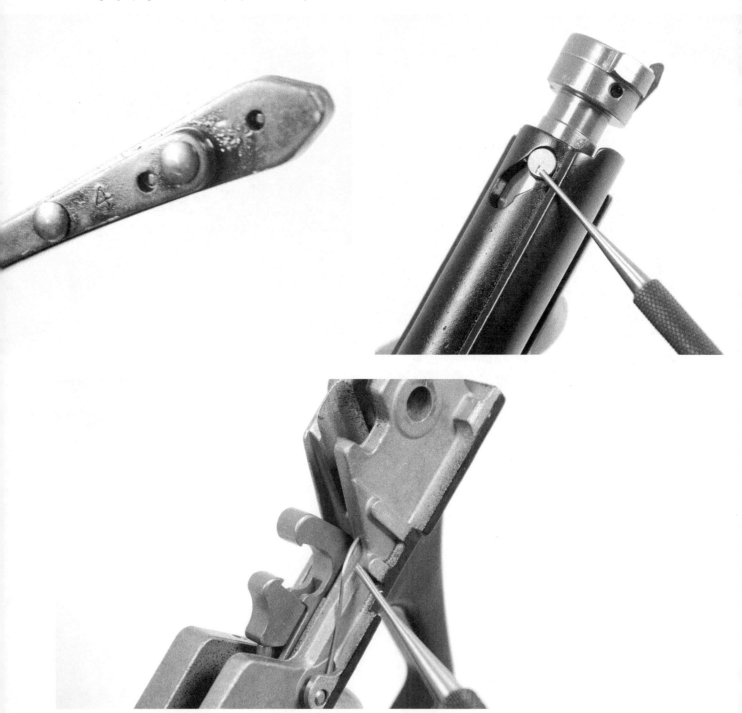

3. When reinstalling the feed latch release spring, rest the long front leg onto the housing. This will allow easier access to it when placing the leg back onto the feed latch release.

Ruger Red Label

Data:	Ruger Red Label
Origin:	United States
Manufacturer:	Sturm, Ruger & Company Southport, Connecticut
Gauges:	12, 20
Overall length:	43 inches (with 26-inch barrel)
Barrel length:	26 & 28 inches
Weight:	7 to 7-1/2 pounds

One of the slimmest and most well-balanced of all over/under designs, the Ruger Red Label was introduced in 20-gauge only in 1977. Five years later the gun was also offered in 12-gauge. Internally, the Red Label has typical Ruger engineering- all parts have an extra margin of strength. The gun shown here is an early 20-gauge version.

Disassembly:

1. Operate the forend latch, and remove the forend.

2. Operate the barrel latch, open the action, and remove the barrel unit.

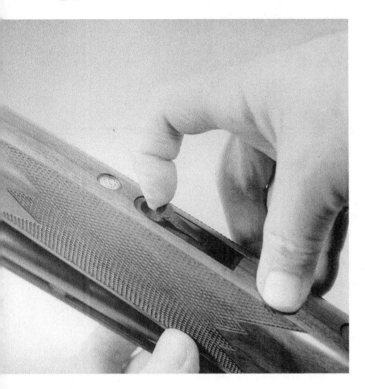

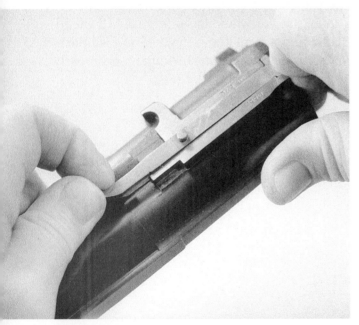

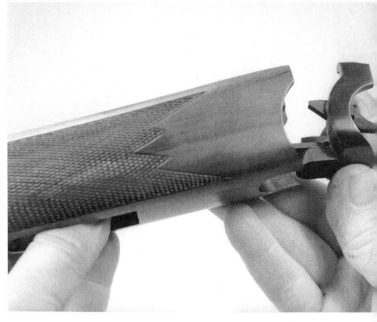

3. To remove the ejectors and their springs, push them all the way forward, and tip the front end outward. Control the powerful springs.

4. Remove the screw on the inside of the forend. Tip the front of the forend iron inward, then remove the assembly toward the rear.

5. Use a tool to depress the plungers of the ejector trip levers, keeping control of the plungers and springs, and move the levers off their posts inward for removal.

6. The forend latch lever is retained and pivoted by a cross pin. Control the plunger and spring when the pin is drifted out.

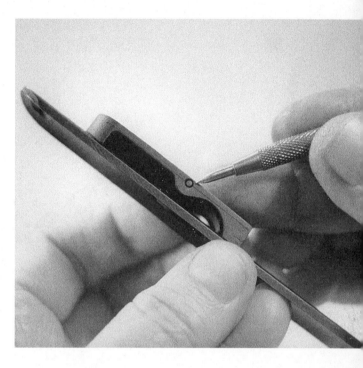

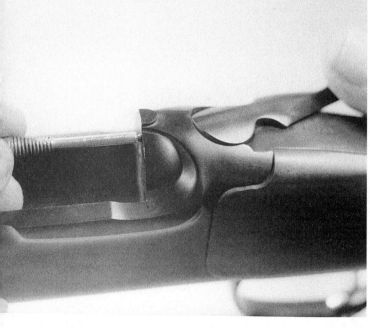

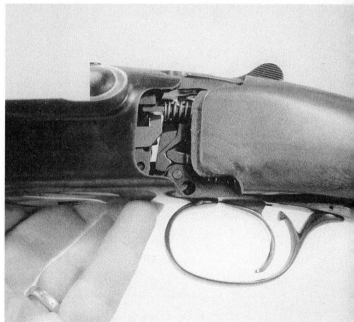

7. Depress the barrel latch detent to bring the latch lever back to the closed position.

8. Remove the two Phillips-type screws in the recoil pad, and remove it from the stock. Use a long-shanked screwdriver to take out the stock bolt and washer, and remove the buttstock toward the rear.

9. Push back the right hammer until a small hole is visible in the spring guide at the rear, and insert a small pin or drift punch in the hole to trap the spring. Repeat this operation on the opposite side, with the left hammer.

10. Push out the hammer pivot pin.

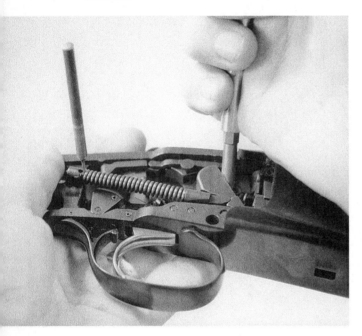

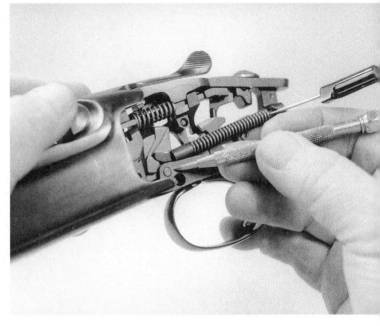

11. Pull the trigger and push the right hammer all the way forward. Turn the guide and trapped spring to the position shown, and remove it.

12. Tip the right hammer back and move it upward, then remove it toward the side. The left hammer and spring assembly are not removed at this time, but there is access to the firing pins, if one needs to be replaced.

13. Use a tool to push the barrel latch spring slightly forward, out of its recess, and push the rear end of the barrel latch spring guide out toward the left. A hole is provided in the guide bar for insertion of a tool to trap the spring, but this is more useful for reassembly.

14. Remove the barrel latch spring assembly toward the left. A small roll pin retains the base piece at the rear, if the spring needs to be removed.

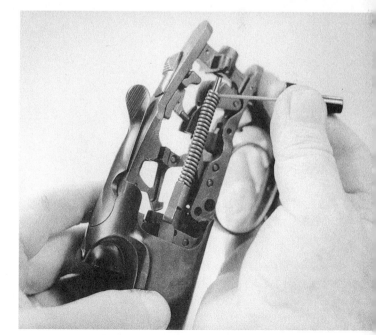

15. With the safety in off-safe position and the trigger depressed, move the left hammer upward, then tip it outward for removal.

16. Remove the left hammer spring and guide.

17. Drift out the small roll cross pin at the lower rear of the receiver.

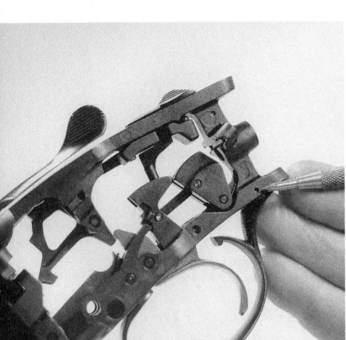

18. The trigger guard will spring outward when the pin is removed. Take off the guard downward.

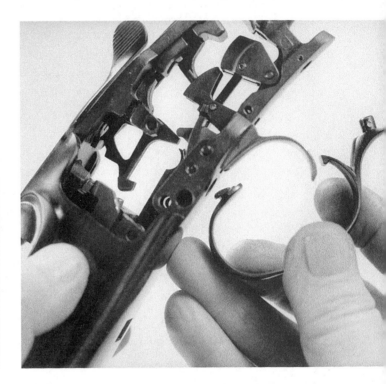

19. Drift out the trigger stop cross pin.

20. Push out the trigger cross pin.

21. Move the trigger downward until the selector cross pin is exposed, and push it out.

22. Remove the trigger downward.

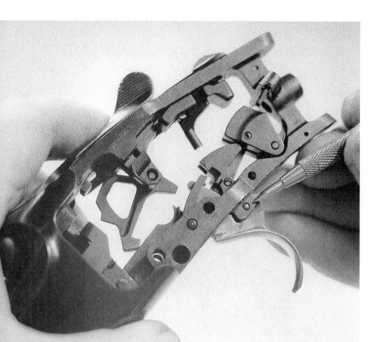

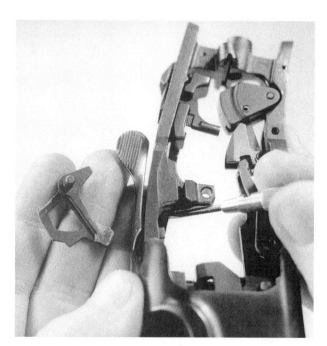

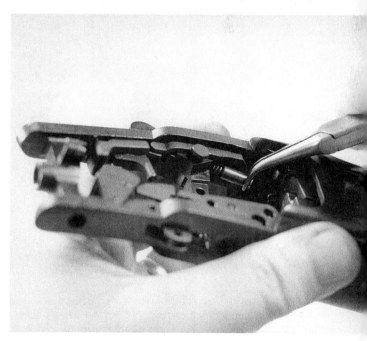

23. With the safety in on-safe position, depress the plunger, and take out the hammer interruptor toward the right. The plunger and spring will be stopped by the safety connector bar.

24. Move the safety to off-safe position, and take out the interruptor plunger and spring.

25. Drift out the safety bar retaining stud toward the right.

26. Remove the safety bar.

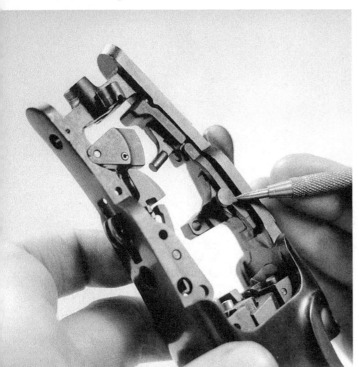

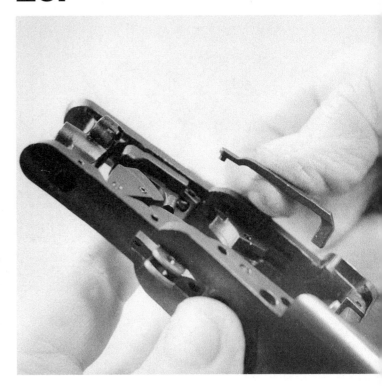

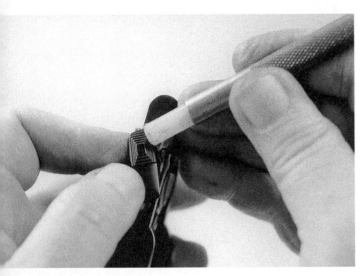

27. With the safety in on-safe position and the thumbpiece to the right (with the "U" exposed), use a non-marring tool such as a nylon drift to bump the rear of the thumb-piece toward the right. Caution: Cover the parts with a shop cloth, as the thumbpiece plunger and spring will be freed upward as the edge of the thumb-piece clears.

28. Keeping the plunger under control, turn the thumbpiece to the position shown.

29. Move the safety block downward and remove it toward the right. Take care that the three plungers and their springs are not lost.

30. Turn the thumb-piece back to center and remove it upward.

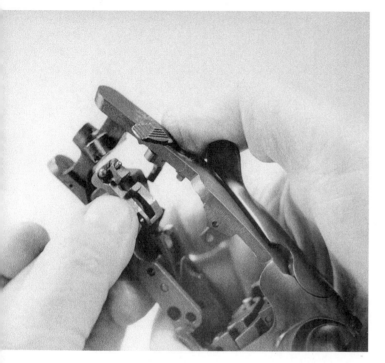

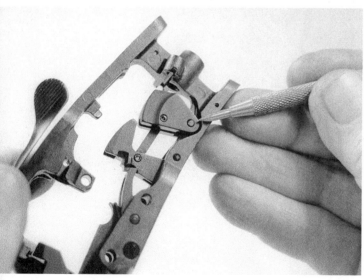

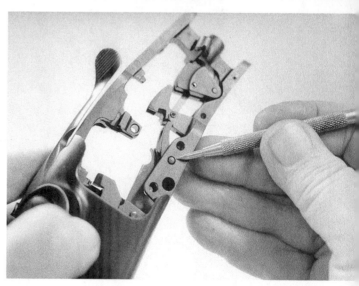

31. Removal of the cross pin in the inertia block will allow the block and its torsion spring to be taken out, along with the link and the attached sear selector. The link is attached to the two parts by roll cross pins. Unless removal is necessary for repair, this system is best left in place. Caution: The inertia block spring will be released when the pivot pin is removed.

32. A single cross pin pivots and retains both sears, and also retains the torsion spring that powers them. If this system is to be taken out, control the spring.

33. Use a non-marring tool to bump the barrel latch lever base upward, with the latch in central position. Hold a shop cloth over the top of the receiver when this is done. After the lever is removed, the detent pin can be taken out rearward.

34. As the latch lever clears its recess, the small retaining plunger and strong spring will be released at the front, slightly off-center toward the right. This is the reason for covering the top as this operation is done.

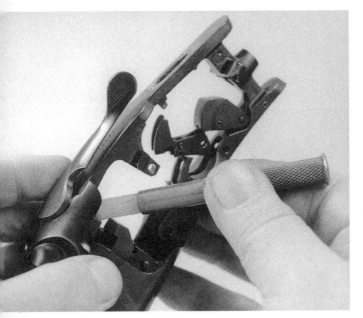

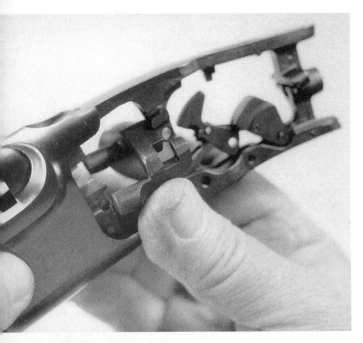

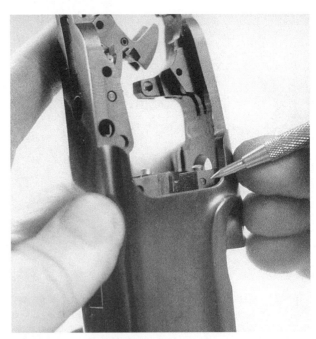

35. Move the locking block rearward, and take it out toward the left.

36. Both firing pins and their return springs are retained by cross pins. The upper retaining pin is drifted out toward the right, and the lower one toward the left.

Reassembly Tips:

37. Drifting out this cross pin will allow removal of the cocking cams and their separate springs toward the rear, and the cocking rods toward the front. The torsion springs will be released as the pin is removed, so control them. Each cam also has a separate bushing.

1. As the trigger is moved into place for replacement of the cross pin, depress the hammer interruptor upward so it won't bear against the trigger and make alignment difficult.

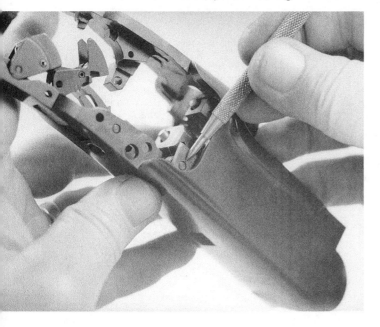

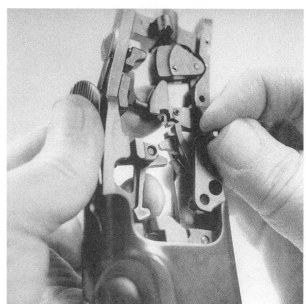

2. When the trigger limit pin is reinstalled, be sure the trigger is pulled for clearance.

3. Before the hammers and hammer spring units are reinstalled, insert a tool on each side to engage the sears with the selector. Then depress the trigger for sear clearance as the hammers are put into position for insertion of the cross pin.

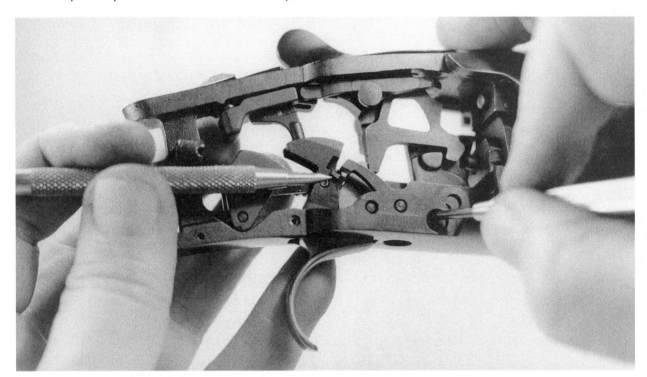

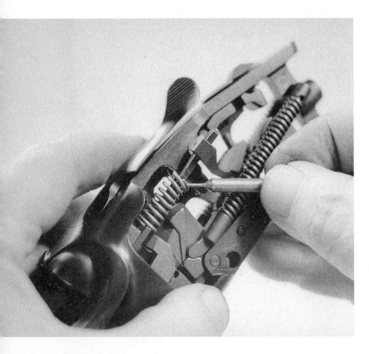

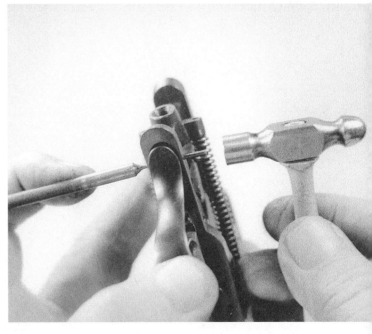

4. When installing the barrel latch spring assembly, the spring can be pre-compressed and held with a tool inserted in the mid-hole in the guide.

5. As the trigger guard is reinstalled, use a drift to hold it for insertion of the cross pin.

Saiga 12

Data:	Saiga 12
Origin:	Russia
Manufacturer:	Izhmash
Gauges:	12, 20, .410
Magazine Capacity:	5 rounds
Overall Length:	45 inches
Height:	7 inches
Barrel Length:	19 inches
Weight:	7.9 lbs

The Saiga shotgun is no more or no less than an AK-47 that shoots shotgun shells. 20 gauge and .410 chamberings are available as well as this 12 gauge model. An aftermarket of surprising size has arisen to service this gun, as the presence of a detachable box magazine makes it very suitable for competition and self-defense purposes. While it is based on the AK series of rifles and most of the mechanisms are similar, these steps should not be used when working on the Saiga's rifle cousins, as there are some differences in the gas system and trigger mechanisms instituted to allow them to be imported. These guns are imported by a variety of companies, such as USSG, RWC, and Legion.

Disassembly:

1. With magazine removed, hammer cocked and safety off, depress the guide rod plunger and push the guide rod into the receiver cover until the cover unlatches.

2. Remove the cover by lifting up the back end and pulling to the rear.

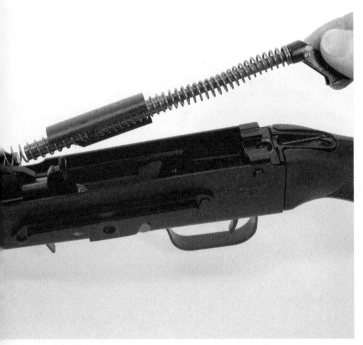

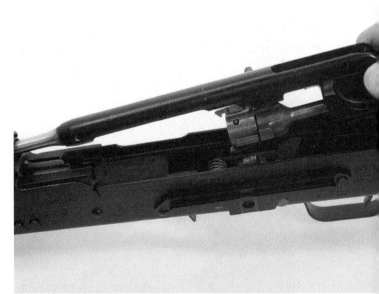

3. Remove the guide rod and return spring assembly by pushing the guide rod out of its slot in the receiver, lifting, and pulling it out to the rear.

4. Retract the bolt carrier assembly all the way to the rear and lift it from the receiver, then pull the assembly to the rear to withdraw the piston from the piston tube.

5. To remove the bolt from the carrier, push the bolt assembly all the way to the rear of its movement then rotate the upper/right side extractor out until it clears the carrier. The bolt can now be pulled out of the carrier to the front.

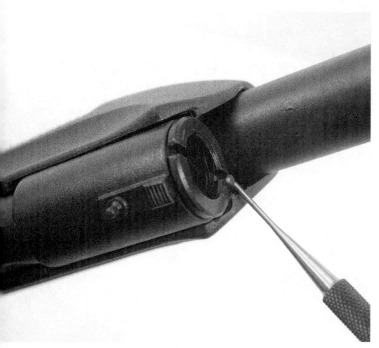

6. Unscrew the piston stopper plug by depressing the plug detent and unscrewing the plug until it comes out of the tube.

7. Remove the piston by inverting the shotgun and pointing the muzzle down. Fouling may require the piston be pushed out from the rear with a rod.

8. Drive out the magazine catch pin to release the mag catch and spring.

10. Remove the sear/disconnector by pulling it out from under the hammer spring and then up and out of the receiver. The hammer limiter will also fall from the sear/disconnector piece.

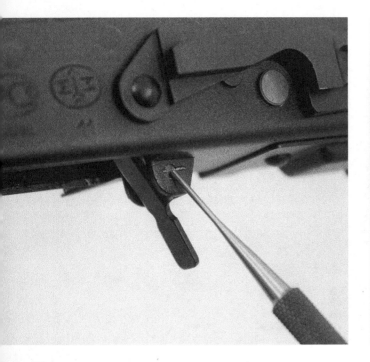

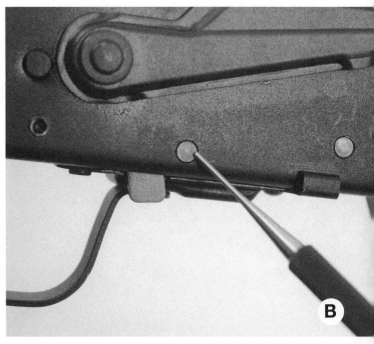

9. To remove the sear pin this long thin spring must be slightly pushed towards the bottom of the receiver to clear the groove in the pin (Picture A). The sear pin can then be pushed out of the receiver to the left.

11. While difficult to see in the photo, the long spring must then be displaced from its groove in the hammer pin. Using a small punch or screwdriver, simply push it inward toward the hammer spring until a small click is heard.

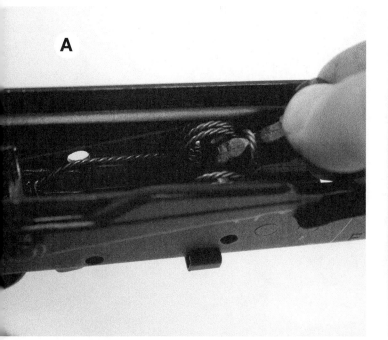

A

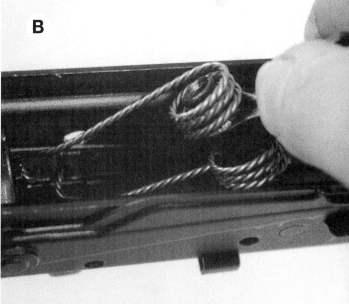

B

12. Remove the hammer by pushing out the hammer pin from right to left, then lifting it from the receiver (Picture A). It will have to be turned slightly as the hammer pin's cylinder is wider than the bolt rails of the receiver (Picture B).

13. Remove the bolt stop and bolt stop spring.

14. Rotate the safety lever up and pull it out to the right side of the receiver.

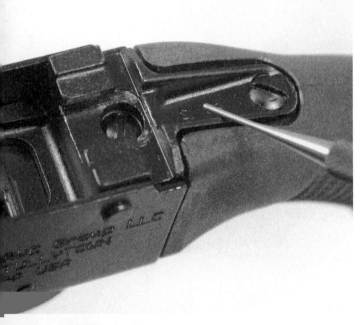

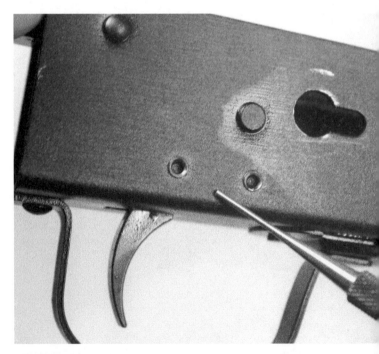

15. There are three screws on the rear trunnion; two on top and one in the bottom which also penetrates the trigger guard. Remove these screws to release the buttstock.

16. The trigger and its connector piece can be removed by driving out these two pins. This should only be done for repair or replacement, since these two pins are actually long rivets.

17. Remove the front sling swivel to release the forend.

18. Pull the forend front down and then pull the forend forward toward the muzzle.

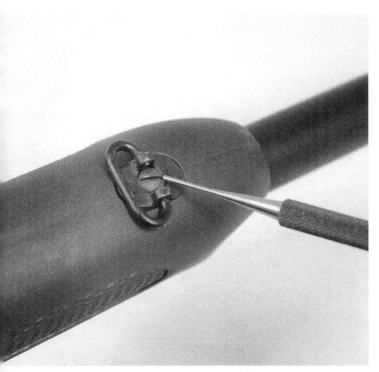

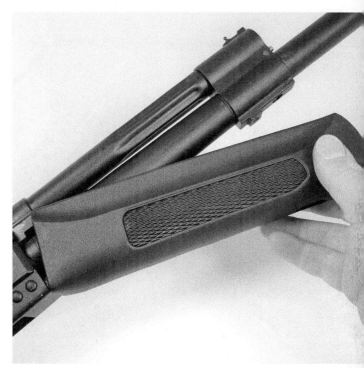

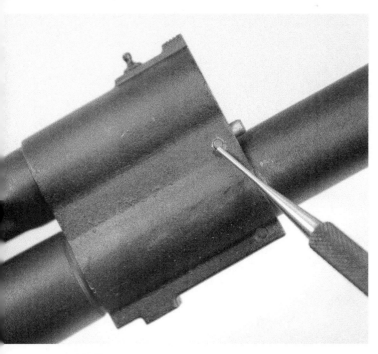

19. To remove the gas plug detent and spring, press out this pin.

20. The gas piston tube can be removed by driving out this pin. However, this should only be necessary if the tube needs to be replaced, and this pin is very tightly set.

21. The front sight is staked in and should only be removed when replacement is warranted.

22. The rear sight is held by a simple dovetail. Drive it out to the right.

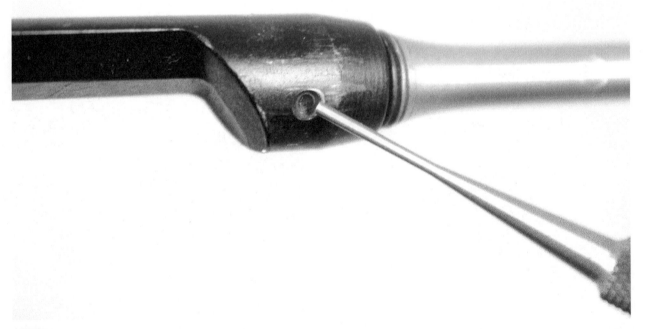

23. The operating rod on the front of the bolt carrier is retained by dimples punched into the piece. There should be no need to remove it, which would require drilling the dimples out to free the rod to be unscrewed.

24. Drive out this pin in the bolt to separate the bolt face from the locking lugs (Picture A). The forward half of the firing pin and firing pin spring can be removed from the bolt face, and the rear half of the firing pin will fall from the bolt lug section through the front (Picture B).

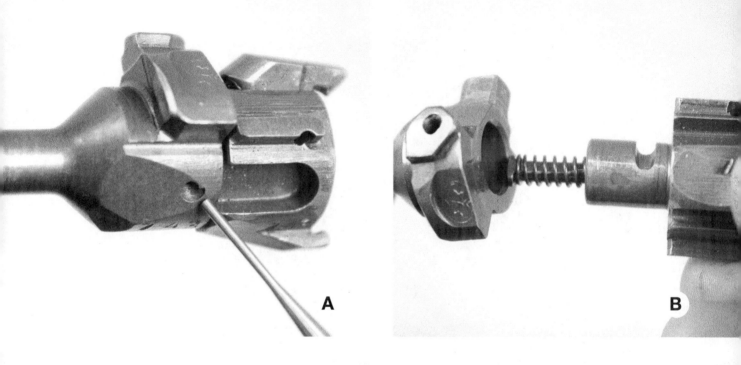

A

B

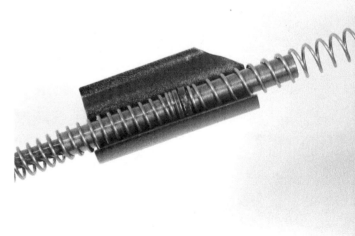

25. Drive out this pin to remove the extractor and spring.

26. The return springs and bolt guard can be removed by sliding them off the front of the guide rod.

Reassembly Tips:

1. A picture of the following tip cannot be clearly shown due to parts obscuring the step. The short leg of the bolt stop spring points to the rear and this spring should be installed, with the bolt stop before the hammer or sear is installed. Then install the hammer, running the hammer pin through the bolt stop hole and fully through the receiver. Then hold the bolt stop spring with a punch through the right receiver wall as the sear is installed. Push through the sear pin as the punch is retracted to keep the bolt stop spring captured.

2. While conducting the previous step, take care to lift the hammer spring's legs over the sear so that they rest on the sear. If the sear is placed over the legs, the legs will be trapped and the sear will have to be reinstalled again, correctly.

Savage Model 30

Similar/Identical Pattern Guns:

The same basic assembly/disassembly steps for the Savage Model 30 also apply to the following guns:

Savage Model 30AC	Savage Model 30D
Savage Model 30E	Savage Model 30F
Savage Model 30FG	Savage Model 30H
Savage Model 30J, K, T, Series A, B, C	Savage Model 30L
Savage Model 30 Slug	Savage Model 30T
Savage Model 30AC Takedown	Sears "Ranger" Model 40N
Springfield Model 67	Springfield Model 77
Stevens Model 67	Stevens Model 77
Stevens Model 77-SC	Stevens Model 79-VR

Data:	Savage Model 30
Origin:	United States
Manufacturer:	Savage Arms Company Westfield, Massachusetts
Gauges:	12, 20, and 410
Magazine Capacity:	4 rounds (3 in 410)
Overall length:	47-3/4 inches (with 28-inch barrel)
Barrel length:	26 to 30 inches
Weight:	6 1/4 to 7 pounds

When it was introduced in 1958, the Model 30 was offered in 12-gauge only, but the other chamberings were soon added. For a time, it was even available in a left-hand version. A number of sub-models have been made over the years, with letter suffixes denoting special features. Mechanically, the Springfield Model 67 and Model 77 guns are very similar, but there is some variation in the shape of certain parts. The gun was made under the Stevens and Springfield names until 1989.

Disassembly:

1. Open the action, and unscrew the takedown knob at the front of the forend piece until it stops. Turn the barrel clockwise (front view) until it stops, then remove the barrel toward the front. The takedown knob can be removed, if necessary, by taking off the C-clip at the rear, inside the barrel loop.

2. Removal of the small vertical screw at the front of the magazine tube will allow removal of the magazine end piece, magazine spring, and follower toward the front. Caution: The spring is under tension, so control it and ease it out.

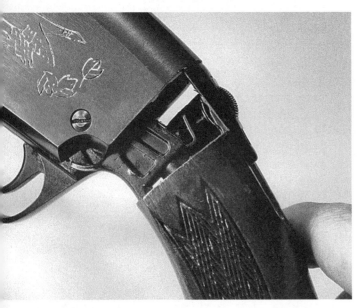

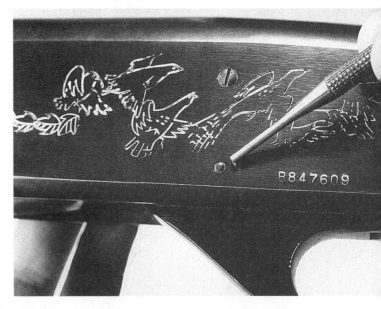

3. Do not attempt to disassemble the receiver components without first removing the stock. Take off the buttplate, and use a B-Square stock tool or a long-shanked screwdriver to back out and remove the stock bolt, lock washer, and washer. Take off the stock toward the rear.

4. Drift out the cross pin above the front of the trigger group toward the left.

5. Remove the cross screw at the lower rear of the receiver.

6. Remove the trigger group toward the rear and downward.

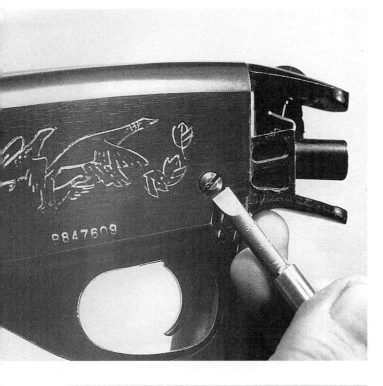

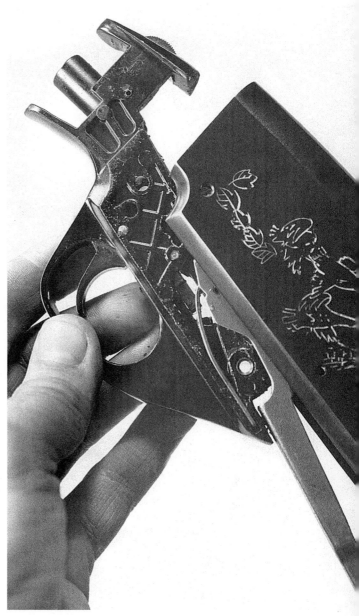

7. Detach the slide latch from its stud on the left side of the housing, and remove it upward. The slide latch release spring is held in place by a riveted stud on the left side of the latch, and is not removed unless necessary for repair.

8. Spring the right wing of the carrier off its pivot stud, and remove the carrier spring toward the right. Spring the left wing of the carrier off its stud, and remove the carrier.

9. The carrier dog is cross pinned on the right rear wing of the carrier, and the pin is riveted in place. If removal is necessary for repair, be sure the wing is well supported.

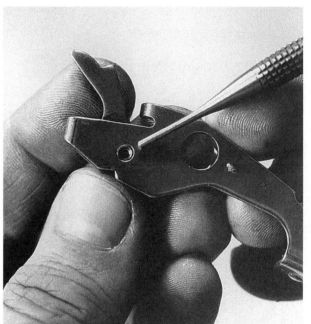

10. Restrain the hammer, pull the trigger, and ease the hammer down to the fired position. Drift out the hammer pivot toward the left, and remove the hammer upward.

11. Remove the hammer spring and plunger from their well in the trigger housing.

12. The inside tip of the slide latch spring is bent down inside the housing to retain the spring, and it should not be removed in normal disassembly. If necessary for repair, straighten the bent tip, and remove the spring toward the left.

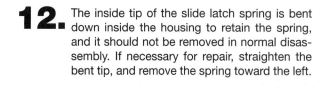

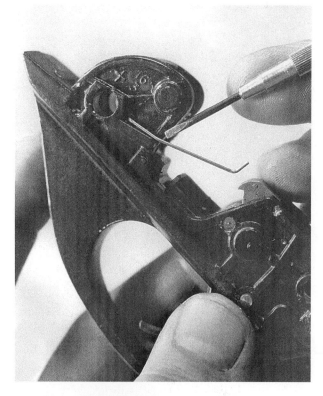

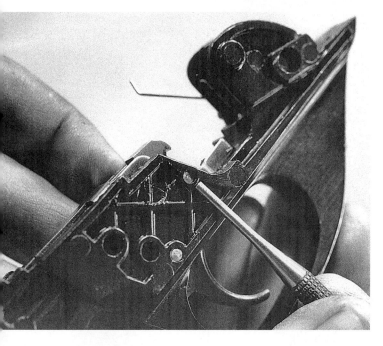

13. Push out the sear cross pin toward the left.

14. Remove the sear, and the combination sear and trigger spring, toward the front and upward.

15. Remove the C-clip from the safety button shaft.

16. Remove the safety button upward, and take out the safety spring toward the side.

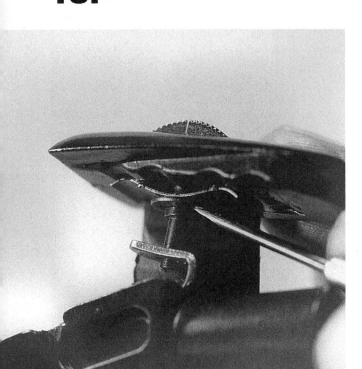

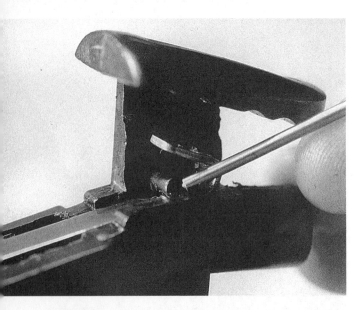

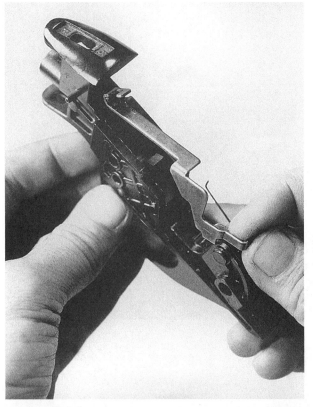

17. Use a roll pin punch to drift the safety bar retaining pin toward the right. It is not necessary to remove the pin, just move it over for clearance.

18. Remove the safety bar toward the front and upward.

20. Remove the trigger assembly upward. The sear trip can be removed from the trigger by drifting out its cross pin toward the right, but the left tip of the pin is riveted, and unless necessary for repair it should be left in place. If it is removed, take care not to deform the trip or the trigger. The trip spring will be released if the pin is removed.

19. Drift out the trigger cross pin toward the left.

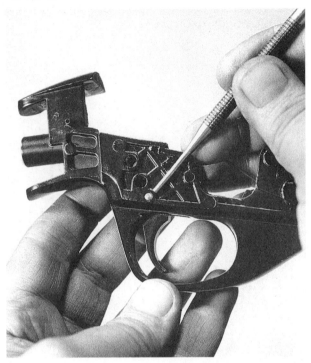

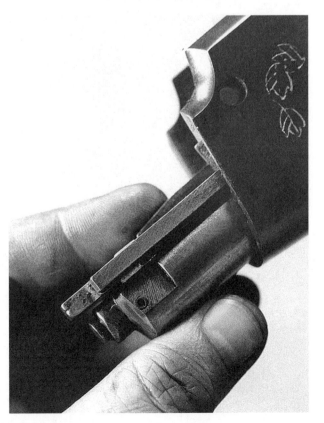

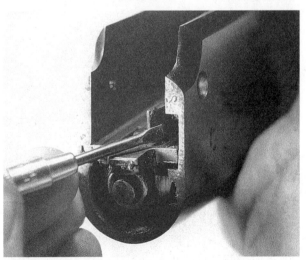

21. Move the bolt all the way to the rear of the receiver, and use a fingertip or tool to spring the rear tip of the action slide bar inward, disengaging the bar from the bolt slide piece.

22. Remove the bolt and slide piece from the rear of the receiver.

23. The slide piece is easily detached from the bottom of the bolt, and the tension spring is then removed from its hole on the underside of the bolt.

24. The bar contact lug on the slide piece is staked in place on the left side of the slide piece, and is occasionally found to be loose, so take care that it isn't lost during disassembly. It can easily be restaked in place.

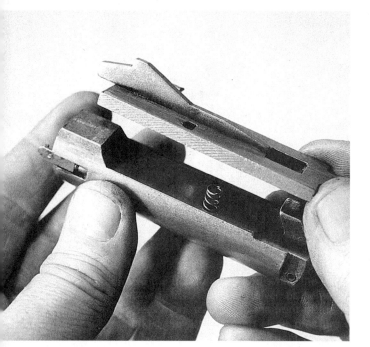

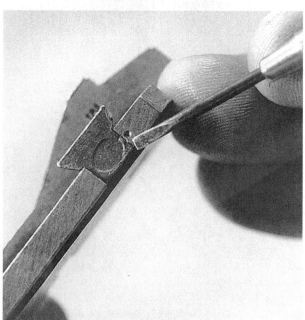

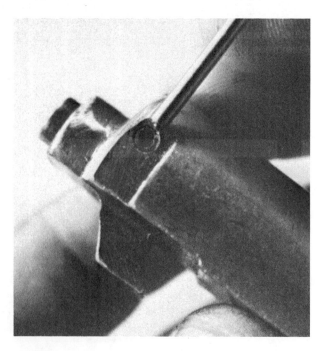

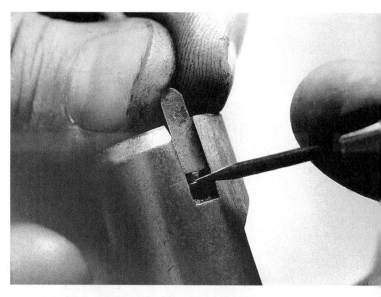

25. Drift out the roll cross pin at the rear of the bolt, and take out the firing pin and its return spring toward the rear.

26. The plunger for the right extractor has a recessed groove for insertion of a small screwdriver to depress the plunger toward the rear. The extractor is then lifted out of its recess in the bolt. Keep the plunger under control, and ease out the plunger and spring for removal toward the front.

27. The left extractor is simply tipped out toward the left until it snaps out of its recess. Restrain the plunger and spring, and remove them toward the front. Keep the extractors and their springs separate, as they are not interchangeable.

28. There is no provision for a special wrench on the forend cap nut. To remove it without marring, use a nylon drift punch and a small hammer to start it, as shown, then unscrew it by hand, counter-clockwise (front view). When the nut is removed, the action slide assembly can be slid out toward the rear, and the forend wood taken off toward the front.

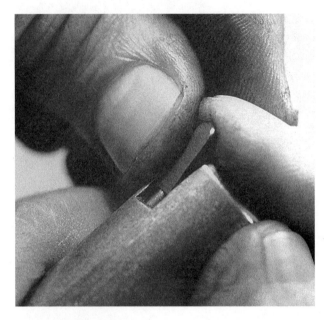

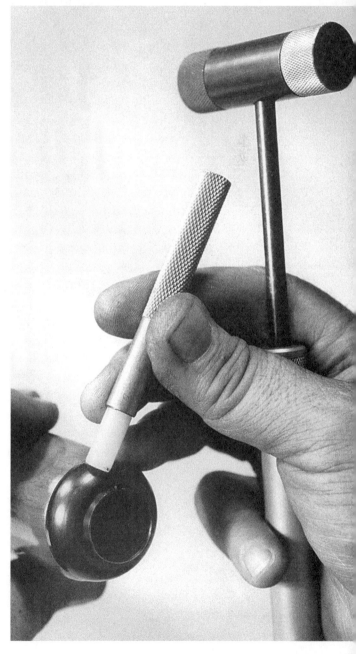

29. Move the rear base ring of the forend tube forward, and lift the front tip of the action slide bar out of its recess. Turn the base ring to align its barrel clearance recess with the slide bar, and take off the bar toward the front.

30. The action slide tube is retained on the magazine tube by a raised welt in a lengthwise slot. If removal is necessary, the slide tube can be pushed off toward the front, springing the welt inward. In normal takedown, it is best left in place. It is also possible to unscrew the magazine tube from the receiver, taking off the slide tube toward the rear. Again, it is best left in place.

31. Removal of the screw on the right side of the receiver, below the ejection port, will release the shell stop to be taken out inward. It will be necessary to insert a tool on the inside to stabilize the retaining nut as the screw is removed, setting the point of the tool in one of the notches provided in the nut. A twin-pointed offset screwdriver is useful in this operation, contacting both of the notches on the nut.

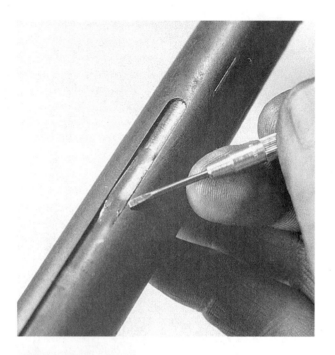

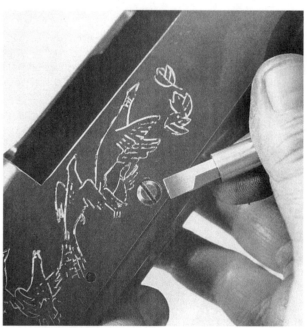

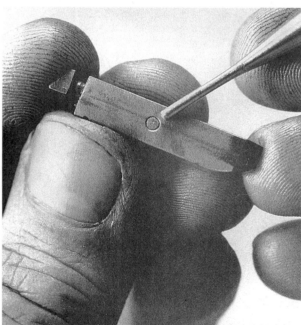

32. Removal of the small screw on the left side of the receiver near the top will release the ejector assembly to be taken out from inside the receiver.

33. Drifting out the small pin in the ejector housing will allow removal of the ejector plunger and spring toward the front.

Reassembly Tips:

1. When replacing the shell stop screw and nut, it will be necessary to insert a tool inside the receiver to contact the nut while tightening the screw. As mentioned in step 31, a twin-pointed offset screwdriver is ideal for this operation.

2. When replacing the hammer pivot, note that the rebated section of the pivot must go on the left side, to clear the slide latch. Also, be sure the lower front step of the hammer is above its ledge in the housing before the pivot is replaced. If the hammer is tilted forward when the pivot is installed, it cannot be cocked.

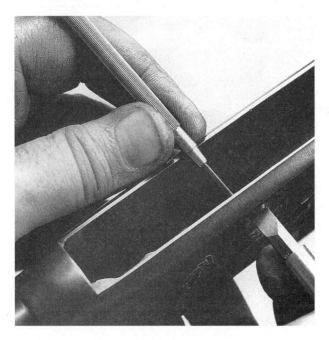

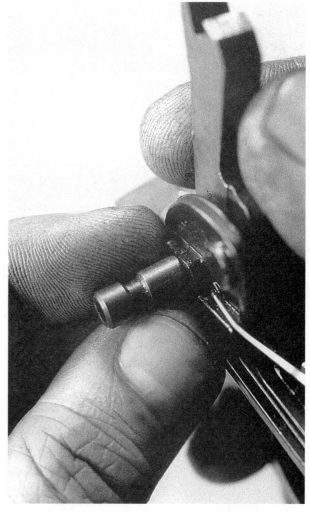

3. When replacing the slide latch, be sure the latch spring engages its groove in the side stud of the latch, as shown.

Savage-Stevens Model 311

Similar/Identical Pattern Guns:

The same basic assembly/disassembly steps for the Savage-Stevens Model 311 also apply to the following guns:

Fox Model B-C	Fox Model BST
Fox Model B-D-B-E SeriesB, Series F	Savage Model 5000
Sears "Ranger" 400	Sears Model 101.7
Sears Model 5100	Stevens Model 5100
Stevens Model 530	Stevens Model 530A
Stevens Model 530M	Stevens Model 530ST
Stevens Model 311R	Stevens/Springfield Model 311
Stevens Model 311A, C, D, Series F, Series H	Stevens/Springfield Model 511A
Stevens/Springfield Model 511	

Data:	Savage Model 311
Origin:	United States
Manufacturer:	Savage Arms Company Westfield, Massachusetts
Gauges:	12, 16, 20, and 410
Overall length:	44-1/2 inches
Barrel length:	26 to 30 inches
Weight:	7 to 8 pounds

The venerable Model 311 double began as a true Stevens gun in 1931, and was wisely retained in the line when the Savage company obtained the Stevens firm in 1936. The Model 311 is a classic example of the simple, solid and reliable American double gun. As with most so-called "hammerless" guns, it has pivoting internal hammers. While there have been some minor changes during its nearly 50 years of production, the basic mechanism is the same, and the instructions can be applied to all Model 311 guns, early or late. Some models of the Fox double, and the Springfield Model 511, have internal mechanisms that are practically the same.

Disassembly:

1. Pull the front of the forend away from the barrels until its spring-catch releases, and remove the forend downward and toward the front.

2. Operate the barrel latch, and tip the barrels down beyond their normal opened position. Remove the barrels upward.

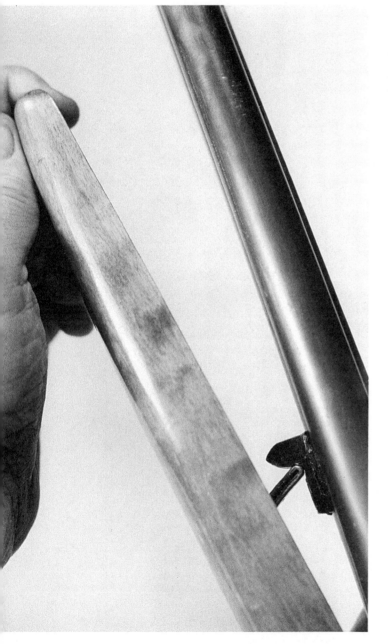

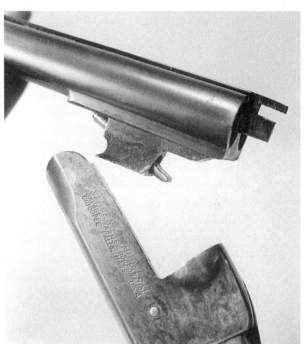

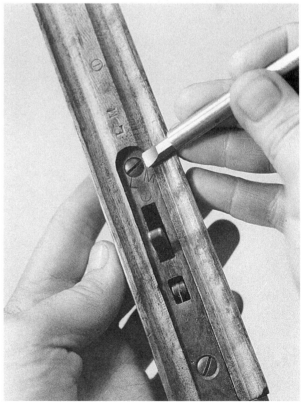

3. Remove the two screws on the inside of the forend, and remove the forend iron upward.

4. The heavy forend latch spring and its small round-wire positioning spring are retained by a cross pin. The smaller spring is under slight tension, so restrain it as the pin is removed.

5. Remove the screw on the inside at the rear of the forend iron, and take off the ejector block toward the rear.

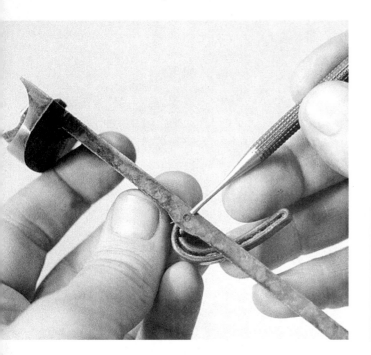

6. Remove the small screw on the underside of the barrel underlug, and take out the cocking plunger and its spring toward the rear.

7. Remove the large screw on the underside of the barrel underlug, and take out the ejector toward the rear.

8. Insert a tool in the slot at the center of the breech face, and depress the barrel latch detent, releasing the latch lever to return to center.

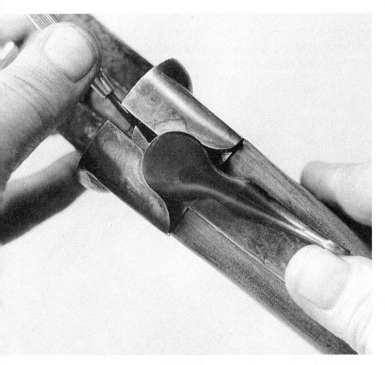

9. Back out the screw in the rear tail of the trigger guard, unscrew the guard from the receiver, and remove it. Note that on some Model 311 guns, the front of the guard is also retained by a separate screw, and an angle-tip or offset screwdriver will be required for removal.

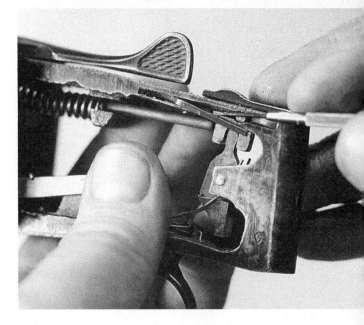

10. Remove the buttplate, and use a B-Square stock tool or a long-shanked screwdriver to back out the stock bolt. Remove the bolt, its washer, and the stock toward the rear.

11. Pull the triggers to trip the sears, allowing the hammers to fall to the fired position. Insert a small screwdriver beneath the tail of the safety spring, from the rear, and lift it just over the edge of its recess. Turn the tail downward, and lift the front cross arm of the spring out of its hole in the receiver. After the spring is removed, turn the left side of the receiver downward over the hand, and tap it until the safety positioning and retaining plunger drops out.

12. Remove the safety button upward.

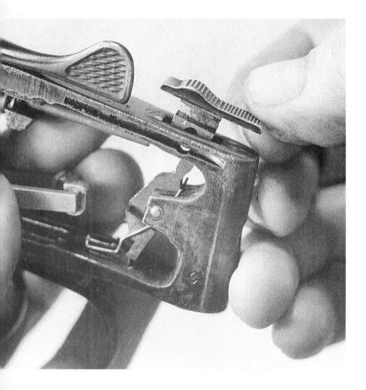

13. Drift out the cross pin at the rear of the receiver. This will release the safety lever and the right and left trigger springs for removal. The springs are under some tension, so restrain them during removal.

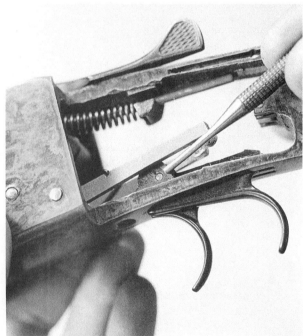

14. Drift out the trigger cross pin, and remove the two triggers downward.

15. Drift out the sear cross pin, and remove the sears and their double spring toward the rear. The sear spring is under some tension, and will tend to angle the cross pin after one end clears the receiver wall. Exert pressure on one sear to keep the pin straight during removal. Another method is to unhook both arms of the spring from the sears before removal of the pin.

16. Drift out the main cross pin that retains both hammers and the cocking lever. This should be done in stages, taking out each of the three parts as the pin clears them. Caution: The hammer springs are quite powerful, and are under tension, so keep the hammers under control.

17. Remove the hammers toward the rear.

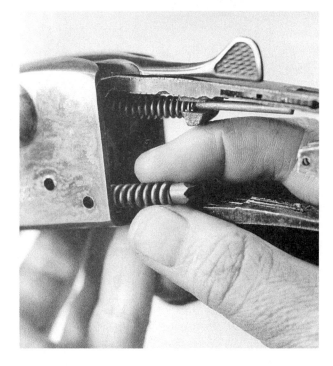

18. Remove the hammer springs and plungers toward the rear.

19. After both hammers are removed, the cocking lever can be moved out toward the rear. During removal, take care that the small return spring at the rear of the cocking lever is not deformed. Drifting out the cross pin will allow removal of the spring.

20. The firing pins and their return springs are retained by large screws beside each firing pin, inside the receiver. The screws, firing pins, and the springs are taken out toward the rear.

21. Insert a small screwdriver on the left side to lever the barrel latch spring forward until it can be pushed toward the left, out of its seat in the upper tang of the receiver. Caution: This spring is quite strong, and is under tension, so control it. Also, do not attempt to move this assembly by pushing on the rear tail of the spring guide, as it is easily deformed. After the spring is released, move the spring and guide downward, then remove them toward the rear.

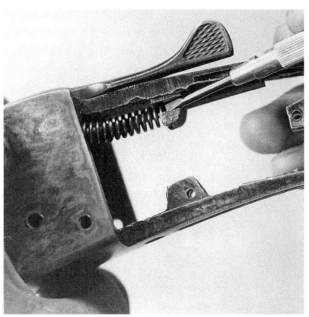

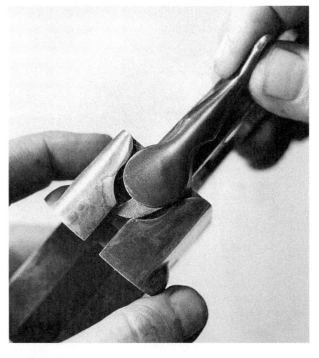

22. The barrel latch lever is retained on the inside of the receiver by a vertical screw. There is no direct access, so an offset screwdriver or one with an angled tip must be used. Remove the screw downward.

23. Remove the barrel latch lever toward the rear.

24. Lift the latch lever detent and its spring out of its recess in the receiver.

1. When replacing the triggers in the receiver, note that the rear trigger goes on the left side, the front trigger on the right, as shown.

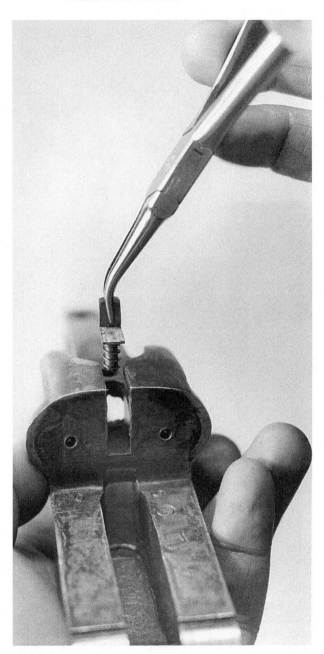

2. When replacing the hammers in the receiver, note that the cocking lobes of each hammer must go toward the center, as shown.

3. When replacing the cocking plunger in the barrel underlug, be sure it is fully inserted before putting in the retaining screw, to insure that the screw nose enters behind the coil spring.

4. When replacing the safety lever at the rear of the receiver, be sure that it is installed with its pivot hole at the rear, and its lower clearance cut toward the front, as shown.

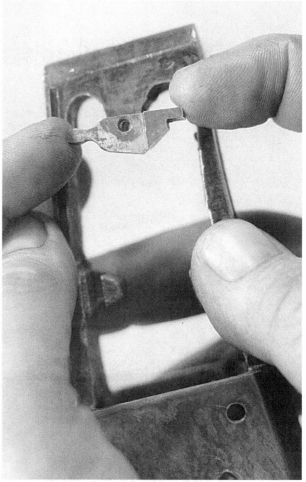

When installing the hammers, be sure the recess at the rear tip of the hammer spring plungers engages the lobe at the bottom of each hammer. Grip the forward portion of the receiver in a padded vise, and use a tool to press each hammer forward until the hammer hole aligns with the cross pin hole. If a hammer is installed and will not cock, this indicates that the plunger has slipped off the lobe during installation. Check this by lifting the cocking lever with a tool after the hammers are installed.

Savage Model 755A

Similar/Identical Pattern Guns:

The same basic assembly/disassembly steps for the Savage Model 755A also apply to the following guns:

Savage Model 720	**Savage Model 720C**
Savage Model 720P	**Savage Model 726**
Savage Model 726C	**Savage Model 726P**
Savage Model 740C	**Savage Model 745**
Savage Model 750	**Savage Model 750AC**
Savage Model 750SC	**Savage Model 755**
Savage Model 755C	**Savage Model 775**
Savage Model 775A	**Savage Model 775SC**

Data:	Savage Model 755A
Origin:	United States
Manufacturer:	Savage Arms Company, Chicoppe Falls, Massachusetts
Gauges:	12 and 16
Magazine Capacity:	4 rounds
Overall length:	46-1/2 inches
Barrel length:	26 to 30 inches
Weight:	6 to 8 1/2 pounds

Although the Savage autoloaders relied greatly on the basic Browning long-recoil design made famous by the Auto-5, there were some elements that were entirely different. The line began in 1930 with the Model 720, which even had the appearance of a Browning. By 1949, when the Model 755 arrived, some of the components, such as the trigger group, were pure Savage. The Model 720, 775, and other variants listed above are mechanically much the same as the Model 755, and the instructions will apply. The Model 755 faded from the scene in 1956.

Disassembly:

1. Pull back the operating handle to lock the bolt open, and set the safety in the on-safe position. Depress the barrel slightly toward the rear, and unscrew and remove the magazine end cap. Take off the forend and barrel toward the front.

2. The ejector is mounted in a slot at the left rear of the barrel extension, and its post is riveted on the outside of the extension. If removal is necessary for repair, it is drifted out toward the right.

3. Remove the friction piece and the compression ring toward the front. The circular friction piece spring is easily removed from the friction piece. If the gun has been used with light loads, the compression ring may be found, reversed, at the rear of the recoil spring. Take off the recoil spring toward the front.

4. Insert a screwdriver in the open end of the magazine spring retainer, and pry it outward, moving the screwdriver to raise it equally around its edge. Caution: The magazine spring will be released, so control it and ease it out. Remove the spring and follower toward the front.

5. Removal of the small screw near the front on the right side of the receiver will allow the magazine tube to be unscrewed from the front of the receiver, if this is necessary for repair. In normal takedown, it is best left in place.

6. Restrain the bolt, depress the carrier latch button, and ease the bolt forward to closed position. Remove the buttplate, and use a large screwdriver to back out the stock retaining bolt. Remove the buttstock toward the rear, and take off the spacer ring at the rear of the receiver.

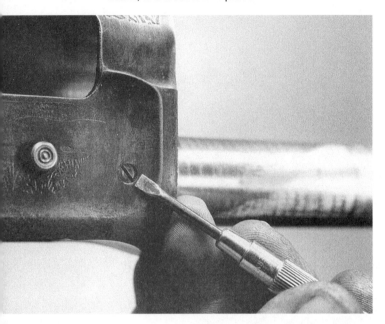

7. Remove the lock screw and the main screw at the front of the trigger housing on the left side. The main "screw" is actually a pin, and is simply pushed out toward the left.

8. Remove the lock screw and the main screw at the lower rear of the receiver on the left side.

9. Remove the trigger group downward.

10. Move the safety to the off-safe position, restrain the hammer, pull the trigger, and ease the hammer down to fired position. Push out the hammer pivot, and remove the hammer and its spring upward. The spring is under slight tension, so restrain it as the pin is removed.

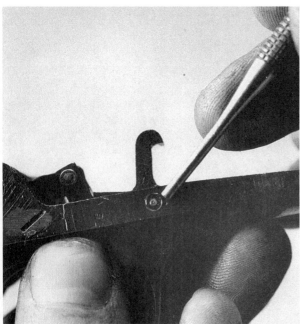

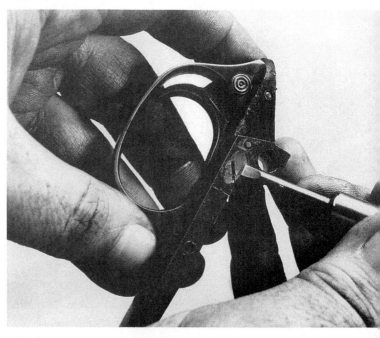

11. Drift out the sear pin, and remove the sear and its spring upward. There is an adjustment screw in the front extension of the sear, and if properly set, it should not be disturbed.

12. Remove the trigger stop screw, located on the right side, just forward of the trigger pin. This screw is usually staked in place, and removal may require some effort.

13. Push out the trigger pin, and remove the trigger upward. Caution: The trigger spring is under compression, and will exit with some force if not restrained. The disconnector and its spring are mounted on the front of the trigger by a cross pin that is riveted in place, and this should not be removed unless necessary for repair.

14. Drift out the cross pin at the upper rear of the trigger housing, holding a fingertip over the small hole at the upper rear to arrest the safety spring. Remove the spring and plunger upward, and take out the safety button toward either side.

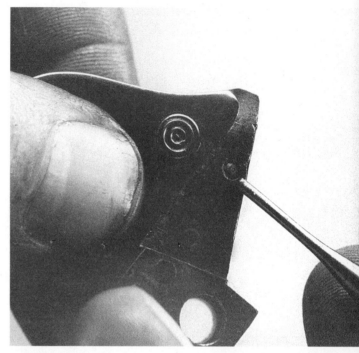

15. Insert a screwdriver in the bottom of the receiver and pry the carrier spring off its post at the rear, unhook it from its front post, and remove it. Caution: Restrain this spring during removal.

16. Take out the lock screw and the carrier pivot screw on each side of the receiver.

17. Remove the carrier from the bottom of the receiver. The carrier dog and its spring and plunger are mounted on the right rear wing of the carrier by a cross pin. If removal is necessary for repair, the pin is drifted out toward the left. Note that the carrier dog spring is quite strong, so control it and ease it out.

18. Retract the bolt until the bolt spring follower passes the small detent hole on the left side of the spring housing, and insert a drift punch or a small pin to arrest the follower and spring.

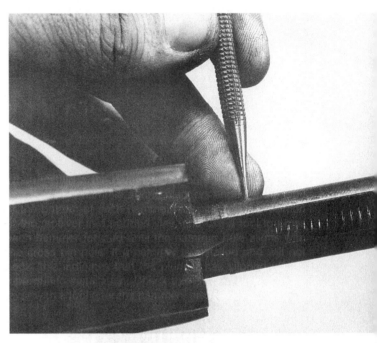

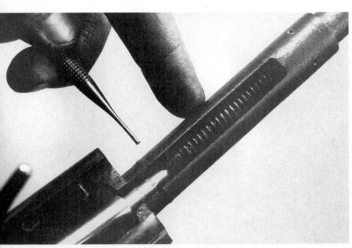

19. Move the bolt forward, and swing the link bar outward. Insert a screwdriver or some other heavy tool to bear on the front of the bolt spring follower, and exert slight pressure toward the rear. Remove the detent pin or drift from the access hole, and slowly release the spring tension, removing the spring and follower from the bottom of the receiver. Caution: This is a strong spring, and it is compressed, so keep it under control.

20. Move the operating handle unit toward the rear, and position the bolt so the cross pin that retains the link bar lever is in alignment with the access hole on the left side of the receiver. Use a very small drift punch to nudge the cross pin toward the left, and out the access hole.

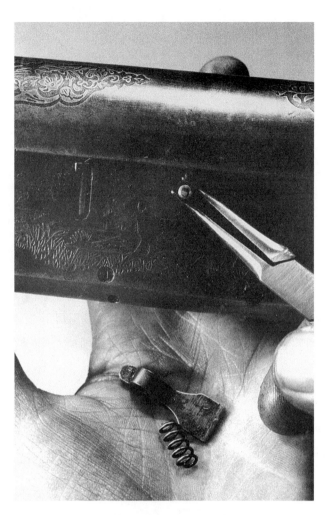

21. Since the pin is only partially accessible on the right side, it is not possible to drift it straight through. When it has emerged enough on the left side, grip it with pliers and pull it out. Keep a hand under the receiver as the pin is removed, as the link bar lever and its spring will be released downward.

22. Swing the link bar back inward, and remove the bolt assembly toward the front.

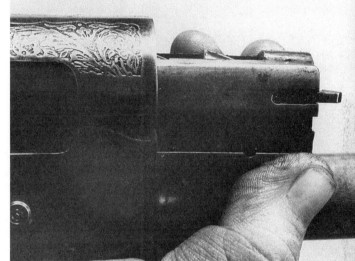

23. Move the operating handle forward, and take it out through the ejection port.

24. Remove the carrier latch pivot lock screw, on the right side of the receiver.

25. Remove the carrier latch pivot screw from the lower right edge of the receiver.

26. Remove the carrier latch, the latch button, and the latch spring from inside the receiver. Repeat this operation on the opposite side, taking off the shell stop.

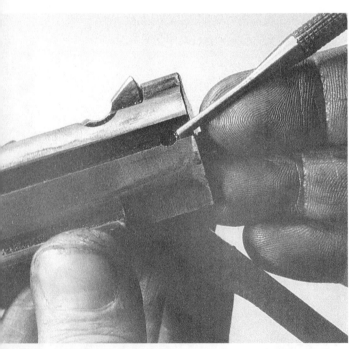

27. Drift out the cross pin at the rear of the bolt toward the right, and remove the firing pin toward the rear.

28. Push the link bar upward through the bottom of the bolt, tipping the locking block out the top of the bolt, and remove the assembly upward. Drifting out the cross pin will allow separation of the link bar and locking block, but the pin is riveted and should be removed only for repair purposes.

29.
The extractor is retained by a vertical pin at the front of the bolt on the right side. Drift out the pin, and remove the extractor toward the right. Caution: Restrain the plunger and spring, and ease them out toward the front.

1.
When installing the carrier spring, set it on its post at the rear, and engage its shorter arm with the lobe of the carrier. Then, push the longer arm inward and engage it behind the flange on the front post. During this operation, keep a thumb on the rear of the spring to keep it on the rear post.

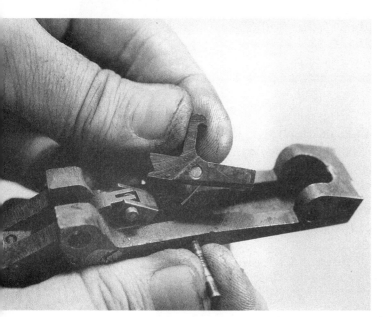

2.
When replacing the sear in the trigger housing, it will be necessary to use a slave pin to hold the spring in the sear until the cross pin is installed. The sear is shown with the slave pin in place. A slave pin will also help when the trigger and its spring are installed.

3.
Replacing the hammer and its spring also calls for the use of a slave pin, but it is possible to replace the hammer without one.

SKB Model XL900MR

Similar/Identical Pattern Guns:

The same basic assembly/disassembly steps for the SKB Model XL900MR also apply to the following guns:

Ithaca Model 300	**Ithaca Model 900**
SKB Model XL900	**SKB Model 100**
SKB Model 1300	**SKB Model 1900**

Data:	SKB Model XL900MR
Origin:	Japan
Manufacturer:	SKB Arms Company, Tokyo
Gauges:	12 & 20
Magazine capacity:	5 rounds
Overall length:	50 inches (with 30-inch barrel)
Barrel length:	24, 26 & 30 inches
Weight:	7 pounds

Except for a few external features, the Model XL900MR and the regular Model XL900 are identical. These two SKB models were imported into the U.S. very briefly, in 1979 and 1980, but apparently quite a few of them were sold. Ithaca briefly imported the SKB semi-auto and gave them their own model numbers. The present importer of the current SKB line is Guns Unlimited of Omaha, Nebraska.

Disassembly:

1. Lock the action open, and set the safety in the on-safe position. Unscrew and remove the magazine end cap.

2. Remove the forend toward the front.

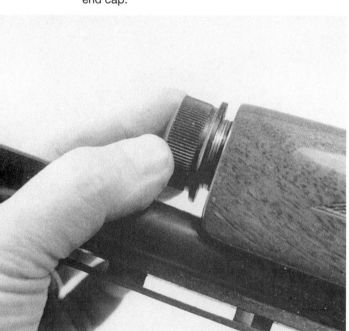

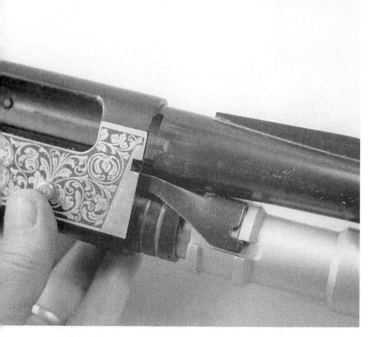

3. Move the barrel forward to the point shown.

4. Restrain the bolt, push the carrier release button, and ease the bolt forward. Remove the barrel toward the front.

5. The bushing at the front is retained by a very small screw, and the gas seal rings at the rear can be spread and removed if necessary for repair. In normal takedown, this system is left in place.

6. Push out the two trigger group retaining pins.

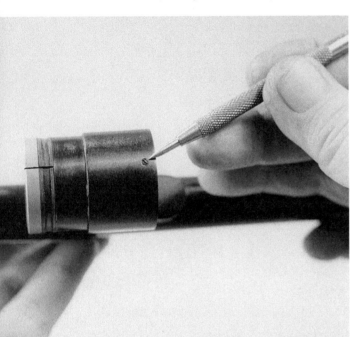

7. Remove the trigger group downward.

8. Move the bolt forward until the wider portion of the slot is aligned with the bolt handle. Remove the bolt handle toward the right.

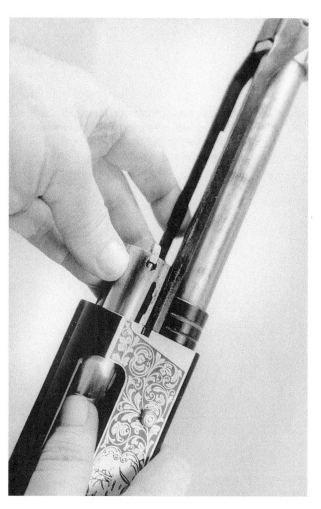

9. Remove the bolt and action slide assembly toward the front. The bolt is easily detached from the action slide.

10. The action slide is detached from the piston by tilting it upward, as shown.

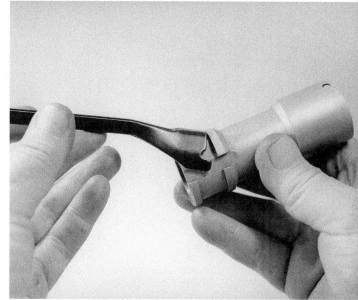

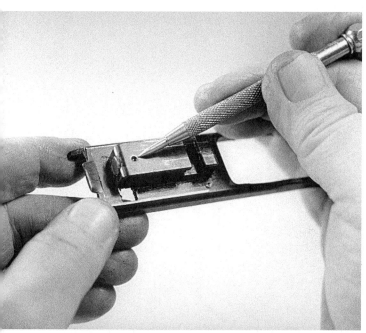

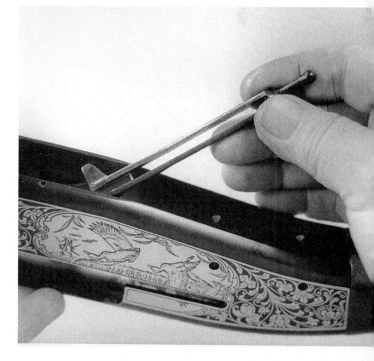

11. The bolt buffer is staked in place, and it retains the bolt handle plunger and spring. This system is not routinely dismountable.

12. Lift the rear of the bolt spring strut, and turn the strut for removal.

13. A vertical roll pin at the rear of the bolt on the right side retains the firing pin and its return spring. The pin is drifted out upward. Removal of the firing pin will free the locking block for removal downward.

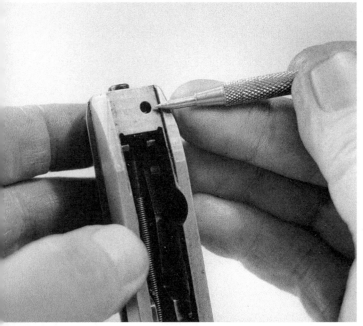

14. Insert a small tool between the extractor and its plunger, and depress the plunger rearward. Tip the extractor out toward the front. Caution: Control the plunger and spring.

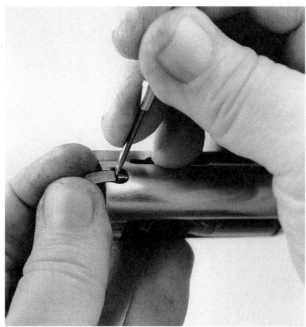

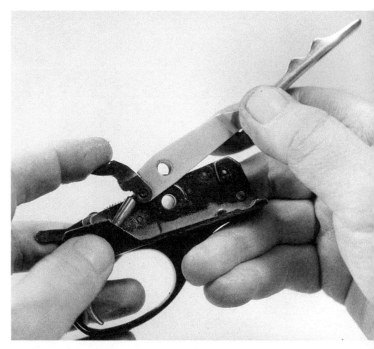

15. Restrain the carrier plunger and spring on the right side of the trigger group, and push out the carrier pivot.

16. Remove the carrier upward. The carrier dog pivot is heavily riveted in place, and should be removed only for repair.

17. Remove the carrier plunger and spring.

18. Move the safety to off-safe position, and depress the safety sear, the lever at left rear. Restrain the hammer, pull the trigger, and ease the hammer down to the forward position.

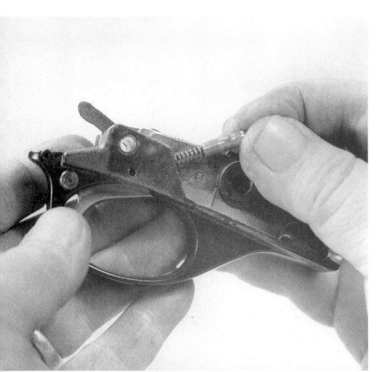

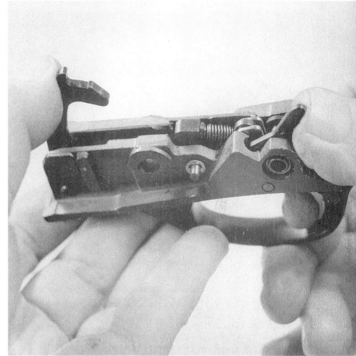

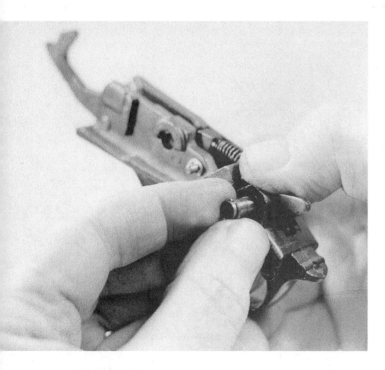

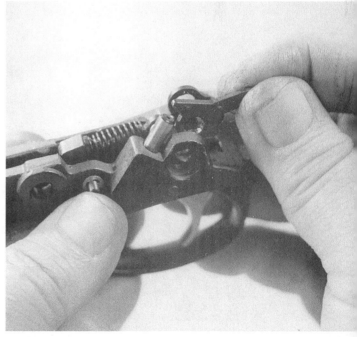

19. Restrain the safety sear, and remove the rear cross pin sleeve toward the left.

20. Remove the safety sear upward and toward the rear.

21. Remove the safety sear plunger and spring.

22. Remove the combination trigger and sear spring.

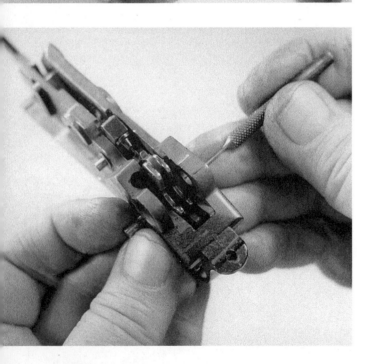

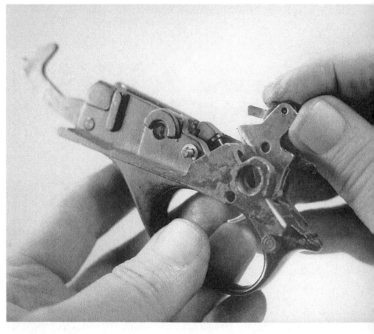

23. Push out the trigger pin toward the left.

24. Remove the trigger assembly upward. The trigger arm is easily detachable by pushing out the pin at the top.

25. Remove the sear pin toward the left, and take out the sear upward. Do not remove the C-clip on the sear pin.

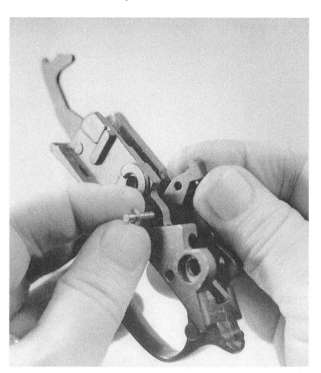

26. Insert a slim tool to nudge the hammer spring assembly out upward. The hammer spring housing can be spread to release the spring, if necessary for repair.

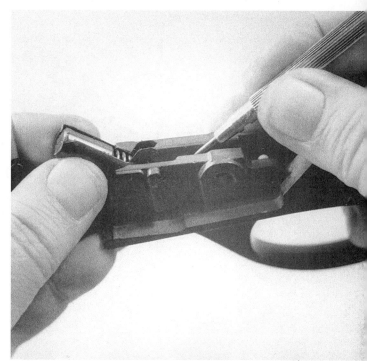

27. Drifting out the cross pin will release the hammer for removal.

28. Pushing out the cross pin at the rear of the trigger group will release the safety spring and plunger. Cover the opening at the top as the pin is removed, to arrest the spring. With the spring and plunger removed, the safety button can be removed toward either side.

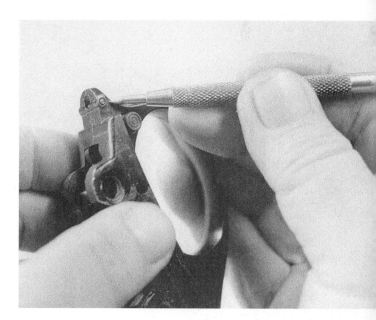

29. Just inside the receiver lower edge on the right side is a small lengthwise spring clip that retains the carder latch pivot pin. A small and sharp tool with a bent tip is necessary for taking off the clip toward the rear. The latch pivot can then be pushed out upward, and the carrier latch and its button and spring can be taken out inward. In normal takedown, this system is best left in place.

30. Removal of the stock retaining nut requires a 19mm socket. Beneath the nut are two spring washers and a heavy solid washer. Remove the stock.

31. Depress the bolt spring end piece, and push out the retaining cross pin. Caution: Control the spring, Remove the end piece, spring, and follower toward the rear. If removal of the magazine spring and follower are necessary, they are retained by a standard keeper ring at the front of the magazine tube. Again, control the spring.

Reassembly Tips:

1. When replacing the bolt spring strut, note that it must be installed as shown, curving downward at the rear.

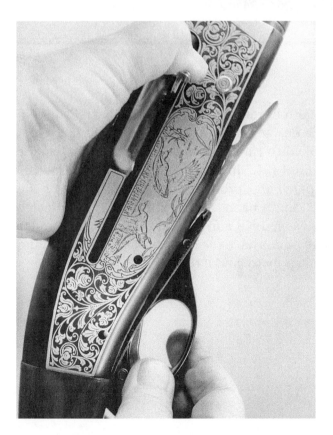

2. When replacing the trigger group, the bolt must be drawn slightly rearward, to insure proper engagement of the safety sear.

L.C. Smith Double

Similar/Identical Pattern Guns:

The same basic assembly/disassembly steps for the L.C. Smith also apply to the following gun:

Marlin L.C. Smith

Data:	L.C. Smith Double
Origin:	United States
Manufacturer:	L.C. Smith Gun Co., Syracuse, New York Hunter Arms Company Fulton, New York Marlin Firearms Co., North Haven,Connecticut
Gauges:	12, 16, 20, 410
Overall length:	42 to 50 inches
Barrel length:	26 to 34 inches
Weight:	5-3/4 to 7 pounds

Lyman Cornelius Smith began making his double-barrel shotgun in 1877, and it was a design that would last for nearly 100 years. The business was sold to Hunter Arms in 1890, and they made the L.C. Smith gun until 1945. In that year, Marlin purchased the Hunter Arms Company, and produced a small quantity of the guns under the L.C. Smith name until around 1951. The design was used again between 1968 and 1972 by Marlin. With minor variations, all of these guns have the same basic mechanism, and the instructions will apply to any of them.

Disassembly:

1. The forend release latch is located on the underside of the forend. Roll it toward the front, and tip the forward end of the forend away from the barrel and remove it downward. Some guns may have a different type of release latch, or no latch at all. On the latter, the front of the forend is simply pulled away from the barrel.

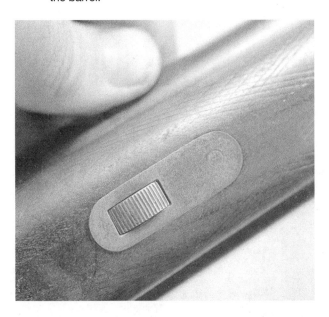

2. Remove the vertical screw on the inside of the forend at the forward end of the forend iron.

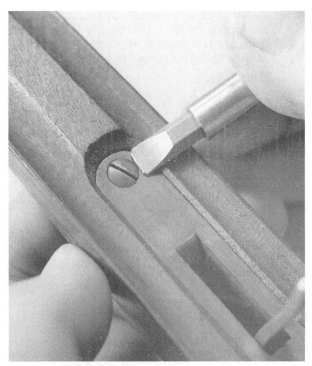

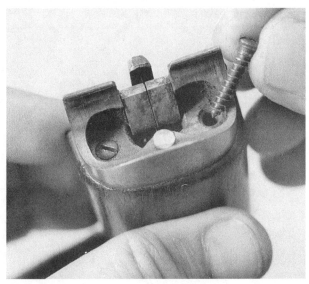

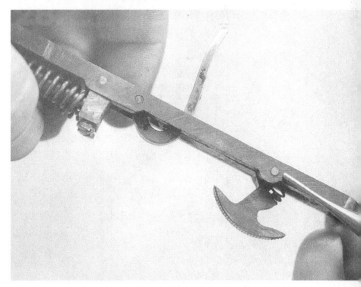

3. Remove the two screws in the recess at the rear of the forend, and remove the forend iron assembly from the forend wood. The external latch plate on the underside can also be removed. It is usually tightly fitted so take care to avoid chipping the wood.

4. The forend release latch is retained on the forend iron by a cross pin. Drifting out the pin will allow removal of the latch downward, along with its spring. The forend retaining spring and its small torsion wire positioning spring are also retained by a cross pin. Restrain the wire spring when drifting out the pin, and remove the retaining spring downward.

5. The gun shown is equipped with selective ejectors, and the ejector plungers and springs are based against a block which is held on the underside of the forend iron by a cross pin. Drift out the cross pin, and remove the assembly downward. The captive spring unit is retained in the block by two screws. When removing the screws, restrain the springs.

6. Operate the barrel latch, tip the barrels downward, then remove them upward. Back out or remove the screw on the underside, in the rear slope of the underlug.

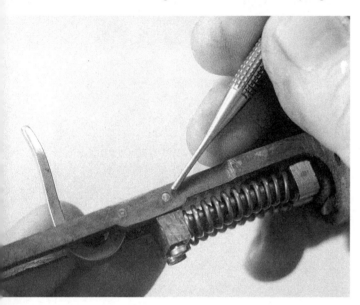

7. Remove the ejectors toward the rear.

8. Drifting out the cross pin (shown at the tip of the tool) at the upper front of the barrel underlug will release the ejector plunger for removal toward the front.

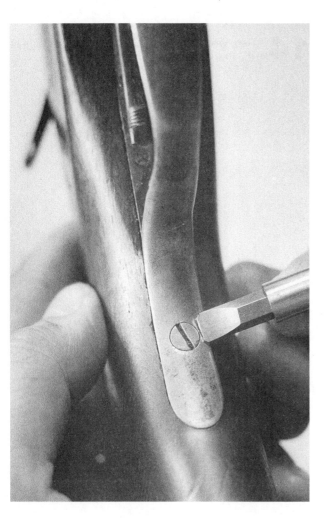

9. Remove the screw on the underside at the rear of the trigger guard, and unscrew the guard counter-clock-wise.

10. Remove the screw near the upper edge of the left lockplate. If there are lockplate retaining screws on each side at the base of the front extension, take them out.

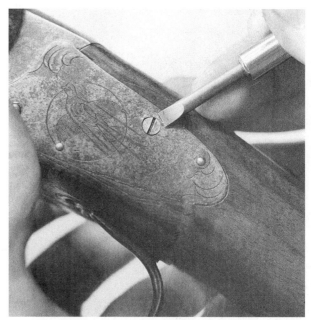

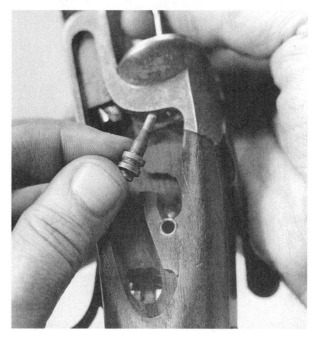

11. Insert a tool from the right side, through the lockplate cross screw hole, to bear on the inside of the left lockplate, and tap it gently to nudge the lockplate out of its recess in the receiver. Swing the rear of the lockplate outward, then remove it toward the rear. Repeat this operation with the right lockplate.

12. When the lockplates are removed, the firing pins will be freed, and can be pushed out from the front and removed toward the rear.

13. Remove the vertical screw in the front tip of the trigger plate.

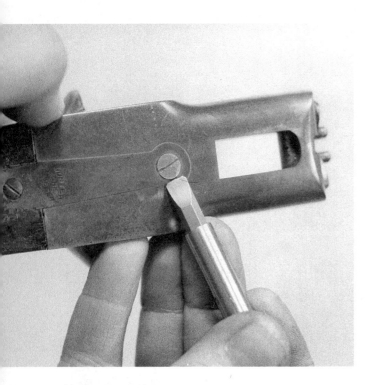

14. Remove the vertical screw on the underside at the rear of the trigger plate.

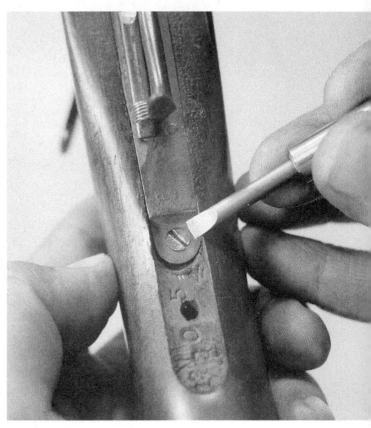

15. Remove the vertical screw on top, just to the rear of the barrel latch lever. After removal of the screw, use a tool to trip the barrel latch detent, inside the slot in the breech face, and allow the lever to move to center position, partially relieving the tension of its spring.

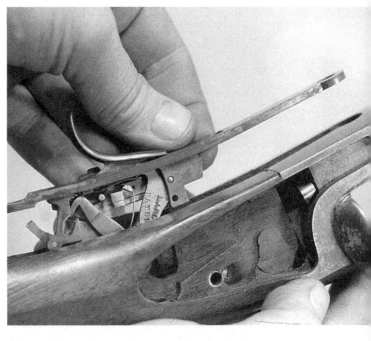

16. Remove the small screw on the underside, just forward of the trigger. Remove the trigger plate assembly downward.

17. Remove the buttstock downward and toward the rear.

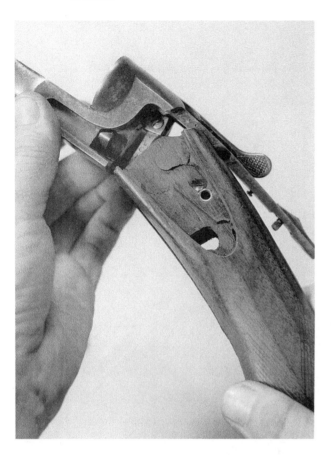

18. Drifting out the trigger cross pin will release the trigger assembly within the plate. Removal of the trigger will require drifting out the front cross pin in the spur link at the top. This will also release the inertia assembly, and it can be taken off upward and toward the rear.

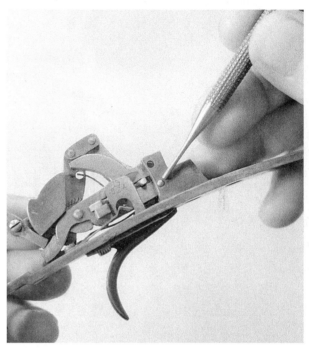

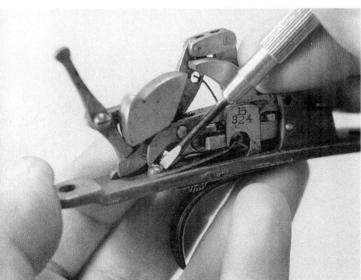

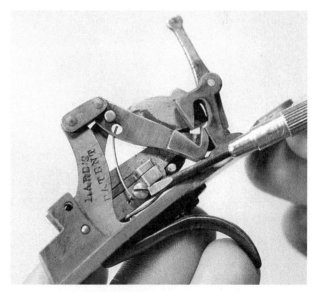

19. After removal of the inertia assembly, taking out this small screw will allow the trigger and change lever spring to be taken off toward the rear, and the change lever (barrel selector switch) can then be removed downward. The safety lever can be taken off by removing its cross screw.

20. On the opposite side of the assembly, a cross screw retains the inertia system spring. This spring must be removed before the inertia assembly is taken off.

21. Depress the sear upward at the rear to drop the hammer to the fired position, and use pliers to compress the hammer spring while removing the hammer spring retaining screw near the post at the rear of the lock. As an alternative to this, if you have a mainspring tool (see Reassembly Tips), leave the hammer cocked and slide the tool onto the spring to keep it under control while removing the retaining screw.

22. Remove the spring toward the rear and upward.

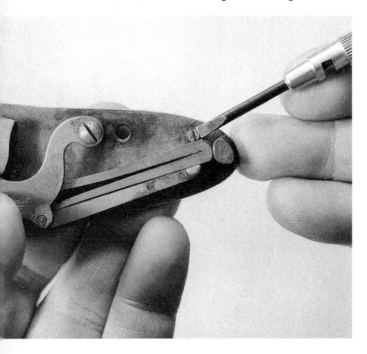

23. Remove the two screws that retain the bridle on the lockplate.

24. Remove the bridle from its posts on the lockplate.

25. Remove the hammer and sear from the lock-plate. Note that the pivots will remain in the sear and hammer. Repeat the takedown procedure with the other lock.

26. Remove the screw that retains the safety positioning spring. Note that the one shown is a round-wire replacement. The original is a blade type.

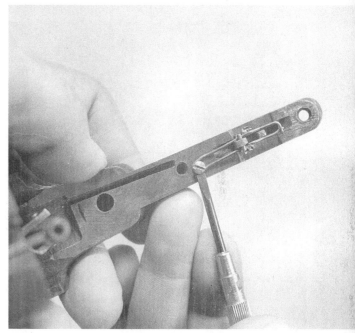

27. Drift out the two small cross pins in the lower lug of the safety button, and remove the safety button upward.

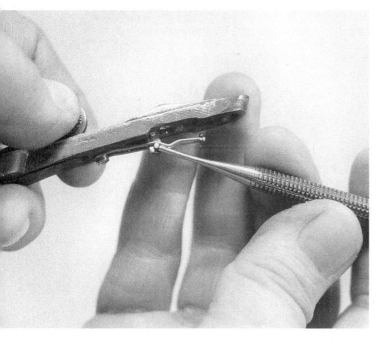
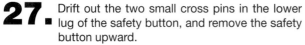

28. To remove the cocking levers, the rear tips of the lever rods are drifted forward, out of the square holes in the lifter lugs at the rear.

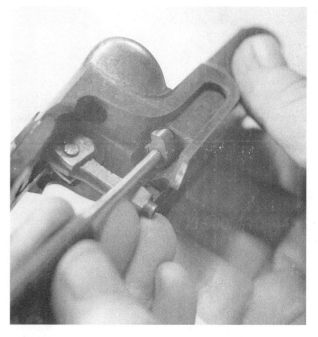

29. Use a drift to tap the barrel latch spring downward, out of its recess in the underside of the receiver, and remove it. Caution: This is a heavy spring, and it is under tension, so proceed carefully.

30. The automatic safety bar, which pushes the safety to the on-safe position when the action is opened, lies in a recess in the underside of the upper tang. The bar is free to be lifted out when the buttstock is taken off. On the gun shown, the safety bar is missing.

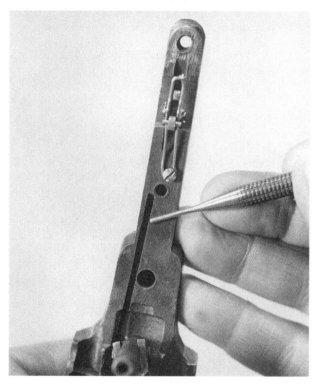

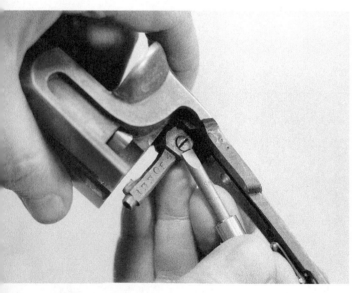

31. Turn the barrel latch lever to the opened position, and remove the cross screw in the barrel latch coupler. Note that this screw is often semi-riveted at its tip, and may be difficult to remove. After the screw is taken out, the latch lever can be removed upward, and the coupler and latch block can be taken out toward the rear.

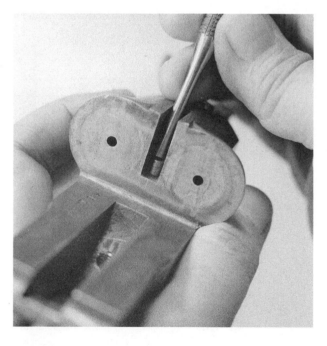

32. Removal of the latch block will release the detent plunger and spring in the slot at the front. Restrain the plunger, and take out the plunger and spring upward.

Reassembly Tips:

1. When replacing the trigger plate assembly, be sure the safety is in the on-safe position, and that the safety lever on the trigger plate is in the on-safe position. The top of the lever must engage with the recess on the underside of the safety button. Insert the rear of the trigger plate assembly first, then swing the front portion up into place. Replace the front screw, but just start it, don't tighten it at this time. With the latch lever in center position, insert a drift punch in the screw hole in the lower tip of the latch lever shaft, and spring the shaft into alignment with the hole in the trigger plate. When it aligns, press the plate into place, and install the barrel latch screw. The other trigger plate screws can then be replaced.

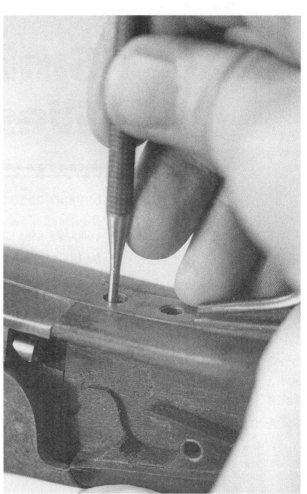

2. Replacing the main springs in the locks can be done much more easily if a mainspring tool is made, as shown. This can be made from any small piece of tough steel. The one shown was made from a broken Poly-Choke leaf. The spring is compressed with pliers, and the tool slid onto the spring to keep it compressed during installation.

3. With the tool in place on the spring, use pliers at the rear, by the stud, to depress the spring below the retaining screw hole, holding it there while the screw is replaced. The hammer can then be cocked, and the compression tool removed. Before replacing the locks in the receiver, be sure the trigger or triggers are fully forward, and the safety is in the on-safe position.

Smith & Wesson 916

Similar/Identical Pattern Guns:

The same basic assembly/disassembly steps for the Stoeger IGA Uplander English also apply to the following guns:

Noble Model 60	Noble Model 60ACP
Noble Model 60AF	Noble Model 66CLP
Noble Model 66RCLP	Noble Model 66RLP
Noble Model 160	Noble Model 166L
Smith & Wesson Model 916T	Noble Model 66XL
Smith & Wesson Model 96	

Data: Smith & Wesson 916
Origin: United States
Manufacturer: Smith & Wesson
Springfield, Massachusetts
Gauges: 12, and 20
Magazine capacity: 5 rounds
Overall length: 48 inches (with 28-inch barrel)
Barrel length: 20 to 30 inches
Weight: 7-1/4 pounds

This gun had its beginnings in 1952, in Haydenville, Massachusetts, under the Noble name. When the Noble company expired in 1972, Smith & Wesson acquired the design, corrected several troublesome design points, and introduced it as their Model 916 in 1973. It was a good, solid, slide-action gun, and when first offered had a fixed barrel. Later guns had detachable barrels. Except for this difference, the instructions will apply to any Model 916 and, in some areas, to earlier Noble guns. The Model 916 was discontinued in 1984, when Smith & Wesson dropped all shotguns from their line.

Disassembly:

1. Cycle the action to cock the hammer, and set the safety in the on-safe position. Remove the buttplate, and use B-Square stock tool or a long-shanked screwdriver to back out the stock bolt. Remove the stock bolt, its washer, and the buttstock toward the rear.

2. Drift out the cross pin above the front of the trigger group at the lower edge of the receiver toward the right.

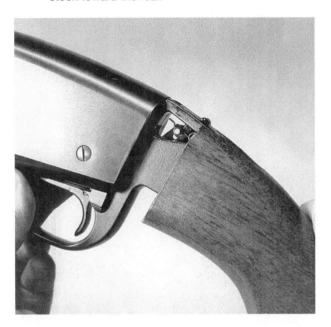

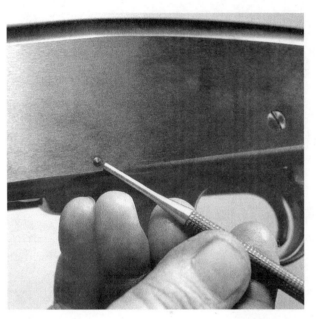

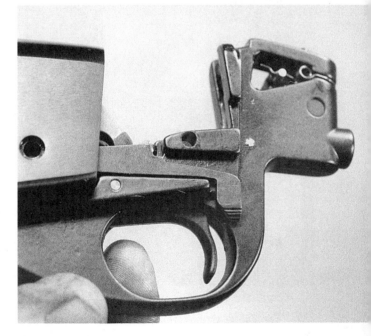

3. Remove the cross screw at the lower rear of the receiver toward the left.

4. Move the trigger group straight out toward the rear.

5. The shell stop will be released inside the receiver as the trigger group is removed, and can be taken out the bottom of the receiver.

6. Remove the carrier pivot screw from the right side of the trigger group, and note that this screw has a reverse thread. Unscrew it clockwise. Remove the carrier toward the right.

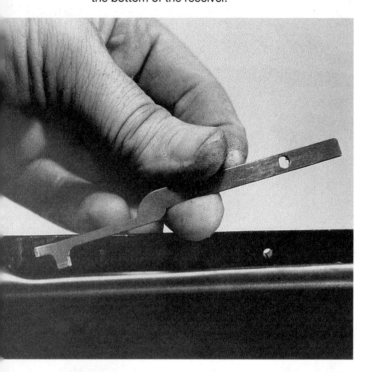

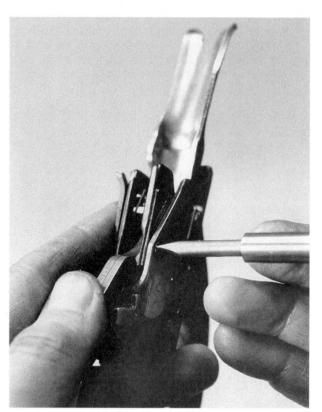

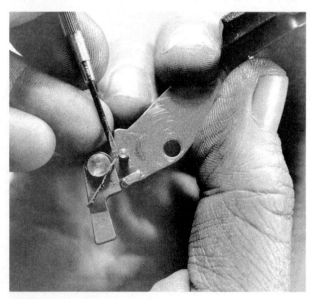

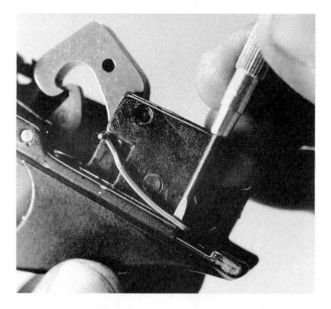

7. The carrier dog is retained on the rear of the carrier by a heavily riveted stud, and is not removable in normal takedown. The carrier dog spring can be removed, if necessary, by unhooking its arms and flexing it over the mounting post.

8. Insert a sharp screwdriver behind the front of the carrier spring, and pry it out toward the right for removal.

9. Remove the slide latch screw on the left side of the housing, and note that this one also has a reverse thread. Unscrew it clockwise.

10. Remove the slide latch toward the left, and take out the latch spring upward.

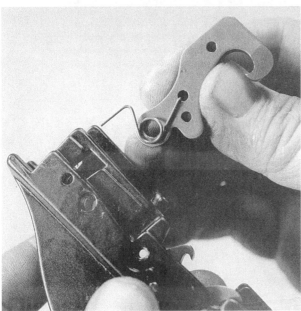

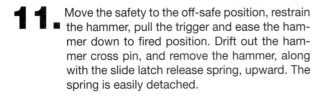

11. Move the safety to the off-safe position, restrain the hammer, pull the trigger and ease the hammer down to fired position. Drift out the hammer cross pin, and remove the hammer, along with the slide latch release spring, upward. The spring is easily detached.

12. Remove the hammer spring and plunger upward and toward the front.

13. Push the sear cross pin toward the right, just far enough to clear the sear.

14. Remove the sear upward.

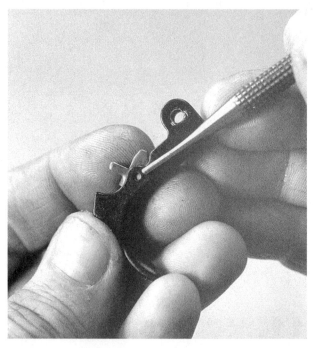

15. Remove the sear pin toward the right, and take out the trigger and the combination sear and trigger spring upward.

16. Drifting out the cross pin in the trigger will allow the trigger detent trip to be removed upward.

17. The trigger detent is mounted on a pin that is riveted on the left side of the housing, and should not be removed unless necessary for repair.

18. Insert a drift punch through the coil of the safety spring, and lever it out toward the left until the coil clears the side of the housing. Remove the spring toward the right rear.

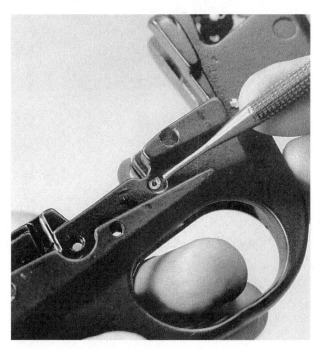

19. Push out the small cross pin in the lower extension of the safety button toward either side, and remove the safety button upward.

20. Drift out the safety lever cross pin toward the left.

21. Remove the safety lever upward.

22. Move the bolt and slide assembly to the rear, and insert a screwdriver through the ejection port to remove the ejector screw. Remove the ejector toward the right.

23. Move the bolt and slide assembly toward the rear until the rear edge of the extractor recess is even with the rear edge of the ejection port. Tip the bolt down at the rear, move it forward, and move the action slide toward the rear, disengaging its bar from the bolt. Tip the bolt further, until it is in the position shown.

24. With the action slide moved to the rear, detach the bolt slide piece inward, and remove it.

25. Tip the bolt back to its normal position, and remove it toward the rear.

26. A cross screw at the rear of the bolt on the left side is backed out to free the firing pin and its return spring for removal toward the rear. Restrain the firing pin as the screw is removed, and ease it out.

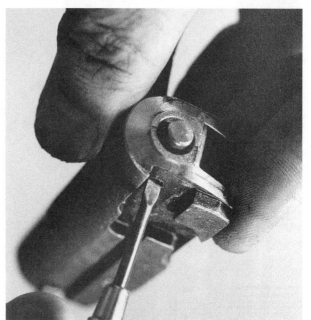

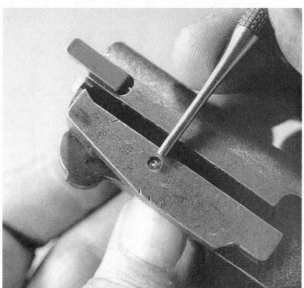

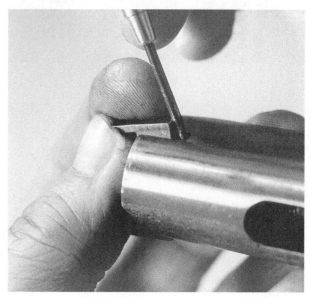

27. A cross pin near the front of the bolt retains the secondary shell stop and its coil spring, and these are removed downward after the pin is drifted out toward the right.

28. Insert a small screwdriver between the extractor and its plunger, and tilt the screwdriver toward the front, forcing the extractor out of its recess. Keep the plunger under control, and ease out the plunger and spring toward the front. Repeat this operation on the opposite extractor.

29. Unscrew the knob at thefront of the magazine tube. Caution: The magazine spring will be released. Control it, and ease it out. Remove the spring and follower toward the front.

30. Remove the magazine tube toward the front.

31. The action slide and forend assembly is now easily removed toward the front. Unscrewing the knurled nut at the front of the forend will allow the action slide tube and bar to be removed from the forend toward the rear.

Reassembly Tips:

1. When replacing the safety system, note that the safety lever goes on the right, and the lower extension of the safety button on the left. Note that the cross pin is ribbed to grip the button extension, and the ribbing is offset from the center of the pin. The pin must be inserted as shown for proper contact.

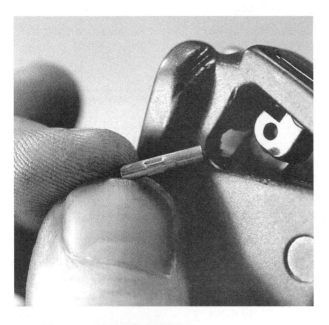

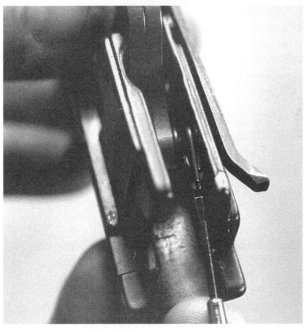

3. When replacing the slide latch, be sure the front inner projection of the latch goes below the front arm of the slide latch release spring on the side of the hammer.

2. When installing the trigger/sear cross pin, be sure the trigger detent is tipped toward the rear, to properly engage the detent trip on the trigger.

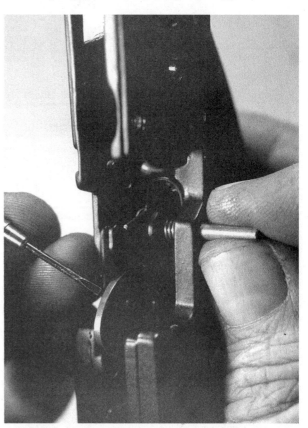

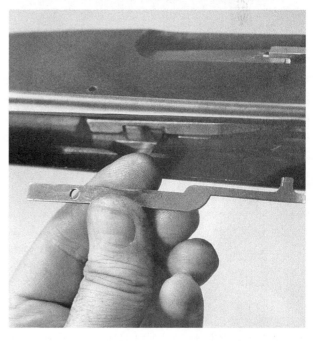

4. When installing the main shell stop inside the receiver, open the bolt slightly to insure that the upper tab of the shell stop properly engages its recess in the action slide bar.

Smith & Wesson 1000

Similar/Identical Pattern Guns:

The same basic assembly/disassembly steps for the Smith & Wesson 1000 also apply to the following gun:

Mossberg Model 1000

Data:	Smith & Wesson 1000
Origin:	United States
Manufacturer:	Smith & Wesson Springfield, Massachusetts
Gauges:	12, and 20
Magazine capacity:	3 rounds
Overall length:	48 inches (with 28-inch barrel)
Barrel length:	26 to 30 inches
Weight:	6-1/2 to 7-1/2 pounds

The Model 1000 was initially offered, in 1973, in 12-gauge only, with the 20-gauge version arriving about 3 years later. The gas system of this gun is unlike any other, with a connector ring on the outside of the magazine tube, a cross pin mating it to an internal piston. A heavy valve at the end of the tube compensates for the varying pressures of different loads, and the gas system parts are plated with hard chrome. The gun is relatively uncomplicated, and takedown and reassembly are not difficult. The Model 1000 was discontinued in 1984, when Smith & Wesson dropped their line of shotguns. It was offered briefly (1986-87) by Mossberg as their Model 1000.

Disassembly:

1. Pull back the operating handle and lock the bolt in the open position. Set the safety in the on-safe position. Unscrew the forend cap and remove it, and take off the forend. Remove the barrel toward the front.

2. Remove the pressure compensator valve from the front of the magazine tube.

3. Remove the piston connector ring spring from its groove on the outside of the ring, and take it off toward the front.

4. Push out and remove the piston connector pin toward either side.

5. Remove the piston connector ring toward the front.

6. Remove the piston toward the front.

7. Restrain the bolt, depress the carrier release button, and ease the bolt forward to the closed position. Push out the two trigger housing retaining cross pins at the lower rear of the receiver.

8. Remove the trigger group downward.

9. Restrain the carrier, and push out the carrier pivot toward the left.

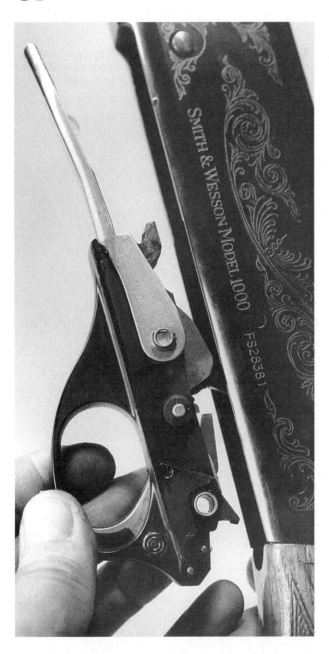

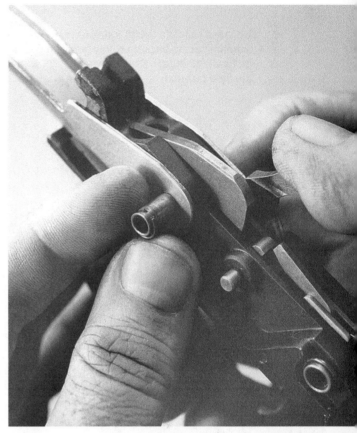

10. Move the carrier upward at the rear, then re-move it toward the front. Take out the carrier plunger and spring from their hole on the right side of the housing. The carrier dog is mounted on the right rear wing of the carrier by a heavily-riveted cross pin, and is not removed in normal takedown. If removal is necessary for repair, the pin must be driven out toward the right. Note that there is a small guide pin inside the carrier spring, and take care that it isn't lost.

11. Move the safety to the off-safe position, restrain the hammer, tip the auto safety (arrow) forward, and pull the trigger. Ease the hammer down to the fired position.

12. With the hammer pivoted all the way over toward the front, the hammer spring and plunger can be lifted out of their well in the housing and removed.

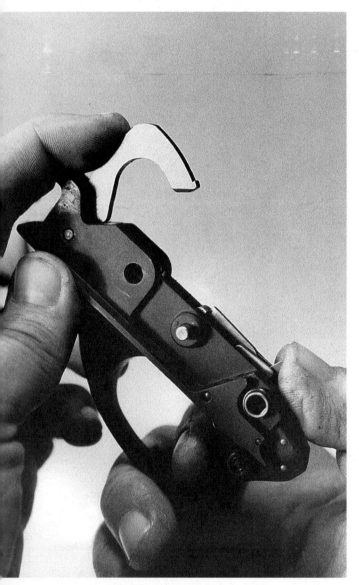

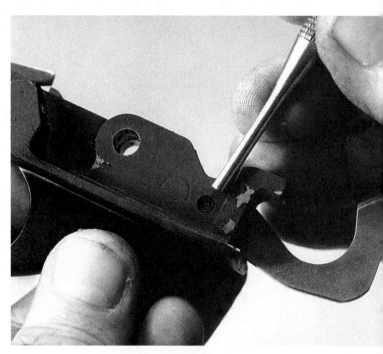

13. Drift out the hammer cross pin toward the left, and remove the hammer.

14. Push out the rear cross pin sleeve toward the left. Note that the sleeve is also the pivot for the auto safety.

15. Push the auto safety downward and toward the front, partially relieving the tension of its spring, and push out the small cross pin that retains the auto safety spring.

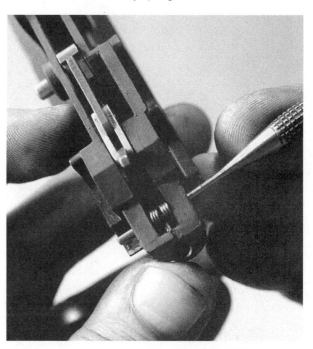

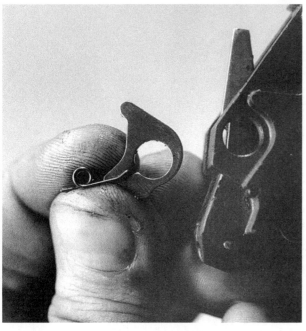

16. Remove the auto safety and its spring upward and toward the rear. The spring is easily detached from the open center of the auto safety.

17. The sear pin is easily pulled out toward the left, and the sear is removed forward and upward, along with its spring.

18. Push out the trigger cross pin, and remove the trigger upward. The connector is mounted in the trigger by a heavily-riveted cross pin, and this is not removed in normal takedown.

19. Push out the small cross pin at the extreme rear of the housing, holding a fingertip over the hole at the upper rear to arrest the safety spring. Remove the spring and plunger upward.

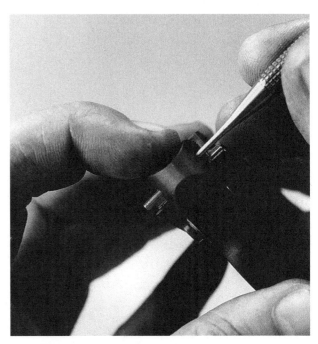

20. Remove the safety button toward either side.

21. Grip the operating handle firmly and pull it straight out toward the right.

22. Remove the slide and bolt assembly toward the front, and detach the bolt and slide piece from the action slide bars.

23. The action slide bars are easily detached from the slide tube by swinging them outward, then unhooking them toward the front.

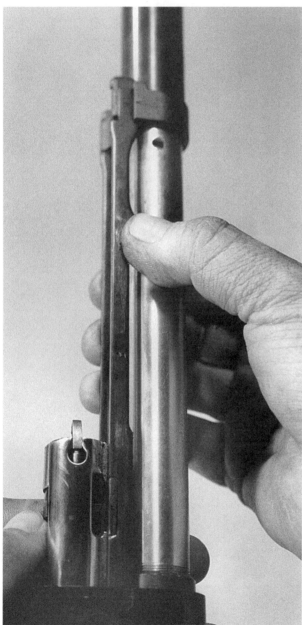

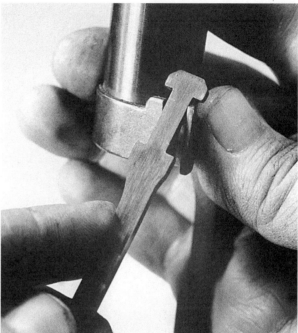

24. The bolt is easily detached from the slide piece.

25. The large cross pin at the rear of the slide piece can be pushed out in either direction to free the link bars at the rear. A small cross pin at the center of the slide piece is drifted out toward the right to free the operating handle retaining plunger and spring. Caution: This is a strong spring, so restrain the plunger and ease it out.

26. Drift out the large vertical roll pin at the rear of the bolt, and remove the firing pin and its return spring toward the rear.

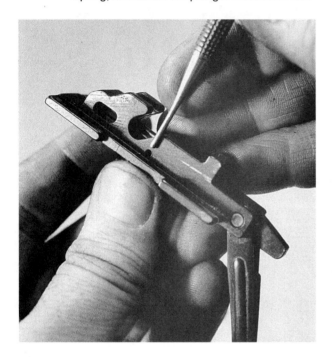

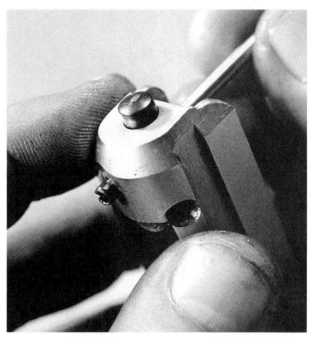

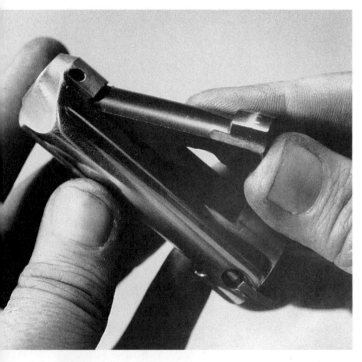

28. Insert a small screwdriver between the extractor and its plunger, depress the plunger toward the rear, and lift the extractor out of its recess. Keep the plunger under control, ease it out, and remove the plunger and spring toward the front.

27. Tip the locking block upward at the front, and remove it.

29. It is possible to spring the magazine spring retaining washer out of its detent holes at the front, allowing removal of the spring and follower. Unless necessary for repair, though, this system is best left in place. If removal of the magazine tube is necessary, unscrew the tube retaining nut at the base of the tube, and unscrew the tube from the receiver. The capacity reducing pin, which serves the same purpose as a plug, can be removed by driving it out toward the right.

30. The carrier release on the left side and the shell stop on the right side are retained by vertical pins in the receiver walls. The pins are retained by small spring clips set in narrow recesses, just inside the lower edge of the receiver on each side. The clips are slid out toward the rear, and the pins are drifted out upward to free the parts for removal, along with their attendant springs.

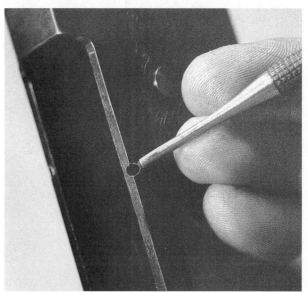

31. Remove the buttplate, and use a screwdriver with a wide, thin blade or a socket wrench of proper size to back out and remove the stock mounting bolt and its captive washers. Remove the stock toward the rear.

32. A screwdriver with a wide, thin blade is required to remove the plug screw at the rear of the action spring housing. Caution: The spring is under tension. Take out the spring and follower toward the rear. The spring housing is also removable by backing off the nut at the rear of the receiver and unscrewing the tube, but in normal takedown this is best left in place.

Reassembly Tips:

1. When replacing the piston, note that the smaller hole goes at the rear, and the large hole at the front must be oriented vertically.

2. When installing the combination sear and trigger spring, be sure the rear tip of the spring is engaged with the stud on the trigger connector before the sear is moved down into place.

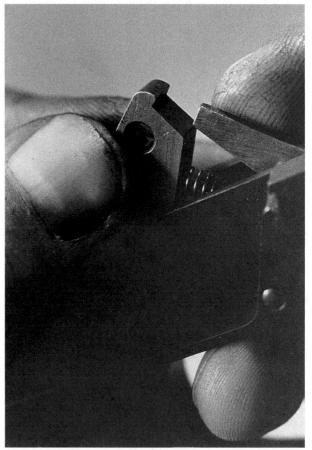

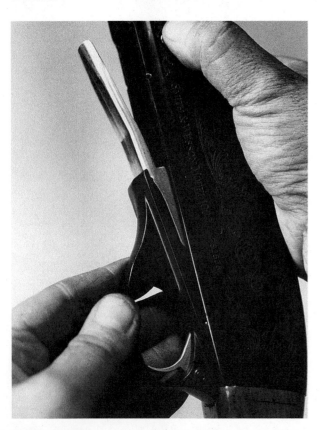

3. When replacing the trigger group, insert the rear end first to insure that the auto safety properly contacts the action spring assembly, and depress the carrier latch as the front of the trigger group is moved into place for replacement of the cross pins. Also, retract the bolt slightly during final seating of the trigger group, as added insurance that the auto safety is properly engaged.

When replacing the safety button, be sure the plunger contact area is oriented toward the plunger at the upper rear (see step 20).

Snake Charmer II

Similar/Identical Pattern Guns:

The same basic assembly/disassembly steps for the Snake Charmer II also apply to the following guns:

New Generation Snake Charmer **Snake Charmer**

Data:	Snake Charmer II
Origin:	United States
Manufacturer:	Sporting Arms Mfg., Inc Littlefield, Texas
Gauges:	410
Overall length:	28-5/8 inches
Barrel length:	18-1/4 inches
Weight:	3-1/2 pounds

The original Snake Charmer was designed by Homer Koon and made by his company in Dallas, Texas. The company was later purchased by Sporting Arms Manufacturing, and moved to Littlefield, Texas. In 1989, the new firm introduced Snake Charmer II, the main difference being the addition of a hammer-block manual safety. A more recent addition is the New Generation Snake Charmer, which has a black carbon steel barrel.

Disassembly:

1. Remove the large Phillips screw on the underside of the forend, and take off the forend downward.

2. Open the action, and remove the barrel pivot screw. Remove the barrel unit upward.

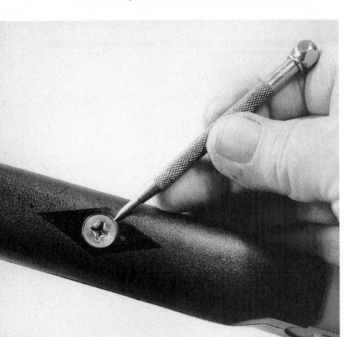

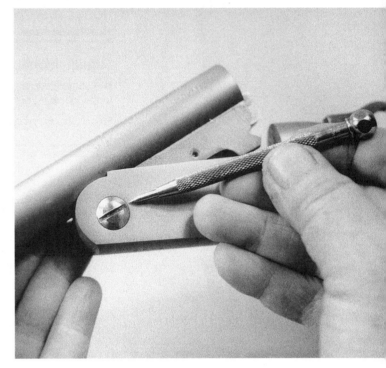

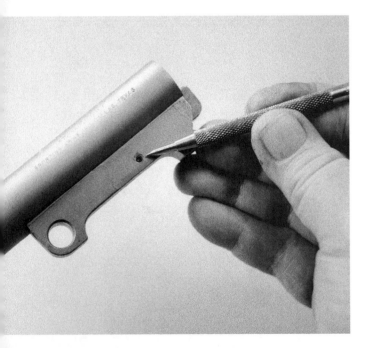

3. The ejector is retained by a roll-type cross pin. Restrain the ejector when the pin is drifted out, and remove the ejector and its strong spring toward the rear.

4. Drift out the small pin just forward of the trigger pivot toward the right.

5. Drift out the small rear cross pin toward the right.

6. Drift out the trigger cross pin toward the right. Note that the larger cross pins in the receiver are splined at the right tip, and all must be driven out toward the right to avoid damage.

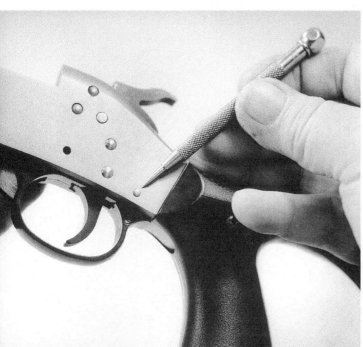

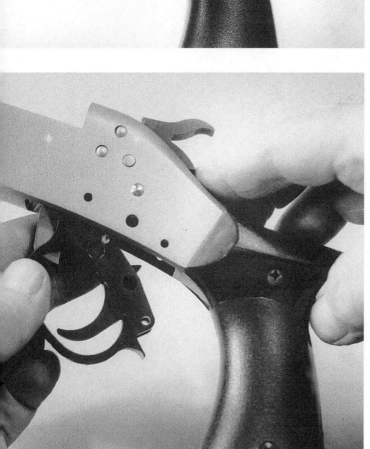

7. Remove the trigger guard unit downward and rearward.

8. Remove the trigger from the guard unit.

9. Remove the combination trigger and barrel latch spring and its plunger from the guard unit.

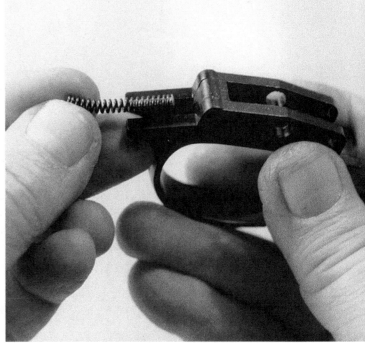

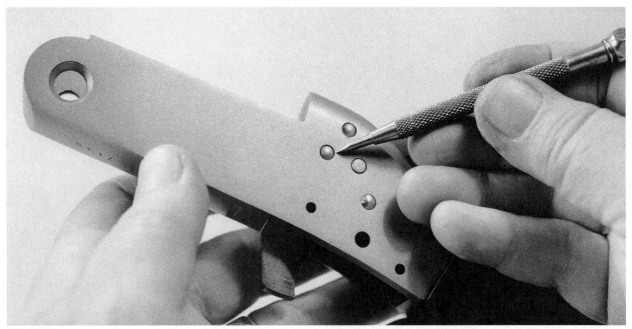

10. Drift out the barrel latch pivot toward the right.

11. Remove the barrel latch downward.

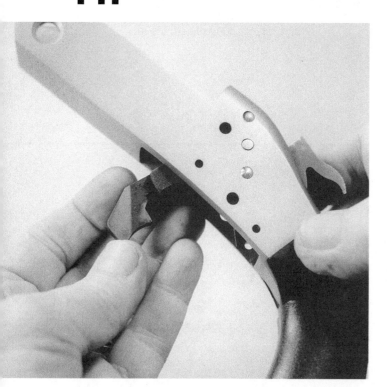

12. Drift out the hammer pivot toward the right.

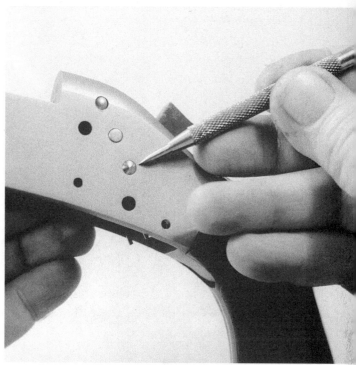

13. Remove the hammer upward.

14. Remove the hammer spring downward.

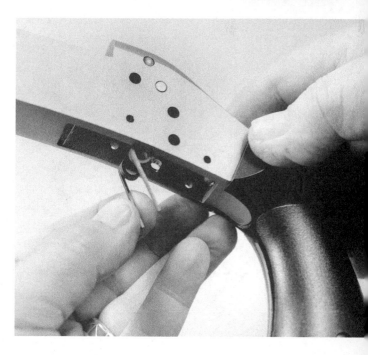

15. The manual safety is retained by a spring washer on the inside of the receiver. With a sharp tool, it is possible to work the washer off the shaft and remove the safety. However, damage to the spring washer is possible, and this could affect operation of the safety. In normal takedown, this system is best left in place. If repair is necessary, the receiver should be returned to the factory.

16. Drift the retaining pin at the top of the receiver out toward the right, and remove the firing pin and its return spring toward the rear.

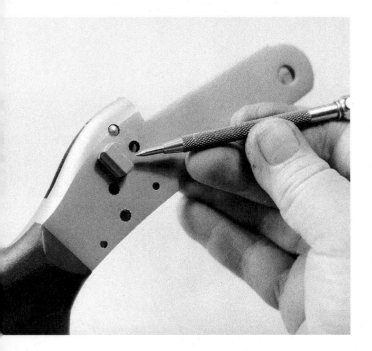

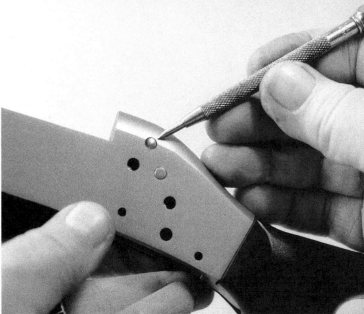

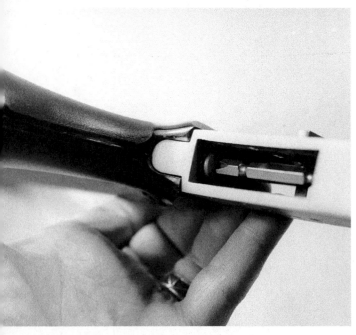

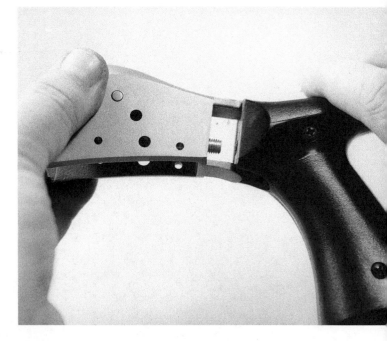

17. Insert a Phillips screwdriver from the front, and remove the stock mounting screw, located inside the receiver at lower rear.

18. Remove the stock toward the rear.

19. Remove the shell storage lid.

20. Remove the three Phillips screws in the left side of the stock, one at the rear and two in the pistol grip. Note, for reassembly, that the upper screw in the grip is shorter.

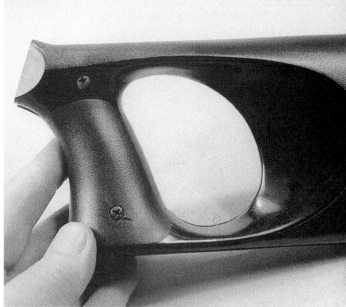

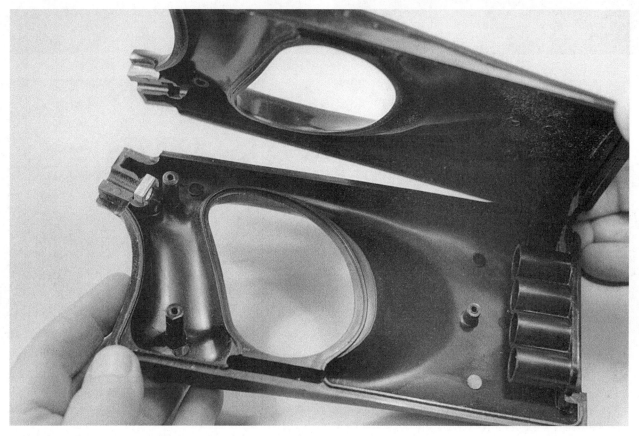

21. Lift off the left half of the stock. The shell storage plate and the stock screw nut can be lifted out of their recesses in the stock.

Reassembly Tips:

1. When replacing the cross pins in the receiver, remember that the larger pins are splined at the right tips, and they must be drifted in toward the left.

2. Reinstalling the guard unit and trigger can be done without a slave pin, but it is much easier if one is used, as shown.

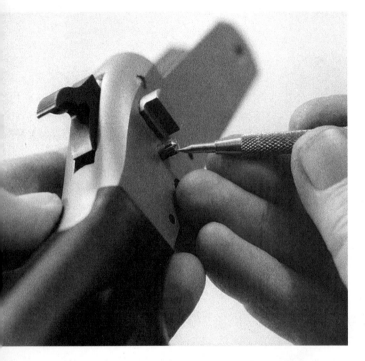

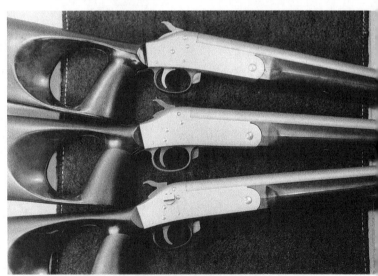

3. When replacing the guard unit in the receiver, be sure the front of the spring enters its recess in the back of the barrel latch. Angle the guard as shown, and the spring should engage properly. As the guard is pushed into place, pull the trigger to clear the hammer steps. Replace the front cross pin, then the trigger pin. Use a drift to align the unit as the rear pin is replaced.

Three versions of the Snake Charmer are shown here. The gun at the top and the second gun are original H. Koon production. Note that the very early gun at the top has an internal trigger pin that does not extend through the receiver. The lower gun is the currently made Snake Charmer II. It should be noted that on the two early guns, the splined cross pins are installed from left to right. So, check this carefully before drifting out the pins.

Stevens Hammer Double

Data: Stevens Hammer Double
Origin: United States
Manufacturer: J. Stevens Arms & Tool Co., Chicopee Falls, Massachusetts
Gauges: 12 and 16
Overall length: 38-1/4 inches (with 22-inch barrel)
Barrel length: 22 inches on gun shown, others offered
Weight: 7-1/2 pounds

Joshua Stevens began making guns in Massachusetts in 1864, and the firm became J. Stevens Arms & Tool Co. in 1886. The firm was bought by Savage in 1926. The old external-hammer double shown here was typical of the Stevens shotguns made from 1886 to around 1910. No model designation is known-it was referred to simply as "The Double Gun" in early catalogs.

Disassembly:

1. Pull the front of the forend away from the barrels, and remove it downward.

2. Operate the barrel latch, open the action, and remove the barrel unit upward.

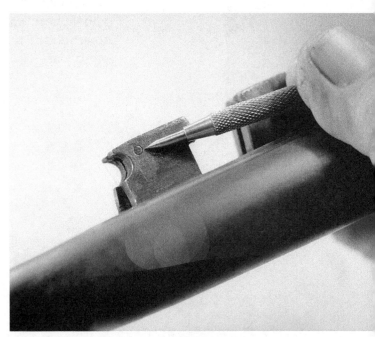

3. The ejector is retained by a screw on the underside of the barrel unit, between the locking lugs. The ejector is removed toward the rear.

4. The ejector lever is pivoted and retained by a cross pin in the forward lug. The lever is taken out downward.

5. With the hammers at rest, remove the cross screw that retains the locks.

6. Insert a slim drift from the opposite side, and gently push the rear of the lock outward for removal. repeat this operation for the other lock.

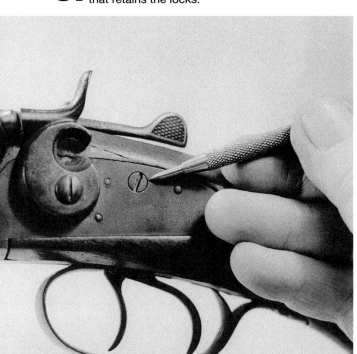

7. Remove the two screws in the plate on the inside of the lock. The two screw posts will be released, so take care that they are not lost. When removing the front screw, put slight rearward pressure on the hammer, and release the tension slowly after the screw is out.

8. Insert a tool to gently pry the plate off the sear and tumbler pivots. The hammer spring will jump up at the front, but it will not fly out. Remove the plate.

9. Remove the hammer spring.

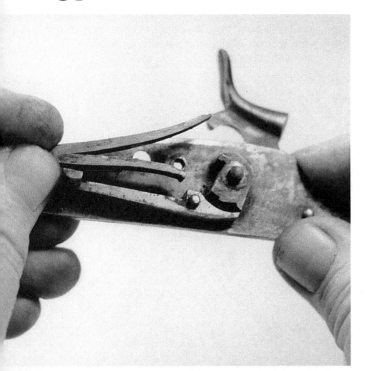

10. Remove the sear. The sear pivot pin is tightly fitted, and it is not removed in normal takedown.

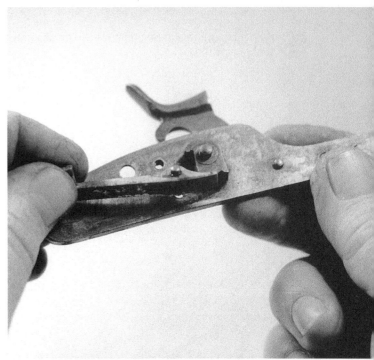

11. Remove the hammer retaining screw.

12. Use a slim drift in the screw hole to nudge the tumbler shaft out of the hammer. This will free the hammer and the tumbler for removal from the lockplate.

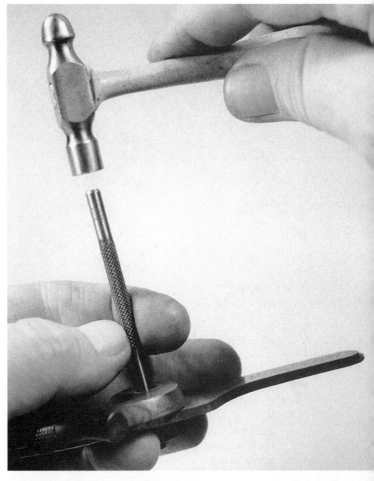

13. Remove the screw at the rear of the trigger guard.

14. Push the barrel latch lever aside for clearance, and remove the screw at the center of the upper tang.

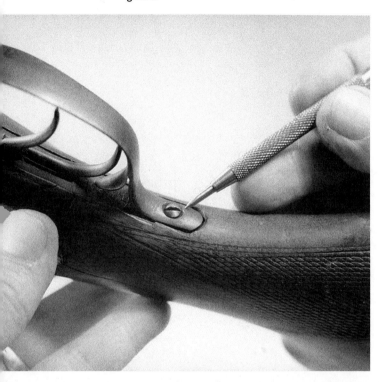

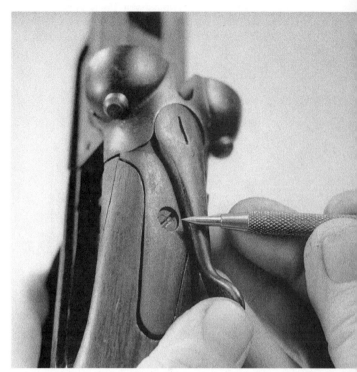

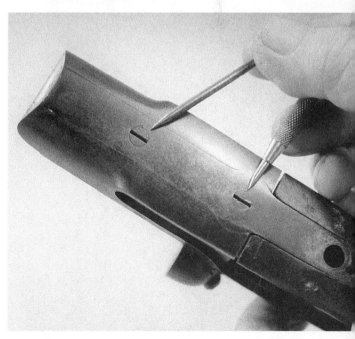

15. Turn the trigger guard slightly to clear the rear trigger, and remove the guard downward.

16. Remove the two screws on the underside of the receiver. Keep them in order, as they were finished in place, and will fit well only in their original locations.

17. Remove the trigger plate from the bottom of the receiver. It may be tight, and may require nudging with a drift from inside the receiver.

18. Removal of the lower plate will free the buttstock to be taken off.

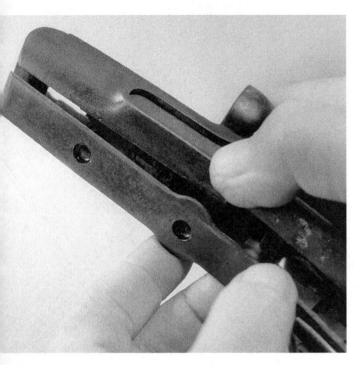

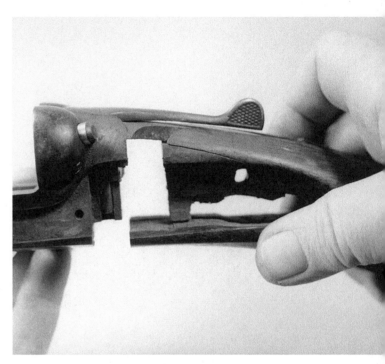

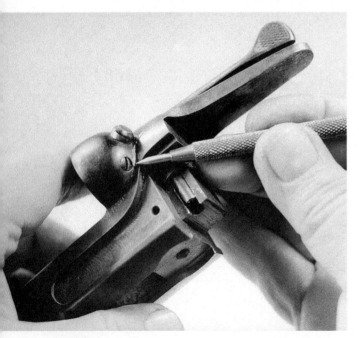

19. Remove the small screw below the firing pin.

20. Remove the firing pin toward the rear. Repeat the operation on the opposite side.

21. Remove the locking block post screw.

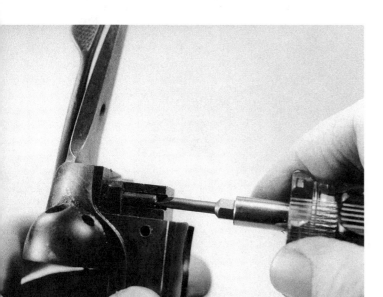

22. Remove the locking block toward the rear.

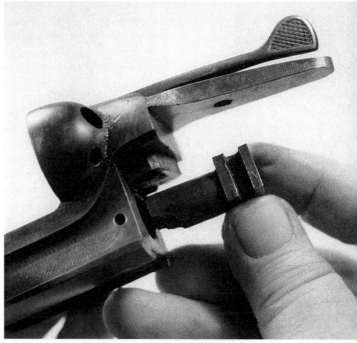

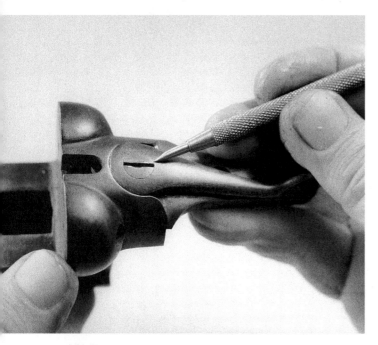

23. Remove the barrel latch lever screw.

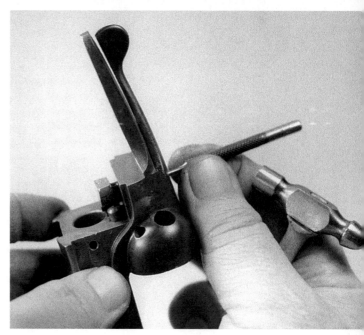

24. Use a small drift in the screw hole to nudge the lever base downward. As the base clears the spring plunger, the plunger will be released, so restrain it.

25. Remove the latch lever base downward.

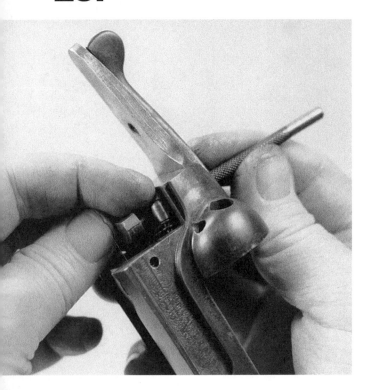

26. Remove the latch lever plunger and spring.

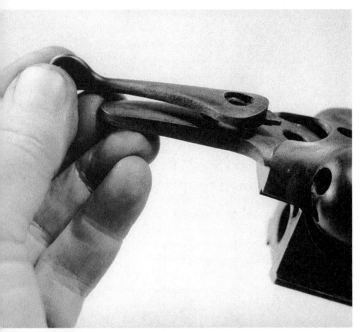

27. Remove the latch lever toward the rear.

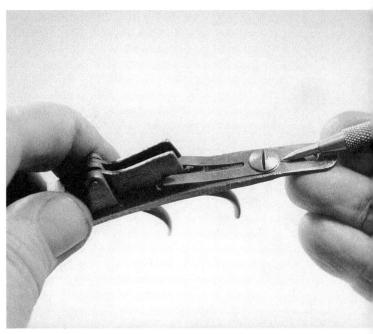

28. The twin-bladed trigger tension spring is retained by a vertical screw at the rear.

29. The triggers are pivoted and retained by a cross pin. The pin will usually have an enlarged head on one side, so drift it out in that direction.

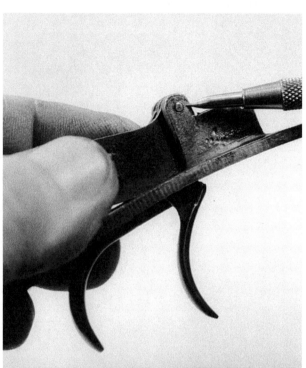

30. The forend iron is retained by two vertical screws.

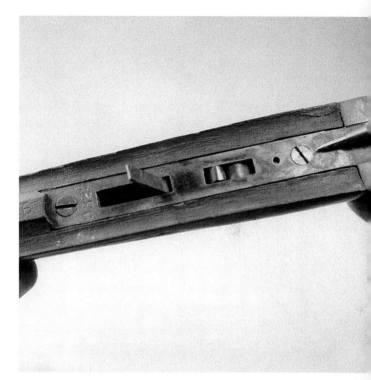

31. The positioning spring for the forend latch spring is retained by a vertical screw on the underside of the forend iron.

32. The forend latch spring is retained and pivoted by a cross pin.

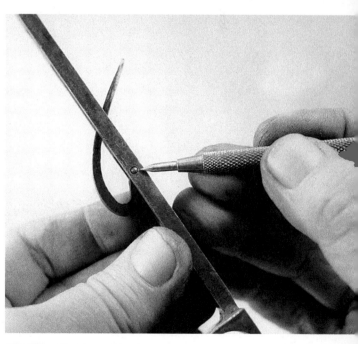

Reassembly Tips:

1. When replacing the hammer and tumbler on the lockplate, be sure the tumbler is oriented as shown in relation to the hammer.

2. Insert the ends of the spring in their seats in the sear and tumbler, then use the hammer to compress the spring for installation of the inner plate screws and posts. Before this is done, put the plate in place on the pivots. It is left off in this view to show the spring engagement.

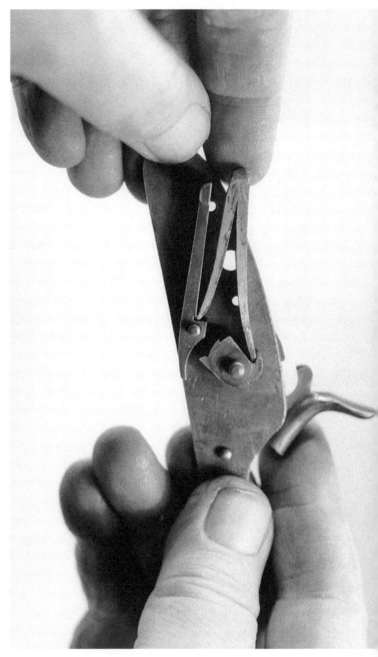

3. When installing the rear post and screw, it will be necessary to grip the sear and the spring, as shown, for clearance of the screw post.

When replacing the firing pin retaining screws, keep the screw heads even with the surface of the receiver. Avoid over-tightening, as this will bind the firing pins.

Stevens Model 59B

Similar/Identical Pattern Guns:

TThe same basic assembly/disassembly steps for the Stevens Model 59B also apply to the following guns:

Stevens Model 39A **Stevens Model 58**

Stevens Model 59A **Stevens Model 59C**

Data:	Stevens Model 59B
Origin:	United States
Manufacturer:	Savage Arms Company, Westfield, Massachusetts
Gauges:	410
Magazine capacity:	5 (2-1/2 inch), 4 (3-inch)
Overall length:	44 inches
Barrel length:	25 inches
Weight:	6 pounds

Made between 1937 and 1967, the Model 59B had a box-magazine counterpart, the Model 58. Except for the difference in feed systems, the two guns were mechanically identical. These takedown and reassembly instructions can be applied to all variations.

Disassembly:

1. Remove the bolt stop screw, located on the left side of the receiver. Open the bolt, hold the trigger back, and remove the bolt toward the rear.

2. Remove the inner magazine tube, and back out the stock mounting screw, located on the underside, just forward of the trigger guard. Remove the action from the stock.

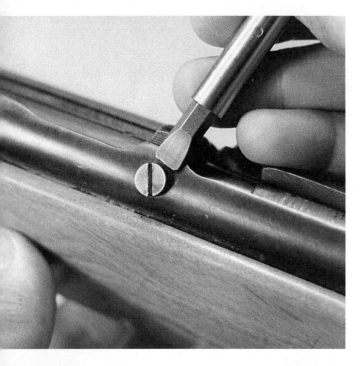

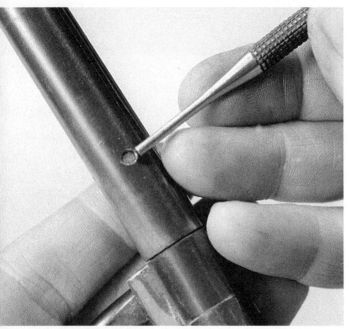

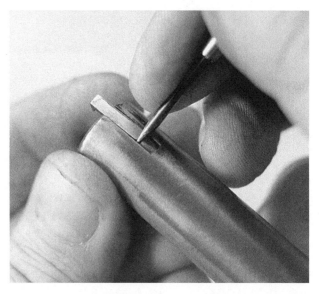

3. Drift out the cross pin in the forward section of the bolt, and take off the forward section toward the front.

4. Insert a small screwdriver between the rear edge of the extractor and the extractor plunger, and depress the plunger, holding it back while lifting the extractor out of its recess. Repeat the operation with the other extractor. Caution: Take care that the screwdriver doesn't slip, and ease out the plungers and springs.

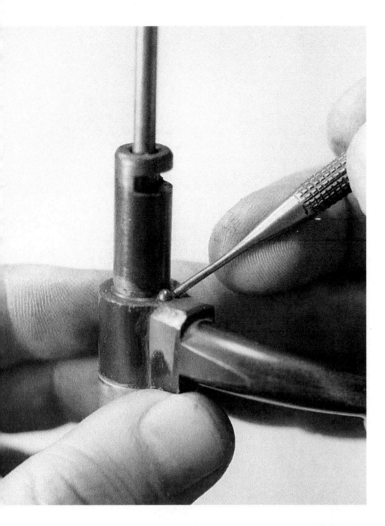

5. Remove the bolt head stop plunger and its spring from the front of the bolt handle base.

6. Depress the striker safety lever, located just to the rear of the bolt handle, to allow the striker to go all the way forward. Turn the cocking piece counter-clockwise (rear view), and let the striker go forward to the fired position, as shown.

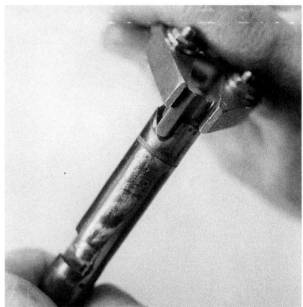

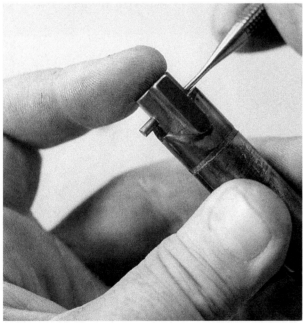

7. Drift out the cocking piece cross pin toward the left.

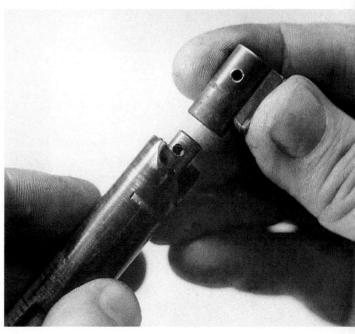

8. Remove the cocking piece toward the rear.

9. Insert a drift through the transverse hole in the striker rod, and use a smaller drift punch to push forward on the striker spring washer. Keeping the washer depressed, use a small screwdriver to move the striker spring retainer out of its slot in the bolt. When the retainer is out, the spring will push the washer back against the drift in the cross hole.

10. Remove the striker assembly toward the rear. To remove the spring and washer from the striker shaft, press the washer against the edge of a partially-opened vise, and take out the drift punch. Release the spring tension slowly.

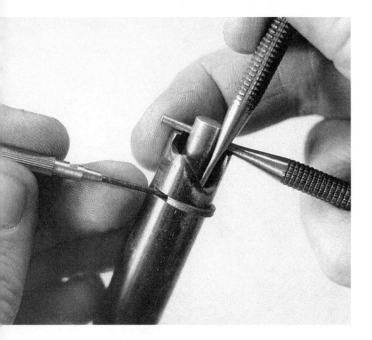

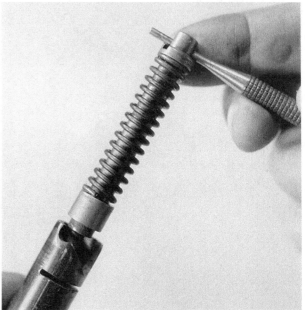

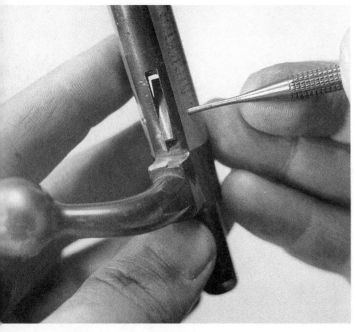

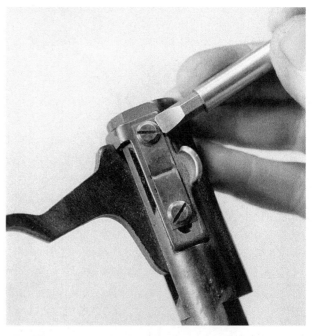

11. A cross pin in the bolt retains the striker safety block and its spring.

12. The safety and its positioning spring are retained on the right side of the receiver by two post screws, and removal is toward the right.

13. Drifting out the cross pin on the underside of the receiver at the rear will allow removal of the trigger and its spring downward.

14. Remove the screws on each side at the upper rear of the lifter housing.

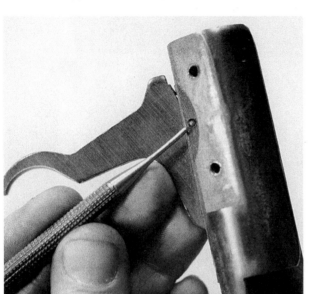

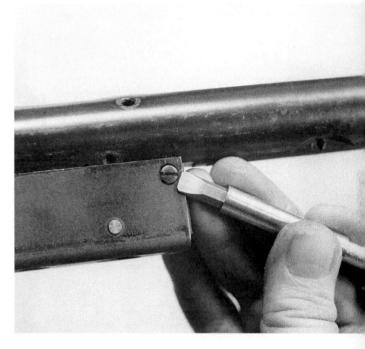

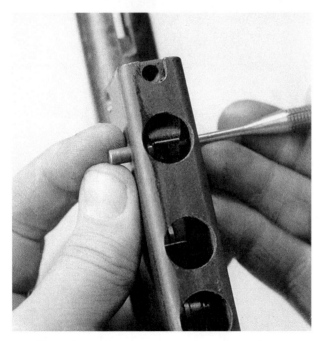

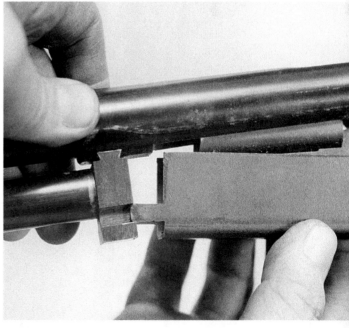

15. Drift out the lifter pivot pin toward the left.

16. Slide the lifter housing toward the rear, tip its rear end downward, and remove it.

17. Move the lifter forward, then remove it downward.

18. Removal of the lifter lever spring loops from the grooved ends of the cross pin will allow the spring to be taken off, and the pin pushed out. The lever is then free for removal.

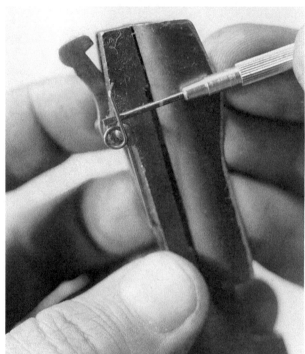

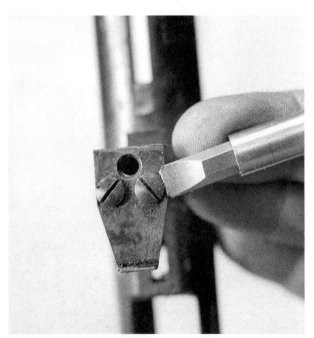

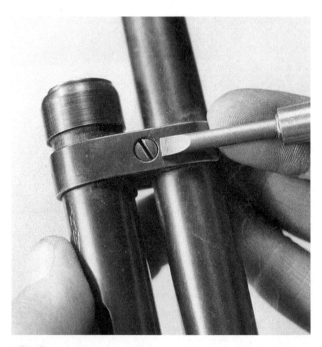

19. The lifter positioning spring is retained on the bottom of the carrier post by two screws.

20. Removal of the cross screw in the magazine tube hanger will allow the hanger and tube to be taken off toward the front.

Reassembly Tips:

1. When replacing the carrier assembly, push it back to engage its positioning spring, and the spring will hold it in place, as shown, during replacement of the carrier (lifter) housing. When inserting the pivot pin, be sure the holes are all in alignment.

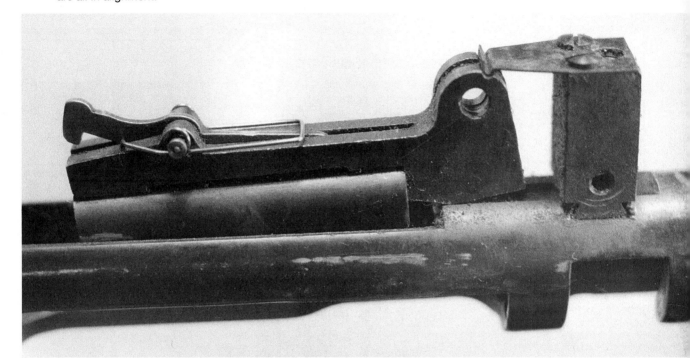

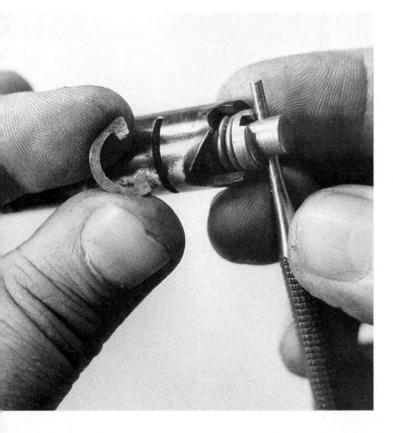

2. When replacing the striker assembly in the bolt, note that the notches in the rear face of the washer must be aligned with the inner projections of the retainer as it is inserted into its slot.

Stevens Model 520

Similar/Identical Pattern Guns:

The same basic assembly/disassembly steps for the Stevens Model 520 also apply to the following guns:

Sears "Ranger" Model 31   **Stevens Model 620**

Stevens Model 621

Data:	Stevens Model 124C
Origin:	United States
Manufacturer:	Savage Arms Corporation, Chicopee Falls, Massachusetts
Gauges:	12 only
Magazine Capacity:	2 rounds
Overall length:	47 inches
Barrel length:	28 inches
Weight:	7 pounds

The Model 520 was made from 1915 to 1930, and during that time it was also sold by Sears as their Model 31 "Ranger." The gun was designed by John Moses Browning, and many Model 520 barrels have a marking that includes the words "Browning's Patent," a cause of some confusion. The Stevens Model 620 and Model 621, made from 1927 to 1953, are similar mechanically, and some of the takedown procedures may be applied.

Disassembly:

1. Open the action, and using the lengthwise ridges on the magazine tube as a grip, turn the tube clockwise (rear view) until it stops.

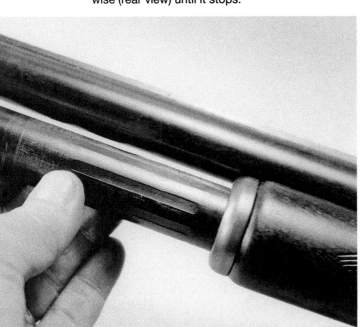

2. When the tube is turned, the tube base at the receiver will move forward to the point shown, withdrawing its side lugs from their recesses in the front of the receiver.

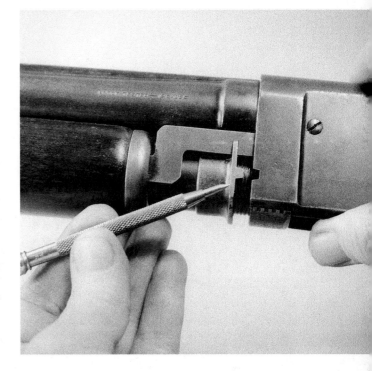

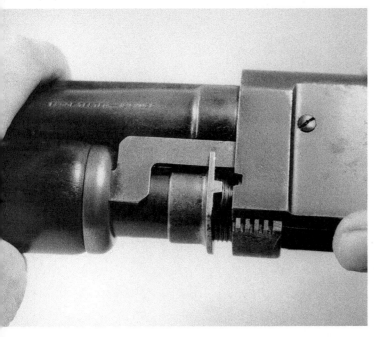

3. Move the barrel and magazine assembly downward to the point shown. It will be stopped by the bar of the action slide.

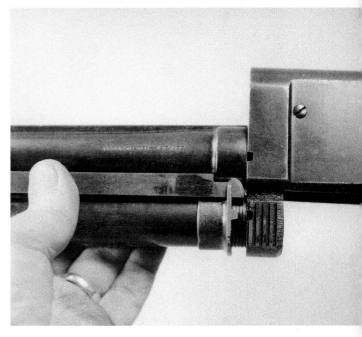

4. Move the action slide all the way forward until it stops, drawing the bar completely out of the receiver. Then, remove the barrel and magazine assembly downward.

5. A single screw attaches the magazine end piece to a lug on the barrel. Taking out the screw allows removal of the end piece, magazine spring, and the follower. Control the spring as the end piece is taken off. The tube can then be unscrewed from the barrel unit, and the fore-grip is taken off the tube toward the rear. Unscrewing the front cap ring will allow the wood to be removed from the action slide toward the front.

6. Remove the stock mounting bolt.

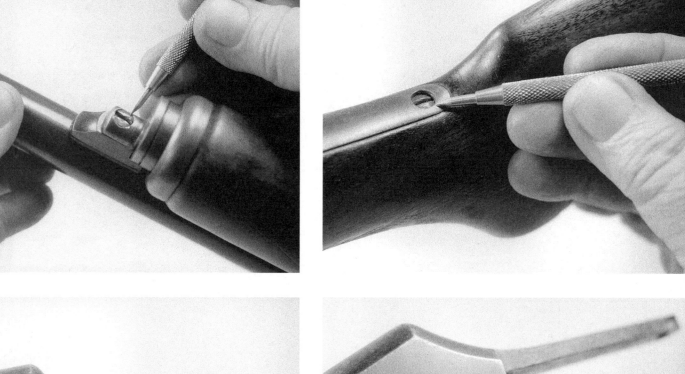

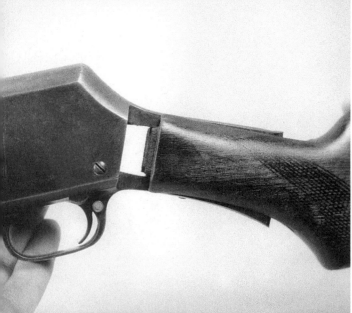

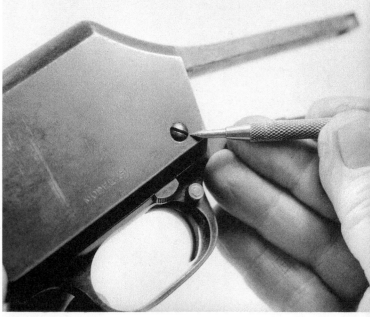

7. Take off the buttstock toward the rear.

8. Remove the cross screw at the lower rear of the receiver.

9. Drift out the cross pin at the lower edge of the receiver.

10. Remove the trigger group downward.

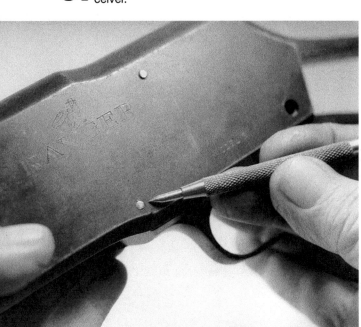

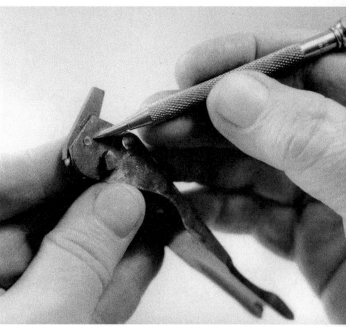

11. Move the bolt forward in the receiver. Swing the carrier outward, move it inward off its pivot post, and remove it.

12. The carrier dog pivot is a riveted part, and removal should be only for repair purposes. If the pivot pin is driven out, a plunger and spring will be released.

13. Keep the bolt slide plate pushed rearward, and push the bolt forward out of the receiver.

14. In some guns, it may be necessary to remove the bolt stop screw before the bolt can be taken out. It depends on the degree of wear.

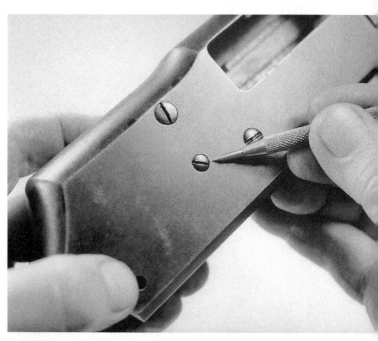

15. Remove the access screw on the right side at the rear of the ejection port, and take out the screw inside the left wall that retains the ejector. Remove the ejector.

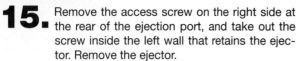

16. This is the pivot post screw for the carrier. There is no need to remove it in normal takedown.

17. This screw retains the shell stop on the inside of the receiver. It is often staked in place, and should be removed only for repair purposes.

18. Push the mounting post of the carrier spring inward.

19. Remove the carrier spring from inside the receiver.

20. Lift the carrier latch button out of its recess in the trigger group.

21. Depress the carrier latch at the front to free the hammer. Restrain the hammer, pull the trigger, and ease the hammer down to forward position. Remove the hammer spring screw.

22. Remove the hammer spring.

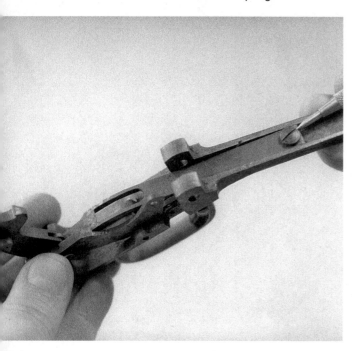

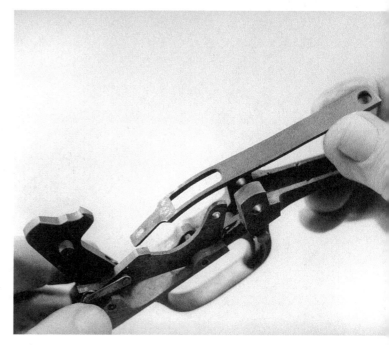

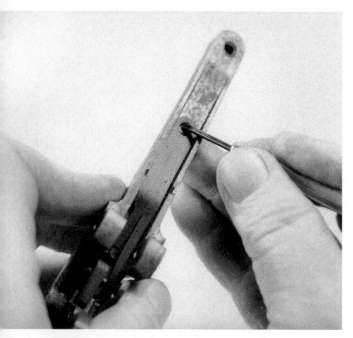

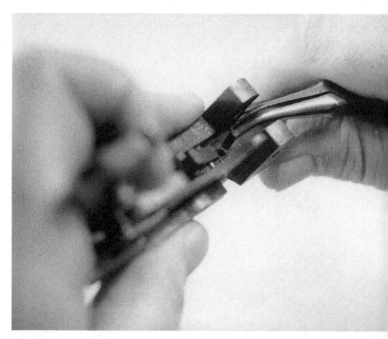

23. Use a too] to slide the combination slide latch and safety spring rearward. The spring has side wings that are in a slanted track on each side, and it is removed upward and toward the rear.

24. With the safety in mid-position, remove the safety plunger upward.

25. Remove the safety button.

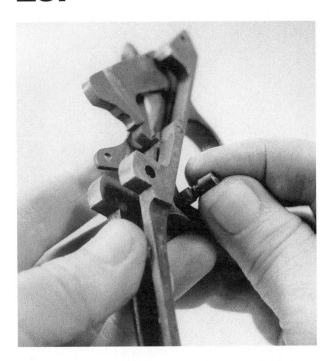

26. Drift out the trigger pin toward the right.

27. Remove the trigger upward.

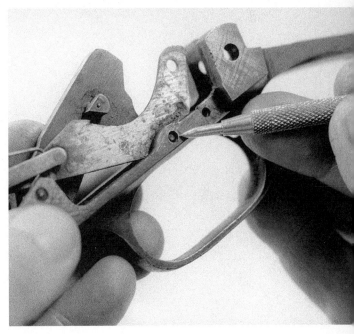

28. Drift the slide latch pin halfway to the right.

29. Lift the slide latch upward at the rear, unhook it from the trip spring at the front, and remove it.

30. Remove the cross pin, and take out the sear and its torsion spring. The spring is easily detachable from the center of the sear.

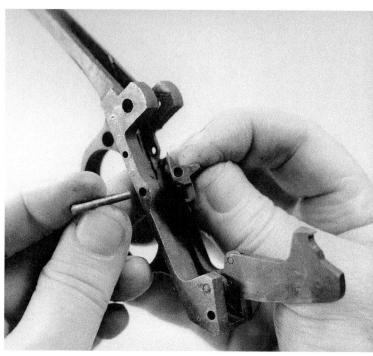

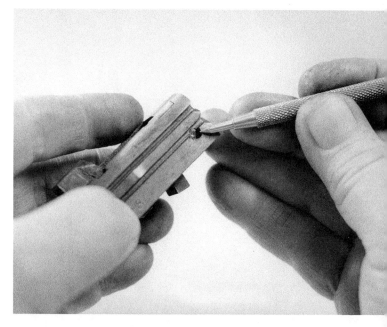

31. Drift out the hammer pivot toward the right, and remove the hammer and trip spring. A small spacer sleeve will also be released on the right side of the hammer. Be sure it isn't lost.

32. The firing pin is retained by a cross pin at the rear of the bolt, and the firing pin is taken out rearward. The retaining pin is driven out toward the right. Removal of the firing pin will allow the locking block to be taken out upward.

33. The extractors are retained by vertical pins, and the pins are drifted out downward. The right extractor has a lengthwise plunger and a strong spring, so control the spring and plunger as the extractor is taken out.

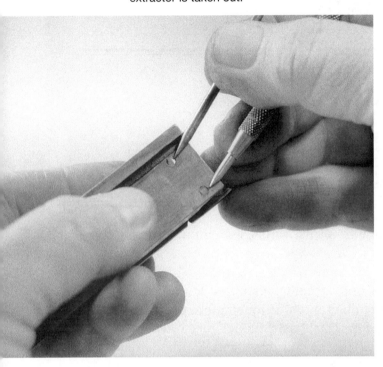

Reassembly Tips:

1. When the trigger is reinstalled, the sear must be lifted to engage the front projection of the trigger, as shown.

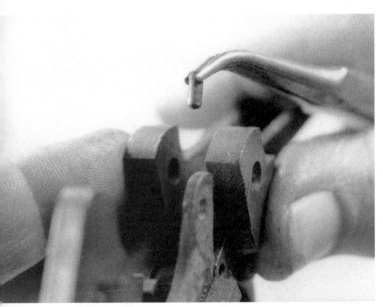

2. When replacing the safety plunger, be sure the rounded end is downward, toward the safety.

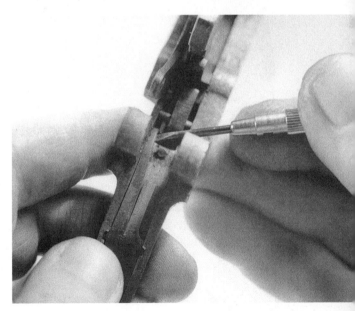

3. As the combination slide latch and safety spring is pushed back into its slanted retaining tracks, it will be necessary to use a tool to lift its longer arm to clear the trigger and engage the shelf on the slide latch. This also applies when the shorter arm reaches the safety plunger.

Stoeger Condor

Data:	Stoeger Condor
Origin:	Brazil
Manufacturer:	Stoeger (E.R. Armantino)
Gauges:	12, 16, 20, 28, .410
Overall Length:	44 inches
Height:	7.25 inches
Barrel Length:	28 inches
Weight:	7 lbs. 6 oz.

The Stoeger Condor in all its variations came onto the scene and the scene was impressed with its features. These features, such as ejectors on some models, a removable choke tube system, excellent wood, decent finish, and long forcing cones, tended to be found in factory guns much more costly than what the Condors sold for. This basic model takedown procedure is virtually identical to the Supreme and Youth models. The Supreme has auto-ejectors. The less common 16 gauge and .410 models have fixed chokes. The Competition model also has an adjustable stock comb.

Disassembly:

1. Push the takedown button toward the muzzle and pull the forend from the barrels. Press the top lever, open the action, and continue to roll the barrels out of the receiver.

2. Gently lift the forward end of the left side extractor arm and push the extractor to the rear. This will lift the extractor's hook out of the slot where it lies.

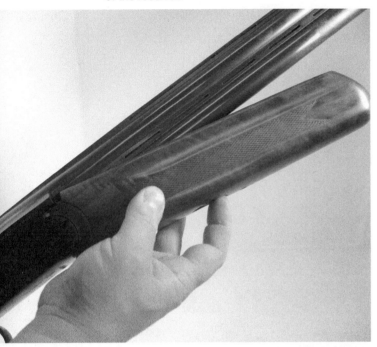

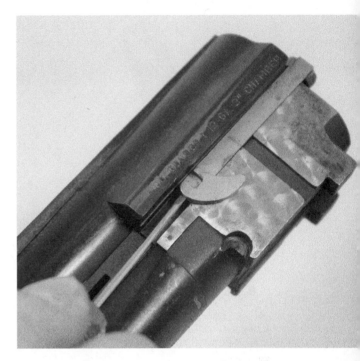

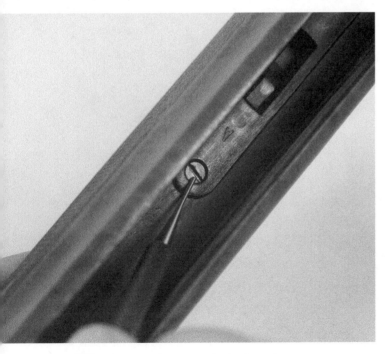

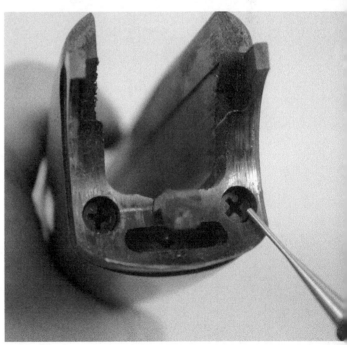

3. Remove this screw in the forend.

4. Remove these two Phillips head screws to release the forend hardware from the forend wood.

5. The takedown button can be removed by driving out this blended pin, however, there is no need to do so unless it needs repair.

6. Remove the two buttpad screws to take the buttpad from the stock.

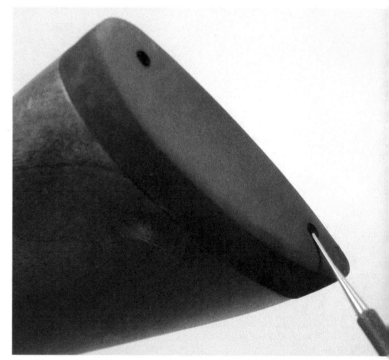

7. The stock can be removed by using a long flat-bladed screwdriver to remove the stock bolt. Then remove the stock from the receiver.

8. Depress the top lever locking pin to release the top lever.

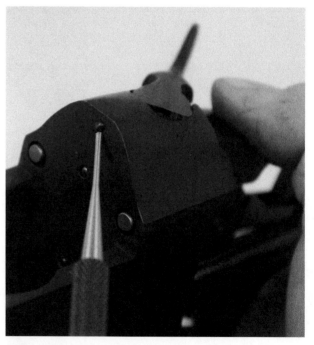

9. With the hammers forward, remove the hammer spring and their guide rods.

10. Drive out the rear trigger guard pin.

11. Drive out the front trigger guard pin and pull the trigger guard straight down and off the receiver.

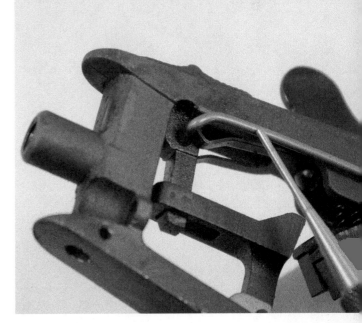

12. The rear of the auto setting safety arm can be pulled out to the side to clear the safety and then pulled out of the receiver to the rear.

13. Drive out the transverse safety retaining pin, then lift the safety lever up and out of the receiver.

14. Drive out the sear pin and remove the two sears and their springs.

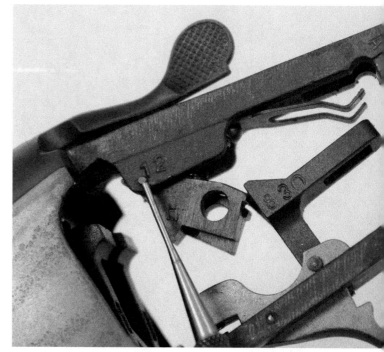

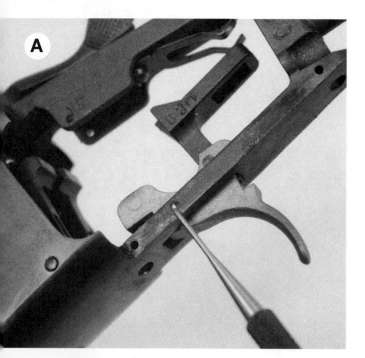

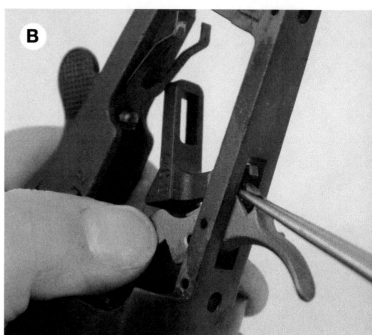

15. Drive out the trigger pin to release the trigger (Picture A). Then remove the inertia block spring and plunger (Picture B).

16. Remove the trigger assembly by lifting and turning it to the side and angling it out of the side of the receiver.

17. Remove the safety spring screw and the safety spring.

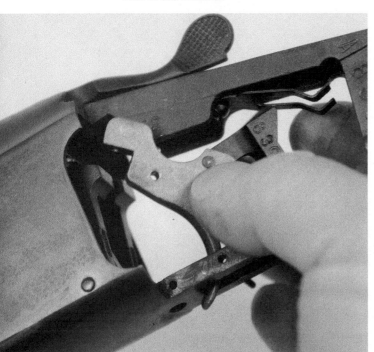

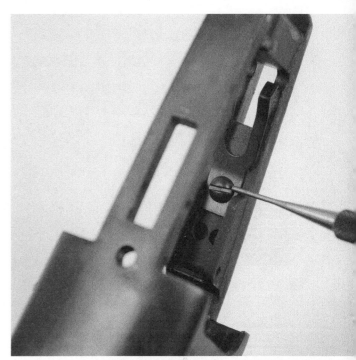

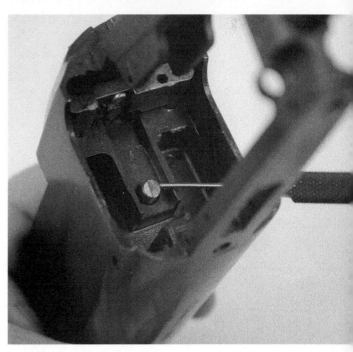

18. Drive out the hammer pin from left to right. Then remove the hammers and the transfer bars in front of them.

19. Remove the bottom firing pin, which was retained by the transfer bars.

20. To remove the cocking bar, pull it back into the receiver then out to one side.

21. This cotter pin must be removed to free the top lever.

22. Slowly lift the top lever so that the locking detent and spring can be controlled. Remove the top lever from the receiver. Then push out the top lever locking pin from the front.

23. Remove the locking block by pulling it to the rear and rotating down.

24. Remove the upper firing pin and return spring, then the top lever spring and plunger to its right.

Reassembly Tips:

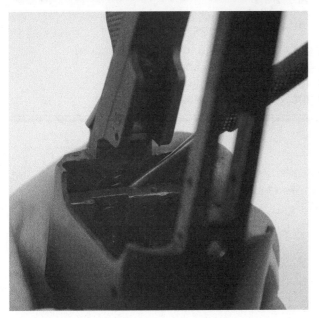

1. When reinserting the top lever, drop it in enough that the locking spring and plunger fall below the upper surface of the receiver. Then, with the lever straight, use a punch to press into the receiver the top lever spring and plunger, while simultaneously pushing the top lever all the way down into the receiver.

2. The hammers will need to be cocked for reassembly. This can easily be done using a screwdriver to push back on the sear notch on the top of the hammer. Take care not to pry against the receiver. Simply push straight back until the hammer over-rotates and the sear catches.

Stoeger IGA Uplander English

Similar/Identical Pattern Guns:

The same basic assembly/disassembly steps for the Stoeger IGA Uplander English also apply to the following guns:

Ladies Model	**Turkey**
Youth	**Coach**
Deluxe Coach	**Uplander Supreme**

Data:	Stoeger IGA Uplander English
Origin:	Brazil
Manufacturer:	E.R. Amantino & Cia, Ltd. Veranopolis, RS, Brazil
Gauges:	12, 20 and 410 (others in basic gun)
Overall length:	40-1/4 inches (English)
Barrel length:	24 inches (English)
Weight:	6 to 6-3/4 pounds

The Stoeger Company (now owned by Beretta) began importing the nice little Uplander double from Brazil in 1996. The basic gun is also offered in 28 gauge, and in a larger 12-gauge version. All are mechanically the same, and the instructions will apply.

Disassembly:

1. Open and close the barrel unit, to cock the internal hammers. The manual safety will automatically move to on-safe position. Push the forend latch rearward, and tip the forend away from the barrels for removal. Open the barrel unit and remove it upward.

2. Remove the two screws on the inside of the forend that retain the forend iron, and remove the iron from the wood. Note that the two screws are of different lengths.

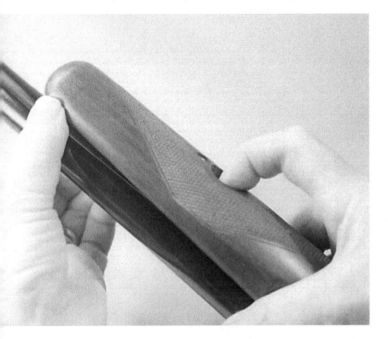

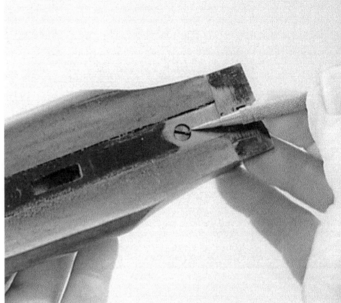

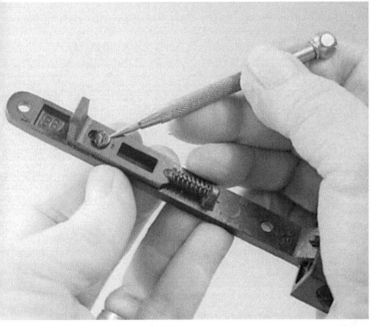

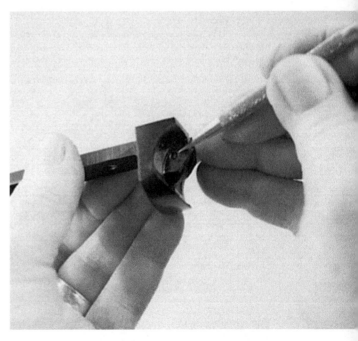

3. The forend latch is retained by a single screw. Note that this screw is not snug, as space must be left for latch movement.

4. The ejector cam lever is pivoted and retained at the rear of the forend iron by a cross pin.

5. The ejector is retained by a recessed screw between the barrel under lugs. After its removal, the ejector is taken out rearward.

6. Remove the two buttplate screws and take off the buttplate. Use a B-Square stock tool, as shown, or a long screwdriver to back out the stock mounting bolt. Take off the buttstock toward the rear.

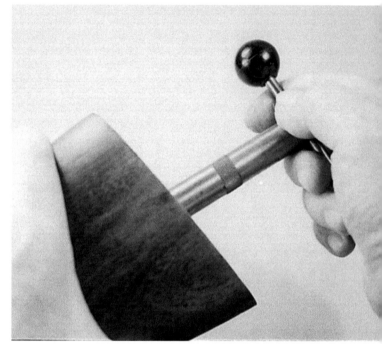

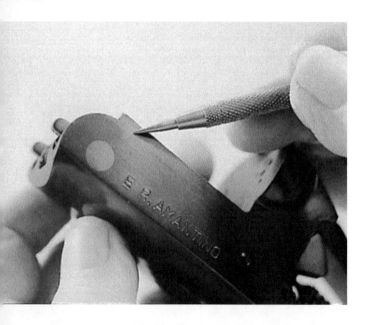

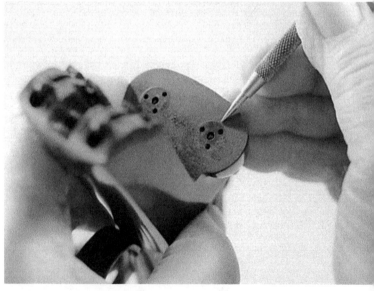

7. The cocking levers should be removed only for repair purposes. Each is retained by a short pivot cross pin, and the ends of the pins are finished-over. Removal will affect the external finish. If necessary, the pins are drifted out from inside, using an angled drift to start them.

8. If the firing pins need to be removed for repair, the hammers must be cocked, and a special three-point tool must be used. The retainers are simply unscrewed, and the firing pins and their return springs are taken out toward the front. In normal takedown, they are best left in place.

9. With the manual safety in off-safe position, pull the triggers and drop the hammers to fired position. Use a proper roll-pin punch to drift out the safety cross pin. Control the safety button as the punch is taken out, as it will be released.

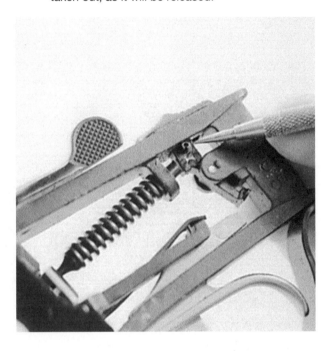

10. Remove the safety button and its plunger and spring upward. It will probably be necessary to insert a tool to lift out the coil spring.

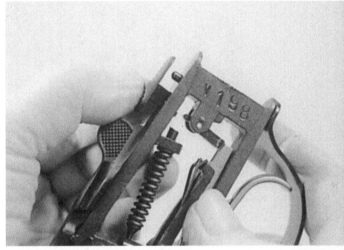

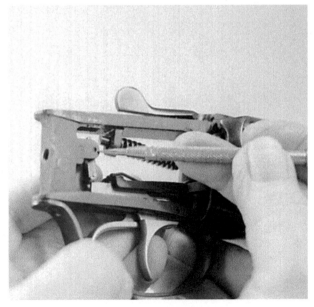

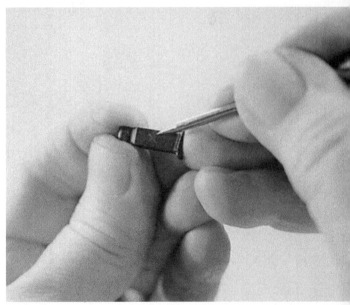

11. Drift out the cross pin that pivots and retains the safety lever, and take out the lever. As you do this, note its orientation, as it must be replaced the same way.

12. When the safety lever is removed, it is a good idea to scribe a mark on its front surface. This will ensure that it is put back in the right orientation. This is important, as its lower end is fitted to properly engage the triggers.

13. To remove the sears, first unhook the spring of one sear, move it to center, and allow its rear arm to drop into the space between the sears and triggers.

14. Use a non-marring drift to move the cross pin just far enough to release the sear on one side.

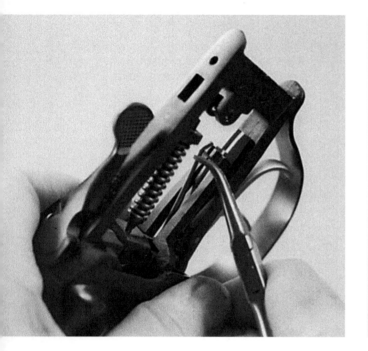

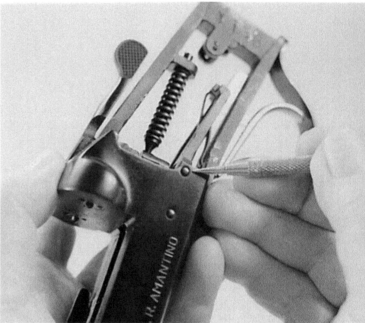

15. Remove the sear toward the rear.

16. Drift the cross pin over a little more, and both sear springs can be removed. Note that the sear springs are not identical, so keep them matched to the sears. The cross pin is drifted all the way out to free the other sear.

17. Remove the screw at the rear of the trigger guard, and use an angle-tip screwdriver to take out the inside front screw and release the guard for removal.

18. Drift out the cross pin that pivots and retains the triggers. Move the triggers forward and downward for removal. Note that the front trigger is on the right, the rear trigger on the left (for reassembly).

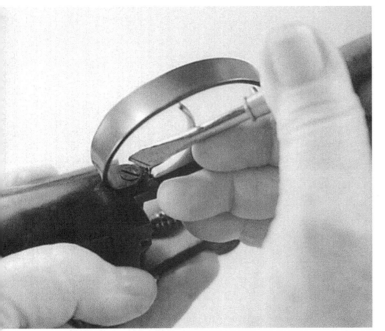 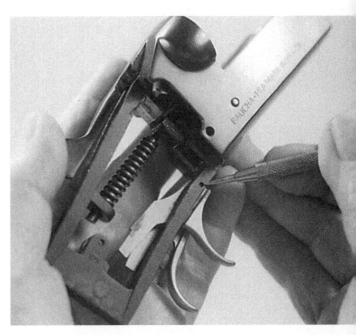

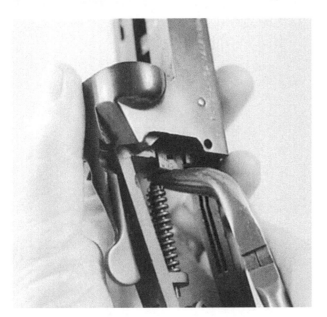 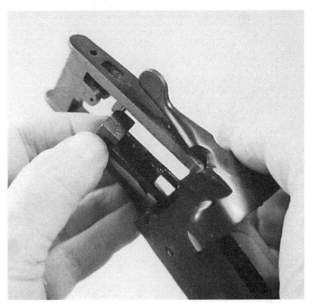

19. Grip the front of the locking block spring guide with pliers, and retract it slightly to move its tip out of the recess in the rear of the block. Caution: Don't let the pliers slip. The spring is strong and the guide can cause injury. A heavy shop cloth wrapped around would be a good idea.

20. Turn the barrel latch lever to start the locking block bar rearward, then pull it out and angle it toward the right for removal.

21. Insert a small tool to depress the plunger of the barrel latch lever spring, and move the latch post upward until it clears the plunger. Caution: Control the plunger and spring and take them out toward the rear.

22. Turn the barrel latch lever toward the side, and remove it upward.

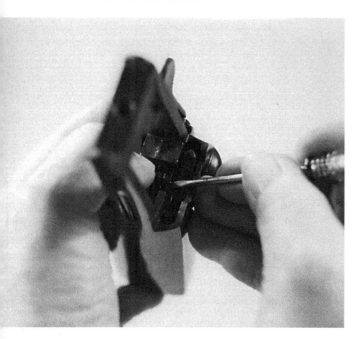

23. The hammers, their plungers and springs, and the cocking rods are removed only for repairs and all are taken out toward the rear. This operation will require that the receiver is held in a padded vise, and a compressor tool must bear on the hammer to restrain it as the indicated pin is drifted across. In normal takedown, this system is left in place.

Reassembly Tips:

1. The locking block spring can be compressed in a vise, and a small drift inserted in the cross hole in its shaft to hold the spring and make reinstallation easier. This advantage would also be useful in removal, but there is no access cut in the spring base to allow it.

2. Remember to reinstall the safety lever with the scribed mark toward the front, to properly engage the triggers. Be sure the lug at its top fits into the fork on the safety button. The roll-pin is more easily inserted from left to right.

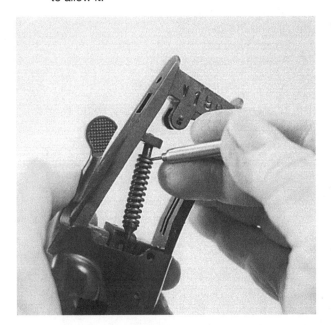

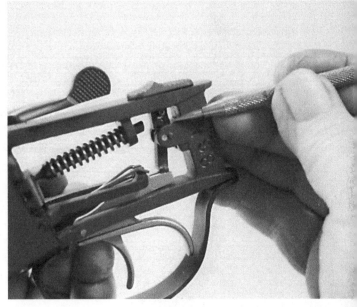

3. Before the forend is reinstalled, the hammers should be cocked. This can be done by putting the levers against the workbench or any piece of wood and forcing them downward. The right lever is shown here in the cocked position, and the left one yet to be done.

When reinstalling the buttstock, avoid overtightening of the stock bolt. If you have a torque-wrench, don't exceed five pounds.

Street Sweeper

Data:	Street Sweeper
Origin:	United States
Manufacturer:	Street Sweeper Atlanta, Georgia
Gauges:	12
Magazine capacity:	12 rounds
Overall length:	37 inches (26 inches with stock folded)
Barrel length:	18 inches
Weight:	9-3/4 pounds

One of the best designs ever produced in a shotgun for law enforcement use, the Street Sweeper has a 12-round rotary magazine and a double-action-only trigger system. Its formidable appearance is an asset, and the rotary magazine allows the spacing of various lethal and non-lethal loads. The Street Sweeper was introduced in 1989. The gun shown here is the "civilian" version. There is also a police version with a 12-inch barrel.

Disassembly:

1. Use pliers to compress the ends of the sling loop arms on the right side until they will enter the tunnel, and remove the sling loop toward the left.

2. Use snap-ring pliers to remove the ring from the right end of the stock pivot. Remove the snap-ring end washer.

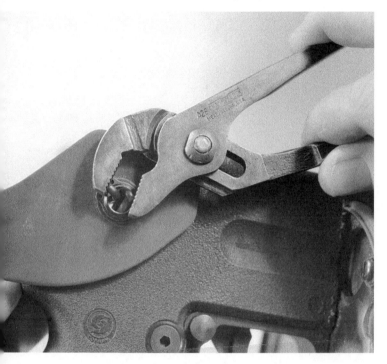

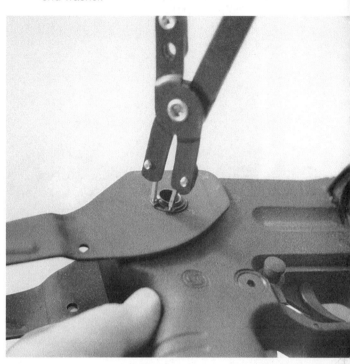

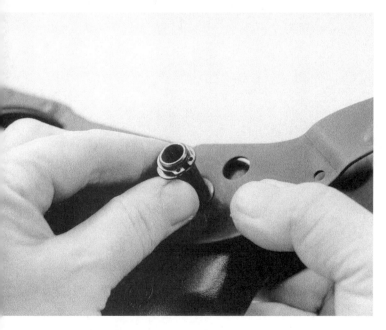

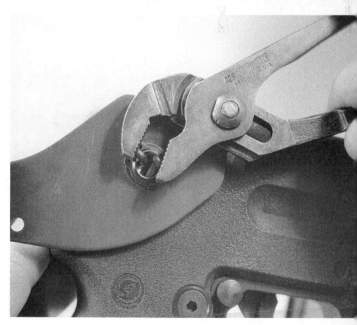

3. With the stock assembly in mid-position, push out the stock pivot toward the left. It is not necessary to remove the left snap ring and washer. Two larger washers, inside the arms of the stock assembly, will be released.

4. Remove the stock assembly toward the rear, along with the washers.

5. It is possible to remove the buttplate from the stock by taking off the small snap-ring. If this is done, control the torsion spring. In normal takedown, this assembly is best left in place.

6. The fore-grip is retained by a large Allen screw and washer.

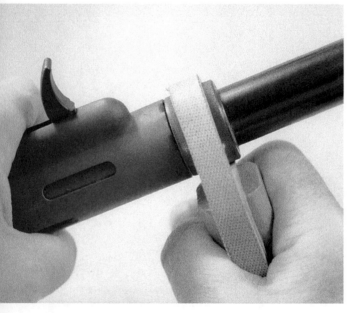

7. Use a non-marring strap wrench to unscrew the barrel jacket nut, as shown. Remove the nut.

8. Nudge the jacket forward, using a non-marring tool against the fore-grip stud. Do not use the ejector handle for this purpose. When the inner flanges of the jacket reach the barrel threads, turn the jacket counter-clockwise for removal.

9. A twin-point wrench is used to remove the nut at the rear of the ejector housing, and the ejector and its spring are taken out rearward, Control the spring as the nut is removed.

10. Put the safety in the on-safe position, and pull the trigger several times until the magazine stops rotation, easing the tension of the drive spring. Remove the four Allen screws, two on each side, above the magazine.

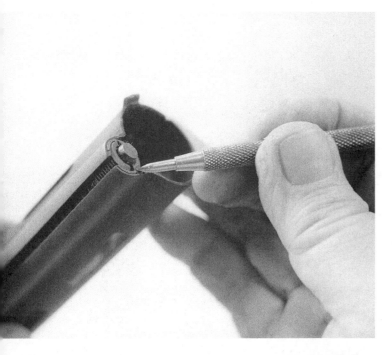

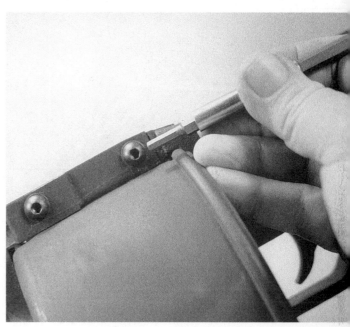

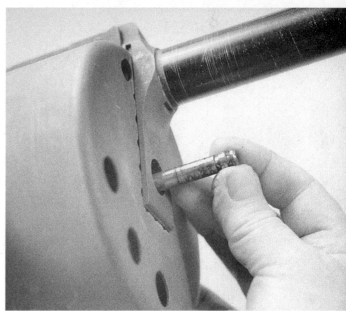

11. Turn the winding key counter-clockwise (front view) to unscrew and remove it.

12. Pull out the magazine pivot shaft toward the front.

13. Remove the magazine assembly downward.

14. Open the loading gate, and turn the rear plates of the magazine housing to the position shown, until the top inner edge of the right plate aligns with the edge of the opening at the top.

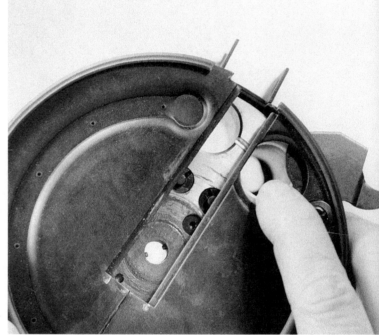

15. Move the left plate to the position shown, depress the right plate very slightly at its lower step, and remove the left plate from the housing.

16. Move the right plate inward, and position the loading gate to align with the exit recess in the housing. Remove the right plate. After the plate is out, the gate can be removed by using a twin-point wrench and screwdriver, but in normal takedown it is best left in place.

17. Lift the magazine out of its housing.

18. The rotation spring mechanism is retained in the magazine by plates at the front and rear, secured by three Allen screws in each plate. This system should not be disassembled in normal take-down. If repair is necessary, it should be done by a gunsmith who is familiar with the mechanism, or it should be returned to the factory.

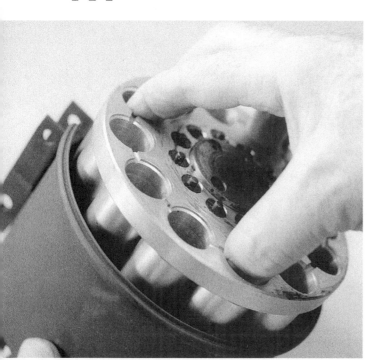

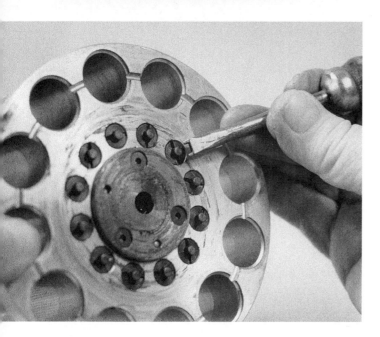

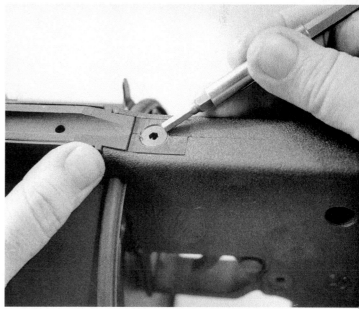

19. The position stop plungers and springs are re-tained by screw-housings that are removable by using a twin-point wrench. In normal take-down, these are best left in place.

20. Remove the Allen screw on top of the grip frame unit.

21. Remove the two Allen screws, one on each side, just to the rear of the safety.

22. Remove the pistol grip unit toward the rear. Keep the trigger pulled as this is done, or flex the guard to clear it.

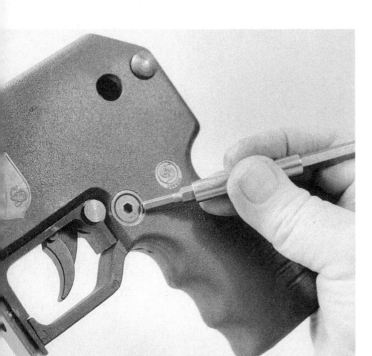

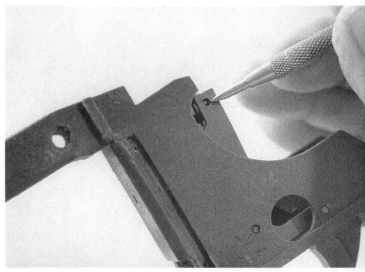

23. If it is necessary for repair, the stock latch button can be removed by holding it with non-marring pliers on the left side, and taking out the screw. The button and spring are then removed toward the left.

24. The firing system of the gun is very simple, but it uses heavy expansion-type springs. If it is not necessary for repair, it is best to avoid disassembly of this system. For access to the firing pin, the hammer spring can be disconnected from the hammer by drifting out this roll-type cross pin. Be sure the hammer is solidly supported.

25. Drifting out this roll-type cross pin will detach the hammer spring unit from the frame.

26. If the hammer spring has been disconnected, drifting out the hammer pivot pin toward the left will allow the hammer to be taken out upward and toward the rear. The double-action lever and its coil spring are retained in the hammer by a cross pin.

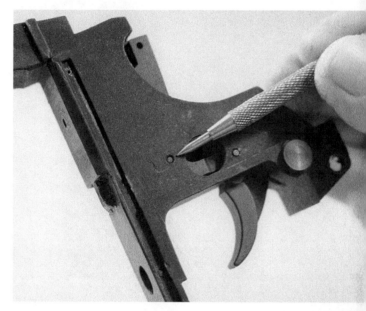

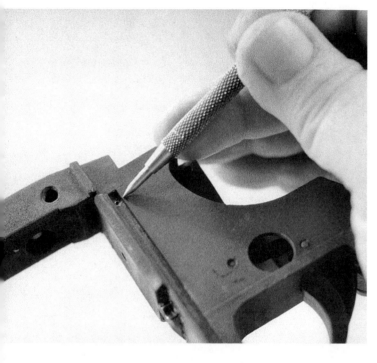

27. The twin trigger springs are retained by a cross pin at the rear of the frame.

28. If the trigger springs have been disconnected, and the hammer assembly removed, drifting out the trigger cross pin toward the left will allow the trigger and the attached thruster assembly to be removed.

29. An Allen screw at the rear retains the safety spring and ball. Control the spring as the screw is taken out. The safety button can then be removed toward either side.

30. The firing pin is retained by a nut on the inside, accessible after the hammer is removed (or its spring disconnected), and the nut requires a twin-point wrench for removal. The firing pin and its return spring are then taken out toward the rear.

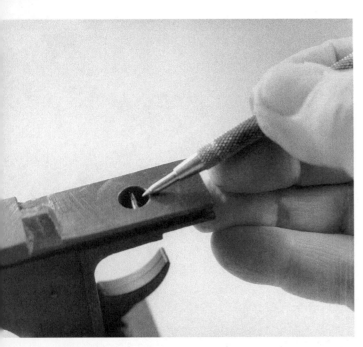

31. This is the index pin for the magazine pivot shaft. It retains no part, and it is not removed in normal takedown.

Reassembly Tips:

1. As the magazine assembly is moved upward into place, the rear flanges may be very tight at the edge of the pistol grip unit. To make this easier, file a slight bevel at that point, as shown. Use hand pressure only in pushing the housing back into place.

2. When installing the magazine pivot shaft, first engage its grooves at the rear with the lugs inside the tunnel. Then, use the indexing cut in its forward tip as a screw slot to turn it until the slot is horizontal, engaging the split rear tip with the index pin in the frame. The pivot shaft should then move easily into place, to the depth shown.

Winchester Model 12

Similar/Identical Pattern Guns:

The same basic assembly/disassembly steps for the Winchester Model 12 also apply to the following guns:

Browning Model 12   **Winchester Model 1912**

Data:	Winchester Model 12
Origin:	United States
Manufacturer:	Winchester Repeating Arms New Haven, Connecticut
Gauges:	12, 16, 20, and 28
Magazine capacity:	5 rounds
Overall length:	47-1/2 inches (with 28-inch barrel)
Barrel length:	20 to 30 inches
Weight:	6-1/3 to 8-3/4 pounds

From 1912 to 1965, the Model 12 was the undisputed king of the slide-action shotguns, and was offered in a wide variety of options in barrel length, choke, stock style, and other features. After the gun was discontinued, public demand induced Winchester to bring it back in 1972, in 12-gauge only, but it was dropped again in 1980. In 1988, Browning made a limited edition of the Model 12 and these instructions also apply. The Model 12 is mechanically uncomplicated, with only one or two tricky points in the takedown and reassembly.

Disassembly:

1. Cycle the action to cock the hammer, and set the safety in the on-safe position. Push the magazine locking pin downward and toward the right, and pull it out until it stops. Using the pin as a lever, rotate the magazine tube counter-clockwise (front view) about one-quarter turn, until it stops.

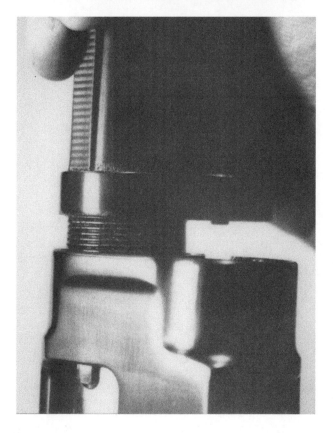

2. Pull the magazine tube forward until it stops.

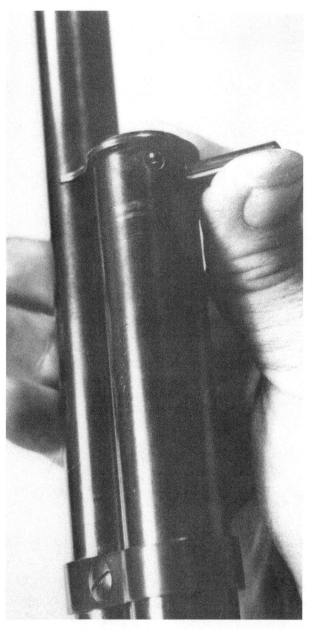

3. Move the action slide and forend assembly forward until it stops, and rotate the barrel and magazine assembly one-quarter turn counter-clockwise (front view). Remove the assembly toward the front.

4. Remove the vertical screw at the rear of the trigger housing.

5. Tip the trigger housing downward at the rear, then remove it toward the rear and downward.

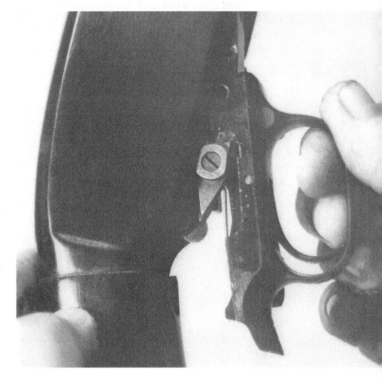

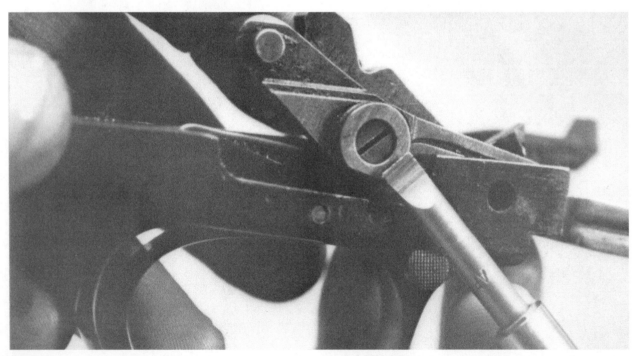

6. Remove the carrier pivot screw, located on the right side of the housing. Note that this screw has a reverse thread, and is removed by turning it clockwise.

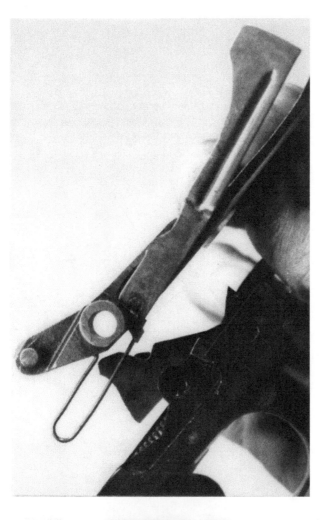

7. Take off the carrier upward, and detach the carrier spring from the rear of the carrier. Note that the shell guide plate is mounted on the right side of the carrier by a riveted pin, and removal is not advisable in normal takedown.

8. The carrier plunger and spring are removable by backing out the screw on the left side at the rear of the carrier. Note that this screw is usually staked in place, and should be removed only for repair purposes.

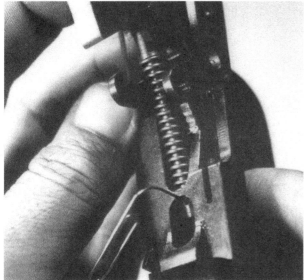

9. Move the safety to the off-safe position, and insert a small pin (an opened paper clip will do) in the small vertical hole near the rear tip of the hammer spring guide. Restrain the hammer, pull the trigger, and ease the hammer forward. The hammer spring will be trapped on the guide by the inserted pin.

10. Lift the front of the slide latch to clear the left tip of the hammer cross pin, and drift out the cross pin toward the right.

11. Exert rearward pressure on the hammer, remove the pin holding the guide and spring, and take off the hammer, guide, and spring upward, slowly easing the spring tension. The spring guide can be taken off the hammer by drifting out the cross pin, but the pin is riveted, and in normal takedown should be left in place.

12. Tip the slide latch upward at the rear to clear the left end of the trigger cross pin, and drift out the trigger pin toward the right.

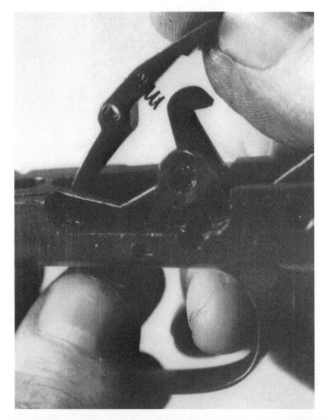

13. Remove the trigger upward, along with the small coil spring mounted in the underside of its forward extension.

15. Move the slide latch upward, and remove it toward the left.

14. Insert a screwdriver from the right side, through the access hole provided, and back out the screw that retains the slide latch.

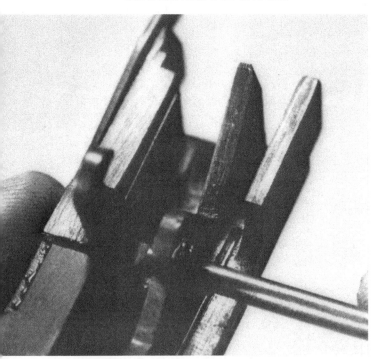

16. The two springs on the slide latch are staked in place on its inside face. Unless necessary for repair, these should not be removed. If removal is necessary, the top spring has an access hole on the outside of the latch to admit a small-diameter drift. The lower spring must be pried out.

17. Set the safety in the on-safe position, and insert a small-diameter drift punch in the hole on the underside of its left end to depress the plunger and spring upward. Remove the safety toward the right, and take out the plunger and spring downward.

18. Tip the rear tail of the shell stop out of its recess, move it toward the rear, then remove it from the bottom of the receiver.

19. Just above the shell stop recess, in the lower left edge of the bolt, the two ends of the bolt retaining lever can be seen. Push the rear end of the lever inward, away from the receiver well, and the rear of the bolt can then be moved downward, out of its locking recess in the top of the receiver. Insert a small screwdriver behind the bolt to nudge the rear tip of the ejector out of its recess in the left wall of the receiver. Remove the ejector and its attached spring from the bottom of the receiver. The spring is staked in place on the ejector, and is removed only for repair.

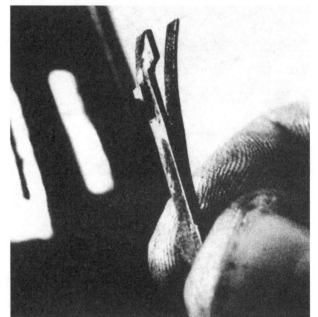

20. Move the bolt almost all the way to the rear of the receiver, tip its rear end outward, then the front, and remove the bolt from the bottom of the receiver.

21. Remove the cross screw on the left side of the bolt, restraining the firing pin retractor as the screw is taken out.

22. Remove the firing pin retractor upward, and take out its spring from the top of the bolt.

23. Removal of the retractor will free the firing pin to be taken out toward the rear.

24. The bolt retaining lever is retained on the left side of the bolt at the lower edge by a vertical pin of small diameter. The pin is drifted out downward, and the lever is removed toward the left.

25. The left extractor and its coil spring are retained by a vertical pin which is drifted out upward.

26. To remove the right extractor, insert a small screwdriver between the extractor and its plunger, depress the plunger toward the rear, and lift the extractor out of its recess. Release the spring tension slowly, and remove the plunger and spring toward the front.

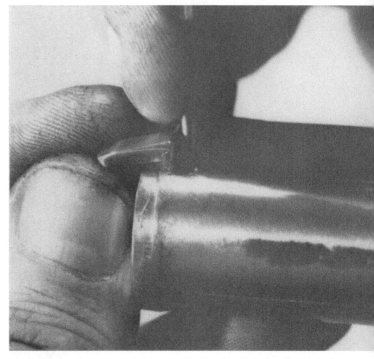

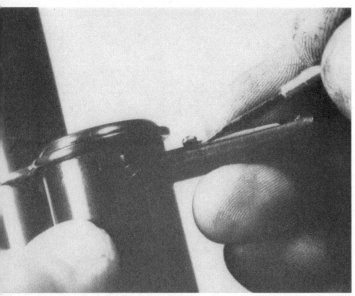

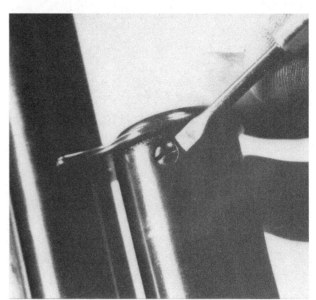

27. The magazine locking pin is removed by depressing the round-wire spring in its slide-slot to clear the rolled tip of the spring, and the pin is then pulled out of the magazine tube.

28. Remove the two opposed screws at the front of the magazine tube, and take out the magazine plug and the plug stop plate toward the front. Caution: The magazine spring will be released, so restrain it and ease it out. Remove the magazine spring and follower toward the front.

29. Remove the two opposed screws in the magazine tube hanger, and move the hanger forward off the tube and barrel. The flat action slide tension spring will be released as the hanger is removed, and the center bushing in the hanger can be taken out. After the hanger is removed, the magazine tube and forend assembly can be taken off toward the front.

30. Use a Brownells Model 12 forend wrench to take off the forend cap nut, and remove the action slide assembly toward the rear. Take out the magazine tube toward the front, and slide the buffer spring off the magazine tube toward the rear.

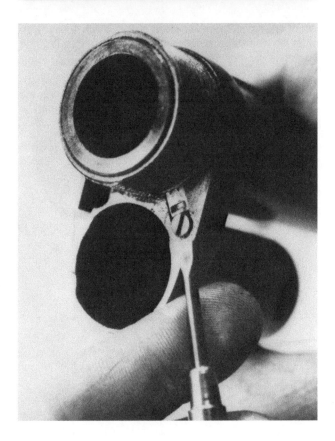

31. Barrel tightness in the receiver is adjustable by backing out the adjusting sleeve lock screw and sliding the lock piece out of engagement with the teeth on the edge of the sleeve to free it. Turning the sleeve clockwise (rear view) will tighten the barrel engagement. If necessary, the sleeve can be completely unscrewed from the rear of the barrel and removed. The buttstock can be removed by taking off the buttplate and using a B-Square stock tool or a long-shanked screwdriver to back out the stock bolt.

Reassembly Tips:

1. When replacing the magazine tube, it is possible to install it incorrectly, in inverted position. There is an index mark on the tube, and an arrow on the underside of the receiver extension. Align these when replacing the end plug, and the tube will be properly installed.

2. When replacing the bolt in the receiver, be sure the rear tip of the bolt retaining lever is pushed inward.

When replacing the shell stop, note that its forward tip must be inserted in a recess at the front before the rear portion is moved into its recess.

When replacing the hammer and hammer spring assembly, use the same method as in takedown, trapping the spring with a pin in the guide at the rear to hold the tension while the hammer cross pin is installed.

Remember that the carrier pivot screw has a reverse thread. When turning it back into place, it must be turned counter-clockwise.

Winchester Model 37

Data:	Winchester Model 37
Origin:	United States
Manufacturer:	Winchester Repeating Arms New Haven, Connecticut
Gauges:	12, 16, 20, and 410
Overall length:	44-1/2 inches (with 26-inch barrel)
Barrel length:	26 to 32 inches
Weight:	6-1/2 pounds

From 1936 to 1963, the Model 37 was the king of the single-barrel outside hammer shotguns. Actually, it didn't have a hammer at all. A hammer-like lever in a slot in the upper tang was attached to a cylindrical striker/firing pin unit inside. In use, the effect was the same as an external hammer. The Model 37 was replaced in the Winchester line by the Model 370 (1968), then the Model 37A (1973), but these guns are entirely different mechanically.

Disassembly:

1. Pull the front of the forend away from the barrel until the retaining catch releases, and remove the forend downward and toward the front.

2. Remove the screw on the underside of the forend. Remove the forend iron upward.

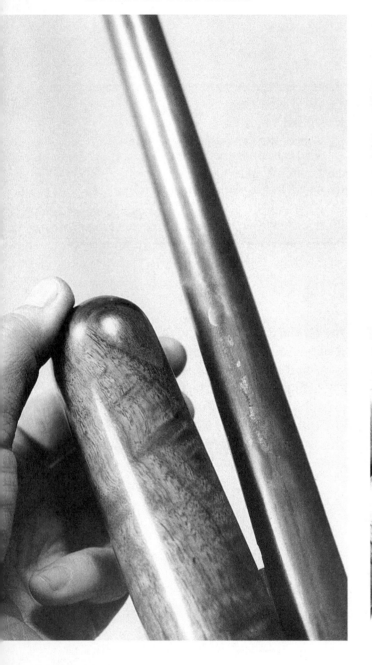

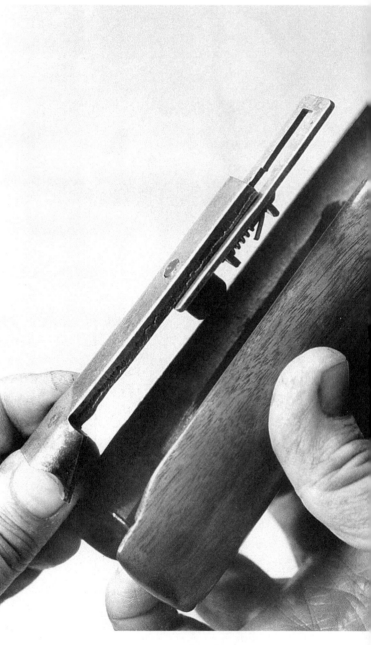

3. Remove the spacer plate at the rear of the forend.

4. Use a screwdriver with a wide and thin blade to remove the mounting stud from the forend iron, and separate the latch plate from the front of the forend iron.

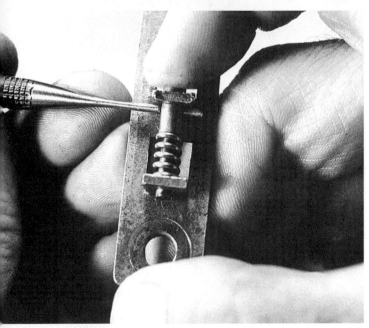

5. Restrain the forend latch plunger, and push out the cross pin in the latch housing to release the plunger and spring for removal toward the front.

6. Operate the barrel latch, tip the barrel down beyond its usual opened position, and take the barrel off upward.

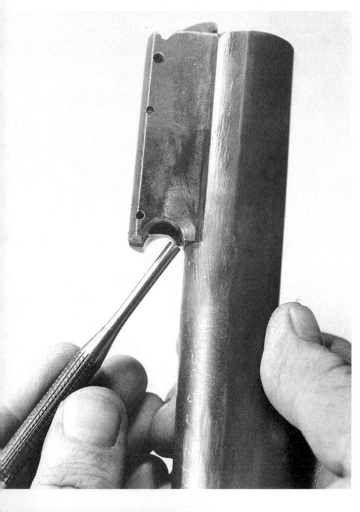

7. Set a drift punch against the upper lobe of the ejector catch, and tap it with a hammer to push the catch arm toward the rear, releasing the ejector to snap out, partially relieving the tension of its spring.

8. Drift out the cross pin at the front of the barrel underlug.

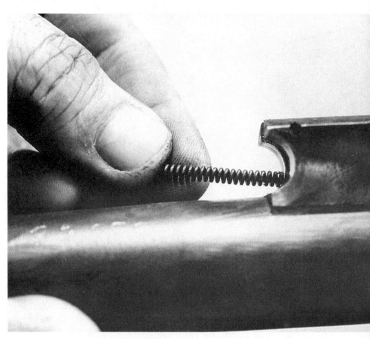

9. Remove the ejector catch toward the front and downward.

10. Remove the ejector spring toward the front.

11. Lift the ejector upward, and remove it toward the rear.

12. Drifting out the large and small cross pins at the lower rear of the barrel underlug will allow removal of the ejector guide.

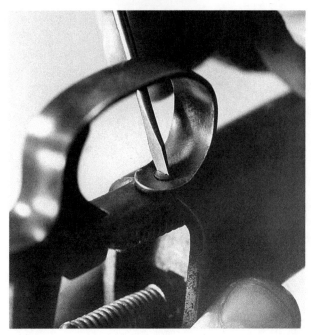

13. Remove the buttplate, and use a B-Square stock tool or a long-shanked screwdriver to back out the stock mounting bolt. Remove the bolt, washer, and buttstock toward the rear.

14. Remove the screw at the rear of the trigger guard. Remove the screw at the front of the trigger guard, using an off set or angled-tip screwdriver, as shown. Take off the guard downward.

15. Grip the rear tip of the guide for the combination trigger and barrel latch spring with sharp-nosed pliers. Depress the guide and spring slightly toward the front, lift the guide fork from its notch on the trigger and remove the guide and spring toward the rear.

16. Push out the cross pin in the rear fork of the striker, near the top of the cocking lever.

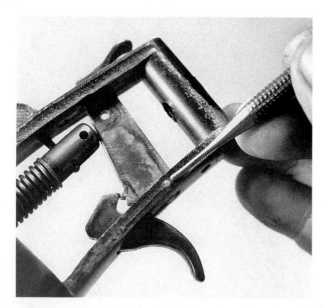

17. Push out the cocking lever pivot pin, in the lower tang of the receiver.

18. Remove the cocking lever upward.

19. Drift out the trigger cross pin.

20. Remove the trigger downward.

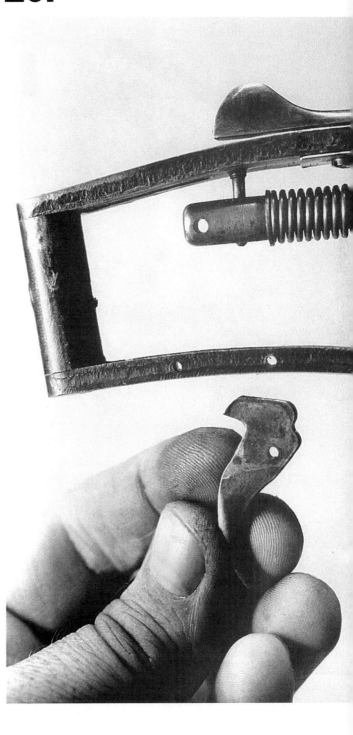

21. Move the barrel latch lever toward the right, and remove the screw in the upper tang, just forward of the cocking lever slot.

23. Drifting out the cross pin in the striker assembly will allow removal of the striker spring and its end-washers toward the front. Caution: The spring is powerful. If removal is not necessary for repair, it's best to leave this assembly intact.

22. Move the striker assembly to the rear, then remove it toward either side.

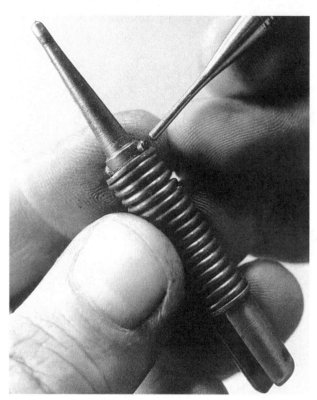

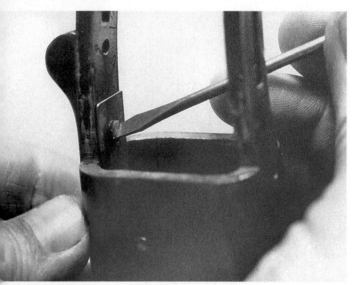

24. The barrel latch lever is retained by a spring plate on the underside of the upper tang, and the plate is held by a vertical screw. There is no direct access, and an offset or angled-tip screwdriver must be used to remove the screw. Take off the plate downward and toward the rear.

25. Remove the barrel latch lever upward.

26. Drift out the large cross pin at the rear center of the receiver.

1. When replacing the barrel latch lever retaining plate, note that it is slightly curved, and that the concave side of the curve goes downward, as shown. Be sure the front of the plate engages its recess in the base of the lever.

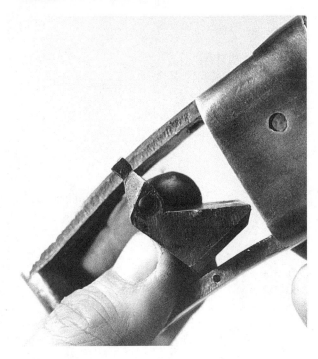

27. Remove the barrel latch block toward the rear, and out either side.

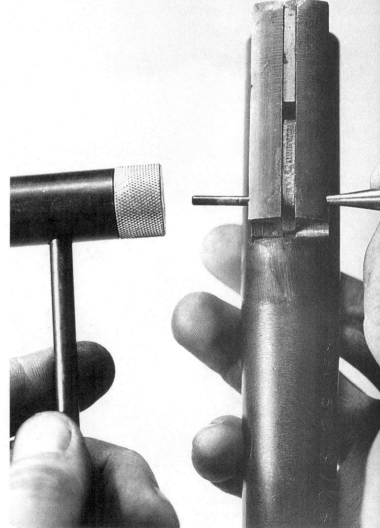

2. Note that the rear tip of the guide for the combination trigger and barrel latch spring is angled, and be sure it is installed with the angle downward, as shown.

3. When replacing the ejector catch, use a tool at the front to push the catch toward the rear, compressing the spring, and insert a drift punch through the cross hole to hold the catch in position for insertion of the cross pin.

Winchester Model 97

Similar/Identical Pattern Guns:

The same basic assembly/disassembly steps for the Winchester Model 97 also apply to the following guns:

Winchester Model 1897   **Winchester Model 97 Trench Gun**

Winchester Model 97 Solid Frame

Data:	Winchester Model 97
Origin:	United States
Manufacturer:	Winchester Repeating Arms
Gauges:	12 and 16
Magazine capacity:	5 rounds
Overall length:	47-1/2 inches (with 28-inch barrel)
Barrel length:	20 to 32 inches
Weight:	7-1/2 to 7-3/4 pounds

A slight reworking of John M. Browning's original design of 1893, the Model 1897 was in production for 60 years. By the time it was discontinued, in 1957, nearly a million of these guns had been sold. It was offered in both fixed barrel and takedown versions, and was also made with a short barrel for police and military use. The mechanism is fairly complicated, and complete takedown and reassembly may present some difficulties for the amateur.

Disassembly:

1. Push the magazine locking pin downward and toward the right, and pull it out until it stops. Using the pin as a lever, rotate the magazine tube about one-quarter turn counter-clockwise (front view), until it stops. Pull the magazine tube toward the front until it stops.

2. Move the forend and action slide assembly forward until it stops, and rotate the barrel and magazine assembly about one-quarter turn counter-clockwise (front view) until it stops. Remove the barrel, magazine, and action slide assembly toward the front.

3. Remove the buttplate, and use a B-Square stock tool or a long-shanked screwdriver to back out the stock bolt. Remove the buttstock toward the rear.

5. Remove the carrier pivot pin toward either side.

4. Remove the carrier pin retaining screw, located in the top left rear of the carrier, beside the hammer.

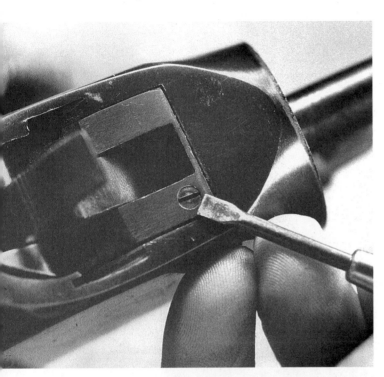

6. Remove the small screw on the right side of the receiver, just forward of the trigger cross pin.

7. Drift out the trigger cross pin.

8. Cock the hammer, push the carrier release button on the right side, and insert a tool between the bolt and carrier to nudge the carrier downward. Remove the carrier downward and toward the front.

9. Slide (or tap with a nylon hammer) the trigger guard unit out toward the rear.

10. The trigger and its spring are easily removed from the top of the guard. There is also a trigger stop screw at the rear inside the guard, and it is easily backed out. If this is done, though, it will have to be readjusted during reassembly.

11. Remove the screw on the right side of the bolt, just below the extractor.

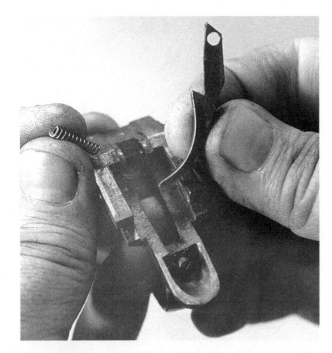

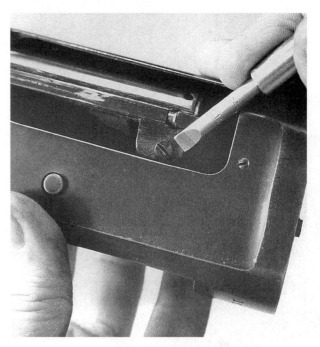

12. Insert a tool beneath the bolt, through the ejection port, and move the front of the slide hook downward, out of its recess on the left side of the bolt. Remove the hook from the bottom of the receiver.

13. Move the bolt all the way to the rear of the receiver, and lift it off upward.

14. Remove the screw on the left side of the receiver near the top, and take off the ejector toward the left. Note that the ejector block is mounted on a short pin-like projection in the receiver wall, just to the rear of the ejector opening, and if it has to be removed, it is drifted inward.

15. The right and left shell stops are retained on the inside of the receiver by vertical pivot screws in the lower edge of the receiver on each side. Back out the screws, and take off the shell stops inward.

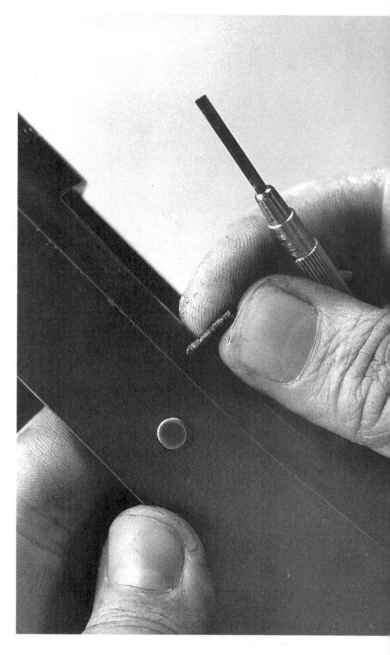

16. The shell stop springs are mounted in slots on the inside of each shell stop, and are easily driven out if necessary for repair.

17. The carrier release button is retained inside the receiver by a round-wire spring that is keyed into a tiny hole in the receiver wall. Use a tool of very small diameter to push the tip of the spring inward, then use sharp-nosed pliers inside the receiver to move the spring forward, releasing the button for removal.

18. The two tiny screws on each side at the front of the receiver retain the barrel chamber ring. After the screws are removed, the ring is taken out toward the front. The larger screw on the front of the receiver is the extension stop screw, and holds no part.

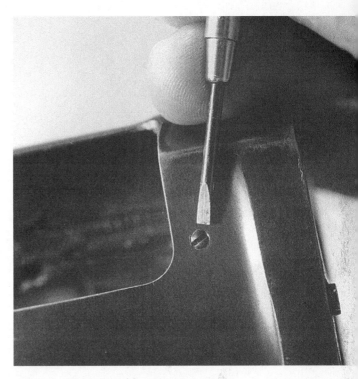

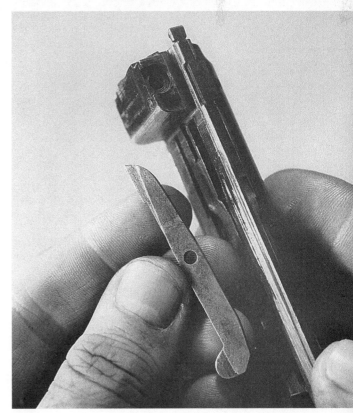

19. Drift out the cross pin at the rear of the bolt toward the left, and remove the firing pin toward the rear. Remove the screw on the left side at the center of the bolt.

20. Remove the firing pin retractor downward, and take out its small coil spring from the underside of the bolt.

21. The left extractor, which is tempered to be its own spring, is retained by a vertical pin which is driven out upward.

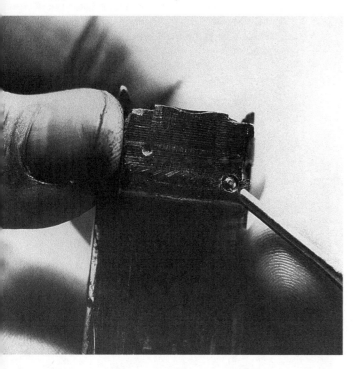

22. The right extractor is removed by inserting a small screwdriver between the extractor and its plunger. Depress the plunger toward the rear, and lift the extractor out of its recess. Keep the plunger under control, slowly release the spring tension, and remove the plunger and spring toward the front.

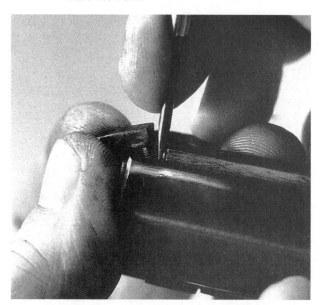

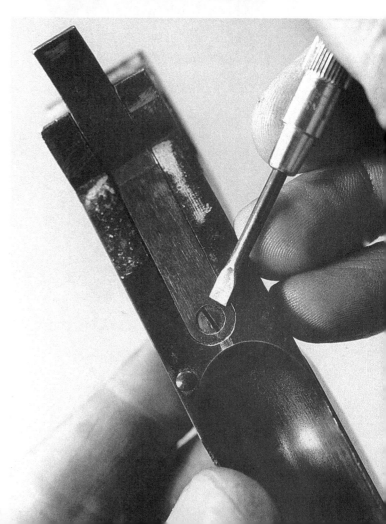

23. Restrain the hammer, and press the tail of the sear upward to release the hammer. Ease the hammer down to its full forward position

24. Remove the sear spring screw on the underside of the carrier, and take off the spring downward.

26. Remove the slide latch pivot pin retaining screw.

25. Drift out the sear pin, and remove the sear.

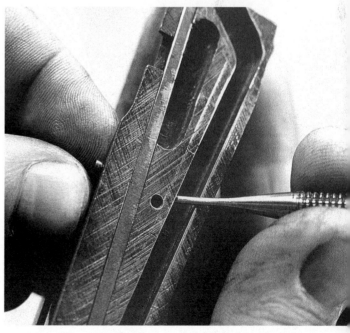

27. Remove the slide latch spring retaining screw, and take off the latch spring, detaching its tab from behind the latch bar.

28. Insert a slim drift in the access hole in the lower edge of the action slide track, and push out and remove the slide latch pivot downward. As the pin emerges, it can be grasped and pulled out.

29. Remove the slide latch toward the left.

30. Swing the shell guide plate upward, and remove the slide latch release plunger toward the right.

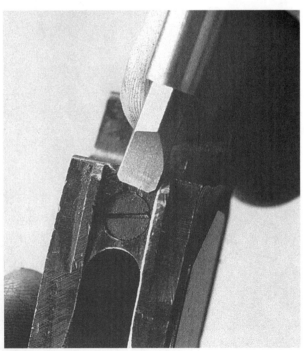

31. Remove the hammer spring tension screw.

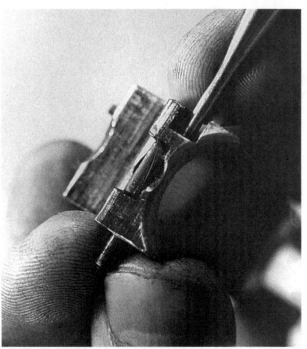

32. Drift out the hammer spring pin toward the right.

33. Be sure the shell guide plate is still swung up out of the way, and drift out the hammer pivot pin toward the right.

34. Remove the hammer upward. The hammer stirrup cross pin should be removed only for repair purposes.

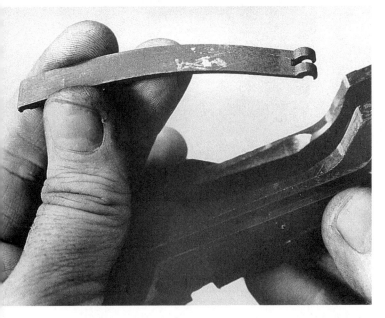

35. Nudge the hammer spring toward the rear. When it has cleared the front bridge of the carrier, the spring can be removed upward.

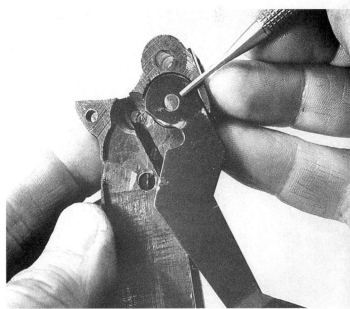

36. The shell guide plate is riveted in place on the carrier, and removal is not recommended in normal takedown. If necessary for repair, it can be taken off, but a new pivot-rivet will likely have to be made.

37. To remove the magazine lock pin, depress the round-wire spring in the slot in its side, and pull out the pin.

38. Remove the two opposed screws at the front of the magazine tube, and take out the plug and plug stop ring toward the front. Caution: The magazine spring will be released, so control it and ease it out Remove the spring and follower toward the front.

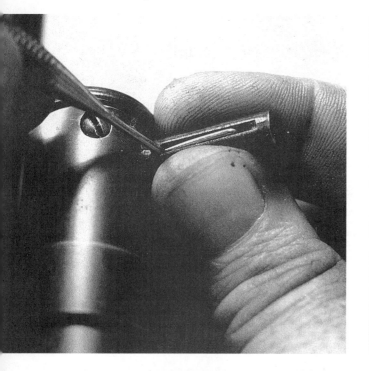

39. Remove the screws on each side of the magazine hanger, and move the hanger off toward the front. When the hanger is removed, the screw bushing at its center can be taken out. The action slide and magazine assembly can now be removed toward the front.

40. Use a Brownells Model 12 forend wrench to remove the forend cap nut, and take out the magazine tube toward the front. The buffer spring can be slid off the magazine tube toward the rear. The action slide can now be removed from the forend toward the rear.

41. Barrel tightness in the receiver is adjustable by backing out the adjusting sleeve lock screw and sliding the lock piece out of engagement with the teeth on the edge of the sleeve. Turning the sleeve clockwise (rearview) will tighten the barrel engagement. If necessary, the screw, sleeve, and lock piece can be removed.

1. When replacing the magazine lock pin, use pliers to squeeze the tip of its spring inward to make reinsertion easier.

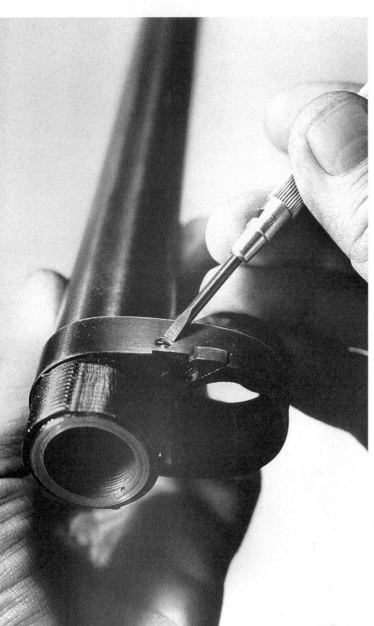

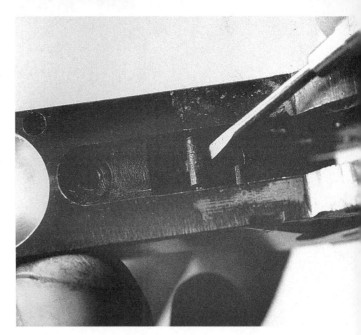

2. When replacing the hammer, insert a tool on the underside of the carrier to tip the stirrup into engagement with the hooks on the hammer spring before tightening the spring tension screw.

3. When replacing the trigger assembly, it will be necessary to use a slave pin to hold the trigger and its spring in place while the guard unit is slid back into the receiver. The assembly is shown with the parts and slave pin in place, ready to be installed.

4. When replacing the carrier cross pin, remember that the groove in the pin must be on the left side, to contact the retaining screw.

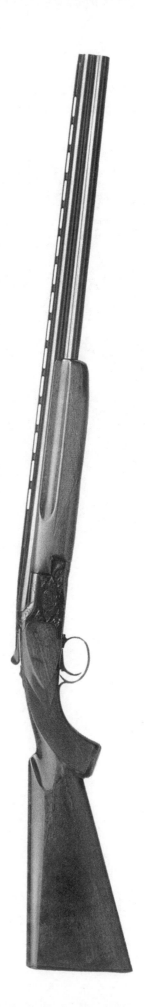

Winchester Model 101

Data:	Winchester Model 101
Origin:	Japan
Manufacturer:	Olin Kodensha Co., Ltd., for Winchester, New Haven, Connecticut
Gauges:	12, 20, 28, and 410
Overall length:	47 inches (with 30-inch barrels)
Barrel length:	26 to 32 inches
Weight:	6-1/4 to 7-3/4 pounds

Winchester's first over/under shotgun was introduced in 1963, initially in 12-gauge only. By 1966, it was also available in 20- and 28-gauge and 410-bore, and in a wide variety of styles and options. There is even a version with an accessory single barrel unit for the trapshooter. The Model 101 was discontinued in 1987. Mechanically, the Model 101 is no more complicated than any other over/under design, but with all guns of this type the amateur should proceed with caution.

Disassembly:

1. Open and close the action to cock the internal hammers. Operate the forend latch, and swing the latch bar outward. Tip the forward end of the forend away from the barrels, and remove the forend downward and toward the front.

2. Operate the barrel latch, tip the barrels down beyond their normal open position, and remove the barrels upward.

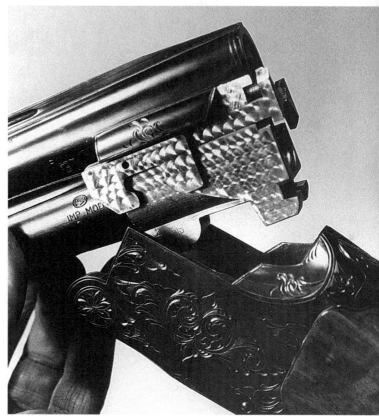

3. Remove the three vertical screws on the inside of the forend, tip the forend iron upward at the front, and remove it toward the rear.

4. Use a nylon punch from the inside to nudge the forend latch housing downward for removal. Tap it equally at each end, to avoid chipping the recess.

5. The forend latch bar is cross pinned to its housing. Backing out the small screw on the inside of the lever will release the lever catch plunger and its spring for removal.

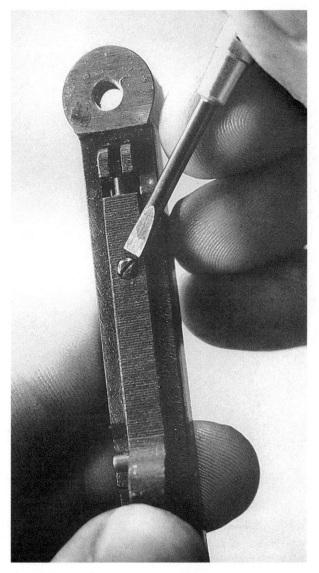

6. Trip the ejector sears downward, allowing the ejector hammers to move toward the rear. Grip the rear neck of each spring guide with sharp-nosed pliers, and move the guide tips out of the recesses on the backs of the hammers. Caution: Even at rest, these springs have considerable tension, so control them and ease them off.

7. A single cross pin retains both ejector hammers, and the pin is drifted out toward the right. The ejector hammer sears and their springs are retained by cross pins at the upper rear of the forend base, and these pins are contoured and finished with the outside of the base piece. Unless absolutely necessary for repair, these should not be removed.

8. To remove the ejectors, slide each one to the rear, and insert a tool into the hole in each ejector to depress the retaining spring. The ejectors can then be slid off toward the rear.

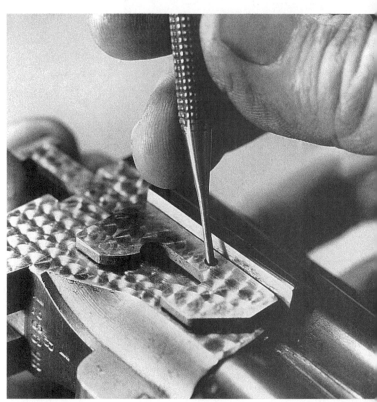

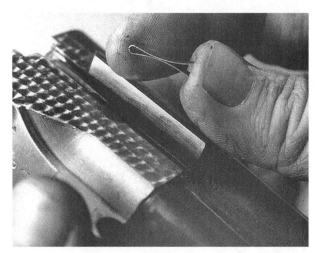

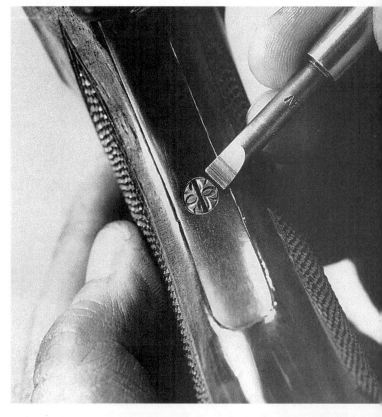

9. After the ejectors are removed, be sure to take out the retaining springs from their recesses on each side, as they will be completely freed when the ejectors are taken off, and might fall and be lost.

10. Insert a finger or tool in the front of the receiver and depress the barrel latch lever detent, allowing the latch lever to return to center. Leave the safety in the on-safe position. Back out and remove the screw in the rear tail of the trigger guard.

11. Lift the tail of the guard from its recess in the stock, turn the guard straight out toward either side, and remove the guard from the bottom of the receiver.

12. Remove the buttplate, and use a B-Square stock tool or a long-shanked screwdriver to take out the stock bolt and its washers. Take off the buttstock toward the rear.

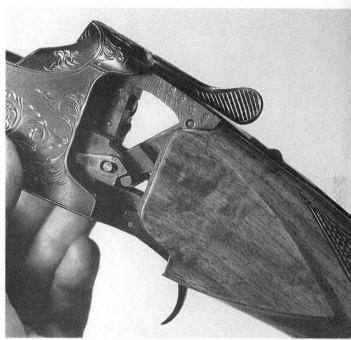

13. Drift out the upper firing pin retaining pin (arrow) toward the right, and remove the upper firing pin and its spring leftward and toward the rear.

14. Drift out the lower firing pin retaining pin toward the left, and remove the lower firing pin upward and toward the rear, along with its spring.

15. Move the safety to the off-safe position and pull the trigger to drop each hammer to the fired position. Grip the forward tip of the hammer spring guide on each side with sharp-nosed pliers, moving the guide tip out of its recess on the back of each hammer. Caution: These springs are under tension, even when at rest, so control them and ease them off.

16. Drift out the trigger cross pin.

17. Move the trigger forward, then downward, moving the trigger and inertia block assembly out the bottom of the receiver. Drifting out the cross pin in the trigger will allow removal of the inertia block, plunger, and spring from the trigger. Caution: The spring is under tension, so ease it out.

18. Drift out the cross pin that retains the sears, and remove the sears and their springs downward. Restrain the sears during removal of the pin, as the springs are under tension. The upper end of the sear and hammer spacer will be freed as the pin is removed.

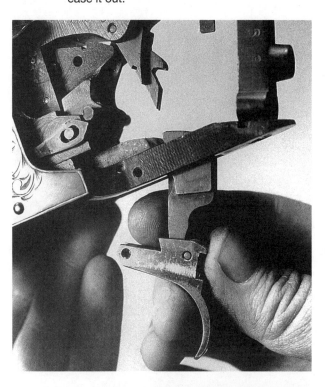

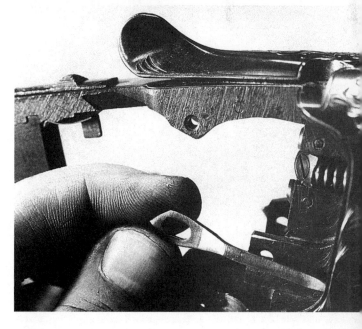

19. Taking care not to damage the rear tips of the ejector trip rods, drift out the cross pin that retains both hammers. Remove the hammers, and the hammer and sear spacer, toward the rear.

20. Remove the ejector trip rods toward the rear, and keep them separated, as they are not interchangeable.

21. Insert a small screwdriver from the rear to lift the front of the safety spring out of its recess, and turn the spring out toward the side. Remove the spring downward, and take off the safety button upward.

22. When the safety button is removed, take care that the small filler block (arrow), located between the lower extensions of the button, is not lost.

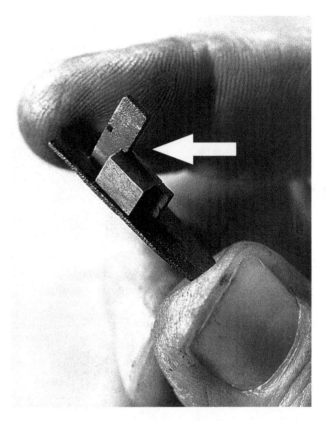

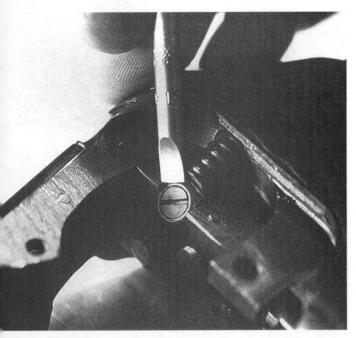

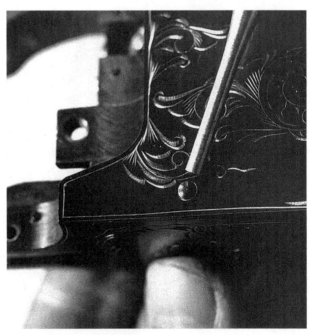

23. Remove the screw that retains the barrel latch lever spring base, and take off the base and spring toward the rear.

24. Drift out the bottom frame plate pin.

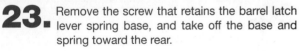

25. Insert a drift punch from the top, in front of the breech face, and tap the bottom plate free.

26. Move the barrel latch lever detent forward, then remove it downward, along with its spring.

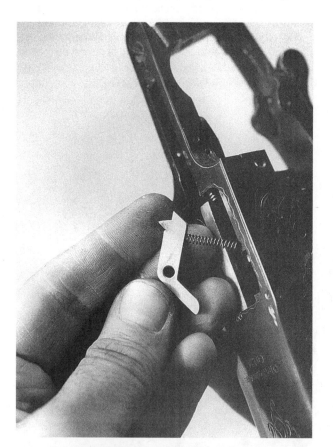

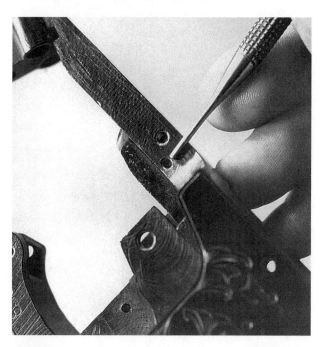

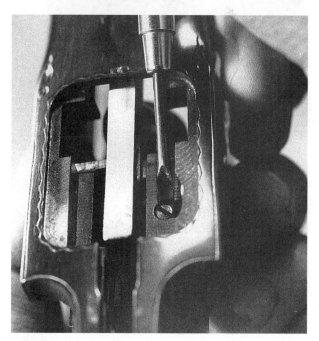

27. Drift out the cross pin that is the rear base for the cocking slide spring, and remove the spring and guide toward the rear.

28. Unscrew and remove the pinion screw from the underside of the barrel latch block.

29. Move the barrel latch block to the rear, stopping it short of contact with the trigger spring. The block may be tight as it is moved out of its normal position, and may need to be nudged with a non-marring drift punch. When the block is moved back, the cocking slide can be moved toward the rear, tilted downward, and taken out the bottom of the receiver.

30. Removal of the barrel locking block will require that the tang spacer, the heavy vertical piece at the rear of the receiver, must be taken out. Remove the screws at the top and bottom of the spacer, and use a nylon drift and hammer to tap it out of its grooves toward the side. When the spacer is taken out, the trigger spring will be released for removal at the bottom, and the barrel locking block can then be moved out toward the rear.

31. Remove the screw at the top of the barrel latch lever, and insert a drift to nudge the latch lever post downward. Remove the post from the bottom of the receiver, and take off the latch lever upward. Note that these parts are very tightly fitted, and if their removal is not necessary for repair or refinishing, it's best to leave them in place.

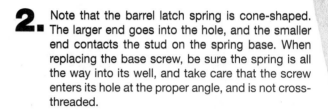

Reassembly Tips:

1. When replacing the barrel latch lever detent and its spring, be sure the spring enters its recess in the receiver, and use a short slave pin, as shown, to hold the lever in place while the bottom plate is re-installed.

2. Note that the barrel latch spring is cone-shaped. The larger end goes into the hole, and the smaller end contacts the stud on the spring base. When replacing the base screw, be sure the spring is all the way into its well, and take care that the screw enters its hole at the proper angle, and is not cross-threaded.

3. The spacer plate that goes between the hammers and sears has a hole at each end, and the holes are of unequal size. The smaller hole is for the sear pin, the larger one, at the bottom, for the hammer pin. When installing the hammers and the sears, be sure the holes in the spacer plate are aligned for passage of the cross pins.

When replacing the trigger and inertia block assembly, insert a tool at the rear to depress the trigger spring downward for clearance. When the trigger is installed, be sure the spring lies on top of the trigger at the rear.

Winchester Model 1200

Similar/Identical Pattern Guns:

The same basic assembly/disassembly steps for the Winchester Model 1200 also apply to the following guns:

Sears Model 200

Sears "Ranger" Model 120

Sears "Ranger" Youth

Sears "Ranger" Combo

Winchester Model 1300

Winchester Model 1300XTR

Data:	Winchester Model 1200
Origin:	United States
Manufacturer:	Winchester Repeating Arms New Haven, Connecticut
Gauges:	12, and 20
Magazine capacity:	4 rounds
Overall length:	49 inches (with 28-inch barrel)
Barrel length:	26 to 30 inches
Weight:	6-1/2 pounds

In 1964, when it was first introduced, the Model 1200 was available in 12- and 16-gauge. The latter chambering was dropped before long, in favor of the 20-gauge. Until the arrival of the Model 1300XTR in 1978, the Model 1200 was available in a wide range of barrel, choke, and stock options. The Model 1200 has also been made for Sears under their brand name, and those guns are mechanically identical, so the instructions will apply. In 1978, Winchester's designation was changed to Model 1300. The last Model 1200 was made in 1981.

Disassembly:

1. Open the action, set the safety in the on-safe position, and unscrew the magazine end cap and remove it. Move the action slide slightly toward the front to give clearance inside the forend at the rear, and take off the barrel toward the front.

2. Close the action, and push out the cross pin at the lower rear of the receiver toward either side.

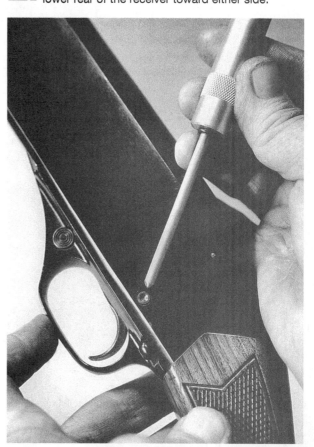

3. Tip the trigger housing downward at the rear, then remove it downward and toward the rear.

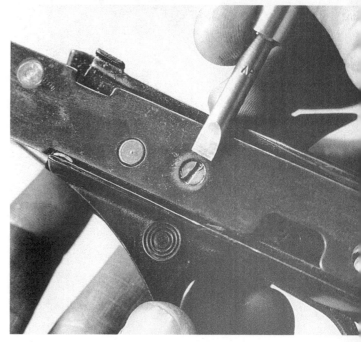

4. Remove the screw in the left sideplate of the trigger housing.

5. Remove the left sideplate toward the left.

6. The left shell stop is heavily riveted on the front of the left sideplate, and is not intended for routine removal.

7. The carrier pivot is permanently attached to the right sideplate. Restrain the carrier, and take off the right sideplate toward the right. The right shell stop is also permanently attached to the right sideplate.

8. Slowly release the tension of the carrier spring, and remove the carrier upward and toward the front. Take out the carrier plunger and spring from the right side of the housing. The carrier dog is retained on the right rear wing of the carrier by a cross pin. If necessary for repair, the pin can be drifted out toward the right.

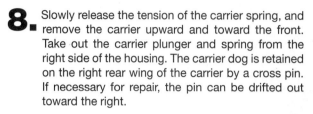

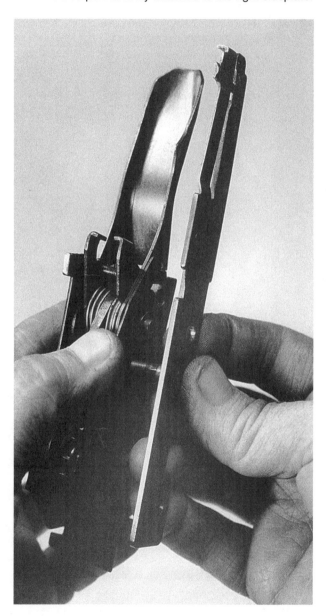

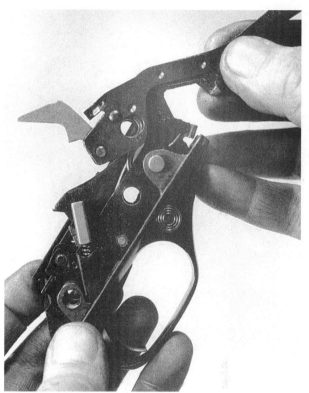

9. Move the safety to the off-safe position, restrain the hammer, pull the trigger, and ease the hammer down to the fired position. Hold a thumb on top of the sear assembly to restrain it, and depress the front of the slide latch. Move the slide latch toward the left and allow it to swing upward, relieving the tension of its spring. Remove the slide latch and its spring toward the left.

10. Release the sear assembly, and remove it upward. While it is possible to remove the sear and its spring from its bracket, this is difficult to do without damaging the bracket. Unless necessary for repair, it's best to leave it intact.

11. Restrain the hammer, and push out the hammer pivot toward the left.

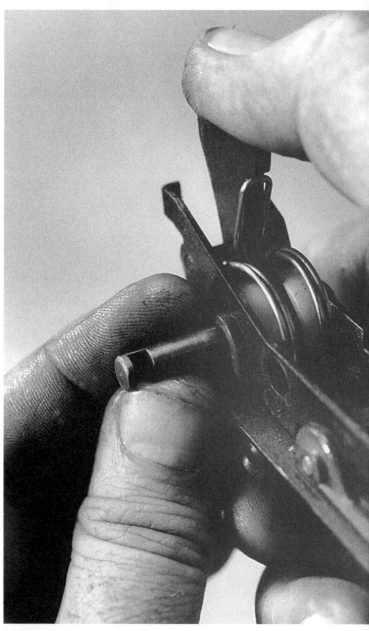

12. Move the hammer assembly forward, then take it off upward. The nylon hammer bushings and the hammer spring are easily detached from the hammer.

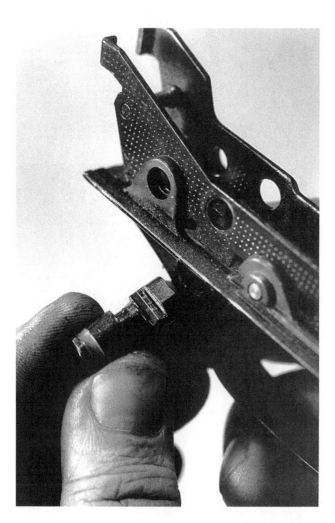

13. Removal of the hammer assembly will have released the safety button, and it can now be taken out toward either side.

14. Remove the trigger pin toward the left, and take out the trigger upward. The stud mounted on top of the trigger should not be disturbed.

15. On late Model 1200 guns, the central frame of the trigger housing is easily detachable, after the parts are removed. If the subframe is removed, take care that the hammer stop pin at the front isn't detached and lost.

16. Remove the slide bridge screw, located in the plate ("slide bridge") on the underside of the bolt.

17. Remove the bolt and slide assembly toward the front.

18. Keeping the slide bridge pressed against the bottom of the bolt, detach the bolt from the action slide bars.

19. Restrain the firing pin at the rear, and remove the slide bridge plate from the bottom of the bolt. Remove the firing pin and its spring from the rear of the bolt.

20. Turn the bolt head until the cam pin is about midway in its track on the underside of the bolt slide, aligning the top of the cam pin with the access hole in the top of the bolt slide. Use a drift punch to drive the cam pin downward. Caution: When the drift is removed, the extractor spring and washer will be released toward the rear. Insert a tool to restrain them.

21. Slowly release the extractor spring and washer, and remove them toward the rear.

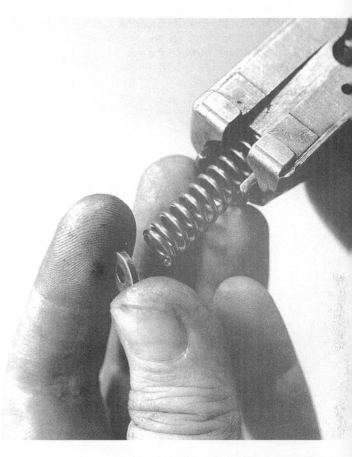

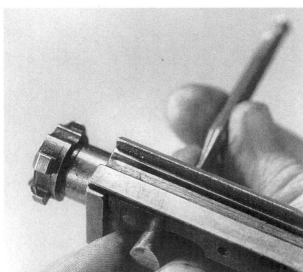

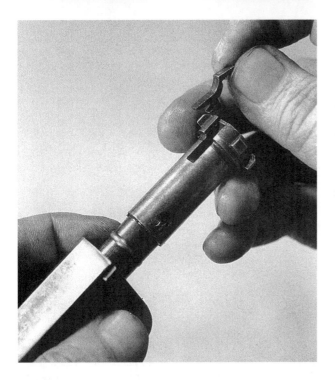

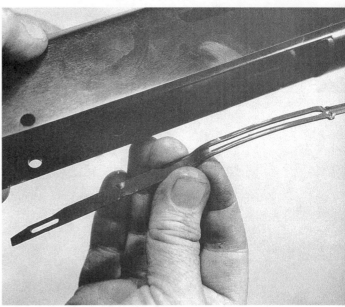

22. Remove the bolt toward the front, and take out the extractor from its recess.

23. When the bolt and slide assembly are removed from the receiver, the ejector will be released for removal. Its long rear tail has an oblong slot which rides on a fixed pin inside the rear of the receiver. Detach the ejector, and remove it.

24. With a piece of steel plate of suitable size to bridge the front of the forend, unscrew the forend cap nut, and remove the action slide assembly toward the rear.

25. Insert a screwdriver in the open end of the magazine spring retainer, and pry it outward, moving the screw driver to raise it equally around its edge. Caution: The magazine spring will be released. Control it, and ease it out Remove the spring and follower toward the front.

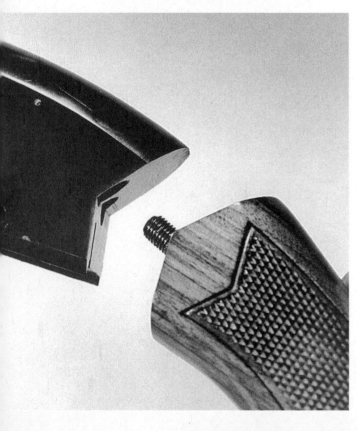

26. Remove the buttplate, and use a B-Square stock tool or a long-shanked screwdriver to back out the stock bolt. Remove the buttstock toward rear.

Reassembly Tips:

1. It is possible to install the bolt in the bolt slide upside down. Remember that the extractor must be on the right side when the bolt system is reassembled. Also, remember that the firing pin passes through the cam pin, so the central hole (arrow) in the cam pin must be oriented for this. Note that the short end of the cam pin goes at the top. Insert a tool from the rear to compress the extractor spring and washer when replacing the cam pin. A large roll-pin punch is ideal for this, as its central nose at the tip will fit into the washer hole.

2. When replacing the hammer and hammer spring assembly, be sure the right lower tail of the spring enters its slot inside the trigger housing, to bear on the detent steps of the safety button. Also, note that there is a flat on one side of the hammer pivot pin, and this must be oriented to match the flat on the inside of the hammer bushings. If not, the bushings will be damaged, and the slide latch will not work properly.

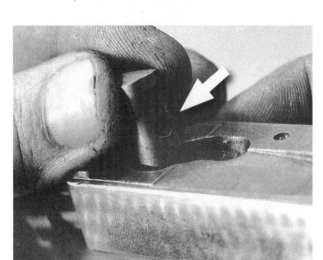

3. When installing the sear assembly and the slide latch and its spring, note that the sear spring must rest on the rear slope of the trigger. Also, be sure the rear tail of the slide latch spring enters its slot at the lower rear, where it becomes the detent for the retaining cross pin. The slide latch spring is shown in position for replacement of the slide latch.

4. When the slide latch is installed, its front opening must fit on the left tip of the hammer pivot, as shown.

5. When replacing the trigger housing in the receiver, carefully hook the front edges of the sideplates into their recesses (arrows), then swing the housing up into place at the rear.

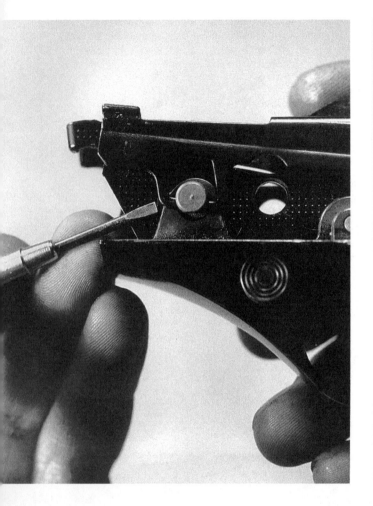

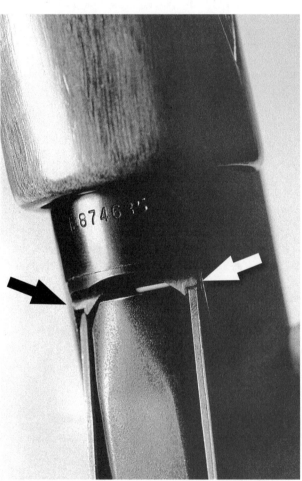

Winchester Model 1400

Similar/Identical Pattern Guns:

The same basic assembly/disassembly steps for the Winchester Model 1400 also apply to the following guns:

Winchester Model 1400 Mark II   Winchester Model 1500XTR

Data:	Winchester Model 1400
Origin:	United States
Manufacturer:	Winchester Repeating Arms New Haven, Connecticut
Gauges:	12, and 20
Magazine capacity:	2 rounds
Overall length:	49 inches (with 28-inch barrel)
Barrel length:	22 to 30 inches
Weight:	6-1/2 to 6-3/4 pounds

Like its slide-action counterpart, the Model 1200, this gun was available for a time in 16-gauge. Both guns were introduced in 1964. The Model 1400 was slightly redesigned in 1968, and was then designated the Model 1400 Mark II. The stock was restyled, and the carrier release system was changed. Otherwise, the mechanism is virtually the same, and except for the carrier release area the instructions can be applied. The Model 1500XTR is mechanically the same.

Disassembly:

1. Pull back the operating handle to lock the bolt open, and set the safety in the on-safe position. Unscrew the magazine end cap and remove it, and take off the barrel and forend toward the front.

2. Restrain the bolt, depress the carrier latch, and ease the bolt forward to the closed position. Push out the cross pin at the lower rear of the receiver toward either side.

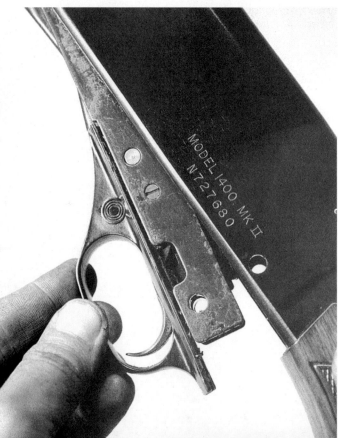

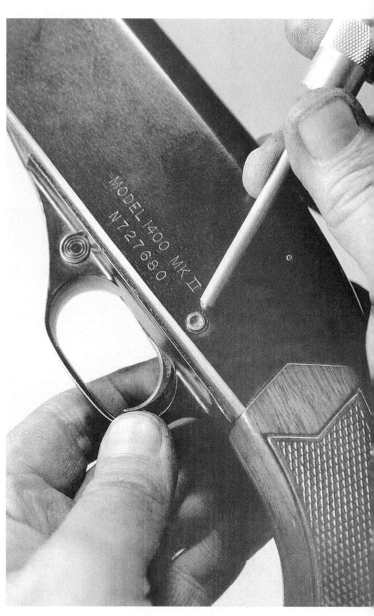

3. Tip the trigger housing downward at the rear, and remove it downward and toward the rear.

4. Remove the screw in the center of the left sideplate on the trigger housing.

5. Take off the left sideplate. Note that both the right and left shell stops are heavily riveted on the sideplates, and are not designed to be routinely removed.

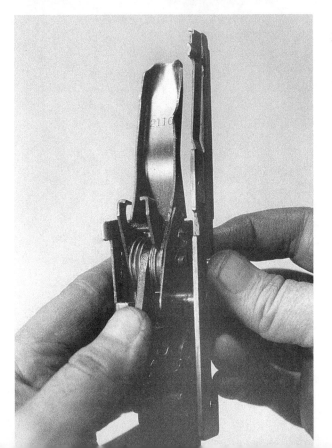

6. Restrain the carrier, and take off the right sideplate. Note that the carrier pivot is permanently mounted on the right sideplate, and the carrier will be released as the plate is removed.

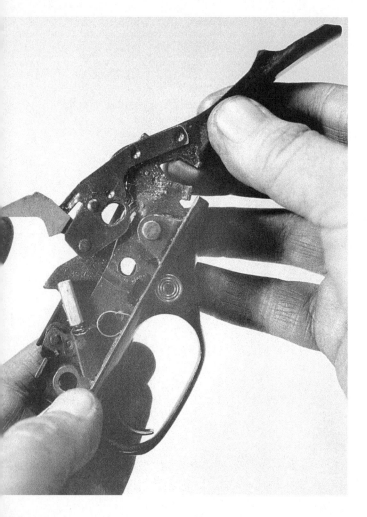

7. Slowly release the tension of the carrier spring. Move the rear of the carrier upward, and take off the carrier toward the front. Also, remove the carrier spring and plunger, and take off the carrier support spring. The carrier dog is cross pin mounted on the right rear wing of the carrier, and is not removed in normal takedown. If removal is necessary for repair, the pin is drifted out toward the right.

8. Move the safety to the off-safe position, restrain the hammer, pull the trigger, and ease the hammer down to the fired position. Depress the front of the disconnector and move it toward the left, holding a thumb on top of the sear assembly to restrain it. When the disconnector is moved out far enough to clear, allow it to swing upward, relieving the tension of its spring. Remove the disconnector and its spring toward the left.

9. Removal of the disconnector will have released the sear assembly, and it can now be taken off upward. The sear and its spring can be removed from the sear bracket by drifting out the cross pin toward the left, but extreme care must be taken to avoid damage to the bracket. In normal takedown, this unit is left intact.

10. Restrain the hammer, and push out the hammer pivot toward the left.

11. Remove the hammer and hammer spring assembly upward. The nylon bushings and the spring are easily removed from the hammer.

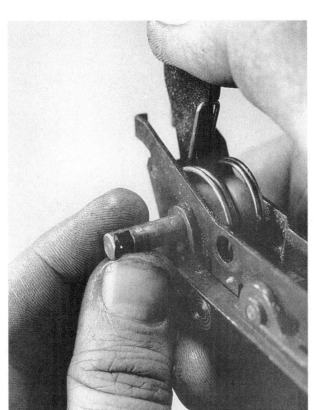

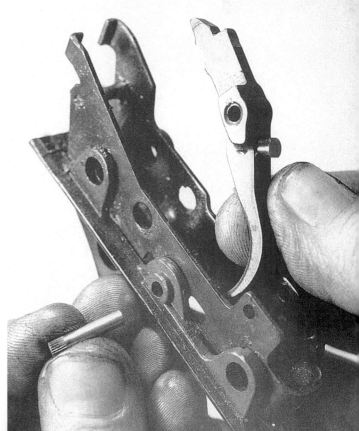

12. Remove the safety button toward the left.

13. Drift out the trigger pin toward the left, and remove the trigger upward. The stud set into the top of the trigger should not be disturbed.

14. After the parts are removed, the central subframe is easily detached from the trigger housing.

15. Insert a tool at the front to retract the recoil spring, and lift the piston pin out upward. Caution: Keep the spring under control.

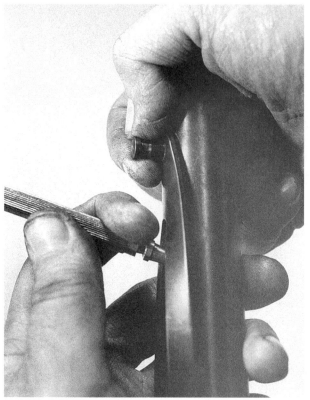

16. Keeping the spring restrained with a tool, remove the piston from the front of the magazine tube.

17. Slowly release the spring tension, and remove the spring from the front of the magazine tube. Caution: The recoil spring is quite powerful. Don't let it get away.

18. Tilt the action slide bars upward at the front, move the bolt toward the rear, and remove the action slide toward the front.

19. Insert a screwdriver through the bottom of the receiver, and remove the bridge plate retaining screw. Restrain the firing pin, and lift the bridge plate at the rear to free it. Remove the firing pin and its spring from the bolt.

20. Insert a screwdriver at the rear of the receiver to unhook the ejector from its post, and remove the ejector toward the front.

21. Tip the operating handle upward, turn the plate as shown, and remove it through the ejection port.

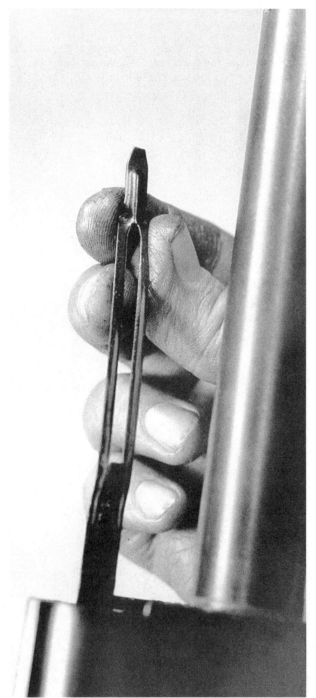

22. Remove the bolt from the bottom of the receiver.

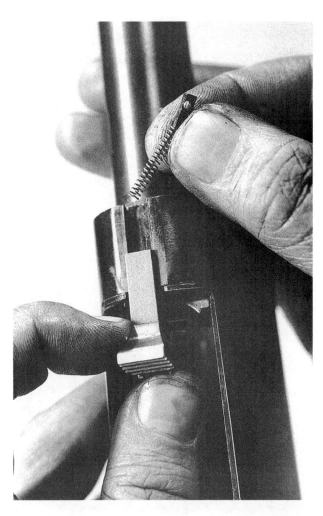

23. Drifting out the roll pin in the front tip of the carrier latch will allow removal of the carrier latch spring and retainer toward the front, and the latch toward the rear. Caution: When the pin is out these parts will be released in both directions, so restrain them and ease the spring tension slowly. In normal takedown, it's best to leave the carrier latch in place, as its front edges are easily broken during removal. The magazine system is another area that should not be disturbed, as removal and replacement is particularly difficult, with a good chance of damage to the parts.

24. Position the bolt in its slide piece to align the cam pin with the access hole in the top of the slide, and drift the cam pin out downward. Caution: The extractor spring and its washer will be released toward the rear as the cam pin clears, so restrain them and ease them out

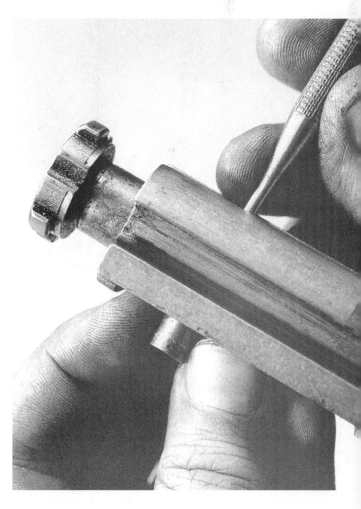

25. Remove the bolt from the bolt slide, and take out the extractor from its recess.

26. Remove the buttplate, and use a B-Square stock tool or a long-shanked screwdriver to back out the stock bolt. Remove the buttstock toward the rear.

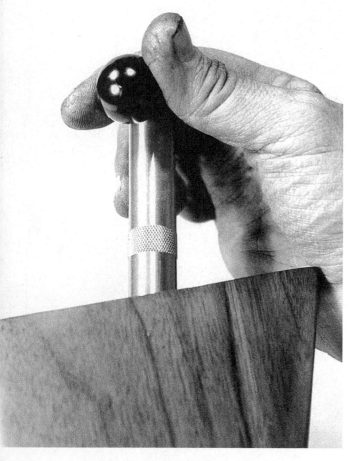

Reassembly Tips:

1. When replacing the cam pin, note that its cross hole must be oriented for passage of the firing pin, and that the end nearest to the hole must be toward the top of the bolt. Also, note that it is possible to install the bolt in the slide piece upside down, so be sure the extractor is on the right side. A large roll-pin punch is useful for compressing the extractor spring and washer before insertion of the cam pin.

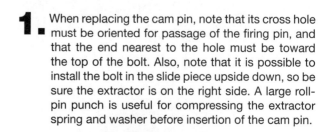

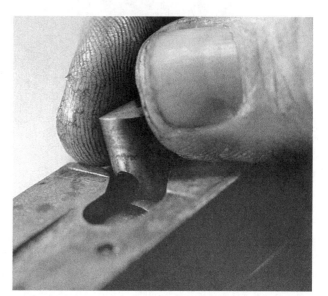

2. When replacing the gas piston, note that the two small holes at the front of the piston must be at the top.

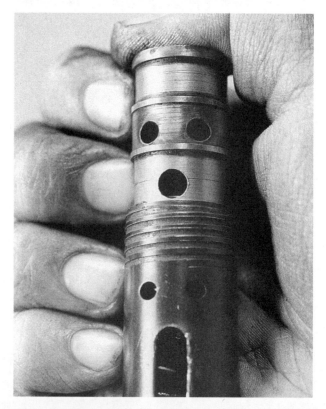

3. When installing the hammer and hammer spring assembly, be sure the right lower tail of the spring enters its slot in the trigger housing, and contacts the detent steps on the safety button.

4. When replacing the hammer pivot, be sure that the flat on the side of the pivot pin mates with the flat inside the nylon bushings, or they will be damaged.

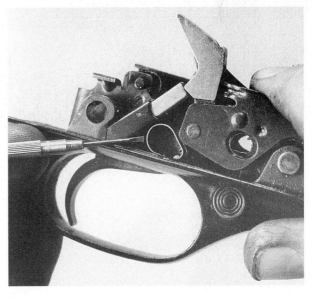

6. Before replacing the right sideplate and carrier pivot, be sure the carrier support spring is properly installed, as shown.

When replacing the trigger housing, carefully engage the front tips of the sideplates with their recesses in the receiver, then swing the rear of the housing upward into place.

5. When installing the disconnector, note that its opening at the front must engage the notch in the left end of the hammer pivot, as shown.

Winchester Model 1887

Similar/Identical Pattern Guns:

The same basic assembly/disassembly steps for the Winchester Model 1887 also apply to the following guns:

Winchester Model 1901

Data:	Winchester Model 1887
Origin:	United States
Manufacturer:	Winchester Repeating Arms New Haven, Connecticut
Gauges:	10 and 12
Magazine capacity:	5 rounds
Overall length:	49 inches (with 32-inch barrel)
Barrel length:	20, 22, 30 & 32 inches
Weight:	8-3/4 pounds

There are very few lever-action shotguns, and the Winchester Model 1887 was the first. It was replaced by the Model 1901, a slight redesign with no major mechanical differences. The Model 1901 was made until 1920. Firing modern shells in these guns is not advisable. The Model 1887 was designed by John Moses Browning.

Disassembly:

1. Open the action, and use non-marring pliers to compress the mainspring. Lift the front hooks of the lower arm of the spring from their grooves in the cross pin, and remove the spring toward the rear.

2. Push out the action pivot pin toward either side.

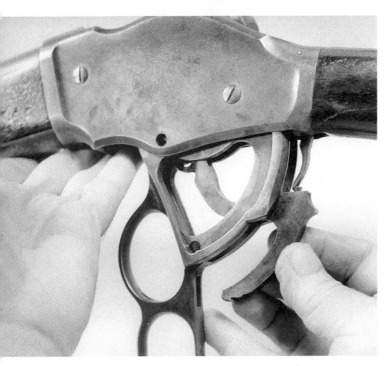

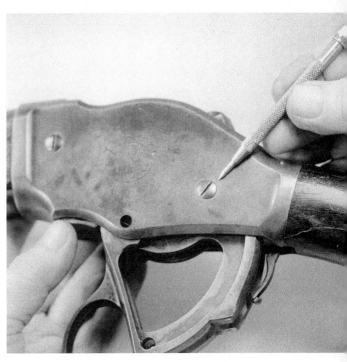

3. Move the hammer downward, and remove it through the rear opening of the lever unit.

4. Remove the carrier pivot screws, one on each side.

5. Remove the lever and bolt unit, and the carrier assembly, downward.

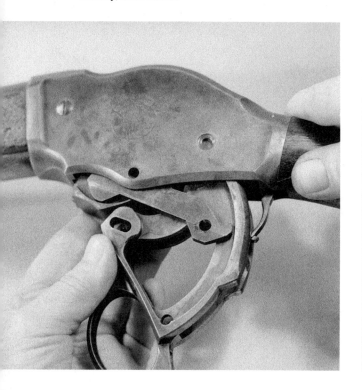

6. On removal, the carrier will separate into two parts.

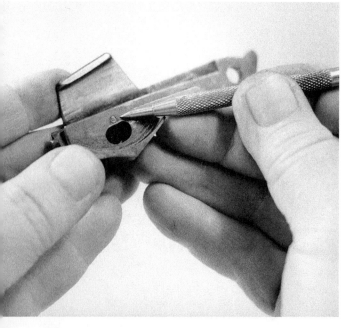

7. Drifting out the cross pin in the main carrier unit will allow removal of the shell lifter. The pin is drifted out toward the right.

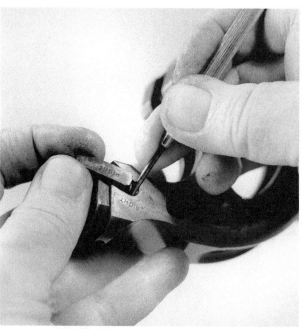

8. Insert a small tool to depress the extractor plunger, and lift the extractor out of its recess. Repeat the operation on the other extractor. Control the plungers and springs.

9. Remove the extractor plungers and springs.

10. A cross pin in the bolt retains the two-piece firing pin and its return spring. Drift the pin out toward the right, and remove the parts rearward.

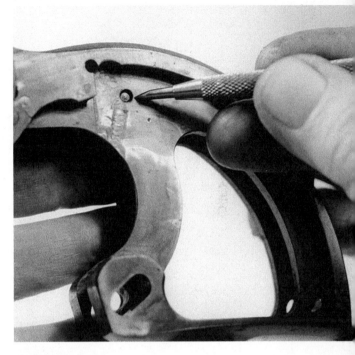

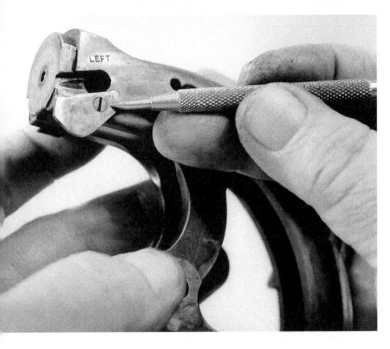

11. The carrier trip plate is retained by a screw, and the plate is taken off toward the left.

12. Remove the stock mounting bolt.

13. Remove the buttstock toward the rear.

14. Remove the trigger spring screw.

15. Remove the trigger spring.

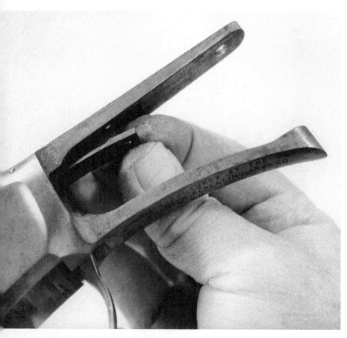

16. Drift out the trigger cross pin.

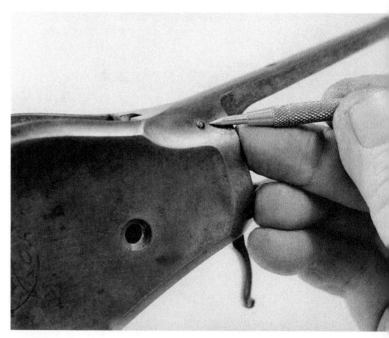

17. Move the trigger forward, and remove it downward.

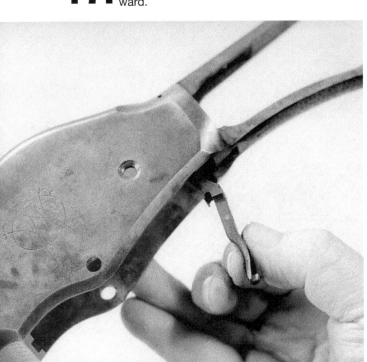

18. Very early Model 1887 guns will have a single screw retaining the forend panels. Remove the screw, or two screws, if the gun is a later version like the one shown.

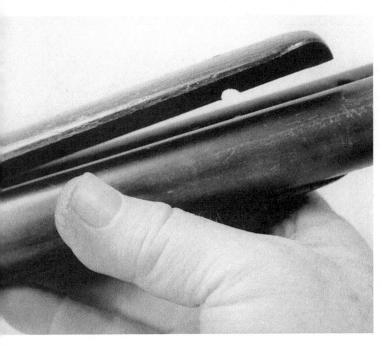

19. Tip the forend panels outward at the front, then remove them toward the front.

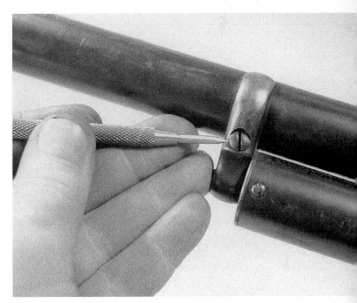

20. On early Model 1887 guns, the magazine is retained by a vertical screw at the front. Later versions, as the one shown, have a barrel band. Remove the cross screw in the band, and use a non-marring tool to nudge the band forward for removal.

21. Remove the screw in the side of the magazine tube.

22. Remove the end piece, the magazine spring, and the follower toward the front. Control the spring as the end piece is taken out.

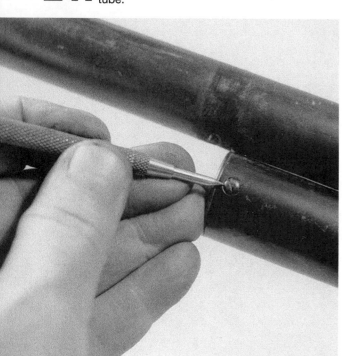

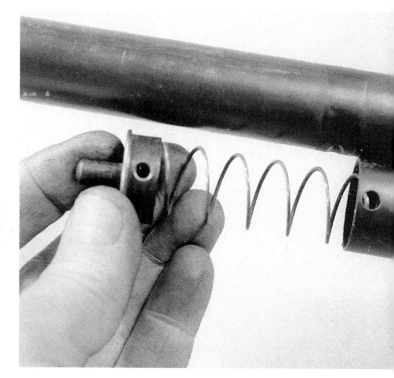

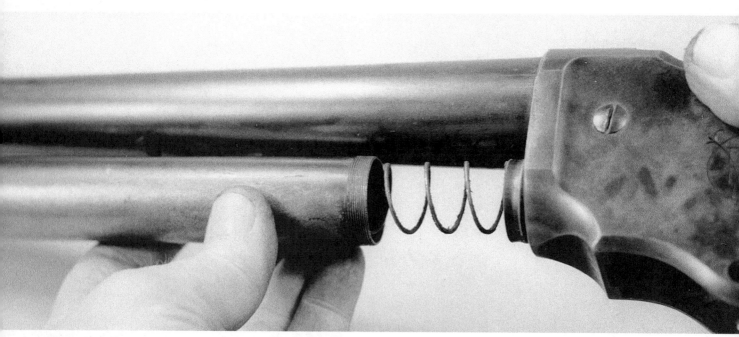

23. If the end piece is very tight, the tube can be unscrewed from the receiver without removal of the end piece, and the spring and follower can be taken out rearward.

24. The plug screw on the left side retains no part, and in normal takedown it is best left in place.

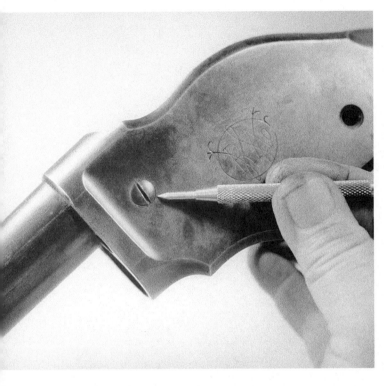

25. On the right side, the larger screw is the carrier stop screw, and the smaller screw is an extractor guide. These, also, are not removed in normal takedown.

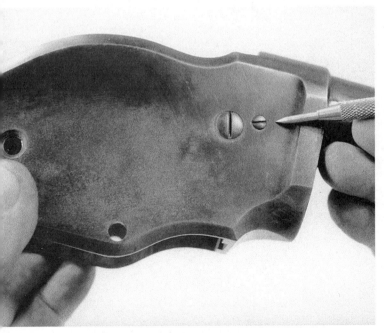

Reassembly Tips:

1. If the magazine tube has been removed, it is not screwed back in tightly. There is an index mark on the tube and the receiver for alignment, but these marks are often faint. Just be sure that the cross screw grooves on the tube and on the barrel are properly matched for passage of the screws, as shown.

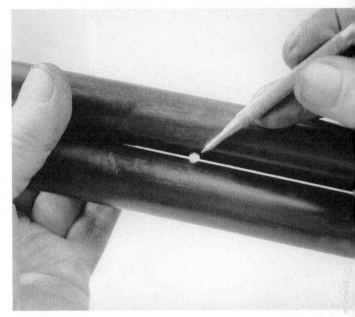

2. Remember that the trigger must be inserted and moved back into position. Use a drift to align the holes before insertion of the cross pin.

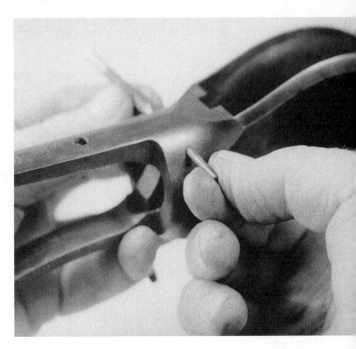

3. There is no chance of mixing up the extractors, as each one, and the sides of the bolt, are clearly marked "LEFT" and "RIGHT."

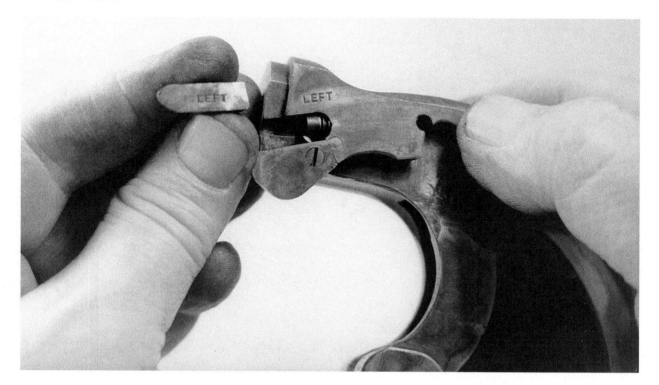

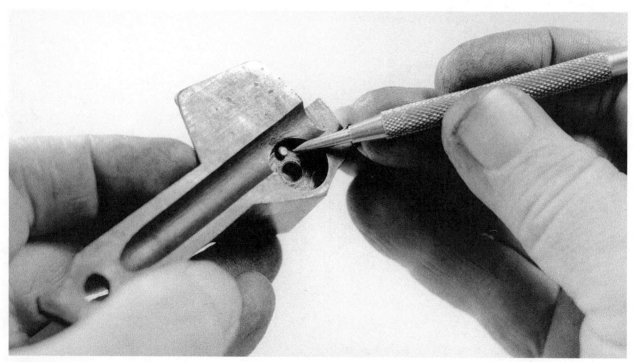

4. If the shell lifter has been taken out, the pin must be even with the left side of the carrier unit, and should protrude slightly into the well on the right side, as shown.

Winchester Super X1

Data:	Winchester Super-X Model 1
Origin:	United States
Manufacturer:	Winchester Repeating Arms New Haven, Connecticut
Gauges:	12 only
Magazine capacity:	3 rounds
Overall length:	46 inches
Barrel length:	26 to 30 inches
Weight:	7-1/2 pounds

As early as 1968, Winchester engineers were beginning preliminary design of a gas-operated autoloader that was intended to be a counterpart to the slide-action Model 12, with similar looks and handling characteristics. The design was finalized and introduced in 1975 as the Super-X Model 1. There are several unusual features, including a two-piece non-tilting bolt and a short- stroke steel rod to transfer the piston stroke to the bolt slide, a system totally unlike all other gas-operated shotguns. The Super-X Model 1 was discontinued in 1981.

Disassembly:

1. Pull back the operating handle and lock the bolt in the open position, and set the safety in the on-safe position. Unscrew and remove the magazine end cap, and take off the forend and the barrel toward the front. Move the rubber O-ring and the steel gas-seal ring off the magazine tube toward the front.

2. Move the piston sleeve assembly off the magazine tube toward the front.

3. The piston head can be removed from the front of the sleeve by taking off its retaining ring, and the internal and external piston rings can be taken off by snapping them out of their grooves. However, this system can be effectively cleaned without disassembly, and is best left in place in normal takedown.

4. The piston rod and its spring can be removed from their mount at the rear of the sleeve by drifting out the rod, as shown.

5. Remove the forend spacer plate toward the front.

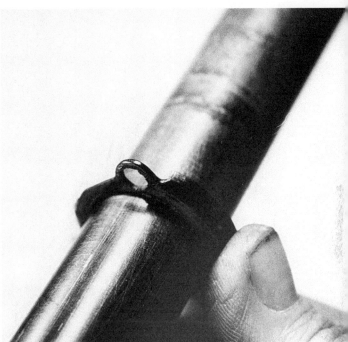

6. Insert a screwdriver at the front of the magazine tube and pry the magazine spring retainer outward, moving the screwdriver to raise the retainer equally around its edges. Caution: The magazine spring will be released, so control it and ease it out. Remove the spring and follower toward the front. If necessary, the magazine tube can be unscrewed and removed toward the front.

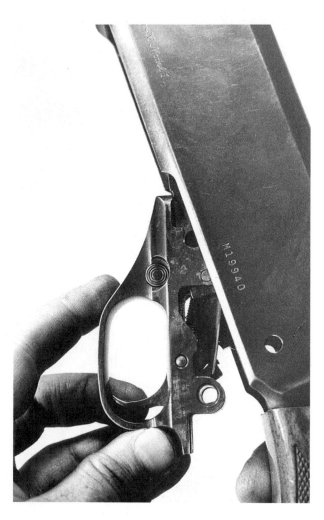

7. Restrain the bolt, depress the carrier latch button, and ease the bolt forward to the closed position. Push out the cross pin at the lower rear of the receiver toward either side. Tip the trigger housing downward at the rear, and remove, it toward the rear and downward.

8. Move the safety to the off-safe position, restrain the hammer, pull the trigger, and ease the hammer down to the fired position. Insert a small screwdriver at the rear of the hammer spring, in front of the sear, and another tool from the side, beneath the spring. Pry the spring toward the front and lift it from below, nudging it out of its notch at the front of the sear and trigger assembly. Caution: The spring is under tension, so keep it under control.

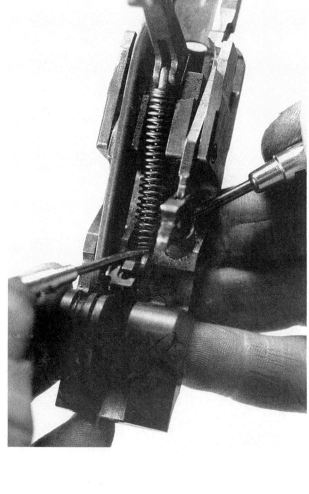

9. Swing the hammer strut upward, and remove the concentric large and small hammer springs, along with the rear spring guide.

10. Swing the hammer strut up out of the way, and insert a drift punch from the right, through the hole in the right carrier pivot, to push out the solid left carrier pivot.

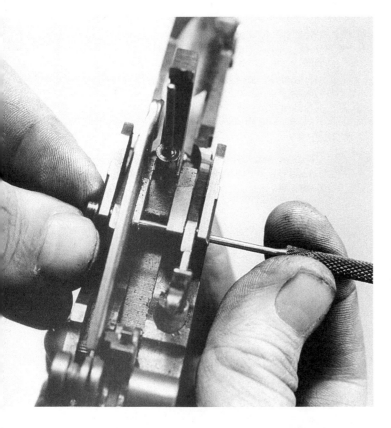

11. Insert a large drift punch from the left, through the hole just cleared, and push out the right carrier pivot toward the right. Restrain the carrier as the pin is removed, as it will be released.

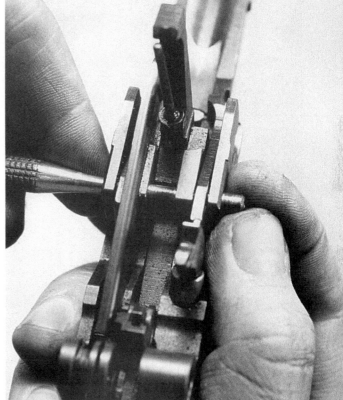

12. Move the rear of the carrier upward, then remove the carrier toward the front. Take out the carrier spring and plunger from their recess on the right side of the housing. The carrier dog, on the right rear wing of the carrier, is retained by a cross pin, and removal is not necessary in normal takedown. If necessary for repair, the pin must be drifted out inward, toward the left. Be sure the carrier wing is well supported.

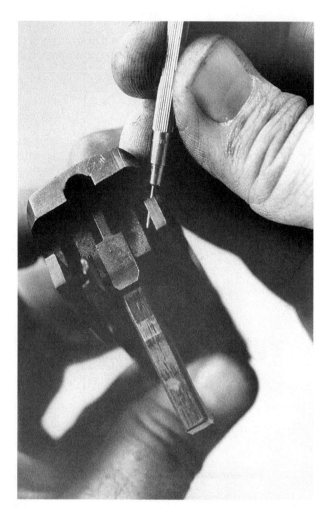

13. Hold the trigger to the rear to relieve sear tension on the hammer, and insert a small tool at the front of the housing to nudge the hammer pivot out toward the left. A small hooked tool made from a bent paper clip is useful for extracting the hammer pivot.

14. Remove the hammer upward. If necessary, the cross pin in the hammer can be drifted out toward the right to free the hammer strut for removal.

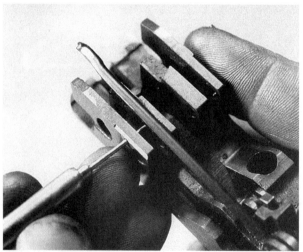

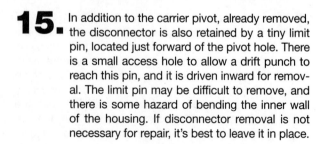

15. In addition to the carrier pivot, already removed, the disconnector is also retained by a tiny limit pin, located just forward of the pivot hole. There is a small access hole to allow a drift punch to reach this pin, and it is driven inward for removal. The limit pin may be difficult to remove, and there is some hazard of bending the inner wall of the housing. If disconnector removal is not necessary for repair, it's best to leave it in place.

16. Insert a drift on the right side, through the access hole in the sear pivot, and push out the trigger pin toward the left. Remove the trigger assembly upward.

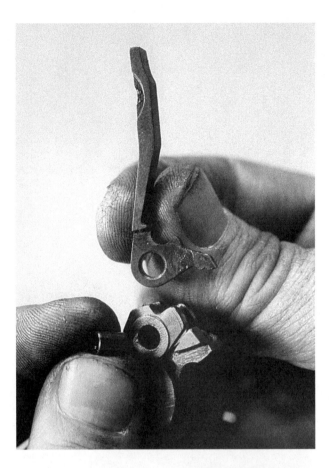

17. Push out the pivot sleeve at the top of the trigger, and remove the sear toward the front.

18. Drifting out the cross pin at the rear of the trigger will allow removal of the disconnector upward. Caution: When the cross pin is removed, the disconnector plunger and spring will be released, so restrain them and ease them out. There is a small Allen screw in the top of the disconnector, and this screw should not be disturbed.

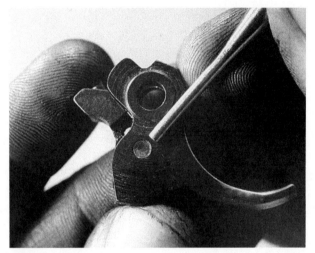

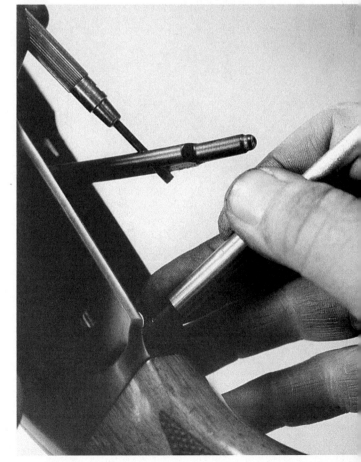

19. Set the safety half-way between its two positions, and insert a tool from the top to bear on the front edge of the safety at the center. Tap the tool to tilt the safety slightly, then push it out toward the right. Caution: The plunger and spring will be released as the safety clears, so restrain them and ease them out.

20. Insert a screwdriver inside the receiver at the rear and depress the bolt spring follower, Lift the bolt slide ink bar outward.

21. Grasp the operating handle firmly, and pull it straight out toward the right. Move the bolt back in the receiver until its lower side lugs align with the exit cuts inside the receiver. Lift the bolt out the bottom of the receiver, depressing the firing pin at the rear to clear the bolt spring follower.

22. The carrier latch is retained in the right wall of the receiver by a vertical pin. The pin is drifted out upward, into the receiver, to free the latch and its spring for removal.

23. Remove the buttplate, and use a large screwdriver to back out the stock mounting bolt. Remove the bolt and washer, and the buttstock, toward the rear.

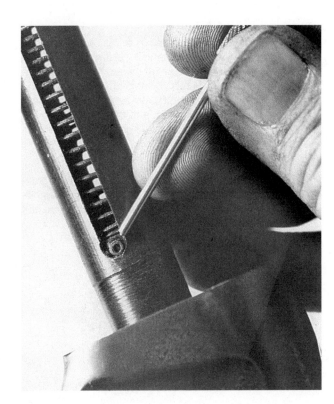

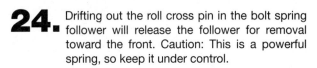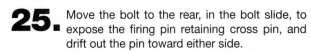

24. Drifting out the roll cross pin in the bolt spring follower will release the follower for removal toward the front. Caution: This is a powerful spring, so keep it under control.

25. Move the bolt to the rear, in the bolt slide, to expose the firing pin retaining cross pin, and drift out the pin toward either side.

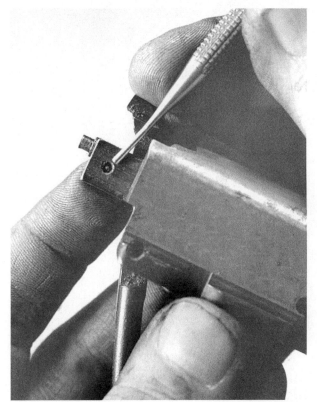

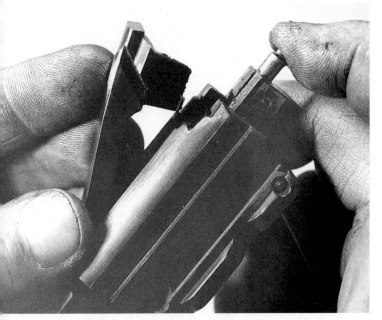

26. Removal of the cross pin will allow the firing pin to move toward the rear, but it is not released. Depress the firing pin toward the front, and lift the locking block upward at the rear. Remove the locking block upward, and take out the firing pin and its spring toward the rear.

27. Remove the bolt from the bolt slide toward the front.

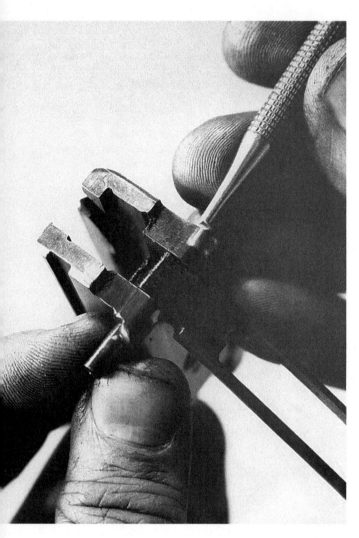

28. Drifting out the cross pin at the rear of the bolt slide will release the link bar for removal. The pin is easily pushed out toward the left. The operating handle retainer and its spring are held in the floor of the bolt slide by a slanted pin, accessible from the top, and this pin is driven out downward. Restrain the spring, and ease it out.

29. Push out the small cross pin at the lower front of the bolt, and remove the carrier pawl and its coil spring downward. The pin is pushed out toward the right.

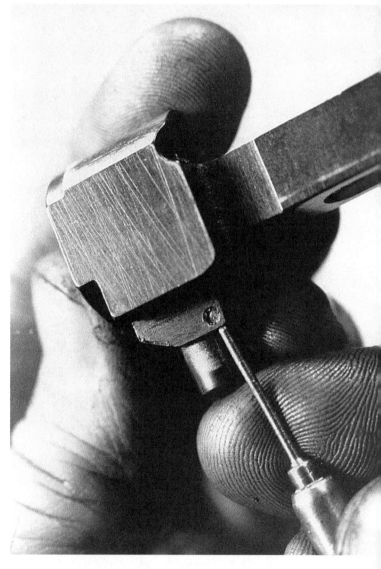

30. Insert a small screwdriver between the extractor and its plunger to depress the plunger toward the rear, and lift the extractor out of its recess. Keep the plunger under control, and ease the plunger and spring out toward the front.

Reassembly Tips:

1. When replacing the firing pin in the bolt, note that the side with the extensive relief cuts goes on the right.

2. When replacing the locking block, hold the bolt assembly and firing pin as shown, set the front of the block into its recess at the front, rest it on the firing pin at the rear, and depress the firing pin until the locking block drops into place. Take care that the firing pin isn't turned, as the cuts must align with the tail of the locking block. Also, remember that for replacement of the firing pin retaining cross pin, the firing pin must again be depressed to align its retaining cut with the cross pin hole.

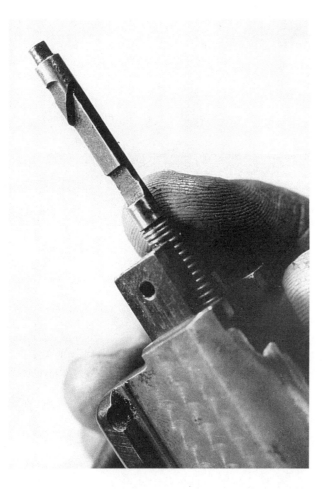

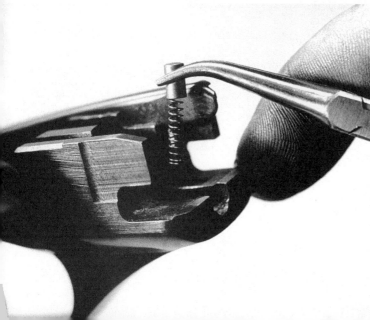

3. The sear spring and plunger are more easily installed after the trigger and sear are in place. Tip the disconnector to the rear, and tilt the front of the sear upward, then insert the spring and plunger and tip the sear back down.

4. Note that the left carrier pivot is reduced at one end, and that end must go toward the right when the pivot is installed.

5. When compressing the hammer spring assembly, take care that the hollow rear guide slips onto the solid front guide (the hammer strut), and keep the springs from kinking as the unit is compressed. There is a recess at the tip of the rear guide, and a small drift punch or a pointed tool can be lodged in the recess to aid in guiding the spring assembly into position.

Winchester Super X2

Similar/Identical Pattern Guns:

The same basic assembly/disassembly steps for the Winchester Super-X Model II also apply to the following guns:

Magnum Turkey   **Camo Waterfowl**

Sporting Clays

Data:	Winchester Super X2
Origin:	United States
Manufacturer:	U.S. Repeating Arms Co., New Haven, Connecticut
Gauges:	12 only
Magazine capacity:	4 rounds
Overall length:	47 inches
Barrel length:	26 inches (others offered)
Weight:	7-1/4 to 7-1/2 pounds

The Super X2 is an extensive redesign of the earlier Super X1, and there are important mechanical differences. The Super X2 has self-adjusting gas operation, and is offered with a stock and forend of either walnut or black synthetic material. FN in Belgium makes the gun for U. S. Repeating Arms.

Disassembly:

1. Pull the bolt handle to the rear, and leave the bolt in locked-open position. Unscrew the magazine cap, and take off the forearm and the barrel toward the front. The metal insert at the front of the forearm is not routinely removable.

2. Remove the gas piston toward the front.

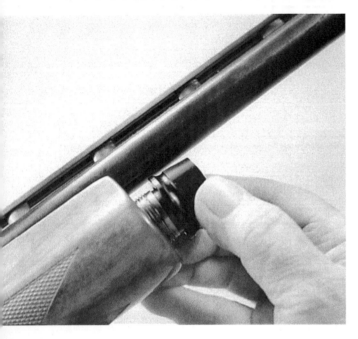

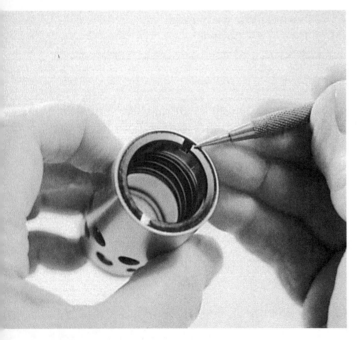

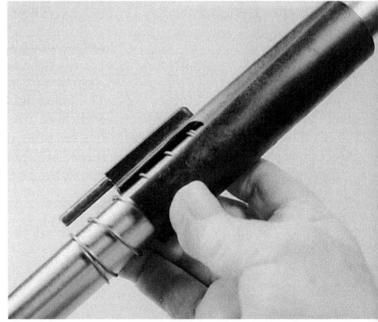

3. Using a special wrench, it is possible to remove the internal components of the gas piston. In normal takedown, this system is best left in place.

4. Remove the gas sleeve and its spring. The steel pin at the rear of the polymer sleeve is not routinely removable.

5. To remove the magazine spring and follower, depress the retaining tab, and ease out the retainer. Caution: Control the retainer and spring.

6. Restrain the bolt, depress the release button, and ease the bolt forward until it stops. Put the manual safety in on-safe position. Use a suitable tool, a roll-pin drift or the Brownells tool shown, to push out the two trigger group cross pins.

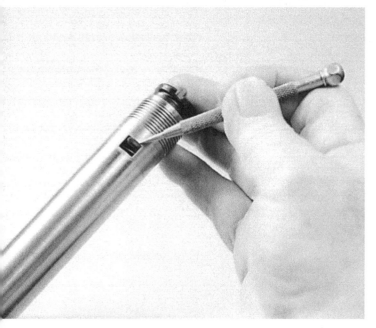

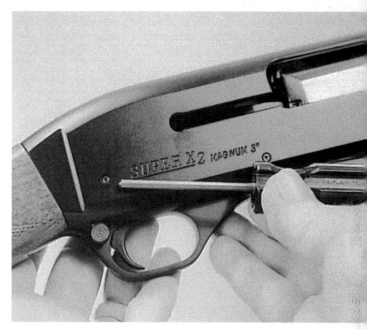

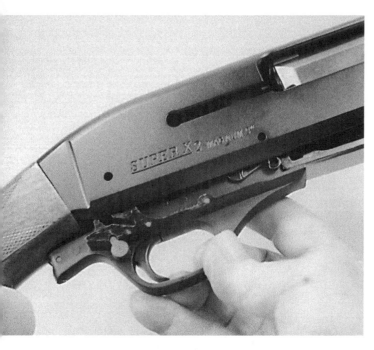

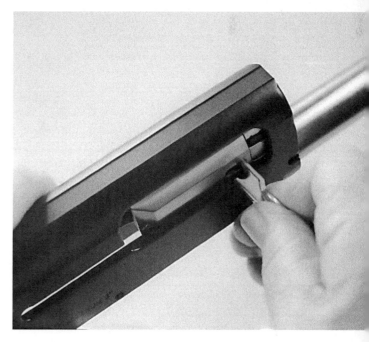

7. Remove the trigger group downward.

8. Grasp the bolt handle firmly, and pull it out toward the right.

9. Move the bolt and bolt slide forward out of the receiver. They are easily separated.

10. The bolt slide link, the connector to the bolt spring, is retained at the rear of the slide by a cross pin which is staked in place. It is removed only for repair.

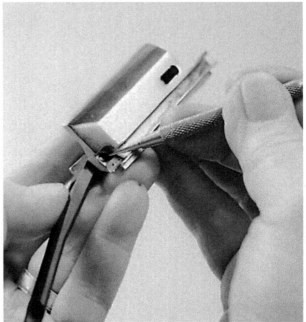

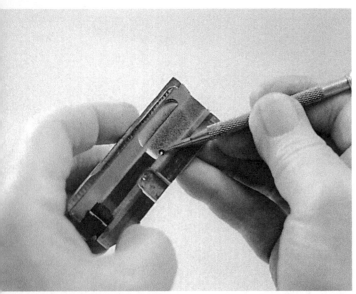

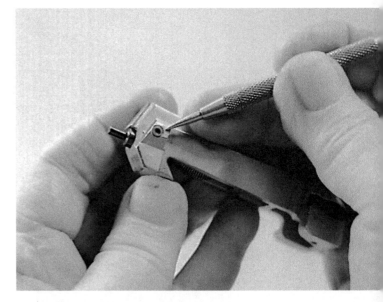

11. The bolt handle detent plunger and its coil spring are retained in the slide by a vertical roll pin. Again, remove this system only for repair. If the pin is drifted out, cover the hole at the front of the slide to arrest the plunger and spring.

12. The firing pin and its return spring are retained in the bolt by a cross pin at the rear. If this pin is removed for repair, restrain the firing pin as the drift is taken out.

13. The extractor is pivoted and retained by a vertical pin that is drifted out upward. The pin is staked at the top, and removal should be only for repair. Restrain the extractor, ease it off, and take out its angled plunger and spring.

14. Before disassembly of the trigger group, be sure the manual safety is in on-safe position, to insure against inadvertent hammer fall. Use a small sharp tool to carefully lift the rear base of the carrier spring out of its recess, and remove the carrier spring assembly. Caution: Control the parts during removal.

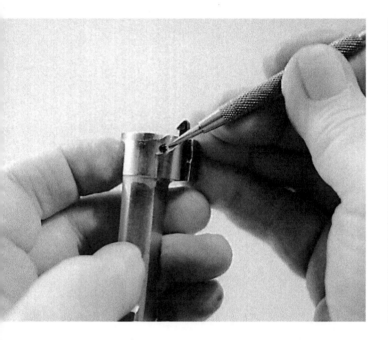

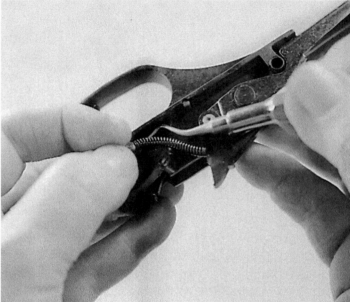

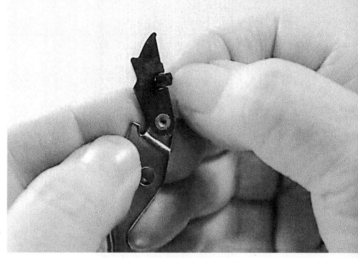

15. Remove the spring clip in the right end of the carrier pivot, sliding it out upward. Caution: Take care that this small clip does not get away and become lost. Move the carrier pivot out toward the left, and remove the carrier.

16. If necessary for repair, the spring base in the carrier dog can be turned to the position shown, and can be taken out to either side. The carrier dog is riveted in place on the carrier, and it is not routinely removed.

17. Move the manual safety to off-safe, restrain the hammer, pull the trigger, and ease the hammer forward to fired position. Unhook the trigger and disconnector spring from its notch in the disconnector.

18. Push out the rear group cross-pin sleeve. The trigger/disconnector spring will be released for removal.

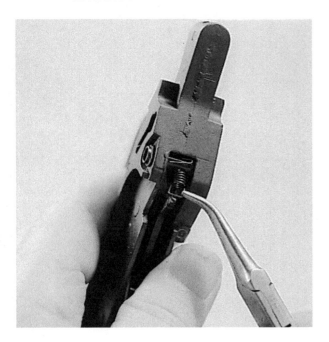

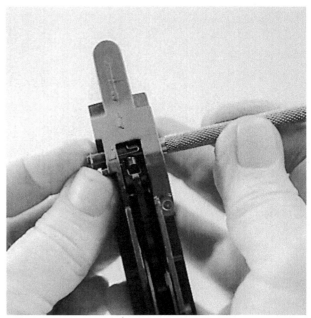

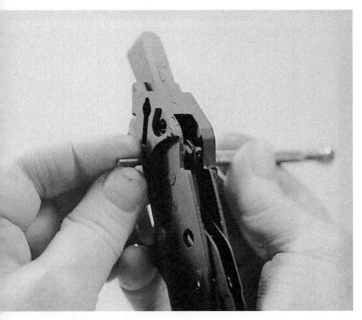

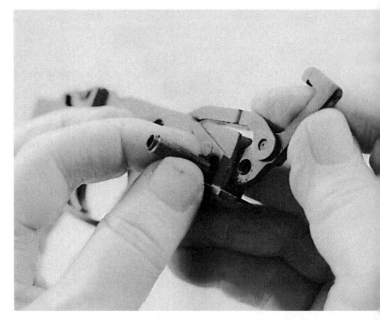

19. Push out the trigger cross pin. The trigger is not removed at this point.

20. Push out the front trigger group cross-pin sleeve, which is also the hammer pivot. Remove the hammer toward the front. The hammer spring strut must be lifted at the rear to clear.

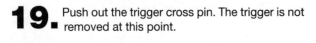

21. Remove the trigger and attached disconnector upward. The cross pin is easily removed to separate the parts.

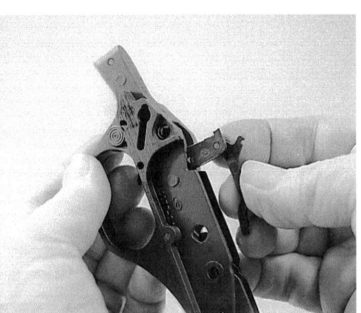

22. Restrain the sear, and push out the sear pin.

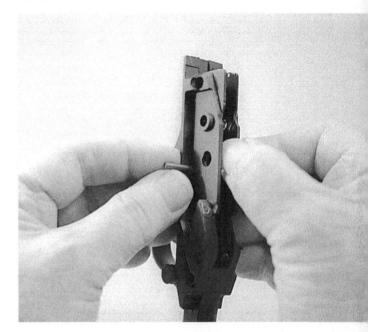

23. Remove the sear and its attached torsion spring, forward and upward. The spring is easily detached.

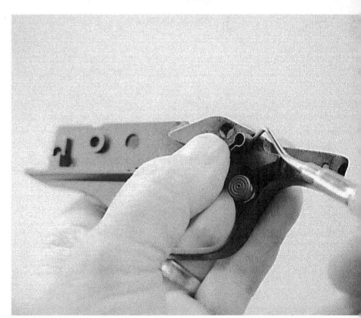

24. Carefully pry out the safety detent spring.

25. Remove the safety. After the safety is taken out, the detent plunger is easily removed.

26. If necessary for repair, the carrier buffer pad can be pried out of its recess.

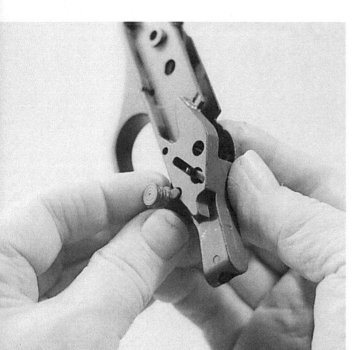

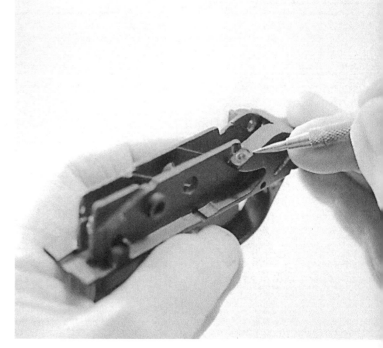

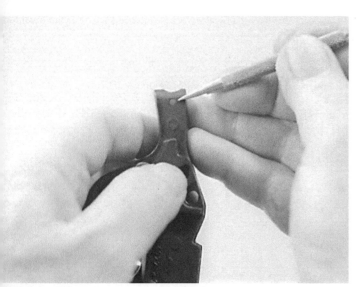

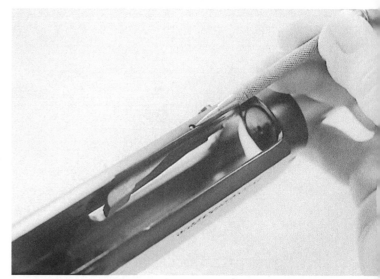

27. To remove the hammer spring and its plunger, insert a tool at the rear to slightly compress the spring, and drift out the retaining cross pin. Caution: Control the spring.

28. The bolt latch assembly, which also contains the shell stop, is pivoted and retained in the receiver by a vertical pin. The pin is secured by a small spring clip in a recess inside the receiver. The clip is pushed off rearward, and the pin is pushed out upward. If removal is not necessary for repair, this system is best left in place.

29. Removal of the recoil pad will give access to a 3/4-inch nut and spacer that retain the buttstock. There is also an oblong steel plate in the stock recess. Remove the stock toward the rear..

30. To remove the action spring and follower, insert a tool at the rear to slightly compress the retainer, and push out the cross pin. Caution: Control the retainer and spring.

Reassembly Tips:

1. When installing the combination trigger and disconnector spring, note that it goes back on the sleeve in the orientation shown.

2. When installing the carrier spring assembly, remember that the upper tip of the spring guide rod must enter the small hole in the spring base on the carrier dog.

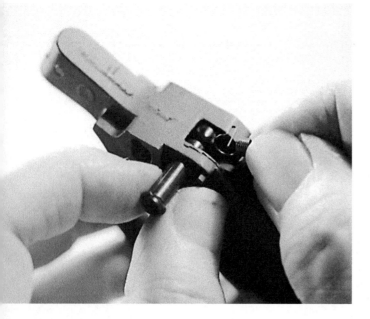

As the bolt and bolt slide are moved back into the receiver, be sure the rear tip of the bolt slide link engages the cupped end of the recoil spring follower, and keep it in engagement while the bolt handle is reinserted.

Winchester Super X3

Similar/Identical Pattern Guns:

The same basic assembly/disassembly steps used for the Winchester SX3 also apply to the following guns:

Browning Gold

Browning Silver

Winchester Super X2

Data: Winchester Super X 3
Origin: Belgium
Manufacturer: FN Herstal, Belgium
Gauges: 12, 20
Magazine Capacity: 4 rounds
Overall Length: 47.75 inches
Height: 7 inches
Barrel Length: 28 inches
Weight: 6.5 lbs

The manufacturers of the Winchester line of firearms continue to change, now residing with FN Herstal in Belgium and imported by Browning. However, the classic lines of guns live on and are joined by newer samples such as the Super X3. The third generation of the Super X line, it has little relation to the first model, with the second model simply based on the Browning Silver line, with some cosmetic alterations to personify it. The 12 gauge SX3 differs from the 20 gauge and has no latch retaining the charging handle, but in other ways is just like the 20 gauge. The Browning Gold model is very similar as well, the greatest difference being a magazine cutoff. Any of these models will follow generally these steps for the SX3.

Disassembly:

1. With the bolt locked back and the safety on "safe" remove the magazine cap. Pull the forend off the front of the shotgun.

2. Pull the barrel from the front of the gun.

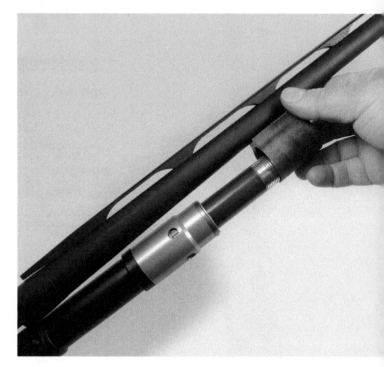

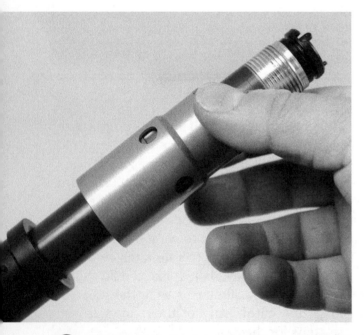

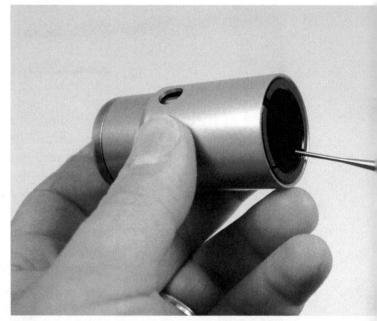

3. Pull the piston, the sleeve assembly, and the piston sleeve spring from the front of the magazine tube.

4. The piston assembly can be disassembled by unscrewing the large slotted ring at the rear of the assembly. However, it is best to avoid disassembly unless something needs to be replaced, as it is easily cleaned in assembly.

5. Depress the bolt release and gently allow the bolt to come all the way forward. To remove the operating handle, reach inside the receiver, under the bolt, and depress the latch on the bottom of the bolt carrier. Then pull the handle straight out to the right.

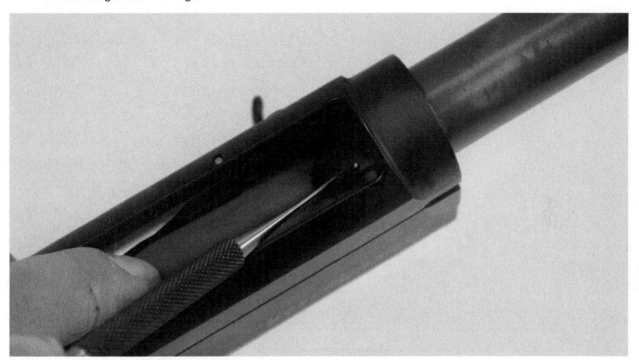

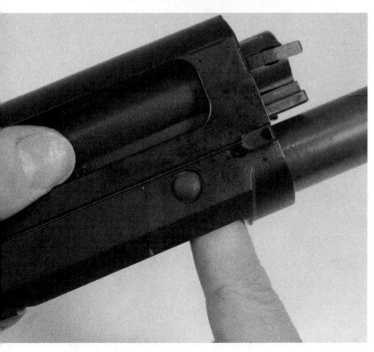

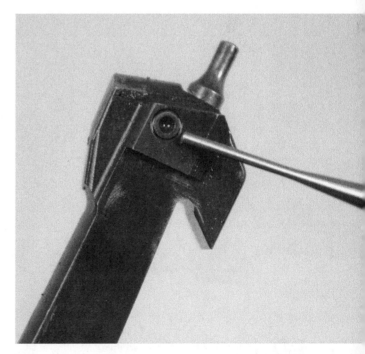

6. Remove the bolt assembly by depressing the latch on the bottom, then pulling it out of the front of the receiver. The bolt will easily lift out of the carrier.

7. The firing pin retaining pin is staked in and should be removed only for replacement. Removing this pin will release the firing pin and firing pin spring.

8. Drive out the extractor pin from top to bottom, then remove the extractor and extractor spring.

9. If necessary for repair, the link pin can be driven out from right to left. This will free the link and the detent and spring in front of it.

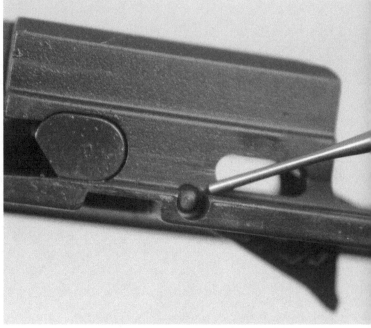

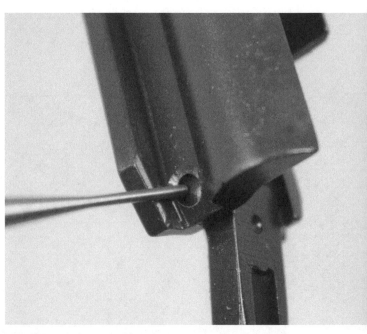

10. The bolt cam piece is not integral with the bolt carrier and is pinned in place in the carrier. The pin is staked and should not be removed unless the cam piece needs replacement.

11. This pin retains the operating handle latch, detent, and spring.

12. Push out these two pins to remove the fire control group.

13. To disassemble the fire control group, first unlatch the front carrier spring from the group frame, then lifting the carrier assembly, pull the spring's short leg from the carrier pin.

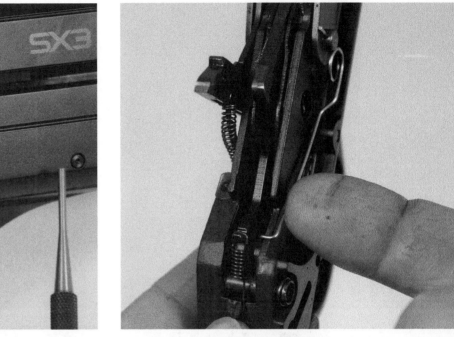

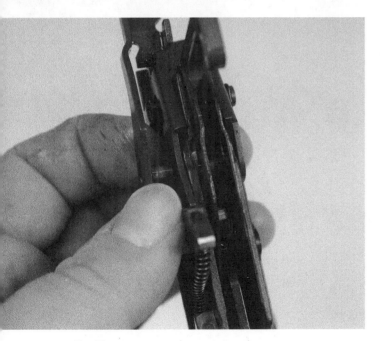

14. Ensure that the hammer is forward, then pull to the left the front carrier assembly. This also frees the rear carrier assembly and the rear carrier spring and guides. Do this carefully to keep control of the spring and multiple parts.

15. Unhook the trigger/disconnector spring.

16. Remove the trigger guard bushing.

17. Remove the hammer pin and pull the hammer from the housing.

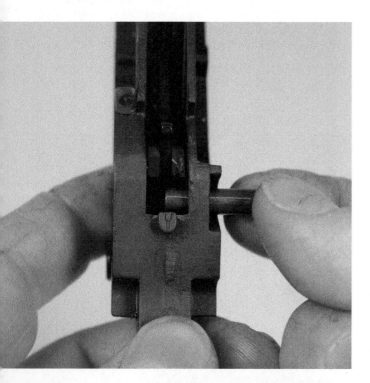

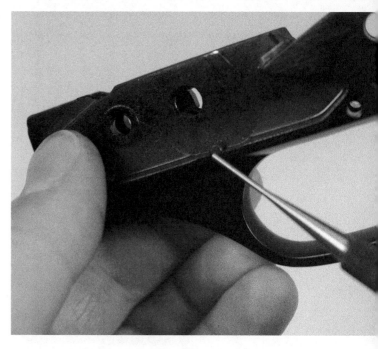

18. Push out the trigger pin. The trigger can now be pulled up and out of the housing.

19. Remove the sear pin and lift the sear and sear spring from the housing.

20. Push out this pin to release the hammer spring and detent. Control the spring as it is still compressed.

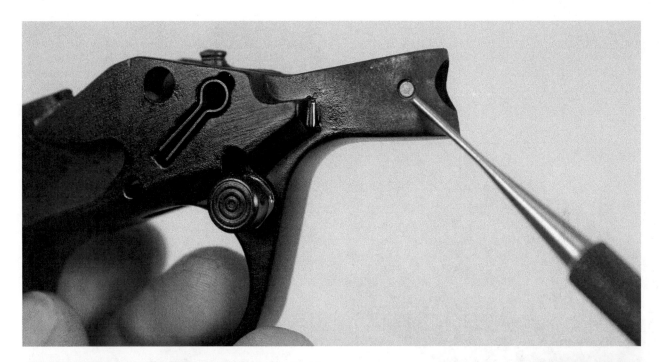

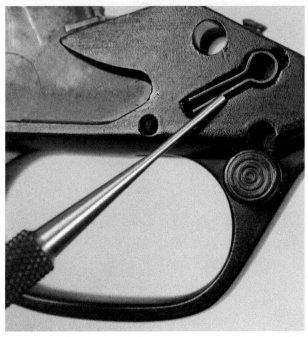

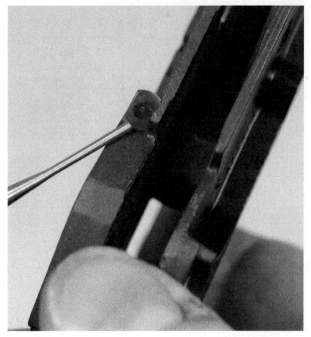

21. Remove this spring to relieve tension on the safety button. Once the spring has been removed, the button can be easily taken out to either side and the safety detent will fall out of the bottom of the housing.

22. There is a synthetic pad on the left side of the housing that should be left unless replacement is needed.

23. This pin retains the shell latch/bolt release. It should be driven out from top to bottom. Control it as its spring is still under some compression.

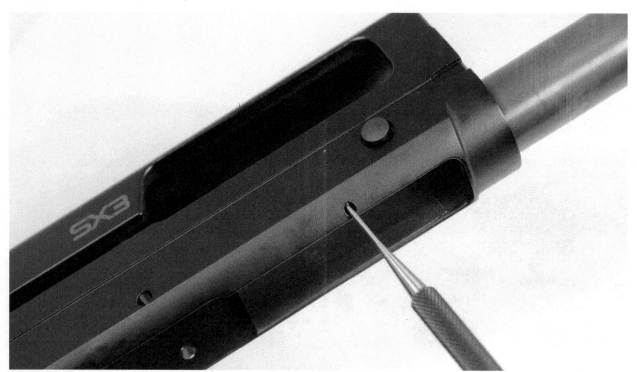

24. Remove the magazine spring retainer by depressing this latch with a screwdriver. Slowly pull the retainer out of the magazine tube. With the retainer removed the magazine spring, limiter and follower can be pulled from the tube. The spring is still very compressed so control it.

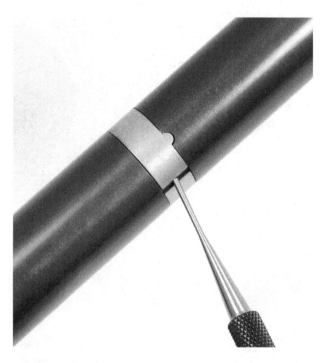

25. There is a seal ring around the magazine tube. Leave it alone unless it is damaged.

26. The buttpad can be removed by unscrewing the two stock screws.

27. Pull any spacers present and the internal stock support from the stock.

28. Remove the stock bolt nut to remove the nut. Then remove the action spring support, the plate beneath the nut.

29. Remove the stock. Then the stock spacer in front of the stock can be removed. Note the orientation.

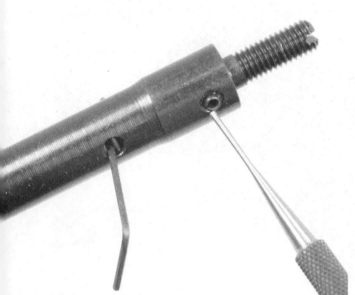

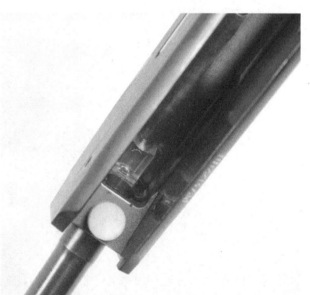

30. This roll pin retains the action spring retainer. Use a small diameter pin to hold the spring in place, then drive out the pin. Firmly control the retainer when unscrewing the retainer piece as the action spring and detent are under considerable compression. Do not attempt to remove the action tube.

31. The synthetic bolt buffer and the spongy pad beneath the trigger group can be left alone unless they need to be replaced.

Reassembly Tips:

1. When reinstalling the sear, first install the sear and sear spring under their rails in the housing. Install the trigger, but not the trigger bushing. Next install the hammer over the sear. The disconnector can then be lowered and inserted under the sear, followed by reinstalling the trigger bushing.

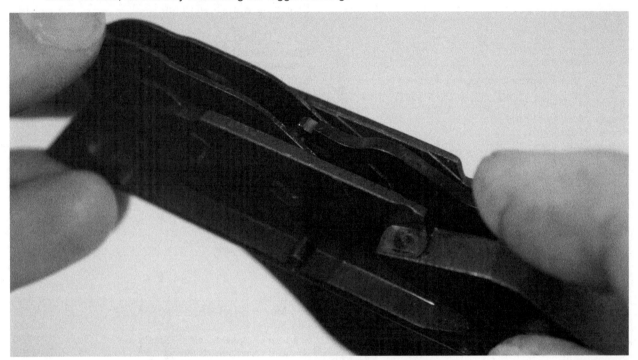

2. Note the orientation of the trigger/disconnector spring. The long leg goes to the rear.

3. When reinstalling the bolt handle, remember to depress the latch on the bolt's underside when inserting the handle.

Index/Cross Reference

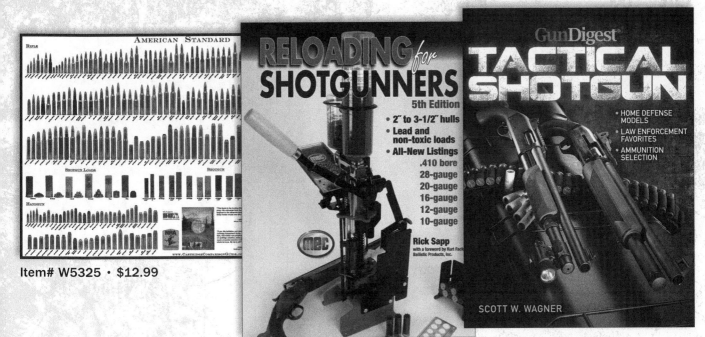